Influencing within Organizations

There are many 'how-to' books on influencing, but few of these are based on rigorous research. There are also many academic studies that analyse the art of influencing, but most are either difficult to find, or else provide little in the way of practical advice.

Influencing within Organizations is unique. It provides readers with vital information on probably the single most important survival-success skill of the twenty-first century – influencing. By tracking down the most trustworthy academic studies, and translating their conclusions into specific, behavioural steps on effective influencing, this book gives the reader a practical guide to influencing that is thoroughly grounded in the relevant theory and research.

The second edition is fully revised and expanded, to include the most up-to-date material. The chapter topics include:

- applying for a job (now two chapters)
- verbal and non-verbal influencing
- impression management
- networking
- influencing in a group
- public speaking

This is a highly practical guide to influencing in organizations, which combines the academic rigour and practical relevancy to make this text an essential purchase for all students of organizational behaviour and theory, communication and political persuasion as well as for anyone interested in the art of influencing.

Andrzej Huczynski is Senior Lecturer in Organizational Behaviour at Glasgow University. He teaches influencing skills to undergraduates and postgraduates, as well as on in-company, executive programmes. He is author of numerous books on organizational behaviour.

Influencing within Organizations

Second edition

Andrzej Huczynski

Routledge
Taylor & Francis Group

LONDON AND NEW YORK

First edition published by Pearson in 1996

Second edition, first published 2004
by Routledge
11 New Fetter Lane, London EC4P 4EE

Simultaneously published in the USA and Canada
by Routledge
29 West 35th Street, New York NY 10001

Routledge is an imprint of the Taylor & Francis Group

© 2004 Andrzej Huczynski

Typeset in Perpetua and Bell Gothic by
Florence Production Ltd, Stoodleigh, Devon
Printed and bound in Great Britain by
The Cromwell Press, Trowbridge, Wiltshire

British Library Cataloguing in Publication Data
A catalogue record for this book is available from
the British Library

Library of Congress Cataloging in Publication Data
A catalog record for this book has been requested

ISBN 0–415–31162–4 (hbk)
ISBN 0–415–31163–2 (pbk)

For Janet, Sophie, Gregory and Tom

Contents

Illustrations

FIGURES

TABLES

Preface

INTRODUCTION

This book is written for final year university students and recent graduates. These are young men and women at the start of their careers who are competing against others to secure their first job, and then, once inside their chosen organization, fighting others for promotion. I believe that to gain a competitive career advantage, the most useful tool that they can possess is knowledge of how to influence people. Beyond this primary-target audience, the book will be useful to anybody who, at some time or another, has to influence those around them.

My interest is particularly focused upon (but is not exclusively restricted to), the graduate job application process. The major, global corporations devote vast resources to the recruiting and selecting of suitable graduate candidates. They spend millions of pounds each year on recruitment agencies and consultants who, together with the company's own human resource management staff, subject hapless recent graduates to the selection ritual. The latter undergo selection methods which include application forms, psychometric testing, telephone interviewing, individual interviewing, assessment centres and ever more sophisticated, elaborate and expensive devices.

This book gathers together all the known and verified information about influencing in general, and that which is concerned with graduate job application in particular. It considers motivation, personality, power, assertiveness, influencing strategies and all the different bits of knowledge which are relevant to candidates entering the organization of their choice, and influencing others once they are in it. As the author, I was particularly interested in the more subconscious aspects of influencing, especially the thinking biases that affected our judgements. The book deals also with marginal knowledge about influencing. That is, with knowledge and techniques which, although not empirically verified, nevertheless do appear to be effective, as judged by practice. I wanted a book which, although based on solid psychological, social psychological and sociological research, would be sufficiently prescriptive to offer specific guidance to these young people. It was important that they should be able to use the knowledge. Not just in a general way ('do this, avoid that'), but also specifically. Which words should they use, which approach was most appropriate for the situation, what should they wear and so on.

This book therefore is a guide to the important process of influencing. It helps readers develop the knowledge and skills necessary to influence individuals and groups, in a variety of work and social situations. The major situation being that of securing one's first graduate job. It takes a more eclectic approach than most others on this subject. It has chapters on many popular topics such as assertiveness, public speaking, running meetings, and so on. However, it avoids duplicating existing publications, and instead considers each of these topics from an exclusively young recruit, influencing perspective. That is, it asks what young graduates can do to alter the content, process or the situation, in order to make themselves more influential. Conceptually, the book is positioned amongst the literature on how to introduce organizational change, self-improvement and salesmanship. As a guide to influencing, it offers a survival manual to those entering organizations and those seeking to rise within them. It is thus pitched somewhere between Niccolo Machiavelli's, *The Prince*, and Douglas Adams', *Hitch-hiker's Guide to the Galaxy*.

Many, perhaps the majority of books on this topic, have been written by 'persuasion peddlers'. That is, authors who have no scientific background, systematic training in, or understanding of, how influence can be systematically applied. They have not even bothered to familiarize themselves with the existing, extensive body of research knowledge that contains a wealth of repeatable, verifiable facts on the topic of human thought and behaviour, and how both of these can be changed. The result is much pseudo-science and misinformation, which goes undetected and uncorrected, leading to errors and mistakes. Of the well-researched books on influencing that exist, many have narrowly focused on only one or two aspects of the process, to the neglect of the others. To overcome these two major deficiencies, this book is research based, drawing upon social psychological and communications studies going back some fifty years, and takes an eclectic view of the subject of influencing. To achieve breadth of coverage within an acceptable total length, I have dispensed with the presentation of competing theories, ideas and frameworks, and have opted instead to present an integrating perspective which offers the best 'value-for-reading or prescription'. For each of the topic areas, I have selected the most useful theory, research study or applications. Information about influencing techniques is presented at four levels:

- *Action*: The specification of *what* the individual has to say or do in order to exercise influence over another.
- *Explanation*: An explanation of *why* that action is likely to work, if there is one.

- *Citation*: Information about *where* the idea is described in greater depth.
- *Origination*: The original *source* of the idea, usually an account of an experiment described in an academic psychological journal.

This book describes the influencing technique and explains how it operates. In preparing this book, great use has been made of the research and writings on influencing of hundreds of authors. It only references the citation and the origination, it does not discuss the experiment or study itself. Extensive references are intentionally provided for those wishing to explore the relevant article or book in greater detail. Thus, the majority of recommended actions contained in this book are research based, while the remainder represent accepted most effective practice. As with any body of knowledge, there is an element of controversy and contradiction. Many books about organizations seek to be reader-friendly, demanding little of readers. This one is pitched between such friendliness and academic complexity. While it addresses the reader in the second person singular, it will require you to struggle sometimes, to re-read and indeed to reflect.

Finally, rather like a government health warning on cigarettes packets, this book is concerned with what you, the reader, might say and do, should you choose to use a particular influencing technique. The author's approach is value neutral, neither advocating nor attacking any particular technique. Hence, where words appear such as *ought*, *should* or *must*, they appear as directions to things that influencers need to do or say, if they have decided to apply a particular technique. They should not be interpreted as writer recommendations. All the influencing tactics reported in this book exist. Somewhere, they are being used by some people on others. Because they exist, they have been researched, and the summary of that research forms the basis of this book. It is however, up to individual readers to decide whether a particular influencing tactic is appropriate for them.

OBJECTIVES

The objectives of this book are to enable you to:

- Define the concept of influencing.
- Distinguish the elements of verbal and non-verbal influencing.
- Understand the elements of impression management.
- Recognize how an understanding of peoples' needs assists your influencing.
- Distinguish different personality types as the basis for influencing attempts.
- Appreciate how people make decisions.
- Understand how to modify a person's behaviour through reinforcement.

- List the principles of giving and receiving assertive feedback.
- Identify your preferred influencing strategy.
- Gain insights into the influencing process as it affects a group.
- Understand the principles of influential public speaking.
- Appreciate the importance of networking.
- Identify and plan to extend your bases of power.

BOOK STRUCTURE

Since influencing is the subject of this book, it is impossible not to duplicate some material. Some chapters focus on types of behaviour (e.g. verbal and non-verbal), while others consider the situations in which such behaviours might be used (e.g. job selection interviews). Some of these situations (e.g. meetings), are scaled-down versions of similar ones (e.g. public speeches). Some chapter sections dwell on an interpersonal strategy (criticizing), while others consider the theoretical basis of that strategy (e.g. assertiveness). Moreover, the research literature permeates the different strategies, approaches and contexts. The aim has therefore been to eliminate duplication to a point where repetition actually becomes a positive feature. As you progress through the book, you will suddenly realize that some theory, research finding or behavioural technique, is as applicable here, as it was in a different context. When such linking begins to occur, you will realize that you are beginning to grasp the totality of the ideas, their *gestalt*.

Get involved in the book. Because such a wide variety of topics are dealt with, the content has necessarily been compressed. As a result, the number of examples, illustrations and anecdotes has had to be limited. Instead, you are invited to stop reading periodically, and to reflect on the idea, and on your experience, and thus actively to manufacture examples for yourself. When you come to a suggestion or an explanation of why that suggestion works, pause, and think if you have experienced it in the past, or try to imagine how you might use it in the future. So, participate in the reading process, as this will help you not only to retain the ideas, but also to apply them. This book seeks to increase your skills of influencing others in organizations and elsewhere. Finally, let me leave you with some words, thoughts and epigrams that you will encounter in this book.

THE INFLUENCING BELL

Because
Life is not fair
First impressions last.
Coming second doesn't count.
To percolate you need to circulate.
There is no dress rehearsal in life.
People like people like themselves.
Failing to prepare, is preparing to fail.
It's not what you know, it's who you know.
If you can fake sincerity, you've got it made.
Minimize your enemies, maximize their friends.
To succeed, you just need an edge over the others.
Saying no at the start, is easier than saying no, later.
The person who never made a mistake, never made anything.
You don't get a second chance to make a good first impression.
Don't be loyal to a company, because a company won't be loyal to you.
It's not what you know, it's what you do with what you know that counts.
How you feel inside and how you appear to others, are two different things.

Acknowledgements

The author would like to thank generations of his honours students who have attended the 'Art of Influencing' course and who, through their ideas, discussions and suggestions, have contributed to the content of this book. Particular thanks are due to Asleigh Anderson whose research into graduate selection methods is drawn upon extensively in Chapters 4 and 5. The author is also grateful to Janie Ferguson of the Glasgow University Library who provided bibliographical advice, and to the staff at Routledge for assisting in the preparation of this book.

Chapter 1

Introduction

To succeed, you just need the edge over the others.

INTRODUCTION

Let me begin by asking you three questions. First, in men's athletics, who is the current world record holder for the 100 metres sprint? Second, who is currently the second fastest athlete over this same distance? Third, what is the time difference between the two? Even if you are not an athletics fan, you will probably be able to answer the first question. It is most unlikely however, that you will know the answer to the second. This stresses one of the underpinning philosophies of this book. *Coming second doesn't count.* People who come first get remembered, while those who come second get forgotten. This is true not only in athletics but in job applications, promotions and in other aspects of organizational life. This book changes the old sporting adage that, 'it does not matter whether you win or lose, it's how you play the game'. It is very concerned with winning, and suggests ways of successfully playing that game to do so.

What about the third question? The answer is, hundredths of a second. As you observe professional sports people on television competing around the world, you will notice that the champions tend to win by small margins. Golfers by the odd hole, tennis players by a tie break or one set, jockeys by a head. This is partly what keeps the audiences in suspense, and provides the thrill. At the top level of professional sport or any other professional life, there will be very little difference between the top participants. There is virtually no difference between a roomful of recent university graduates waiting to be interviewed for their first job. The selector could just as well draw straws to make the appointment. Hence, those who win a golf, tennis or racing trophy are not ten, five or even twice as good as the person who came second. On the line, at the decision point, they were just fractionally ahead of the opposition.

This book does not guarantee success. However, it does aim to, 'nudge up your average'. If in ten interpersonal influencing encounters, you typically succeed in four, then this book will help you to push it up to five or six. Drummond (1991) noted that successes were the result of small differences. A job offer may hinge on one interview, or even one part of one interview. A small, influential act may prove to be critical. This brings us to the second principle of this book which is that, *to succeed, you just need the edge over others*. This book provides you with that edge. That edge consists of small differences which, when translated into gains, add up to more than the sum of their parts. Small gains are also easier to achieve than big ones. At the individual level, it is easy to choose to use certain words and avoid others. It does not involve any major personality transformation. Externally, no one bothers to oppose isolated and apparently trivial acquisitions. Only when the gains have accumulated, do they realize what has happened. Both types of changes are important to make because, to quote Walther (1993), *there is no dress rehearsal in life*. You have to get it right, first time!

EDUCATIONAL AND WORK ORGANIZATIONS DIFFER

Many new graduate recruits into organizations naively believe that to succeed and to be promoted, it is sufficient for them to work hard, and that this will be recognized and rewarded. In short, they believe that life is fair! Their fallacious belief is founded on their only real experience of large organizations, their school and university. Unfortunately, the behaviour that is effective within educational institutions, is rarely effective in work organizations. There are at least three ways in which organizational life differs from school or university experience. First, interdependence with others is much lower in most educational contexts. For the most part your academic performance was not related to that of your classmates. Provided you studied hard, you would pass, irrespective of how well or badly your colleagues performed. Indeed, if you sought their assistance too much, you might even have been accused of cheating. In contrast, if school life is golf, organizational life is football. You are only as good as the other members of your team. You rise and fall depending on how well you all perform together. Baumeister (1982) commented that the stress in organizations on teamwork, has emphasized the virtues of sociability, co-operative spirit, flexibility and adaptability. The ability to work with others is crucial, as career success depends on good relations with co-workers and bosses. If you want to progress, you need to appear to others as productive, successful and capable. If you gain the approval of your team members, you not only gain access to rewards, but also increase their dependence on you, and thus increase your ability to shape their actions in the future (Turner, 1991; Feldman and Klich, 1991).

A second lesson from school was that the success of your fellow students did not impact on you. If everybody passed the examinations, then everybody was allowed to proceed to the next class, the next year, and from primary to secondary school and on to university. In organizational life, you are in competition with your colleagues for the senior, more desirable jobs. Organizations are pyramidal in structure, with fewer jobs available the higher you go. Constable and McCormack (1987) estimated that out of 2.5–3 million managers in Britain, 1.6 million were in supervisory or junior management; 800,000 were in middle management; and only 350,000 were in senior management. Thus, at the middle level, there are half as many posts as at the base level, and at the top level, there are half as many posts as at middle level. The figures suggest that, however good your performance, if you are seeking promotion, you will be competing for an ever declining number of posts. These estimates were made prior to a severe reduction in middle and junior management posts during the 1990s. Such de-layering of organizations has reduced the number of rungs in most company promotion ladders. Given the arithmetic, it is obvious that good work performance alone, will be insufficient to gain you promotion. Finally, in your academic environment you were a generally passive consumer of education. You were the client. In an organization, you are expected to be a producer. At your job interview, you will be asked how you think can contribute to organizational goals and profits. This is a question that shocks many first time job applicants. Once in an organization, your contribution to company goals will be assessed, and your performance and influencing skills, will determine your success.

INFLUENCING AND ORGANIZATIONAL SUCCESS

At the beginning of your organizational career, you will be an enthusiastic young professional or manager who tries hard to be competent and improve your company's service to its customers and its profitability. Consider this not unusual scenario: on joining your new company, you become so interested in your job that any other activities, such as networking or career planning, appear as irrelevant distractions. You believe that working hard, putting in a good performance will be noticed and rewarded. Part of your expected reward from the company, is being provided with the resources to allow you to do a good job. However, you start to find that, as your responsibilities grow, you spend an increasing amount of your time in competition with others for these limited resources. You dislike this activity; find it unpleasant; do it badly; and thus you frequently fail to get what you need.

Slowly, you begin to develop negative attitudes towards your colleagues who are more astute influencers. These people often succeed in securing the resources and promotion which you have failed to do. You see these influential, successful people as time-wasters who could be better employed teaching students, making sales, providing medical care, making cars, or whatever you feel that they are supposed to be really doing. You begin to mix with people like yourself, who have similar problems, and a similar level of failure. After all, it is natural to be

3

attracted to people who are similar to ourselves. Talking to them, your attitudes harden. You become confirmed in the rightness of your beliefs. To those outside of this clique of 'failures', especially senior managers, your attitudes appear cynical and politically immature. The result is that you do not build alliances with others in the organization, do not get sponsored in your career, and do not gain power. Your failure to get the resources and support that you need affects your own performance, and that of your unit or department. Passed over for promotion, senior management decides that you lack the qualities needed to make a successful contribution to the company. They decide to 'let you go'.

This depressing scenario is intended as a warning to those who believe that influencing is an optional extra for career success. That is, a game that you can choose whether or not to play. Certainly, you can choose not to participate, but then do not be surprised if some of the unpleasant consequences described above begin happening to you. You may respond that influencing is a skill that you are born with. That you either have it or you do not. While the natural influencing ability of people differs, influence is as much a science as a native ability. Thus it is possible, and essential, for everyone to improve their influencing and political skills, or else suffer the consequences (Lewicki and Litterer, 1985).

Often, your need to belong will engender a strong loyalty to the company, which the latter also encourages. However, careerwise, this is most dangerous. Observers have warned employees not to give their full loyalty to their company, as companies do not reciprocate it, as redundancy and lay-off announcements regularly confirm. Tom Peters, the famous management guru, advised new company entrants to be disloyal. He suggested that they should be loyal to their craft, loyal to their peers and should not 'sweat the boss' in the hierarchy. Peters felt that in modern times, getting better at what you are doing, serving somebody well, and being good to your network (which you would have to call upon when you were out of a job) was about the only way to enhance the odds of survival.

CAREERIST ORIENTATION TO WORK

Feldman and Weitz described a new work ethic which they called a careerist orientation to work. It incorporated six beliefs. First, that merit alone is insufficient to climb up the organizational ladder. Non-performance strategies are also needed (Feldman, 1985, 1988). It is important that you 'appear' to be promotable, that is, worthy of advancement. Second, social relationships with your manager and co-workers are critical in order for you to advance. Such relationships should appear to be social in nature, but in reality must be used calculatingly to obtain job contacts and inside-organizational information. Third, the image of being a 'team player' is central to career progression. Individuals should still pursue self-interest at work through appearing co-operative and helpful on the surface, while at the same time seeking information about how to topple the competition. Back in the 1950s David Reisman referred to this as 'antagonistic co-operation', which was teamworking that concealed the real struggle for individual survival within the organization. Fourth, individuals' career goal are usually incompatible with those of any single organization. Consequently, in order to progress, you must appear to be loyal and committed to your current employer, while keeping your options open. Fifth, obtaining promotion sometimes requires the use of unethical behaviours. However, it is important not to advocate dishonest or unethical behaviour or even acknowledge its existence. Instead, you should become adept at inconsistency and develop the ability to hold public positions that are either mutually inconsistent or inconsistent with past positions. Finally, significant proportions of work cannot be tangibly assessed. Nor can relative success on those jobs be validated. It is therefore important for you to construct socially the illusion of success and power through symbols such as dress and office design. The book takes an unashamedly careerist orientation to work, and is unlikely to endear its author to the corporate graduate recruitment profession.

IMPORTANCE OF INFLUENCING

Competence in the job without the ability to make things happen in the organization, results in wasted effort. In contrast, job competence complemented by influencing will result in career success. Influencing skills are now a necessary part of any job, whether you are in personnel, public relations, accounting or production. It does not matter if you are a new entrant to the company or a long-serving manager. Gone are the days when salespeople were the only ones who needed influencing skills. The possession of such skills is the key to surviving in today's changing work environment. The ways things get done in the flatter organization structure, especially by those in middle-level line positions or in staff posts, is through influence. Coercion and formal authority are no longer a realistic option. The influence must be subtle and sincere to get decisions made in your favour: upwards with senior management, downwards with those who report to you, and laterally with peers, co-workers and those in other organizations whose support you need. It used to be said that in order to achieve success at the bottom of the corporate ladder, you needed to put in time and acquire your professional and technical expertise. We now know that while such expertise is necessary, it is not in itself sufficient. Knowing your job is only one aspect of being effective. The other part is being influential. Every personal interaction with another person is an influencing interaction.

You will need to use influence when you are dealing with your boss or co-workers at work. What about using influence at home with your parents, girl or boyfriend or partner? What about applying it at the golf club, church, teacher–parent meeting or your residents' association? Whenever people come together, whether inside or outside an organization, there is a need to influence. Politicians and religious leaders know this. They cannot require or order us to vote for them or attend their churches. Instead, they seek to influence us. Back in the work situation, your position of power has its limits over your subordinates. You may be able to require an employee to work until 5.00 p.m. but their contract may prevent you from ordering them to do overtime. Every employee sets down a psychological line that defines their boss's authority. Beyond that line, authority will not work, but influence might.

Over-reliance on formal power may lead you to gain employee compliance rather than their commitment. Workers may do the minimum that they can get away with, because of the way that they have been approached. Because the minimum has been accomplished, the manager cannot complain to the employee. However, over a period of time, the quality of the department's work will deteriorate. By relying solely on authority, managers restrict their ability to improve the performance of their departments or units, and hence endanger their own promotion prospects. Finally, we can say that the use of authority or position power is inconsistent with the democratic values in organizations. Attempts by western companies to respond to the Japanese challenge have been characterized by strategies that involve employees, and give them greater responsibilities over the work that they do. Moreover, cost-cutting exercises, which have involved the removal of a number of organizational levels, have also had an effect. The managerial responsibilities of the eliminated posts have been redistributed amongst those who remain. Much of that re-allocation has occurred downwards. This approach, which has been labelled *employee empowerment*, has changed the role of the supervisor to one of coach or facilitator, rather than of a director. For this reason, the skill of influencing has risen to the top of the agenda for many managers and corporations. Influencing is the change strategy that fits this new value system best. In the future, companies will be hiring and promoting people who are effective influencers. These managers are able to gain the commitment of employees by harnessing the achievement of an employee's personal goals to the company's objectives.

DEFINITION OF INFLUENCING

There are many different definitions of influencing. These all highlight three key variables in the influencing process. Some definitions focus on the *influencer*, the person doing the influencing. They refer to their credibility, trustworthiness or sincerity. Other definitions stress the influencer's *message*, that is, the structure and content of the word-package that they send out. It includes what is said and how it is said, or indeed, written. Still other definitions of influencing focus on the recipient or target of the influential message, the *influencee*. They often define the influencee in terms of how they change their attitudes, values or behaviour.

It is both easy, and not very fruitful, to get bogged down in definitions. Amongst the many confusing and contradictory definitions of the concept, Zuker (1991) probably offers the most useful one. We shall build on it and define influence as, *the ability to affect another's attitudes, beliefs or behaviours — seen only in its effect — without using coercion or formal position, and in a way that influencees believe that they are acting in their own best interests.* Let us consider the definition in a little more detail.

Ability to affect another

Ability is defined as a natural or acquired competence in doing. The ability to influence is not a mysterious gift or talent possessed only by those at the top of an organization with power. Anyone can have influence, at any level in the organization. This book holds that influence can be translated into a set of behavioural skills that can be learned, practised and successfully applied in interpersonal situations.

Attitudes, beliefs and behaviours

The focus here is on *behaviour* and *action*. Changing another's attitudes, values or beliefs is only important to the extent that this affects what other people do and say. We shall see that research shows that changing a person's behaviour, can lead them to change their original attitudes, values and beliefs. The arrow of causation thus points in both directions. Ultimately, influence is about getting others to do what you want. This may be voting for your proposal, lending you money, giving you a discount on a car, giving you a promotion, or appointing you to a new job.

Seen only in its effect

Arthur C. Clarke, the science fiction writer, once wrote that, *any sufficiently developed technology is indistinguishable from magic.* In a similar way, influencing is a process that will be unobservable to both the influencee or an observer. The first they will know of it, is when they have supported your proposal, accepted your suggestion, or agreed to act as you have requested them to. With a few exceptions, if they feel that you are trying to influence them, it is a sign that you are failing.

Without exertion of force or formal authority

Influence is an alternative to the use of coercion or formal authority. Moreover, it is one which has long-term effects, avoids distrust and hostility and, if well executed, is not noticed. People will do things for you, without knowing why,

7

but feeling good about it. Such positive feelings may come partly from their assessments that they are acting in their own best interests, and achieving their own personal goals.

CENTRAL AND PERIPHERAL ROUTE

Petty and Cacioppo (1986) and Chaiken (1987) have distinguished what is one of the most fundamental differences in receptivity to an influencing attempt. Thus, most literature on the subject distinguishes two general approaches towards influencing which they label central route and peripheral route. *Central route* persuasion occurs when interested people focus on your arguments and respond with favourable thoughts. This route involves active and thoughtful processing of a message; careful scrutiny of its content, merit and logic. Computer advertisements often used this method. Studies reveal that we are more likely to take in the information if it has a personal relevance for us and we feel involved in it. The success of this route depends on the quality of arguments presented. What is crucial here is not the message itself but what response it evokes in the person's mind. Our minds are not sponges that soak up whatever message is poured into them. If the message summons up favourable thoughts, it persuades us. If it provokes us to think of contrary arguments, then we remain unpersuaded. In contrast, the *peripheral route* to persuasion occurs when people are influenced by incidental cues such as what the influencer is wearing or how she pronounces certain words. This involves relatively shallow, lazy processing of information. Little attention is given to the message's content, merit or logic. Perfume, car, cigarette and soft drink advertisements use this approach, associating the product with images of beauty, pleasure, glamour and good moods. The focus is upon superficial cues such as influencer variables, rather than message content. The question for the influencer is which route is most appropriate for their message and the audience. This book will consider both influencing routes.

SUCCESSFUL INFLUENCING

We have already noted that the three key variables in the influencing process are the influencer, the message and the influencee. To be an effective influencer, you will have to make adjustments to yourself, for example, how you look, what you say, and what you do. Additionally, you will need to spend more time on crafting your influencing message. This involves decisions on what to say, how to say it, in what communication mode, and at what time. Your choices in both these areas will be determined by your assessment of your influencees, in terms of who they are, and what you want from them. Since the target audience and influencing objective will change over time, to be successful you will need to adapt to each new influencing situation.

Successful influencers must possess awareness, flexibility and control. *Awareness* refers to the state of realization of your own and other people's feelings and behaviours, and how these affect you and them. If your awareness is low or non-existent, you will be unlikely to be a successful influencer, because you lack the means to improve. Learning, self-monitoring and feedback from others can all help to raise your self-awareness, and set you on the road to improvement by highlighting what it is that you do not do well. A second requirement for successful influencing is *flexibility*. This is your ability and willingness to adjust what you say and do to match other people's expectations, so as to achieve your goals. An example of being flexible, is deciding to use certain words and phrases while avoiding others. Your initial attempts may feel rather forced and artificial. The final requirement for successful influencing is exerting conscious *control* over your behaviour, controlling what other people do, and probably enjoying doing so. Obviously, people differ in the extent to which they enjoy controlling others. Some find it utterly distasteful. Riordan (1989) felt that in advice given to male and female managers, a Machiavellian motivation is often assumed (Christie and Geis, 1970; Koester, 1982). The person with the Machiavellian personality is held to be better at self-promotion, audience re-orientation and self-presentation. Machiavellian motives also frequently imply manipulation and egotism.

Successful influencing therefore involves making changes, sometimes dramatic ones, to your behaviour. In his book, *Race and Culture*, Robert Park the famous anthropologist, felt that is was not a historical accident that the first given meaning of the word, *person* in the dictionary, is *mask*. This underscores the fact that everyone is everywhere, more or less consciously, playing a role. Park went on to say that it is in these roles that we come to know each other, and indeed ourselves. Many people consider such flexibility in behaviour as sinister and even manipulative. As promoting deception, destroying real feelings and spontaneity, and turning human beings into insincere puppets. In contrast, Schlenker and Weigold (1990: 827) wrote that, 'It is myopic to argue that self-presentation primarily involves pretence, deception or illegitimacy. Self-presentation involves packaging desired self-identifications so that audiences draw a preferred conclusion . . . There is nothing nefarious, superficial or Machiavellian about packaging. Just as a textbook writer must edit information to present it in a readable, concise fashion, so must people edit information about themselves in everyday life to provide the "best" description possible.'

To what extent is learning and using influencing skills manipulative? One can argue that when we meet another person, we are trying to manipulate them, and they are seeking to manipulate us back. We talk in order to exchange what we want for what they want. This may be information, companionship, agreement, sexual favours, a job, a contract or understanding. Most people would feel that the word 'manipulate' was rather too strong a description for what they were doing. Instead, they would state that they were simply expressing, as efficiently, as they knew how, their natural desire to communicate successfully and efficiently. The context might be a party, interview, appraisal or a team meeting. The basic ethical line taken in this book is that ultimately, it is up to readers to decide which ideas they are willing to apply.

In making this judgement, it is useful to make some observations. First, in response to the charge that changing your natural behaviour results in 'play-acting', one might ask how that differs from foreign language learning, elocution or public speaking training. Neither teachers nor students of these subjects are criticized for being manipulative. In these three examples, the aim is to communicate more successfully with other people so as to inform, amuse, entertain them, as well as to persuade or even dominate them. Some observers feel that influencing is just common sense. Why study the obvious? If the techniques of successful influencing were so obvious, then relations between people, both inside and outside work, would proceed more smoothly than they usually do. Much of the conflict that one observes is a clear demonstration of the lack of people's knowledge, skill and practice in influencing.

Finally, critics have argued that influential behaviour is not spontaneous. Like learning any skill, initial attempts at influencing are unlikely to be spontaneous, just as developing the skill of playing tennis or driving a car, is at first awkward and artificial. O'Connor and Seymour (1990) presented a four-stage learning cycle through which a novice influencer would typically move. This is shown in Figure 1.1. Stage one represents you, the reader prior to reading this book. Although you seek to influence others, you are unaware of how ineffective you are (unconscious incompetence). By reading this book, you will realize how low your skill and knowledge in this area is, and how you could be a more effective influencer (conscious incompetence). The learning and application of the suggested techniques and principles is, at first, artificial, uncomfortable and you are very aware of what you do and say. Nevertheless, the number of your influencing successes will increase (conscious competence). O'Connor and Seymour suggest that after twenty-one days or so of continuous application of the principles and techniques, they will become second nature to you, and you will cease to even notice that you are using them. When your application of them has become automatic, you have arrived at the fourth stage of development, that of unconscious competence.

The starting point for the journey from unconscious incompetence to unconscious competence is increased self-awareness, which can be obtained by feedback from others and through greater monitoring of your own behaviours (Snyder, 1974, 1979). High self-monitors are alert to situational cues that guide them towards the presentation of what they believe are appropriate behaviours in different situations, even if these behaviours are not wholly consistent with their inner dispositions. In contrast, low self-monitors display behaviours that are congruent with inner feelings and beliefs, risking the social impropriety of so doing (Briggs and Cheek, 1988; Lennox and Wolfe, 1984). That is, they fail to adapt to the situations in which they find themselves.

1 Unconscious incompetence

2 Conscious incompetence

3 Conscious competence

4 Unconscious competence

Figure 1.1 *Four-stage learning cycle*
Source: O'Connor and Seymour, 1990

Chapter 2

Non-verbal influencing

First impressions last.

INTRODUCTION

Oscar Wilde said that, 'It is only shallow people who do not judge by appearance.' Since most people do, our non-verbal behaviour becomes a crucial part of the total message that we communicate to others. Professor Arygle found that non-verbal signals had about four and half times the effect of verbal ones (Fletcher, 2000). Mehrabian (1968, 1972) estimated that our understanding of another person is based on 7 per cent of what they actually say; 38 per cent of how they speak; and a massive 55 per cent of silent speech signals such as how they look and behave. Thus, 93 per cent of the total message that we send to others is non-verbal. Ray Birdwhistell found that two-thirds of conversations take place non-verbally. Moreover, global ratings of posture and mannerisms are closely related to positive hiring rates (Young et al., 1979). Here, we are considering those brief, subtle messages that have a powerful effect on our listeners below the level of their awareness. Although the subject of non-verbal behaviour has received wide coverage in the popular press (Spillane, 2000), more scholarly, research-based studies confirm just how powerful and influential non-verbal communication is (Anderson, 1988; Forbes and Jackson, 1980; Imada and Hakel, 1977; Gabbott and Hogg, 2000).

According to Lewis (1991), the impact of non-verbal communication (also called, 'silent speech' or 'body language'), has often been ignored or understated. Three reasons have been offered for this. First, although these types of messages exert a great deal of influence on how we think and behave, they act subconsciously upon us, and typically go unnoticed. Second, silent speech communicates enormous amounts of information, which means that it is difficult to both recognize explicitly and to control. It is for this reason that when our words and our body language contradict each other, others will believe the body language (Moine and Herd, 1984). Finally, despite being our predominant or sole mode of communication up to the age of three years, non-verbal communication, after than time it is lost under the weight of words, even though we remain extremely sensitive to its influence subconsciously.

Despite Sir John Davies's advice, given in the sixteenth century, that one should, 'judge not the play before the play has done', most people do form impressions of others during the first four minutes that they are with them. We, as human beings, exchange hundreds of units of non-verbal information about each other, even during a brief exchange. With so much data available, we can only pay attention to a small part of it. Only a tiny proportion of the available information is ever perceptually selected, even though it is available to be observed. Additionally, in order to process this vast amount of information, the human brain has developed shortcuts to save time. These can work both for and against us. One such shortcut is the *stereotype*. To save time, the brain groups together people who have similar characteristics and allocates traits to them on the basis of this grouping (e.g. Scots are mean; students are lazy). Our stereotypes are based on our own past experiences. In films and television, in order to tell a story in a short time, the characters are stereotyped for us. For examples, the Westerns of the past had the stereotypes of the Good Guy (white hat and clean shaven); the Bad Guy (black hat with beard or unshaved); the Banker (spectacles and a suit); the Sheriff (bald); and the Town Drunk (dishevelled clothes). In a similar way, the people we meet have stereotypical categories into which they place us, and assign positive and negative values. Another shortcut used by our brains is called the *halos–horns effect*. With this, we make judgements about others based on one of their striking features (positive or negative) such as their dress, handshake, posture and the use of the body and its features (including eyes), or how they occupy space.

One human being cannot but react to another in a pre-programmed way. We do it psychologically by using instincts buried deeply inside us. It is a legacy of our survival instinct when we had to make split-second assessments of others as friends or foes, in order to decide whether to stay, fight or flee. Our intellect may sometimes suspend disbelief, but our atavistic instincts are triggered involuntarily. Therefore, the starting point for using non-verbal communication as an influencing tool is to recognize that you involuntarily send off non-verbal messages to those with whom you interact. These people use mental shortcuts to make their assessment of you. Rather than complain of their misperceiving you, you can capitalize on this human perceptual process, by consciously influencing which category they place you in, and by showing them a single striking feature of yourself which will provide you with a positive halo. As we shall see, it is important to make your non-verbal messages congruent with your verbal ones, if you want to influence your listeners. As before, this means becoming aware of the non-verbal messages that you are already sending, and being flexible enough to adjust them and control influencees to your advantage. Such non-verbal communication

13

is not only capable of being learned, but is already extensively being taught (McGovern *et al.*, 1981).

The majority of people pay little or no attention to their non-verbal behaviour. They are then surprised or disappointed that they have not achieved their objective. For example, that they failed to persuade a client of the viability of their plan, or are not offered the job that they wanted, despite having got to the interview. The first impression is necessarily a non-verbal one. The contact sequence between two people is, first, look at their face, especially the eyes; second, their body; third, the clothes; fourth, listen to their tone of voice, and, fifth, shake hands. Research by Anderson (1988) suggests it takes 120 seconds after meeting another person to make that first impression. Within ten seconds, your listener will start making judgements about you – your ability, sense of professionalism and intelligence. People tend to focus first on what they see (dress, appearance, eye contact, movement), after that, on what they hear (rate of speech, tone and volume of voice), and only then on the content of your speech. After four minutes it becomes difficult to change the initial impression that you have made on them. Given the nature of human perception outlined earlier, you need to manage every second of your first contact with any new person. The adage, 'you don't get a second chance to make a first impression' is not just a well-known saying, but has a scientific basis, and is known by psychologists as the *primacy effect*. Indeed, some commentators suggest that if you do create a negative first impression once in a job, it is easier to change your department or company, than try to redeem it. Moreover, that first impression should be of someone who is extroverted, open and outgoing (Chaplin and Phillips, 2000).

There are two contexts in which the management of non-verbal signals is particularly important. The first is the selection interview, and this will be considered in greater depth in Chapter 5. The second context is the longer term, day-to-day interactions with those around you. Bruce (1992) observed that once within the organization, through their repeated exposure to you, your boss and fellow workers will build up a library of information about you, including their own remembered reactions to you. You must ensure that their library contains only suitable, positive reading material. People will 'place you' on their private map of the world by noting your physical attributes (voice, face and accent) and props (clothes, jewellery). Accurately or not, they conclude that an untidy haircut shows lack of self-discipline, that overly ornate jewellery shows vanity, and that your highly polished shoes show personal drive and self-organization.

There are three classes of message that you can send to other people about yourself – that you are inferior, superior or similar to them. Most writers agree that a submissive manner and arrogant behaviour are to be avoided when seeking to influence another person, except in some very specific circumstances which will be outlined later. The strongest recommendation is that you should become as similar to your influencee as possible. It is said that we make the most favourable judgements about those people with whom we have characteristics in common. It is these characteristics that we look for, and recognize without difficulty in others. In short, *people like people like themselves*. Davies (1991a) divided non-verbal behaviour into two broad categories – body language and clothing. In the remainder of this chapter, we shall use this distinction to identify the more and less powerful non-verbal signals, and what you can do to exert flexibility and control. Davies said that although outward appearance need not necessarily reflect internal attitude, other people believe that it does. Through the use of non-verbal behaviour, or body language, you can indicate to others how powerful you feel yourself to be in a situation, and how much power you expect to be given by others. Various facets of body language convey your personal power.

POSTURE

The dictionary defines posture, first, as position or bearing, and, second, as a frame of mind or attitude. The two are related. Good posture conveys a visual impression of self-assurance and knowledge of the situation, while a loose or sloppy stance reduces the impact or the control that you will have over others. Poor posture singles you out as a target for your opponent by making you appear vulnerable. A failure to display a firm image, indicates to observers a lack of strength on your part. If you feel weak and inferior in a situation like an inter-view, and reflect such feelings non-verbally, this can quickly lead to rejection. If in contrast, you control your behaviour, act out a part, and look strong and self-assured, your interviewer will react to what they perceive as your firmness and strength. Your controlled outward appearance will reflect to your inner self, not only creating a positive self-attitude, but also leading you to manifest more posi-tive, productive, new behaviours (Parkinson, 1989). We can distinguish three aspects of posture – sitting, standing and walking. The use of space in any of these three modes communicates a great deal about you to those around. You will be seeking to ensure that your non-verbal gestures are consistently in line with your verbal statements, and that all the time, they communicate *confidence*, *authority* and *conviction*. So what do you need to do?

Sitting

In situations of security and ease, we tend to leave the front of our body exposed, in the same way as animals roll over on their backs. When in the sitting position, uncovering our bodies communicates honesty and trustworthiness. In contrast, when we are defensive or feel under attack, we cover this area of our bodies by crossing arms and legs. Covering your face with your hands, makes you come across as nervous or even deceitful. To appear confident and at ease in a situa-tion, it is best to keep your arms at your side, hands on your lap, and your feet

15

set firmly on the ground. A second thing to remember when in the seated position, is to avoid slumping. While medical research confirms that slumping is bad for your back, social psychologists have found that slumpers are perceived as people who are depressed, defeated and who lack self-respect. So check if you are a chronic seat slumper, and if so, make a conscious effort to remove this habit, possibly by exercising. Sitting upright will make you feel and look more determined, as well as more energetic and purposeful.

At an interview avoid, if possible, deep armchairs that compel you to sit well back in them. If offered an unsuitable chair, decline it politely, giving the excuse of a bad back if necessary. Once you are in a suitable chair, locate your bottom as far back into the chair as possible. Reverse into it, bottom first. Avoid sitting down too quickly in chairs which make rude noises (the whoopie-cushion effect). Next, extend your chin, and keep it as high as possible. Direct your energy upwards so that you feel suspended from the top of your head. Now incline forward slightly, so that only the lower part of your body is touching the chair back. This allows you to fully exploit your height, making it easier to command space. You are now in the power sitting position which gives you an air of authority, which is good for listening, and which will not tire you out. Compare this to the powerless slump position, in which your bottom is located towards the front edge of the chair.

Standing

To look powerful and confident when standing, you need to position yourself where you can be clearly seen. Avoid protecting yourself by standing behind chairs or tables, or hugging the wall or a doorway. Never stand opposite an unknown male, or adjacent to an unfamiliar female. With a man, start with a more side-on position, and gradually work your way round to a more frontal one. With a woman adopt the opposite approach by starting the encounter in a frontal position, and then moving slowly to a more adjacent one. Tall people are regarded as more powerful, dominant, assertive and successful than short ones. We associate greater height with greater authority. Wilson's research, published in the late 1960s, revealed that among men at the time, each extra inch of height above 5 feet 8 inches was worth another thousand dollars on salary (Wilson, 1968). While you cannot increase your height, you can influence the perception of your height. If you reduce your overall height by slouching, you diminish your stature physically and psychologically. Standing correctly can add up to an inch to your height.

A person who stands up straight, transmits more confidence than someone who slouches. The most effective stance for both men and women is nearly military. Keep your head and chin up, rib cage high, and your stomach tucked in. Extend your head until it is stretched as far as it will go to make your spine erect, so that it feels as long as possible, then let your shoulders drop. Your feet should be spread about shoulder width, with your weight evenly distributed over both feet. Keep your knees slightly bent, so that your buttocks tuck under. Never cross your legs while standing. Except when eating, arms should be at the sides, fingers slightly cupped. Avoid folding your arms or hugging your chest with them. When talking to a taller person, rather than coming in close, and having to look up at them, move back until your gaze is level with theirs. Avoid shuffling or swaying when talking. Try to mirror the body position of the person that you are talking to, and whom you may be trying to influence. You may find that you are already doing so unconsciously.

Walking

People typically move in one of two ways, either jerkily and swiftly, or smoothly and slowly. The first style can be off-putting. If you approach another person in a rush, you will appear as furtive, nervous, tense, lacking in control, low status and worried. Only the most junior people in an office rush around. Rushing produces a feeling of suspicion and distrust in other people. They will come to see you as lacking confidence, uncertain and devious. In contrast, the smooth and slow style, puts everyone at their ease, and makes it easier for you to be listened to. Walk slowly, deliberately and walk tall. Take time to review your surroundings. Adopt the manner of a proprietor, not the furtive air of somebody who does not really belong. Imagine you own the place and move accordingly. Never allow yourself to be hurried. As you walk slowly, your stature grows. Wait, absorb and slowly proceed. Wheat (Fortune, 2003) notes that when powerful people stride into a room, they pause in the doorway, suggesting that it is a frame within which others can view their 'picture of power'. Move calmly, coolly and deliberately. Without appearing diffident or lacking in enthusiasm, take your time entering offices and sitting down. By making your movements smooth, fluid and better co-ordinated, you convey the silent message of relaxed confidence, authority, determination, dominance and directness. In this way, you increase your sense of presence. The effect of modifying the way you sit, stand and walk, not only makes your physical presence more striking, but it also helps you to develop a more positive mental attitude. Your emotions and expressions are all intimately linked with your posture.

OCCUPATION OF SPACE

Stechert (1986) noted that the more status someone possesses, the more space they control. Powerful people in business take up more space and have fewer reservations about invading the space of others. In contrast, less powerful ones back off and yield space to others. Dominant people are free to move in the territory of others (the boss freely walks into the subordinate's office or cubicle); they are accorded more space for their bodies (no one crowds the top brass around a meeting table); and the space they control is more desirable (bigger offices with good views). High-status people even take up more space with their privileges, such as their company car parking. The more space you occupy, whether physical or office, the more confidence and authority you will convey. In addition, how we occupy that space is also important for communicating a confident image. Davies (1991a) observed that people who find themselves in new and uncomfortable situations, or who are on their best behaviour such as at an interview, will typically tend to fill up very little space. They position themselves symmetrically so that they will look neat, tidy and contained. Alternatively, they often perch on chairs or stand in doorways. As we relax, we fill up more space, by asymmetrical positioning, letting our arms and legs stretch out to the sides. When with other females, women do spread their bodies more, but when face-to-face with men, one of the unspoken rules, is that the man's body should be wider than the woman's.

It is therefore important to occupy a reasonable amount of space and look comfortable in it. Becoming aware of how you typically stand or sit can achieve this. If you are seated squarely on the chair, you might rest your hands on the table in front of you, thus expanding your personal space. Marking out territory can also be achieved by placing papers and other possessions around you at meetings and elsewhere. This extends your physical influence. You can look comfortable in your marked space by sitting in the power position in your chair, resting your arms on the chair arms or, if seated at a table or desk, steepling your hands together, or resting them on the table.

You will want to avoid invading other people's space unintentionally, and in particular, their intimate zone (Glaser and Smalley, 1992). Doing this can cause friction and be counterproductive. Personal space, defined as the distance between two people when they are sitting or standing, is important. Make sure that you are working at the correct distance to achieve the results that you require. Take into account individual and cultural differences, as well as the nature of the relationship. Table 2.1. shows the preferred distances of different cultures and countries. Learn to work at a variety of distances without feeling alienated or uneasy. The more flexible that you can be in manipulating another's various zones, the greater will be the control that you will be able to exert in the encounter. Keep an arm's length distance between yourself and the other person. When occupying a chair, do not bury yourself in it. Spread out, your torso erect, and place your elbows loosely on the arms of your chair, leaning forward occasionally in a relaxed manner. In this way, you are occupying all the space that is available to you, without invading another's.

If you do want to invade another's space deliberately as a power play, be aware that you will provoke a powerful increase in their arousal. Under certain circumstances, deliberately violating someone's personal space can enhance mutual liking. But only do so if you are rewarding someone with verbal praise.

18

Table 2.1 *Preferred personal zone distances*

Close	Medium	Far
Arabs	British	White North Americans
Japanese	Swedes	Australians
South Americans	Swiss	New Zealanders
French	Germans	
Greeks	Austrians	
Black North Americans		
Hispanics		
Italians		
Spanish		

Source: Lewis, 1991: 108

Under these conditions, closing the distance between you will enhance their liking of you, their interest and their willingness to co-operate. Never stand when somebody is sitting, unless it is your intention to dominate or intimidate them. As we noted earlier, height is a powerful dominance signal.

INVOLVEMENT AND DETACHMENT

Davies (1991a) suggested that you can communicate a sense of involvement by leaning forward towards your influencee, and detachment by sitting back from them, with your fingers over your mouth. Coming over as detached implies defensive behaviour, indicating a person not wanting to risk involvement or partic-ipation. If your influencee is communicating this behaviour to you, ask them directly for a response ('what do you think?') to discover where they stand. We shall consider this and similar strategies in the chapter on influencing a group. Showing interest non-verbally is easy since there is nothing that interests us more than ourselves. When people take an interest in us, we become more interested in them. To communicate an interest in another person, make them feel impor-tant valued and appreciated. Verbally, you could use flattery, or non-verbally, by using gaze directed at them. This is probably the most powerful silent signal that is available to communicate interest in another person.

POSITIONING

How you position yourself with respect to another person is important in building rapport with them. Sitting at the head of an average table conveys importance, while the same position at a long table shows detachment. Sitting at right angles to your influencee builds empathy between you, and is less confrontational than sitting face to face. Obviously, how you can position yourself depends on the furniture available, how it is positioned and whether it can be changed. The role of office furniture in impression management has been extensively studied (Ornstein, 1989; Lewis, 1991; Campbell, 1979). Just as we judge people on the basis of the clothes that they wear, we also judge them on the basis of their office environment. A person with a clean, tidy desk or office is deemed to have a logical and ordered mind. However erroneous this may be, you have nothing to lose, and much to gain, by keeping your desk, cubicle or office space neat. If you have an office area of your own, decorate it to project the image that you want others to have of you. You have the choice of including or excluding plants, family photos, souvenirs, charts, graphs, articles, certificates and so on. Do not make your office too comfortable or permanent, especially if you wish to be seen as someone who is on the move to a more senior position.

In an interview situation, if you have a choice, choose a chair beside the interviewer so that you are at 90 degrees to each other, with no barrier between you. If you are across a desk, shift your chair slightly, so that you are not directly in front of the other person. Once in the chair, always sit asymmetrically, and take up as much space as possible. Choose a chair without sides, that is easy to get in and out of, and puts you at the same height as the other person. Monitor your body language, so as to make sure that you do not come across as desperate for the job, or desperate for your suggestion to be accepted. Look comfortable, as if you are enjoying yourself. When chairs can be moved, the rules for personal distance outlined earlier apply. However, you can get away with sitting closer to a person than you could if you were standing next to them. This is because their chair increases their sense of security, especially when its arms provide a physical barrier between you and them.

CONTROL OF DISPLACEMENT ACTIVITY AND GESTURES

When you experience tension, at a meeting or at an interview, your body prepares itself for a fight or flight response. This is reflected in comforting displacement behaviour such as the clenching of fists, the setting of your jaw, bracing your legs and puffing out your chest. However, like walking, such visible, fast, erratic hand movements convey to observers your inner feelings of pressure. When nervous or tense, you will tend to do things that displace this, such as stroking or rearranging the hair, fiddling with jewellery, tapping a pencil, part covering your face, twiddling your thumbs, or re-arranging your clothes. Glaser and Smalley (1992) strongly warn women to avoid giving signals that they are tense or uncertain when making a point. While such 'displacers' are one way of dealing with tension, they can be off-putting to those looking at you, and more importantly, they send them the message that you are not in control, and are of low status. It is therefore more beneficial to find ways of relaxing yourself before a stressful interaction, and to control your displacement activity during it. Davies (1991a) recommends physically relaxing through controlled breathing, shaking out arms and legs, and easing tension from the neck and shoulders. You can focus your tension on an object, such as having a pen to grip firmly. This diverts your tension in a way that is not distracting for observers. The absence of displacement activity will convey status, and show you as confident, relaxed but purposeful.

The pace and direction of your gestures represents another area of non-verbal communication. Stechert (1986) noted that women are non-verbally submissive to dominant males. In their body movements, men stress gestures that move away from their bodies. To convey power, you should gesture from below your face, moving them out from the body, rather than beginning your gesture at face level, and then moving inwards towards your body. Use gestures such as pointing with hands and forearms in the area between the chin and the waist. These are power gestures which match and confirm your words, and do not distract or contradict them. Used sparingly, gestures can add impact, but if overdone, they can diminish the strength of your delivery.

Men's gestures are dominant ones that show relaxation and aggressiveness at the same time. People with status can afford to be relaxed. Inferiors usually keep a closed posture with their bodies contracted, clothing tidy, and a buttoned-up, closed, rigid posture, which indicates fearfulness. In a group, the high-status speaker will lean back, hands behind head, body in an asymmetrical position taking up the maximum amount of space. Another power gesture for a man is sitting with a leg over a chair. In contrast, women articulate with their fingers, hands and wrists when they gesture, but generally move less than men. In addition they look at speakers more, and smile and nod more than men. They open and close their eyes more slowly, and more intermittently than men, and demonstrate more affiliative behaviour, conveying warmth and expressiveness. Men use behaviour to indicate status and dominance. A woman can exert more power by consciously relaxing in a man's office. She can extend herself over his territory by leaning over his desk; crowding him; spreading her possessions (papers, diary, work materials); and by touching his belongings.

However, women should avoid matching men's dominance gestures with their own submissive ones. For example, when a male crowds a woman, she should not yield by moving back. When he frowns, she does not need to smile. When he stares, she does not need to lower her eyes. Such submissive non-verbal responses reinforce the higher status and power of men in the workplace, and exacerbate gender inequality. The problem for women is particularly acute. Many authors have cautioned women against tilting or nodding their heads. This gesture can make them appear subservient, submissive and timid. Frequently women are unaware of this behaviour. Nevertheless, it reinforces their little-girl image when they are talking to men. When accompanied by a tag question ('What do you think?'), the head tilt makes the woman appear indecisive. Do not bob your head while listening to someone. You may appear to be agreeing with them even if you do not.

In contrast, Fox and Spector (2000) found that successful applicants at interviews (amongst other things), tended to shake or nod their heads, used their hands to make gestures, made direct eye contact and smiled (Amalfitano and Kalt, 1977). Perhaps the solution is to use gestures to amplify and reinforce your words by them, but use steady positive movements, in order to communicate your own ease and confidence to your listener. Beyond the interview, orders and requests gain power if they are delivered with little head movement. Practise relaxed stillness with little distracting movement. The power of stillness recommends that when someone is pressurizing you, slowing down your movement can help you to dictate the pace of response, and prevent their forcing your hand. Aguinis and Henke (2001) highlighted another 'no win' situation. They found that when women used assertive, non-verbal behaviour like direct eye contact (in line with the male stereotype of a manager) they were perceived as using coercive power, thereby creating resistance, reduced organizational commitment and dissatisfaction among their subordinates. When they had a relaxed facial expression, in contrast to a nervous one, they were perceived to possess lower power. It seems that if women fulfil their organizational role expectations, they simultaneously violate their gender role expectations, and may be perceived negatively.

EYE CONTACT

Eye contact is probably the single most researched and discussed aspect of body language. Our eyes reflect brain activity and move around as we think. Glaser and Smalley (1992) wrote that the more eye contact you engage in, the more alert, dependable, confident and responsible you will be judged to be. When used with a high energy level, speech fluency and voice modulation, above average eye contact has a major impact. Davies (1991a) noted that the making and breaking of eye contact played a crucial role in transmitting power. Failure to establish eye contact both signals submissiveness and invites interruption. Averted eyes suggests non-assertion, while steady, sustained eye contact is very powerful. Eye contact should be steady and good when first meeting. This reassures your speaking partner that you are paying attention, and subtly flatters them by conveying that what they are saying has great interest for you. After this, eye contact should be made at frequent intervals while talking and listening. It should be long enough to acknowledge the person. Neither so long that you stare and disturb the other person, nor so short that you appear frightened. Staring relentlessly at others is both unnerving and unnatural.

Never look down, but maintain contact when listening or talking. Keep your gaze on the speaker steady and firm, but get and give some relief by looking away every few seconds. Under normal circumstances, never hold gaze for more than three seconds during the initiation stage of a meeting. Look, then break eye contact briefly. Any violation of this rule can create a negative impression, even though the person receiving the message is unable to explain the reason for their feelings of discomfort. When breaking eye contact with another person, do it downwards. The only exception to this rule is during a power play when it is your deliberate intention to disconcert your opponent. An upward eye break conveys a lack of interest in them, and is likely to throw them temporarily off balance. So normally, break gaze down, left or right, but never upwards.

When speaking to a group, ensure your gaze includes them all, and then establish eye contact with individual members. If one of the group members sends you facial signals of disinterest or disapproval, your natural response is to avoid looking at them. However, you gain power by doing just the opposite. Increase the amount of eye contact you make with your opposer. They may be behaving thus because they need attention. Rather than allowing yourself to be discouraged by their show of self-importance, acknowledge their need for recognition. This will help you to persuade them. If you are on the receiving end of a gaze, refocus your eyes on their feet or watch. Eyes are probably the most important aspect of non-verbal communication. Always initiate the 'eyebrow flash' (the upward movement of the brows when meeting), and whenever possible, always respond to another's eyebrow flash unless you deliberately intend to signal hostility (Lewis, 1991).

On the related issue of looking around, there is a difference of opinion as to whether this denotes high or low status. On the one hand, Stechert (1986) asserts that high-status people do less looking, and that it is only the low-status ones who are most vigilant, needing to monitor the behaviour of others in order to know how to behave, and to discover what they are up to. In this view, the environment controls them, and they need to be constantly on their guard. In contrast, Bedoyre (1990) argued that actual and potential leaders had constantly to be aware of their environment, the monarchs of all that they surveyed. They would look steadily, holding their gaze, while lesser people broke off and looked away. This steady, direct look, neither threat nor gesture of intimacy, is often used by the dominant person at the start of a social encounter. The relative 'level' of people is established at the start of their interaction, and becomes hard to change afterwards. Perhaps these two views can be reconciled by focusing on the *type* of looking done. Stechert's furtive, quick glances, can indeed be held to signal low status, while Bedoyne's use of gaze – the steady and intense look, coupled with controlled walking which says, 'I belong here' can signal high status.

23

Control of your eye contact allows you to send non-verbal impressions to others. Staring is a powerful device for establishing their inferiority, while not looking at the person who is speaking to you or to whom you are speaking, can also reinforce your superiority. The latter, apart from being disconcerting to them, conveys to them in how low esteem you hold them. If you want to convey your interest, intensity, seriousness and self-confidence, you should fix your gaze in the triangle bounded by the person's eyes and nose. Maintain eye contact for about 60 per cent of your total interaction time with them. Less than that and you will be interpreted as shifty, uneasy and lacking in confidence; longer than that, and you will be seen as aggressive. The triangle of facial gaze principle recommends focusing on the eyes and nose in normal conversation, and eyes, nose and mouth for more intimate discussions.

Finally, let us consider lying. Lying is a way of influencing people. Deceiving others and trying to detect deceit is part of daily life, social as well as organizational. What behaviours do people show, and which do they think they show, when telling a lie. There is a gap between believed and actual behaviours.

Vrij *et al.* (2001) found that people are poor at detecting lies, achieving an accuracy of a little over 50 per cent. There are several reasons for this. Often, people do not want to know the truth; conversation rules prevent one person observing a suspected liar properly. Observers often look for the wrong things when attempting to detect deceit, as there are no typical behaviours shown by liars. Finally, observers fail to take personal differences into account, and the differences between liars and truth tellers are usually small.

There is a general, stereotypical belief about what non-verbal behaviours are exhibited when someone is lying. These include smiling frequently; avoiding direct eye contact; looking away; and increased hand, finger and foot movements. Researchers have found these stereotypes to be incorrect. There are huge individual differences in deceptive behaviour, and thus no 'typical' non-verbal behaviour to indicate lying. The explanation of the inconsistency between actual and believed behaviours, is that people are unaware of their own behaviour when they are lying. They have greater self-insight into their para-verbal behaviours. There are some of these characteristics more often seen in liars than truth tellers. These included speaking in a high-pitched voice; making more speech hesitations and errors; waiting longer before giving an answer; pausing more often; and speaking more slowly. Conversely, and perhaps surprisingly, truth-tellers, tell their stories in a more unstructured way; include more unusual details; make more spontaneous corrections to their stories; and admit a lack of memory more often. It seems that liars get caught because of what they say (content), not how they say it (para-verbal), and one of the main reasons is lack of preparation. However, the variability of behaviour mentioned earlier, makes lying difficult to detect (Ekman and Friesen, 1974; Hocking *et al.*, 1979;).

24

FACIAL EXPRESSION

The eyes are the dominant features in everyone's face. Davies (1991a) stated that the bottom half of the face is as important as the top half in conveying comfort and confidence in a situation. The jaw and mouth are common sites of tension, and can communicate your feelings of nervousness or insecurity. The more relaxed your muscles are here, the more you can project the facial expression that you want. The converse is also true. Tension sets your face rigid. In most influencing situations, individual or group, your aim is to keep people listening to you. Hence, an animated face with a changing facial expression is essential. People trust others more when they show their emotions through their faces. Your facial expression tells others how they should respond to you. While you will want to maintain a relaxed animated face so as to keep the interest of your observers, there are some circumstances in which not giving too much away through facial expressions may be a better strategy.

Of the various facial expressions, the smile is probably the most powerful. Correctly used, it is a valuable aid to influencing. It projects warmth, conveys confidence and is useful in establishing rapport. Used inappropriately, when it contradicts your tone of voice or content of speech, it sends a mixed message which is discounted by your listeners. When you are angry, or are trying to sell something, you want to be taken seriously, so do not smile. In this context, women are frequently advised to smile only *when pleased*, rather than to smile in order *to please*. Women, especially younger ones, tend to smile, giggle or laugh when nervous. Such behaviour is often interpreted as girlish and silly. Stechert (1986) noted that smiles are often a gesture of appeasement or submission offered upward in the status hierarchy. Smiles also signal nervousness, apology, greeting and, when used with angry words, soften the negative impact of a message. They are also used when seeking approval (Park, 1979; Shannon, 1987). Bavelas and Chovil (2000) recommend that women should actively control their smiles, appearing warm but serious and confident at the same time.

For this reason, smiles that come too freely and in inappropriate situations, often indicate uncertainty and discomfort. Nervous, mirthless smiling and laughing, can become a habit. Once you become aware of it you will see it and hear it all around you in the office. Women often smile not only to mask negative or disturbing feelings, but also to put others at ease, to encourage others, to fill gaps in the conversation, and to create a relaxed and comfortable atmosphere. Used consciously and sparingly, smiles can be useful in business. When listening to another person, women smile 17 per cent of the time, while men smile 8 per cent. Because women tend to smile more easily and more often, they find the lack of smiles from men confusing. However, an absence of smiles in men does not necessarily indicate that they are feeling less friendly or attentive, although this may appear so to a woman.

25

Whatever your gender, you should avoid compulsive smiling. Your expressions need to match your message. Do not laugh when you are saying something serious. Although it is believed that our features reflect our emotions, others believe that our features can create emotions in us. At a personal level, if you are depressed, by physically forcing yourself to smile, you can become emotionally happier. In such circumstances, you will smile, not because you are happy, but because you want to feel happy. Finally, you should not forget the point about matching. By observing the other person, and matching your expressions, smile or frowns with theirs, you can help to create empathy, and thereby establish a rapport and a more harmonious relationship with them.

TOUCH

Used judiciously, the use of touch can assist in projecting an impression of either warmth, caring or of control. Touch can facilitate compliance and pro-social behaviour from strangers as a product of heightened involvement, increased arousal, perceptions of status or greater awareness to provide assistance (Remland and Jones, 1994). For example, a simple touch on the arm can emphasize a point and leave a lasting impression on the recipient. When proving a certain point, a touch on the arm can emphasize that point in a different way, later guiding the listener to remember it subconsciously (Bates, 1995). Used inappropriately it can backfire and you will come across as patronizing. Depending on the national culture, you can actually cause offence. All in all, touching can be quite a dangerous non-verbal behaviour. In Anglo-Saxon cultures, the single most important, and often only touch, is the handshake. It is usually the only physical contact that you will have with another person. When meeting senior people for the first time, have your right hand prepared to shake theirs, but only shake it, if they offer you theirs first. Do not initiate the handshake in such circumstances. With people at the same and lower levels, for example, work colleagues and subordinates, offer your hand to them first. Smile while you shake hands, and maintain a neutral expression while talking. The brevity of a handshake can understate its importance. It can silently give any signal from intended dominance at one extreme to unequivocal surrender at the other.

There are different types of handshakes, and some of them are shown in Figure 2.1. You should make your handshake brief and firm. Make the contact, apply a moderate pressure, hold it for a second or two, and release the hand. The clasp should communicate confidence. Grasp the other person's full hand and not just the fingers, or high up on the thumb. Women are sometimes unsure of when and how to shake hands, and their uncertainty comes over in this aspect of their body language. Just use straight fingers and flat palm. We are told that a limp, cold handshake can be most off-putting to the recipient, and can be taken to imply the possession of these qualities by its owner. A very tight

WHAT KIND OF HANDSHAKE?

Study these to discover what kind of handshakes you give. You may need to make some adjustments to yours, unless you already shake hands on equal terms.

A Equal terms
Both hands are vertical, with thumbs together and the shake is firm but relaxed.

B Taking control
Hands are turned so that the controlling hand is on top of the open palm. Fine for lovers, but not so good in business.

C The pull
Pulling a person closer may mean a lack of confidence or a need for closer contact.

D Fingers only
Either given or taken, this is the shake of someone who holds back and doesn't give themself.

E The cold fish
Floppy, cold or damp, this handshake is unmistakable and uninviting. Ask your friends to check if you do it unwittingly.

F The clamping vice
Ouch! is the usual response. Used by aggressive people who like to appear tough.

G The protector
A double hand-clasp is warm between friends but implies a need to ingratiate from a stranger. Many politicians use this one.

Figure 2.1 Handshakes

Source: Pilkington et al., 1992: 91

grasp, is similarly said to give the impression of an aggressive person. Avoid the Wet Kipper handshake by keeping your hand dry. If you perspire when nervous, grasp a paper hankie in your pocket just before you go into the interview room. If you want to communicate dominance, use the Great Man or Woman Grip which involves a stronger than normal pressure, and a slightly longer than usual grasp. To convey friendship and a desire for co-operation, use the Get Together Grip, that is, moderate pressure and the hand held a little longer. If you want to add a little assertiveness to your hand signal, then apply slightly greater pressure. Wheat (Fortune, 2003) suggests that the same 'Proctor' (double) handshake is also used when one powerful person meets another. Maintain eye contact throughout the handshake. There is one other touch behaviour that is permissible in Anglo cultures, but which is less commonly used than the handshake. This is the touch or grasp of the upper arm. The 'neutral zone', located between the elbow and the shoulder. Try to initiate a farewell handshake, as this can reinforce positive feelings established during the meeting. It allows you to control final moments of the encounter, subtly communicating the sense of having been in control of the situation throughout. Handshaking is important because of the primacy and recency effects. We tend to remember what was said and done at the beginning and end of social encounters, while the content of the middle is forgotten.

Chaplin and Phillips's (2000) research into handshaking revealed that there were gender differences related to handshaking. Men's and women's handshakes differed on most dimensions. In general, men had a firmer shake than women, and such firmness was more favourably rated. Men with firm handshakes were perceived to be more extroverted, less shy and more open to experience. Women with the firmer handshakes were perceived to be more open to experience than men. Men were found to form more positive impressions from handshakes than women. The implication is that if you meet a male interviewer, you have the opportunity to make a good first impression through the handshake; if you meet a female interviewer, it is important to avoid a poor handshake.

APPEARANCE

Height is an important variable, especially for men. Stechert (1986) noted that dominant people are likely to be bigger than others. Wilson (2000) reported that in the dating game, size does matter! Empirical research found that bachelors tended to be an inch shorter than married men. The explanation is not that women select men for their height, but they use height to guide them on to their real interests – genes, wealth and status. Research has shown that tall men are more successful academically, socially and financially, so women who think tall is their type are believed to crave these other qualities. Beyond sexual attraction, numerous studies have revealed that the western ideal height for men is

6 feet 2 inches (and slowly rising). The connection between height and status is embedded in language. Respected men have 'stature' and are 'looked up to' (*Economist*, 1995–6; Wilson, 1968). The prejudice against short men (5 feet 5 inches and below) appears to be universal and not restricted to western culture. Back in organizations, a 1980 survey found that more than half of the chief executives of American Fortune 500 companies were over six feet tall. By carefully selecting your clothes, you can make yourself appear taller, and thus be perceived as more important. More recent research by Harper (2000) in the UK found that tall men earned 5 per cent more than average men, and 10 per cent more than short men; and that short women were penalized by 5 per cent on average.

Weight

Weight discrimination has been shown by studies, to be much more prevalent in the hiring process than bias against race or gender. Tretheway's (1999) research suggests that male professionals respond negatively to large females who are overweight, believing them to be lazy or lacking in self-control, and thus not to be trusted with professional responsibilities. In contrast, a 'fit' body is seen as exuding confidence and discipline, signalling that its occupant is capable of performing the duties required of a professional woman. Prejudice against overweight women is most severe. A national survey in the United States showed that white women who were 'slightly chunky' earned 6 per cent less than thinner women while white men who were a 'little heavy' received 7 per cent less in salary than slimmer men. Managers in the US appear to be critical of heavy employees because of perceived higher cost such as higher medical insurance bills. Bosses blame overweight people for their condition, and it has become an acceptable bias (Asher, 2000). Roehling (1999) reported that in 1990, the starting salaries of 'normal-weight' people with MBA degrees were on average, $3,000 higher than their overweight counterparts. Another 1998 study, found that mildly obese white women earned 5.9 per cent less than normal weight ones, and those morbidly obese earned 24.1 per cent less. As the size of children and young people continues to grow, these findings are significant. Overweight women earned 5 per cent less than the average, although fat men earned as much as slim ones. Apart from being overweight, a poor complexion can count against you.

Looks

Looks are crucial. Physical attractiveness has been defined as the degree to which one's physical and facial image elicits favourable reactions from others. The frontal face is most generally used for judgements of attractiveness because it is omnipotent and omnipresent. The attractiveness bias leads to the '*what is beautiful is good*' stereotype. Attractiveness affects first impressions in job interviews, subsequent

29

selection placement and promotion decisions. It operates by the tie-breaker effect that states that when the abilities or qualifications of candidates are similar, an applicant's appearance becomes the determining factor (Chiu and Babcock, 2002; Benson et al., 1976). Hamermesh and Biddle (1994) found that people described as attractive, earned more statistically, than average-looking people, and far more than below-average looking people. Cosmetic surgery, although expensive and some would say unethical, can change your features. Over a lifetime of earnings, it may be a sound investment to go under the knife. Many top fashion models do this, but this trend has spread to marketing executives and investment bankers. The study suggests that the majority of people have to do the best with the features they were born with, using make-up and haircuts, in order to increase their physical attractiveness.

But is beauty not in the eye of the beholder and culturally determined? Apparently not. Beauty it appears is recognized universally, transcending all racial and cultural barriers. In a beauty test devised by Dr Stephen Marquardt, and completed by respondents from all around the world, there was 97 per cent agreement as to what constituted a beautiful person. What is looked for in the face? The biological preferences for the sexes are 'recurring themes' (harmony) and symmetry (or balance). Men seek women with big eyes, smooth skin, lustrous hair and luscious lips. Women look for men who possess symmetrical features (Bates and Cleese, 2001). Good-looking people do better at job interviews (Straus et al., 2002); and earn more than ugly ones. Harper (2000) found that the pay penalty for unattractiveness was about 15 per cent for men and 11 per cent for women, which is a little higher than the 8–12 per cent range reported by Solnick and Schweitzer (1999). Another study of Dutch advertising firms, found an association between good-looking executives, higher revenues and business success (Economist, 2003). The most desirable employee is healthy, well groomed and possesses a pleasant expression. Handsome men outperform less good-looking ones in managerial and clerical jobs. Generally, physical attractiveness is beneficial (Perlini et al., 1999). Physically attractive people are judged to be more sociable, dominant, warm, mentally healthy, intelligent and socially skilled than unattractive people. For this reason attractive people are more likely to be hired and promoted (Marlow et al., 1996), and will also earn more (Frieze et al., 1991; Hamermesh and Biddle, 1994). However, good looks are only advantageous to women seeking clerical jobs. Attractive women may be penalized when applying for managerial positions (Heilman and Saruwatri, 1979). A handsome man was seen as likeable and possessing integrity, and his success tended to be attributed to his capability. An attractive female's success was ascribed to luck or connections, and she was perceived as having less integrity (Heilman and Stopeck, 1985a, 1985b).

Why should this be so? The argument is that attractiveness enhances either perceived masculinity or femininity, and is thus a potential asset for both men and women. However, if a job is masculine sex typed, as managerial jobs tend to be, then attractiveness only benefits men. Attractive females, who are perceived as more feminine than less attractive ones, are more negatively evaluated for such jobs, and are seen as possessing less good person–job 'fit'. Why should we be affected in this way? One possible theory is that we tend to view attractive individuals as possessing other positive qualities that could be considered relevant to our liking of them, such as talent, kindness, honesty and intelligence (Cialdini and Goldstein, 2002). Additionally, attractiveness can trigger a heuristic which leads us to mindlessly agree with, and be influenced by, those we see as likeable (Kipnis et al., 1984). Overall, the research data appears to support the view that successful beauty treatment and plastic surgery, can be a career-enhancing investment.

Clothes

Appearance, in terms of clothing, represents a separate category of non-verbal behaviour. Although most of the claims made in dress-for-success manuals have not been scientifically verified, some research has been carried out on the impact on interpersonal impressions (Hamid, 1972; Jackson, 1983; Kaiser, 1985; Rucker et al., 1981; Scherbaum and Shepard, 1987). In one poll, three-quarters of organizations studied, had a formal policy on dress and appearance for at least some of their staff (IRS Employment Trends, 2000). Within company constraints, managing the impression that you communicate through your clothing is important. Impressions of authority can be manipulated to increase your power. You need to *look* like you are in authority. Since distance helps authority, clothes can function as distancing mechanisms. Uniforms, judges' wigs, doctors' white coats are all used in this way. Business suits create a similar effect. Bedoyre (1990) wrote that people have stored patterns of responses for recognizing authority, and that external trigger signs like dress activate these. People assume substance from appearance, and this means that you need to project your authority non-verbally.

The concept of authority in organizations is expressed in the right to manage. Although authority rests on the idea of legitimacy, many managers hesitate to use their authority, simply for fear of looking foolish, if their authority is successfully challenged. Whatever clothing you choose, make sure that it fits the message that you want to communicate about yourself, and avoid anything that might contradict your chosen image. Consider all aspects of appearance (hair, make-up). Choose your clothes to communicate any one of a number of messages, depending on the circumstances. For example, your attractiveness, that you are feeling good, that you are a competent and professional individual; that you fit in with the crowd; that you are different from the crowd; that you are approachable; or that you are in authority.

31

Let your clothes suit your image, and your image should match the job. This may be at the job selection interview, or later, as an organization member. The clothes you wear make a statement about your personality to others. What is important is that you *choose* what statement you wish to make, and ensure that you are consistent in your clothes from day to day. Inconsistency is disconcerting for clients and bosses. It may also lead them to believe that inconsistent dressing is an indication of inconsistent thinking or unpredictable behaviour. Your clothes are amongst the first non-verbal signals that are perceived by another person. Shakespeare's Hamlet said that, 'The apparel oft proclaims the man' (and indeed the woman). Dress to express yourself and not cover yourself up. You should think of your clothes as wrapping 'packages'. These vary in their degree of formality. Alan Pease distinguishes between very casual clothes (No. 1s) to very formal ones (No. 5s), with all others located in between. Categorizing men's clothing is easier than females', as current fashion and individuality play more of a role in female clothing. For men, the range may be from T-shirt, jeans and trainers to dark-blue, pin-striped suit, white shirt, striped tie, long black socks and black, lace-up shoes. Spillane (1993a; 1993b) discussed different aspects of both male and female clothing. There are some general observations that hold true for both men and women. Changing your 'package', alters others' perceptions of you.

The advice offered to women is to 'fit in' and to practise gender management. This involves selectively borrowing masculine modes of appearance that are gender appropriate. For example, muted colours, a tailored suit, and short or medium length hair (Cianni and Rombmerger, 1997). It seems that the way a women dresses can influence her chances of success and promotion in companies (Kimble and Damhorst, 1997). Wearing the appropriate clothes makes a woman feel more confident in her role (Bartlett, 1994). Past examinations of the relationship between fashion and identity amongst women fall into two camps. The 'stitched up' school argues that women's choices in fashion are restricted by social constraints such as patriarchal, capitalist effects. Women are therefore forced to generate a distorted image of themselves, through defensive and misleading use of clothes. Books on female attire, such as *The Women's Dress for Success Book* by John Molloy (1978), may fall into this category. They advise females to conform to some standard, be it a clone of male's dress, or some variation on a theme. Their formality ranges between casual, represented by blouse, jersey and jeans, through to formal, represented by dark-coloured two-piece suit, white blouse and scarf. The 'gaping seams' school of thought, argues that what you choose to wear, reflects your inner self, and that this can be expressed at many levels. It holds that choice of clothes discloses unique and socially shared connotations. Wearers can use their clothes to express pleasure and fulfilment or rebellion and defiance.

However, the situation may be more complicated than popular accounts might claim. The complexity and ongoingness of the process of self-presentation through clothes has been extensively discussed (Guy and Banim, 2000). Wilson (2003) distinguished between female with male management traits that could be possessed by both men and women in an organization. The masculinity of women's clothing has been found to have a positive effect on the perception of masculine management characteristics. At a job interview, women can use dress to convey these, thereby increasing their chances of success. The more masculine the outfit worn by a woman, the more favourable the hiring decision was found to be (Forsythe *et al.*, 1984, 1985; Cash, 1985). However, it appears that the masculinity of the clothing worn by women, does not affect the perception of feminine managerial traits, Wilson reported research showing that female applicants were rated highly on feminine management traits, irrespective of the masculinity of their costume. In contrast, a more masculine costume was necessary to enhance the perception of masculine managerial traits (Forsythe, 1987). However, there may be a limit to how masculinely a woman can be dressed, as negative consequences have been found for women who dress in ways that are considered too masculine (Garber, 1992; Tretheway, 1999). Wilson described this problem for women as a double-bind situation.

Guy and Banim's (2000) research suggests that clothes not only project an image but also promote self-realization. An outfit with a history can affect moods and how a person handles a situation. This suggests that fashion can be used both to influence the opinions of observers, and the moods of its wearer. They recommend that it is not enough to project a positive image. A woman must also mentally feel positive. This means wearing not only what affects another's view of her, but also what influences her herself. They found that women's relationships with their clothes fell into three different groupings, depending on the wearers' perception of themselves. When she felt powerful and in control, she was 'the woman I want to be'. When miserable and lacking self-worth, she was the 'the woman I fear I could be'. When choice was not an effort and she wore what she felt comfortable in, she was 'the woman I am most of the time'. The three self-images can be used consciously to create and manipulate moods. If the woman is required to be confident and optimistic, smarter outfits that take in her knowledge of herself, the situation she is dressing for, and her wardrobe, can help her to project the desired image, making her feel comfortable in the situation and the role. The study revealed that when an anticipated image was achieved, women were less adverse to risk-taking, and trusted their instincts more. When that image was not achieved, self-doubt crept in.

Specific colours for men and women can be evocative. Dark colours on a woman convey high status as with a man. Purple and gold are associated with high power, while greys and beiges do not raise your visibility. Blue, and in particular dark blue, is the colour of conservatism, accomplishment, devotion, deliberation and introspection and is associated with people who succeed through application, earn money, make the right connections in life, and seldom do

33

anything impulsively (Gray, 1982). Warm, bright colours 'advance' towards the eyes of observers, and make their wearers stand out from the crowd. Writers suggest that women should avoid looking too drab or severe, and recommend wearing a scarf in a flattering shade that softens the image, allowing them to stand out without looking too loud. Make-up that uses shades that suit the skin tones of its wearer creates an effect that is subtle without being overdone. Managing your visual image involves being aware of your strengths and using your clothes and make-up to make the best of what you have. If you look good, you will automatically look wiser, more credible and more experienced to others, while feeling better in yourself.

Glaser and Smalley (1992) offer specific advice about women's clothing. They recommend that they wear a well-fitting, tailored jacket, to signal authority. The two-piece suits for women become optional at higher levels. Women should not take a handbag as well as a briefcase to an interview or meeting. Such clutter, they say, signals low status. Instead, a briefcase is sufficient which is carried in the left hand, freeing the right for handshaking. It looks more organized and professional with only one item. Leave your handbag in the car and/or put your wallet in your briefcase. Women should avoid wearing clanking jewellery, slit, mini or tight skirts, revealing blouses or evening-type shoes. They should be feminine and businesslike. The appropriate and acceptable footwear is a low to medium heel and closed toe. While high heels may increase height, which is associated with status, they are tiring to wear and are difficult to keep in good condition. Torn heels or scuffed shoes convey low status. Shoes should be darker than the hemline, and be filled with stockings whatever the weather. Women's fashions tend to change more frequently than men's, and so checking photographs of successful people in the press, will help you keep up to date with changing fashions.

Bryce (1991) made some specific sartorial suggestions for men. He said that coming over as powerful did not mean standing out by looking loud or eccentric, since this reduced status. The suit is the most important and expensive part of a man's wardrobe. The simple rule is buy the best you can afford. One good one, is preferable to two or three cheap ones. Inexpensive suits may look good in the shop when tried on, but they will get crushed by lunchtime. To keep it looking good, shake it out at night, and then let it hang freely for half an hour. It is better to wear a suit every other day, thus giving it a chance to recover from the previous day's wear. With pin-striped suits, quarter-inch stripes give the most authority and wider stripes are more informal. A double-breasted jacket conveys a more closed-up, less approachable image, while single-breasted is more informal. With the exception of interview clothing, work clothing has generally become more casual in recent years. However, what is 'appropriate' will vary from company to company, and from department to department.

Wearing light blue shirts conveys informality, while white shirts always look right at night. With striped shirts, the wider the strip the greater the informality.

Avoid having more than three colours in a shirt. The shirt should be double-cuffed, with the cuff and cuff link showing under the jacket sleeve. This should be about five inches from the tip of the thumb. Suit jackets that hide the bottom of the shirt cuff should be avoided. Just see what wrist skin contrasted with jacket sleeve, without a cuff, looks like! Shirts should always look clean and be well ironed. Trousers should break on the shoes. The back of the trouser leg should be half an inch longer than the front, but turn-ups should be parallel. Belt buckles should not be too large. Replace the worn seat or knees in a suit's trousers immediately. The reason why the combination of a white shirt, dark suit and a deep-red tie is the most formal, is due to the contrast between the colours (white, blue, red) which projects great formality. Stripes of no more than half an inch apart, add to your authority. The fewer the colours on the tie, the greater your authority. Avoid wearing a navy blue tie with a blue suit or club ties. The knot on the tie should fit the collar space, and the tie should come down to the belt, which should match your shoes in terms of colour. Ties are useful allowing you to vary the impression that you want to give to your audience. The sincere tie, with narrow stripes, is good for interviews and presentations.

Spectacles should be as wide as your face, and positioned so that you can look through the middle of the lens. The upper rim of your glasses should be on your eyebrow. They should contrast with your face shape. Square glasses for people with roundish heads and vice versa. Square glasses with thick rims denote power. As with suits, invest in good shoes, which help your image and last longer anyway. Have two pairs so that you can give them a rest after a day's wear. Always have black shoes; look after them and keep them polished. Avoid light-coloured socks (and white ones in particular), as people's eyes are attracted to light or brightly coloured areas. Ensure your socks have a good elastic and are long enough. When sitting on a chair, legs crossed, you want to avoid the presentation of flesh between the turn-up and the top of your sock. Cut your hair into a definite style, and keep yourself well groomed. The exact style chosen is less important. Beards are a problem since facial hair is associated with rebellion and mystery. The stereotypical 'bad guy' in a film wears a dark beard, and there is also the concern about 'chinless wonders'. Since beards obscure and hide facial expressions, they reduce your ability to communicate facially, and may thus reduce the trust you give. All in all, avoid facial hair.

Your choice of clothes communicates how good you feel about yourself and how high your self-esteem is. Employers believe that those who look and act as if they care about themselves are likely to care about their jobs. Despite developments in technology, most interviewers can recognize cheap, low-quality clothing, and make the unfair inference, that they are worn by cheap, low-quality people. Well-cut clothes will make you feel comfortable, and will convey to others that you have the 'measure of yourself'. A style that makes you feel smart will boost your self-esteem (Schlenker, 1980). Clothes can also indicate 'conspicuous consumption', that you are already successful. For all these reasons, you should consider your purchase of work clothes as an investment in yourself.

The general principle of *matching* is one of the recurring themes in this book, and it can usefully guide your choice of clothes. People who wear similar clothes, are attracted to each because they infer similar beliefs, values and attitudes, and even political affiliation (Seitz and Cohen, 1992). This relationship is closely linked to the attractiveness of the person, discussed earlier in this chapter. The unattractive person who dressed poorly was only 68 per cent likely to be hired, rising to 76 per cent when dressed appropriately. However, the attractive person's chances of appointment rose from 82 per cent to 100 per cent when placed in appropriate clothing (Bardack and McAndrew, 1985). Clothes matching involves the influencer achieving an equivalent level of formality or style of attire to that of the influencee. Again, it is based on the premise that people like people like themselves. When we see aspects of ourselves in others, we cannot help but warm to them because we do not have to form another impression. We assume that they represent our own qualities with which we are comfortable. Matching thus creates empathy, increases rapport and creates a bond between two people. In a general sense, therefore researching what the appropriate attire is for the organizational context is good policy (dark suit for a bank, short-sleeved shirt in a factory). For an interview situation, this may involve finding out, through attendance at company presentations, what the typical attire is. By matching expectations and norms, the interviewer can focus on you as a person, rather than as someone who is dressed incorrectly (Floyd, 1999).

Standing apart from the crowd may become a priority once you have been in a job for a time. You may need to increase your visibility to those in a position to promote you. Dress at, or just above the level of the person that you are trying to influence. Dress in a way to be included for the job you want, not the one you have. Take note of what people in the position that you aspire to are wearing, and dress in a similar way. If necessary, this may mean dressing to stand out from your current crowd. You can use a variety of signals to do this – following fashion, accentuating sexuality and colour. Whatever your choice, the dress must be distinctive. People tend to label each other. Find out what your label is, and if you like it, emphasize it ('works hard', 'cares about her staff', 'cares about doing a good job', 'not afraid to make decisions').

Apart from their clothes, both men and women should ensure that all their accessories match their main outfit. While it may be easy to deceive people by appearance, do not give the game away by being inconsistent. Men frequently let themselves down by their unpolished shoes, while women get their make-up wrong. For this reason, 'accessories' are important – not only shoes and gloves (if worn) – but also briefcases, personal digital assistants (PDAs), and perfume or aftershave. These are all your 'props' that need to be carefully selected. They should match the quality and style of your outfit, and complement your other non-verbal messages. A top quality pin-striped suit calls for a leather briefcase. Since accessories such as bags and briefcases are frequently used on a daily basis, they should be chosen carefully and replaced if necessary. Men and women need to ensure that their personal grooming is good. Remove any nicotine stains from teeth and fingers. Recently showered, shaved, clean hair and nails make a good, first impression. Long nails make women look more predatory. Your hair needs to be well styled. Severe, short styles are best avoided as they make both sexes look too macho. Lots of hair, piled high makes your head look bigger, and the rest of your body relatively smaller.

NON-VERBAL ASPECTS OF THE INTERVIEW

Having discussed non-verbal behaviour in general, it is useful to conclude this chapter by discussing some of the research findings of Raffler-Engel (1983) which focused on job selection interviewing. This author discovered that interviewers believed that candidates' personalities could be deduced from the non-verbal cues that they gave, a fact that is acknowledged in the expression, 'I'm going to look him/her over'. At a selection interview, it is the candidate's personality that is the main focus of attention. Does their emotion trigger expression or does expression trigger emotion? Interviewers are intuitively aware of the relationship between expressive behaviour and mental attitude. They look for candidates who, through their bodies, show that they have the intellectual power and physical strength to meet the needs of the organization. Raffler-Engel reported a comment from one interviewer:

> The first thing I noticed was that he smiled and so he was not hostile but friendly. The second thing I noticed was his weight. And I immediately ran all kinds of things through my mind relating to past generalizations that have to do with someone who is that overweight. I started forming opinions about him before we even started talking based on the fact that he was overweight as much as he is; whether or not he could really get around, move around fast, in the fast pace that we keep in a rental store, in and out of the trucks and delivering merchandise and that sort of thing. I can't say that people are slow because they are overweight, it's just the preconceived notion that I have that a person may be slow because he is overweight.
>
> (Raffler-Engel, 1983: 50)

Raffler-Engel highlighted what job interviewers paid particular attention to. First, she confirmed the importance of dress and neatness with, 'image coming through appearance'. The basic requirement for any applicant was that they should be clean and neat. Crumpled or stained clothing, unkempt hair or other signs of untidiness were totally unacceptable. Second, the interviewers looked at grooming. Facial hair on men raised a 'bad guy' stereotype which the candidate needed to quickly counter with a smile and positive handshake. Dress was important and had to be appropriate. Interviewers assumed that if a candidate did not dress well it was because they did not think that the job was worth dressing well for, and that, by implication, they did not really want the job. Other recruiters felt the candidates had to show that, once appointed, they would represent the company well, and would dress accordingly. Interviewees should show respect for the job they would like to perform, and their attire should indicate that they are serious about their plans for the future.

A third qualifier was odour. A bad odour was the most objectionable feature which automatically disqualified a candidate. Unwashed and cheap soap were both worse than bad breath. A light odour of sweat was permissible and unavoidable with the strain of the interview. Similarly, overpowering scent on a woman could trigger the memory of a past, bad experience. The effect of smell (or olfaction) on the human psyche has tended to be neglected until relatively recently (Synnott, 1996; Baron, 1997). Olfaction is the only sense that directly stimulates the more primitive parts of our brain – the limbic system – evoking powerful feelings of passion and love. This is something of which perfume manufacturers are well aware.

The presence of a pleasant scent has been found to impact on various aspects of organizational life. For example, it appears to increase helping behaviour (Baron, 1997), and improves performance on difficult tasks (Martin, Barrett and Watson, 2001). In the selection process, Baron (1983) found that female interviewers rated applicants who wore perfume or cologne more positively than those who did not. However, male interviewers rated those who wore it, both male and female candidates, more negatively than those who abstained. He explained this by reference to the male stereotype that serious things should not come in fragrant packages. This highlights the importance of context in deciding whether or not to improve your smell. Wearing a fragrance can potentially draw attention unnecessarily away from a job applicant's key qualities (e.g. ability, ambition), particularly if the interviewer is male and the interviewee is female. Researchers in the field stress the tightrope that job applicants must walk. The advice appears to be wash, and then apply perfume or cologne sparingly before an interview, but just enough to get noticed.

On the behaviour side, Raffler-Engel found that interviewers used a candidate's posture to assess their interest in the job, and their attentiveness towards the interviewer. Interviewers treated 'leaning forward' (with the bottom lodged in the back of the chair) as indicating excitement, enthusiasm and a sincere interest in the job. They liked candidates who shifted posture when there was a change in argument, or when the conversation touched a high point. They did not like quiet, static individuals, since they were viewed with suspicion – 'what's she holding back?' (McGovern and Ideus, 1978). The motionless candidate made a

very poor impression. Perfect composure was not stillness, but forceful animation. Interviewers did not want a nervous or overbearing candidate, but a shift
of posture or leg position was seen to indicate alertness, confidence, respect and
energy. Most interviewers wanted an assertive candidate.

Above all, the interviewers were looking for rapport. During an interview,
candidates were probed on their courtesy, friendliness and whether or not they
could establish and maintain rapport. This last aspect is evaluated by the interviewer's gut-feel. Rapport has been described by kinesthetists as *interactional
synchrony* (parallel or mirroring image). In this mode, two people share posture
shifts, smile at each other, and even match leg positions. What then are the
rapport qualifiers that Raffler-Engel's interviewers were looking for in candidates? These included posture sharing and the ease with which candidates moved
their body. To encourage posture changes, interviewers would often change their
own seating arrangements during the session from a head-to-head to a side-by-
side position. Or they would invite the candidate to sit in a club chair, or by a
coffee table. While the re-seating took place, they would note the candidate's
movements and ambulation while changing chairs. Slow continuous movements
were held to denote sincerity. Nervous movements were expected by interviewers from young candidates, especially at the beginning of an interview, but
these were expected to subside with time. Fidgeting was universally seen as a
sign of nervousness, but unless it was very distracting or continuous, there was
a great variation in how positively or negatively it was judged by the different
interviewers studied. Some assumed it that it indicated a lack of maturity, a
quality which selectors particularly required in candidates and which they searched
for. Other interviewers considered fidgeting to be the result of tension. Women
interviewers particularly disliked it. The general body behaviour expected of a
successful candidate was one of self-control coupled with assertiveness (Seitz and
Cohen, 1992).

Turning finally, to eye contact, mutual gaze was the non-verbal behaviour that
Raffler-Engel's interviewers were most keenly aware of. Next to neatness, eye
contact was the most important since it was used by them to indicate a candidate's qualities of honesty, confidence, self-pride and determination. A 'shine in
the eye' was considered to show alertness and interest. A lack of eye contact
adversely affected the candidate, by conveying shyness, insecurity, nervousness,
a lack of general motivation, drive and interest in the job applied for, and even
untruthfulness. From this research study, interviewers considered the best candidates to combine courtesy and self-control ('manners') with drive. An assessment
of an applicant's degree of drive and energy was based on an observation of
their bodily motions. For example, forcefulness was deduced from their postural
behaviour and eye contact. Interviewers liked candidates to punctuate what they
said with hand gesticulation. The most important gestures were held to be
'batons', which emphasized a phrase, clause or sentence or a group of sentences.

Such gesticulation was evaluated in relation to what was said, and what it implied about the candidate. It was candidate enhancing, in that it showed their clarity of expression, and indicated a forceful and enthusiastic personality. In contrast, wild and excessive gesticulation was considered negatively as a sign of an over-bearing personality, or as a symptom of more uncontrolled nervous fidgeting. Non-gesticulators ('stills') were judged to be dull, lacking in drive and motivation. All employers wanted energetic individuals. Interviewers believed that the more enthusiastic a person was, the more gestures they had. For some interviewers, over-gesticulation was not possible. Other aspects of the job interview will be considered in Chapter 5.

Chapter 3

Verbal influencing

Faith may move mountains, but words move people.

Anon (in Lambert, 1996)

INTRODUCTION

Ng and Bradac (1993) wrote that, 'facts and logic are often insufficient for persuasion. Facts and logic, the prescribed bases of persuasion, must be adapted to the situation, and it is language and language style that will bear the burden of the mission . . . language is the primary instrument of persuasion'. How do others assess your stature? Performance in the formal role may be an important component, but in many situations, job performance may be difficult to ascertain quickly, or is separate from other contributing factors. One aspect of a person that is quick and easy to evaluate is what they say and how articulate they are. Listeners carry in their heads connections between a person's language and their power. They learn that thoughtful people talk in a certain way, and unthoughtful ones, in other ways. Such learning is held in the form of stereotypical beliefs. They will rate a speaker as competent because, in their stereotype, rapid speech is held to indicate great mental ability, while a non-standard accent indicates low status or low personal control. The difference between peripheral route and central route persuasion was introduced at the start of the book. The former refers to the smaller, more incidental factors, that affect an influencee, and would encompass how they talk, including the words that they use. Verbal influencing thus uses the peripheral route. This chapter focuses primarily on one-to-one conversations, and complements a later one on small group and public speaking.

Influencing is an activity which, above all, involves argumentation, presentation and debate. Only words have the power to bring precision to the communication process. Articulateness has been found to be crucial in successful interdepartmental relations, and can compensate for a low formal position in the company (Bucher, 1970; Hamlin, 1993; Griffin, 1998). In the interview situation, interviewers regularly confuse how well you talk, and the level of your linguistic flexibility, with intelligence and ability. Well-spoken people are judged to be more intelligent and able. Another important dimension of speech was highlighted by Berger and Calbrese (1975) who discussed uncertainty reduction. A primary social drive in humans is reducing their uncertainty about others, hence the importance of mirroring. One human being wants to be able to predict how another will behave. Such uncertainty is affected by an individual's speech style, rate and lexical diversity.

Influential verbal communication depends on what is said and how it is said. Research into low-power forms of communication has contrasted male and female speech (Mulac *et al.*, 1988). Female speech forms are classed as low-power in a comparative, and not an absolute sense. Men dominate the workplace. They got there first, and established the patterns and rules. Women in the workplace have to understand men's ways. Men are more aggressive in behaviour, while women have greater verbal ability. They use their verbal skills to deal with emotions, and act upon their emotions more consistently. Men in contrast discount feelings. However, the differences are not that significant. If women dominated the workplace, their forms of speech would be defined as high-power, and those of men as low-power. Given the reality of organizational life, you need to become aware of any de-powering features of your own habitual speech, and eliminate these from your linguistic repertoire when interacting with others.

Men and women occupy two different sociolinguistic communities. Lakoff (1975) says that women's language is sufficiently different from men's to be classed as a separate dialect. Men and women talk about different topics. Males like to talk about things and activities. Their talk is auxiliary to activity. Office men-talk is not a 'getting to know you' kind of bantering. It is not intimate, but surface talk. It does, however, build a sort of camaraderie. Men build trust through action – checking to see if another man will support them in a difficult situation. They do not find this out through conversation the way that women do. Men will not self-disclose until trust is well established through action. In contrast, females prefer to talk about people and feelings. For them, talk is often the activity. They establish trust with each other through self-disclosure, share secrets and problems, and search for common feelings and experiences. They often establish business relationships through personal conversation. Women assume that others are interested in their personal lives, whereas in reality, they are not. Men do not want to reveal the details of their lives, and are put off by co-workers who ask, 'How are you feeling?' or 'What's the problem?' Just chatting about emotions or personal relationships makes men uneasy. A man is unlikely to want to hear about a woman's emotional life. Men also resist talking about emotions that are part of the job. Women disclose more personal information than men, and tend to initiate more intimate questions and respond with more personal details. Research shows that after a self-disclosure conversation, women feel a kinship with their conversational partner, while men feel less compatibility.

While subordinates may be self-revealing, powerful people whether male or female, keep up their guard. They do not use emotional displays or reveal personal information because such information gives others power over them.

Pauline Frederick commented that when a man gets up to speak, people listen, then look. When a woman gets up, people look, and then, if they like what they see, they listen. Men and women differ in the way that they speak. Although both boys and girls find ways of creating rapport and establishing status, girls tend to learn conversational rituals that focus on the rapport dimension of relationships. In contrast, boys tend to learn rituals that focus on the status dimension (Tannen, 1995). In female culture and polite society, conversation proceeds through orderly turn-taking, with each speaker waiting for the other to signal readiness to give up the floor. Speech is polite and tentative, rather than direct and informative.

Men use a more dominant style and take speaking turns by interruption. They use more interruptions ('let's go to the next topic'), more directives ('write down your answers here'), and maintain the floor by using conjunctions and fillers at the beginning of their sentences ('and another thing'). They grab a speaking turn by butting in. Often just listening to the first half of a sentence to decide what to say. In such a conversation, if you wait for a turn, you will never get in, and black marks will be counted against you. Interruption is both a display of dominance and a controlling device, because incursions disorganize the flow. Men speak firmly and in detail. They offer opinions, suggestions, information and disagreement, which all represent assertions of status. For men, being firm and specific is even more important than being accurate.

Women's speech makes greater use of questions ('What's next?)', justifiers ('The reason I say that is'), intensive verbs ('I really liked her'), shows a greater interest in people than objects (through the use of personal pronouns) and uses a more indirect, qualified style ('Surprisingly, it was an easy assignment'). Women are more likely to use formal, grammatically correct language, and to add qualifiers to their assertions (Glaser and Smalley, 1992; Mulac and Lundell, 1980; Ng and Bradac, 1993; Zahn, 1989). They bridge the distance gap between themselves and others by being friendly and agreeable, and by asking for information and opinions. Stechert (1986) noted that men are comfortable with heavy facts, and use these to display power. Men speak more often and at greater length than women. Monopolizing a conversation ensures that they get their ideas across, enabling their topics to be discussed. Others thus come to perceive them as leaders. Women ask three times as many questions as men. They use attention getters ('guess what' and 'did you know'). Women frequently offer their listeners encouraging cues – head nods, murmurs and facial expressions – that keep the talk going. They also look at their speaking partner more, both in mutual gazes, and when the other person is not looking at them. These studies suggest why women may be perceived as more persuadable and as less credible than their

43

male counterparts (Reardon, 1991). They are more likely than men to use power-less speech forms which suggest uncertainty and emotion. Research on public speaking shows that male speakers are rated as more dynamic than women, who in turn are rated higher on aesthetic quality. This has been termed the gender-linked language effect (Kennedy and Camden, 1983; Mulac, 1976; Mulac and Lundell, 1980, 1982, 1986; Mulac et al., 1985; Tannen, 1990). This research has identified six specific power-reducing speech forms.

LANGUAGE TO AVOID

Hedges and qualifiers (*I sort of liked it*)

These are the clearest indicator of low power. An example is the sentence above. The speaker is responding to a question of whether they liked something. However, since they do not yet know the questioner's opinion, and fear disagreeing with them, and thus possibly losing their favour, they offer a quali-fied, non-committal response, which can be easily adapted once the questioner expresses their view. The responder is actually saying, 'you will probably disagree with me but' or 'I'm not quite sure but'). Apart from being annoying to the listener, using such hedges and qualifiers makes you sound weak, uncommitted and uncertain about what you are saying. Remove the qualifiers and replace them with, 'It seems to me', 'I believe that', or 'I wonder if you'. Only use qualifiers in situations where you are really uncertain, and then say them with a firm voice, and do not drop your head or avert your eyes from the listener, otherwise, your genuine uncertainty will be mistaken for helplessness.

Other hedges include, 'I suppose', 'you know', 'like', 'kind of' and 'well'. All of these signal that you are unsure of yourself, and afraid of imposing your view on others. Women's constant use of questions and hedges, robs them of authority and gives the impression that they are apologizing for expressing any opinion at all. Studies have shown that men use 'women's language' when they are in a submissive role with other, more senior men. Women's speech contains many powerless features since women frequently feel, and are, less powerful than men in organizations. They automatically use less powerful language when there is no need to. Women can gain more power and influence simply by changing the way that they speak. By eliminating hedges, intensifiers and ques-tioning tones, women can be perceived as more convincing, competent, intelligent and trustworthy. If they do not change, then they will have difficulty in gaining credibility, and will continue to set themselves at a grave career disadvantage.

Whereas a man might shout, 'Damn, the lift's broken again!', women would say 'Oh dear, the lift's out of order.' They say 'I'm so angry' or 'I'm very annoyed.' These serve as hedges on the statement, making it sound as if the speaker dare not say just how angry she is. Speaking-in-italics, that is, emphasizing words as if they were italicized, tells listeners how you want them to respond. It gives the impression that the speaker is afraid of not being listened to, afraid that her words will have no impact. Instead she should speak as if she expects to be listened to, and that her words will have an impact.

Irritators (*You know, sort of, kinda, try, yes–but*)

The irritator, *you know*, highlights your lack of confidence in what you are saying, as well as being annoying to have to listen to. It is saying to the listener, 'I know I'm not expressing myself clearly, but you are intelligent enough to know what I mean.' The irritator, *kinda*, represent an apology for not knowing the correct word to use, while *try* is most often used by people who are habitual under-achievers and failures. Users of this word, announce in advance, that they may not succeed in a task, or that they even expect to fail. When asked to do a task, they reply, 'I'll try' or 'I'll do my best.' Both responses signal impeding failure. Translated they mean, 'I have doubts about my ability to do this. Do not count on me'. Once they have failed, the phrase, 'Well, I tried', confirms they had little confidence in their ability to do the job. These powerless phrases impact the listener at the subconscious level, convincing them that their user lacks self-confidence and ability. If you habitually use such phrases, eliminate them and in their place use language that commits you ('I will or will not'). The word, *try*, is as reassuring as a *definite maybe*. Finally, *yes–but* users attempt to avoid intimidation by feigning agreement. The 'but' contradicts the words that follow ('your report is good, but'). In such circumstances it is better to use, *and*, *however* or *still*.

Intensifiers (*I really liked it*)

Avoid the use of empty adjectives and adverbs such as *really*, *very*, *awfully* and *terribly*. As in, 'it was such a difficult meeting', 'I felt terribly bad at letting him down', 'It was all awfully embarrassing'. Intensifier words lack gravitas and substance, and are associated predominantly with women. They should be replaced with more powerful and genderless ones for placing emphasis, such as *absolutely*, *remarkably*, *incredibly*, *excellent* and *outstanding*.

Tag questions and disclaimers (*Don't you agree?*)

Tag questions are those which are added to the end of a sentence statement, while disclaimers are expressions that excuse, explain or request understanding from your listeners. Tags include, 'They are, aren't they?', 'Don't you agree?', 'I liked it, did you?', and 'I don't mean to be rude but'. These should be avoided, especially when spoken with a rising intonation. There is a cultural aspect here. Canadian and US males and females have rising intonation, even when they are not asking questions. A tag takes a firm and decisive statement and turns it into an unnecessary question, for example, 'We must invest in this now – shouldn't we?'. Users of tag questions seek to avoid confrontation in an effort to please everyone, or to gain others' support. Overused, they make you appear wishy-washy and indecisive. Tags are appropriate when checking ('The meeting is scheduled for 10.00 a.m., isn't it?'); small talking ('Looks like rain, doesn't it?'); or requesting the confirmation of something that you hope will happen ('It's OK to use your phone, isn't it?'). Avoid tag questions when giving your opinion, otherwise listeners will think that you are unsure of yourself, and do not actually expect the listeners to agree with you. In this context, the direct question ('Is the meeting scheduled for 10.00 a.m.') or the direct statement ('The file is in the conference room') are to be preferred. Examples of disclaimers would be prefaces to statements which include phrases such as, 'I'm probably wrong but', 'You may not like this but', 'Maybe this is OK' and 'I suppose we could'. Not only do tags and disclaimers reduce your power, but they also invite the listener to disagree, and thus make you look less knowledgeable and intelligent.

Hesitations ('I, *uh*, liked it')

Hesitations and fillers, often called non-words (*um, er, ah, uh, well*) are used when we need time to think. They are used more by women than men. Since they are used less in female-to-female conversations, it has been suggested that women use them to play down their intelligence in front of men, or reduce the fear of coming over too strong. Fillers signal uncertainty and lack of preparation, while increasing the opportunity of your being interrupted. A wide range of hesitations are demonstrated regularly on the radio every Saturday afternoon during post-football match interviews with players and managers. Avoid these irritators by thinking out what you want to say, forming it in your mind, and then speaking it out.

Excessive question asking

Women ask three times as many questions as men, when talking to men. Various reasons have been put forward for this. These include finding a topic of interest, to gain detail and to make better decisions. However, when asking questions of others, you are not giving out your own opinion, and are in fact inviting that of others. Women also tend to open a conversation with a question. This is a speech pattern that signals uncertainty and a desire for attention. For example, before informing others of why an issue is being discussed, they frequently precede the explanation statement with a rhetorical question, 'Do you know why we are discussing this matter? It's because' rather than making the statement, 'Today, we are discussing'. However, questions can be used to control the other person, requiring them to think out responses in the forms of justification and information provision. A question can be used to convey the point that you have the power to quiz.

Other powerless speech forms

There are a variety of verbal behaviours that have been found to detract from influence. Do not give *unnecessary or excessive apologies* ('I'm sorry, we had a power cut'; I'm sorry to be nuisance'). If you have wronged or inconvenienced someone, then an apology is appropriate. However, do not apologize for your thoughts, feelings or a situation over which you have no control. Just state the problem, explain your solution and leave out the apology. Second, *focus on the point* you want to communicate and get rid of any information that is irrelevant. The shorter your request, the more powerful it is. 'I want the department to upgrade my computer' is more powerful than, 'I'm sorry to interrupt, but my PC is not really working satisfactorily, and I think we should consider replacing it'. Third, *avoid excessive personal disclosure*. Women in particular provide personal information to those around them, but such self-disclosure is often considered to be inappropriate in a business context. Finally, you should *avoid over-politeness*. If you want to take a more dominant role and you are a woman, make fewer encouraging murmurs, and sometimes sit silently when *his* conversation topic drops. In his book, Gray (2002) notes gender-based differences in language that are used in organizations.

LANGUAGE TO USE

Walther (1993) used the term, *powertalking*, to refer to a form of speaking which conveyed a positive impression of yourself to your listeners. He felt that this form of speech could be taught since it consisted of the conscious use of certain words and phrases. This same form of speech has an impact on you, since by hearing yourself using these powerful phrases, you begin to think positively, thus gaining confidence in yourself. Positive talking leads to positive thinking, which in turn, leads to positive action. Hence, powertalking and positive thinking interact to your benefit. Despite being developed in the American context, Walter's recommendations, with minor adjustments, have validity in the British environment. In his book, Walther describes numerous powertalking techniques which are listed under eight broad headings.

Projecting positive expectations

Power talkers respond to others positively (saying 'I'll be pleased to' or 'I'd like to' rather than, 'I'll have to'); they make commitments which they keep ('I will do it' rather than 'I'll try to do it'); they focus on positive outcomes ('I want

47

to' rather than, 'I'd hate to'; they recognize limitless expectations ('I haven't yet, and I can' rather than, 'I can't do that'); they are optimistic ('I can improve the situation I'm in' rather than, 'My situation is hopeless'); they avoid conditional phrases ('When will you' rather than 'I wonder if you would'); they seek creative solutions ('That's a challenging opportunity' rather than, 'That's a problem'); they use self-empowering assertions ('I'm getting better at' rather than, 'I'm no good at'); they seek benefits in a situation ('Investing' their time rather than 'Spending' it); they are positive ('This can be done' rather than, 'This is impossible'), and they separate a person from their behaviour ('Your behaviour is bad' rather than, 'You are bad').

Giving appropriate credit

Powertalkers either change their shortcomings or forget about them (thus avoiding the need for excuses or apologies); they describe their beliefs and achievements positively and proudly ('I believe that' rather than, 'It's only my opinion that'); they modestly acknowledge their own role in creating success and do not attribute it to luck ('I planned well and worked hard', rather than, 'I was lucky'); they do their best without apology or justification ('I enjoy doing this' rather than, 'I'm not too good at this'); and they praise others when things go right (actually saying 'I'm grateful for your help' rather than just thinking it).

Learning from experiences, rather than encountering failure

Powertalkers look to learn lessons from failures and grow from them (saying 'I learned' rather than 'I failed'); they look for positive results following unexpected changes or setbacks (saying 'I see opportunities in this development' rather than, 'I can only see problems'); they focus on choices and not regrets (saying 'Starting from now I will' rather than, 'If only I had'); they think and act positively when at a low point (saying 'I can succeed' rather than 'I'm a failure'); when they do describe failure, they see it as a temporary setback (saying 'I'm going to bounce back' rather than, 'I'm going down'); they apply their energy to create more positive outcomes (saying 'That's it, it's over' rather than 'What if things get worse?').

Remaining responsible for their own feelings

Powertalkers say, 'I feel upset when that happens' rather than, 'You make me upset when'); they eliminate phrases that time is out of their control (saying 'I can manage my available time better' rather than, 'I don't have enough time'); they accept responsibility for their actions ('It's my responsibility' rather than, 'I can't help it, it's someone else's fault').

Persuading others to work with them

They replace conflict words with positive ones (saying 'However'; as well as, 'And' instead of 'But'); they keep their options open ('Let's give your idea a chance' rather than 'That's not practical, it'll never work'); they emphasize the benefits that will accrue to influencees when seeking their help (saying 'This will be helpful to you because' rather than 'Will you do me a favour?'); they ask specific questions which can improve relationships ('Can you suggest one thing that I could improve' rather than, 'Is everything satisfactory?'); they focus on the positive ('Here's what I can do' rather than 'This is what I can't do'); they accept and acknowledge the ideas of others allowing them to co-exist with their own (saying 'I understand your view, here's mine, let's look at both of them' rather than 'I disagree').

Speaking decisively

They commit themselves to specific duties and amounts (saying 'I will get this done by' rather than 'I should get this done by'); they add a margin of safety and beat their target (saying 'You will have it definitely by 4.00 p.m.' rather than, 'Maybe I'll be able to have it ready by 3.00 p.m.'); they elicit detailed, useful information by asking open-ended questions (saying 'What questions do you have?' rather than, 'Do you have any questions?'); and they decide what to say and then say it ('I believe' rather than 'I would tend to think that').

Telling the truth

Powertalkers avoid suspicious and misleading phrases (such as, 'Well, to tell you the truth', instead they just tell the truth); when they do not want to do something they just say no (saying 'No, I won't' rather than, 'I don't really want to but I'll see'); they eliminate universal self-criticizing terms (saying 'Sometimes things go wrong for me' or 'A few things did not work out' rather than, 'I always do badly' and 'Everything goes wrong for me'). Finally, powertalkers give respect to those with whom they interact. They remember and use others' names, or ask to be reminded if they have forgotten; they do not take relationships for granted but show the other person appreciation by saying please and thank you; and when they have made a mistake, they apologize. Walther's (1993) prescriptions represent a valuable starting point for people who want to improve their verbal influencing skills, both in the job interview and the general work situation. They have been somewhat brutally summarized here, but his book which elaborates and exemplifies each of the aforementioned techniques, repays detailed study.

To Walther's list, one can one other set of verbal devices – causal attributions. Candidates have to explain their own and others' behaviour to interviewers. Such explanations are called causal attributions (Silvester, 1997). They can either enhance the interviewee's image in the eyes of interviewer or detract from it. Silvester *et al.* (2002) studied three types of attributions. These were the *internal-controllable* ('I didn't get the promotion due to not spending enough time on one particular area of my work'); *internal-uncontrollable* ('I didn't pass my exam because I was too ill to sit it:'); and *external-uncontrollable* ('I didn't get my promotion because my application got lost in the post'). They found that interview candidates using internal-controllable attributions for past negative acts and failures conveyed a more positive impression of themselves than those using the other two types of attributions. They were more highly rated because they were seen as taking responsibility for their actions. In contrast, external-uncontrollable attribution-users were thought to be unwilling to take responsibility for their mistakes.

POLITENESS TECHNIQUES

Politeness techniques are used by everybody and are crucial in establishing and maintaining power relations, and influencing others. How do you use language to create and sustain power in what Morand (2000) calls face-threatening acts? These occur in face-to-face situations, as when you are contradicting, criticizing, disagreeing, interrupting, borrowing something, bumping into someone, imposing or asking for a favour. To establish a power relationship when doing this, draw upon linguistic politeness routines which reduce the loss of face which may occur for the other person. In these contexts, politeness becomes a key element in diffusing or minimizing the conflict and saving face. He identified two types of politeness which he labelled negative (avoid) politeness and positive (approach) politeness.

Negative politeness is very formal and is used to create social distance between the speaker and the hearer. Morand's examples are shown in Table 3.1. It involves using indirect questions, hedges, calling people, 'Sir' and avoiding personal pronouns. The key words used admit the intrusion into the other person's space. A phrase can be used to minimize the imposition, 'I need *just a little* of your time'. Examples include, 'Can I *perhaps* trouble you?'; 'I am sorry to bother you'; '*Excuse* me . . .'; 'Pardon me . . .'. Another means of doing the same is to use honorific or impersonal terms within the situation. Such as, 'Can I help you, *sir?*' and '*Is it possible to request* a favour?'. These negative tactics resemble low-power language discussed earlier in this chapter. Unlike them, they are used consciously to achieve an influencer's objective.

In contrast, positive politeness tactics work through the insinuation of a sense of communality and familiarity between the interacting individuals. These are shown in Table 3.2. It involves showing interest in the influencee, using slang, first names and 'we' and 'let's'. The speaker may call attention to the person's qualities, possessions, interests or wants, and adopts these are their own. He may also seek to establish a common element between the two parties. This can be done by using slang or inclusive words. For example, '*Heya, gimme a hand, willya?*'; 'Hey *bud*, have

Table 3.1 Tactics of negative politeness

Tactic	Example
1 Use indirect questions such as enquiries into the hearer's ability or willingness to comply	'Can you tell me what time it is?'
2 Use hedges: words or phrases which diminish the force of a speech act	'Can I *perhaps* trouble you?'
3 Use the subjunctive to express pessimism about hearer's ability or willingness to comply	'*Could I* ask you a question?'
4 Use words or phrases which minimize the imposition	'I need *just a little* of your time.'
5 Give deference by using honourifics such as Sir or Mr	'Can I help you, *Sir*?'
6 Use formal word choices to indicate seriousness and to establish social distance	'Could you tolerate a slight imposition on my part?'
7 Apologize: admit the impingement, express reluctance	'*I am sorry* to bother you, but . . .'
8 Impersonalize the speaker and hearer by avoiding the pronouns 'I' and 'you'.	'Is it possible to request a favour?'
9 Use the past tense to create distance in time	'*I had been* wondering if I could ask a favour.'
10 State the face-threatening-act as a general rule	'*Regulations require that* I ask you to leave.'

Source: From Morand (2000: 238)

you *gotta* minute?'; '*We're* not feeling well are *we?*'; and '*Let's* . . ., shall *we?*'. Alternatively, it can be done by complimenting or showing concern. For example, '*Nice* to see you; hey *really love* your new car; can I borrow it sometime?'; and 'You look like you've had a really rough week'. This type of speech is still polite but suggests a smaller or no gap in power status between the influencee and the influencer. It is used in social settings or situations in which the speaker wants the individual to feel comfortable, such as a sales situation. The positive politeness tactics are less polite or formal than the negative ones, and they assume a favourable outcome. Also, unlike the negative ones, positive politeness tactics admit that the speaker may be imposing upon the other party.

Morand asserts that positive politeness tactics should be deployed for successful interviewing. Politeness is crucial to an individual's ability to do a job, such as a flight attendant dealing with a disgruntled passenger or a salesperson ingratiating

Table 3.2 *Tactics of positive politeness*

Tactic	Example
1 Notice hearer's admirable qualities or possessions, show interest, exaggerate	'Nice to see you: hey really love your new car; can I borrow it sometime?'
2 Employ phonological slurring to convey in-group membership	'*Heya, gimme* a hand *willya*?'
3 Use colloquialisms or slang to convey in-group membership.	'I know I seem like a *stick-in-the-mud, but what the hell.*'
4 Use ellipsis (omission) to communicate tacit understandings	'[Do you] Mind if I smoke?'
5 Use first names or in-group name to insinuate familiarity	'Hey Bud, have you gotta minute?'
6 Claim common point of view: speaker asserts knowledge of hearer's wants or asserts that hearer has knowledge of speaker's wants	'You know how the janitors don't like it when . . .'
7 Give reasons: assert reflexivity by making activity seem reasonable to the hearer	'I'm really late for an important appointment, so . . .'
8 Use inclusive forms such as 'we' or 'let's' to include both speaker and hearer in the activity	'*We're* not feeling well, are *we*?'
9 Assert reciprocal exchange or tit for tat	'Do me this favour, and I'll make it up to you.'
10 Give something desired – gifts, sympathy, understanding	'You look like you've had a rough week.'

Source: From Morand (2000: 239)

himself with a new client. A subordinate may find knowledge of these two sets of tactics useful when engaging with a face-threatening act with their boss. She can adapt her level of politeness depending on whether the situation requires an insinuation of commonality or a more distancing, cushioning effect. Bosses too, may find these tactics useful when approached by employees lower in the hierarchy, or when approached by their own managers.

DESIRABLE WORDS AND PHRASES

Other writers have also made valuable contributions to influential speaking, suggesting how talkers can convey an impression of control in order to deflect any potential criticism. Davies (1988) offered five specific examples of this. '*Rightly or wrongly'* is a useful phrase with which to pre-empt criticism. Without stating it obviously, you show that you have painstakingly thought about the arguments for and against your decision, you have weighed them up carefully, and have come to a considered decision. The effect is that your listener is reluctant to jump in with an over-hasty criticism of what is essentially a thought-through decision by you. *'It's as you were saying earlier'* gains attention since people always pick up their ears to hear repeated what they have already said. *'There are two ways of looking at this'* is a gentle way of introducing a controversial idea to forestall its immediate rejection. *'What Angela says is quite correct'* is ideal if you want to be one up on Angela. It nicely implies that you are the real expert, and that Angela is merely playing at it. At the same time, Angela can't object, since, on the face of it, you are simply agreeing with her and are backing her up. Davies' final recommendation is to be positive, focusing on what should be done, rather than stating things negatively. She suggested using phrases like: 'I require a *decision* on'; 'I must have a *ruling* on'; 'Clearly then the *decision* rests on'; 'The *options* are'; 'The risks I must *choose* between are'. The words in these phrases make others feel that serious issues are being decided. Everyone likes to feel important, and these words suggest that they are involved in momentous events. Engender excitement by hyping things up a little. Making others feel powerful enhances your own stature.

Let us now consider the individual words. There are several which are particularly influential. For example, 'we', implies togetherness and a feeling of co-operation that can never be stated outright. The word carries a meaning out of all proportion to its size, as in, 'we ought to examine if this is possible'. Using the word, 'no' and its derivatives, is also vital. Listen carefully to what you are being asked to do. Make a judgement as to whether you want to do the task, taking into account your other interests, priorities and commitments. Say that you cannot or do not want to do it, clearly, unambiguously, but graciously. Maybe suggest an alternative person for the task. Be clear that you will not do it, but do not be brusque. End the discussion, either by changing the subject or by physically leaving. Sort out any guilt you may feel later. You can only do so much, time and indeed life, are short. Cialdini (2001a) recommends the word, *'because'*. He identified it as a trigger-word which elicits compliance through appearing to provide a reason. For example, jumping to the head of the photocopier queue by stating, 'Excuse me, I have five pages. May I use the photocopier ahead of you because I have to make some copies?'. More generally, the word, *'because'*, makes your power appear greater, suggesting that you possess information others do not have, and that you have expert power through your knowledge of the subject being talked about at the time (Langer *et al.*, 1978). The following influential words have been shown to affect decision-making (Lambert, 1996). They include those in Table 3.3. These are key words that selectors want to see on your job application form/CV, and want you to speak at your interview. These will be discussed in the two following chapters.

53

Table 3.3 *Desirable words*

Definitely	Good
Clearly	Discover
Leading edge	Money
Achieved	Easy
Specifically	Guaranteed
Renowned	Initiative
Success	Proactive
Impact	Enthusiasm
	Leading

Moving on to powerful phrases, you can experiment with, '*I will.*' Any issue, however small, over which you have authority to say yes or no, gives you the opportunity to increase your power. Affable expressions like, 'Gimme it, I'll sign it' or 'I'll see what I can do', detract from your power. Powertalkers say, 'I will authorize payment; I have the authority to vary the scheme in exceptional circumstances'; 'I will pay the claim'; 'I will sign it; I have the discretion to agree variations in the contract'; 'I will need clear evidence that existing resources are being used to capacity'; 'It is crucial to me that the proposal is properly thought through'; 'I have the power to veto'. In all these contexts, *I*, is a most important word. When you use it, it implies that you and you alone can solve the problem, and that you are thus indispensable. '*Will*' is a powerful word because it means just what it says. Avoid the shortened, '*I'll*', version. Words like, '*power*' and '*authorize*', always add weight, so use them liberally. Phrases such as, '*if you can convince me*', and, '*I will need clear evidence*', work to your advantage because they emphasize that you sit in judgement. The word, '*critical*', has a dramatic impact, while '*strategy*', suggests that you know what you are doing and why.

Being decisively obstructive to others involves some other phrases. Your aim is to thwart them without appearing to do so, by discovering that you are unable to do what they want. Such ostensible impotence can be used to create the impression of power by using language like. *I have no authority to* . . . (impression of authority); *it would be irresponsible of me* . . . (impression of responsibility); and, *it would not be appropriate for me to* . . . (impression of propriety). These are extremely difficult phrases to challenge since you are invoking rules in sorrow rather than in anger. If others feel your power through your deliberate obstruction, they will feel resentful. So you must shed a few crocodile tears to soften the blow. Here are some phrases with which to do just that:

- Personally I'm sympathetic, but you know the rules.
- I only wish I could.
- The problem is I have no discretion.
- You will appreciate, I am sure, that if we do it for one, we have to do it for all.
- I've racked by brains to find a way round this, but this time I think I'm stumped.
- As you know, the rules on this are applied very strictly.
- If I did that, I would be looking for another job tomorrow.
- Unfortunately there is no provision for . . .
- I agree it seems unfair, but there is nothing I can do about it.
- It's a shame we can't do it.

Drummond (1991) said that power was created partly by verbally reminding the other party of their dependence on you. Once you start to speak powerfully, and act the part, that part eventually becomes an aspect of you. Make small easy language changes and experience the effect. The best place to start is on the telephone where you cannot see the other person's face (or they yours) and you are less likely to falter.

STARTING CONVERSATIONS WITH STRANGERS

Social interaction is the basis for the development of common values, which is the basis for mutual liking, which in turn affects the ability to influence. Verbal interaction in the form of conversation, is the foundation for all of this. To influence others, you need to talk to them. Some of these people will be unknown to you. This is particularly true when you attend networking events, a topic to be discussed in Chapter 15. You will thus have to initiate a conversation with a stranger. The procedure is straightforward. First identify the person to whom you want to talk. Most people are delighted at the opportunity of meeting someone new. Thus, if your target is alone and not otherwise engrossed in an activity, they are likely to be receptive. You can recognize if they reciprocate your interest by communicating non-verbal signals of interest back to you. These include smiling at you; looking at you more than once; having their arms or legs uncrossed in an open position if standing; or legs crossed towards you, if sitting. Next, once you have identified someone to speak to, smile, make eye contact and speak.

What you actually say as an opener is relatively unimportant. Glass (1991) highlights the four-step greeting sequence which consists of a smile, an initial facial eye-to-eye contact followed by the total face, the handshake and then the warm 'Hello' or 'How do you do?'. The key thing is to make contact and get things going. There are only three topic openers to choose from: the situation, the other person or yourself. There are also only three ways of beginning: ask a question, give an opinion or state a fact. Although these combinations give you nine possibilities, since you are usually trying to interest or involve the other person, asking a question is usually best. Use an open question that involves more than a yes or no reply from them. If the other person is interested, they will probably give you some free information about themselves, and that will allow both of you to find a common interest, and move the conversation to a more personal level.

When talking about a *situation*, choose one that you are both involved in (attending a course, conference, meeting) is usually the best and easiest. It is less anxiety-provoking than talking about the other person, and is likely to provoke more involvement from them than talking about yourself. Look around and find something that interests or puzzles you – 'Do you know if this trainer usually teaches this course?'. 'Is this conference held annually?'. When talking about the other *person*, remember that most people like to talk about themselves, and will grasp the opportunity to do so. Before starting, observe what the other person is doing, wearing, saying or reading, and think of something that you'd like to know more about – 'I noticed that you hit the key twice there, why did you do that?' (doing); 'That's an interesting insignia on your tie, does it represent a particular group or organization?' (wearing); 'At the meeting you said that the purchase was probable, what exactly did you mean by that?' (saying); 'That's the business section, can you tell me what the exchange rate for dollars is today?' (reading). As an opener, talking about *yourself* rarely stimulates conversation. Never volunteer information about yourself unless asked a specific question. Unless someone asks a specific question about your family, profession, interests or possessions, they are not interested.

KEEPING A CONVERSATION GOING

There is no reason to ever be at a loss for words. During the course of a conversation, the other person will always provide you with free information, that is, data beyond that which you requested or expected. Take advantage of it by making statements or asking questions about it. By doing this, you will channel your conversation in interesting directions. In the following exchanges, the free information is in italics.

> Q: Did you have far to come today?
> A: Not really, *I live in Hammersmith but my car broke down.*

> Q: Have you attended a course on public speaking before.
> A: Yes once, *when I lived in America.*

Once people drop you some free information, if you think that it is stimulating or useful, use it. This is the way that one switches topics in a conversation.

Few interesting conversations ever dwell on a single topic for more than a few minutes.

Q: Did you have far to come today?
A: Not really, *I live in Hammersmith but my car broke down.*
Q: Did you have to abandon it and come by train?

Listen out for free information, not only to keep the conversation interesting, but also to keep it going. Adding the intermittent head-nod is a useful non-verbal signal to keep the conversation going. Your nods indicate affirmation. After you have asked an open-ended question and your listener begins to give an answer, nod your head throughout their answer. When they finish speaking, nod your head another few times. Usually, by the time that you have nodded three or four times, the listener will begin speaking again, and will give you more information. Will you appear a nodding donkey to them? The speaker will respond to your encouragements, rather than to their form. If the person fails to provide you with free information, it either means that you are asking the wrong kind of questions (closed ones instead of open-ended) or that they do not wish to continue their conversation with you.

The more information that you give about yourself in the shortest time, the better your communication exchange will be. Do not say, 'I'm a student', but say, 'I'm studying X at Y University'. This is called offering conversation bait. It encourages them to respond with what they do ('Oh, I studied that at the same university'). You may mention something that you have in common. Description is the best form of communication, because it keeps the other person's interest. Describe why you like something or someone. Respond to the other person's answers by adding personalized comments, then follow that up with a question which relates to that personalized comment. In response to being told that your conversation partner comes from Switzerland, tell him that you have visited Zurich, and follow this up by asking him what he thinks about that city. Talk in terms of the other person's interests, and get them to agree with you early, even on some minor point ('It's a nice party').

Avoid treating the other's response as an invitation for a soliloquy. Most listeners lose interest in a person who only talks about himself. Instead, give a little conversation, ask a question, wait for and listen to the answer, and then respond again. This procedure is called *mutual conversation*. If you want to make a good impression on people and maintain a good relationship with them, you need to give others respect, and enable them to feel important when they are around you. At some point, it will be time to end your conversation. You can do this by breaking eye contact with your listener. Another way is to say, 'Well' or 'At any rate', and physically move, so as to signal the end of the discussion. When you end, do so on a strong note vocally, by projecting your voice and using the proper inflection. You want to leave a positive, departing impression on the other person. Finish with a good firm handshake, if appropriate. The departing impression that you leave is as important as the initial one that you make. The latter should complement and reinforce the former.

In a business meeting, use specific, as opposed to general language, that gets your points across. Avoid 'verbal clutter'. Talk in short sentences using bullet points, rather than in paragraphs. Use words and statements that are short, simple, direct, familiar and concise. Do not say, 'I hope everyone will work together to get the annual report out at the end of the month.' Say instead, 'The report is due out on the 31st. I need everyone's contribution by the 5th of the month'. Women tend to give details since it establishes intimacy, but men find this to be an irritating trait. A conversation can be killed by either a non-response, or by a lack of encouragement, such as, 'is that so?', 'then what?' and 'uhuh'. Without a response or encouragement, the speaker has either to drop the topic, or stop talking altogether. By being silent when talk is expected, the listeners convey disdain and lack of interest. They take the dominant role by manipulating the silence.

NAME REMEMBERING

It is important to take the trouble to learn and remember peoples' names (Glass, 1991; Walter, 1993). Forgetting someone's name is equivalent to saying to them, 'You are not important to me' or 'You did not impress me enough for me to remember your name'. This is not a good start if you want their help or support in a situation such as a job interview, small group discussion or public presentation. Dale Carnegie reminded us that to any person, their name is the sweetest sound in any language. So, when introduced to another person, 'brand' their name in your memory by repeating it immediately, either to yourself or out loud, and using it early in the conversation. You can mentally brand by visually associating some vivid feature of the individual with their name. For example, associating Donald with a duck. If, despite this effort, you still forget their name, you can ask someone else; ask them to repeat their name; or ask them how they pronounce it. Greeting people with their name is a sign of your respect for them. Always err on the side of formality. That is, use their formal title and surname, unless invited otherwise. Being greeted by your first name by a person you have never met before can generate a negative response. Finally, using the person's name during your conversation also has the effect of keeping their attention. In organizations, we use words to influence others. Words are the basic tools of the influencing trade. Yet few people take the time and trouble to analyse the words that they use, in order to make themselves more influential.

Chapter 4

Influencing your job appointment I

People like people like themselves.

INTRODUCTION

Given the large number of people who apply for jobs every year, it is not surprisingly that this topic has received a great deal of attention in the popular literature. The majority of these writings rely on common sense and anecdotal information. They offer useful advice, especially for the first-time graduate applicant. Perhaps you already have a book with a title such as *How to Get Your Dream Job* or something similar. This and the following chapter do not seek to duplicate these books, but instead bring together and summarize the crucial body of neglected research studies into what *really* influences selectors' judgements of job applicants. This literature has revealed that the selection process is far less scientific and much more subjective than most major companies would admit, and is therefore susceptible to being influenced by the well-informed candidate (Feldman, 1990; Knights and Raffo, 1990; Robertson and Smith, 2001). The focus of this chapter is what you need to do to get yourself to the job interview and beyond. It considers the concept of organizational fit; identifies the qualities sought by companies in applicants; suggests how your referees should complete their reference on your behalf; and considers the ever-growing field of psychometric testing. It you successfully follow this advice, you should get yourself shortlisted for an interview, or invited to attend an assessment centre. Both of these selection methods will be covered in the next chapter.

ORGANIZATIONAL FIT

In her analysis of graduate selection methods, Anderson (2001) emphasizes the increasing importance of *organizational fit*. This term refers to company-specific requirements that the selection process is used to assess. Fit concerns issues such as an applicant's appearance, attitude, personality, values and similar attributes discussed here, and in other chapters of this book. Generally speaking, companies are recruiting graduates to a particular management control structure, rather than to a specific job. Hence, the selection emphasis has begun to move away from considering skills relevant to a specific job, and more towards matching the individual candidate with their future work, company mobility requirements, and interactions with a wide range of colleagues. The person offered a position needs to be able to fit into the social environment of the company's culture, its customers and suppliers, and be able to operate within its physical environment, especially that involving IT. Yapp (2003) stated that candidates should expect to be asked not only what they have achieved, but also how they approach their work and, in particular, what their predominant style is when dealing with colleagues, direct reports and customers. Finally, companies are increasingly providing resources on their websites that make it clear exactly what type of person they are looking for. You, as an applicant, can thereby check your fit with the organization, its culture and ways of doing things.

Anderson (2001) conducted in-depth interviews with some UK graduate selectors in order to determine how they assessed whether a candidate *fitted* the organization. Her respondents agreed upon the elements that constituted organizational fit. She reported that if applicants did not match the stereotype that the company was looking for, and thus did not possess the 'right qualities', they were immediately sifted out, despite possessing good academic qualifications and extensive work experience. This may explain the disappointment of many graduates who have worked in part-time, junior-level, company jobs since they were 16, especially in supermarkets, only to find themselves rejected when applying for graduate management positions in those same organizations after graduation.

Thus the starting point for every applicant is to assess their organizational fit using the company website. It contains job profiles and describes the company's work in detail, often including brochures and videos, which are regularly updated. Some sites have chat rooms where applicants can discuss work experiences with recently appointed employees. These and similar resources will allow you to acquire a good understanding of the area – marketing, finance, production – that you are applying for. You have first to understand what a company does before you are able to assess whether you are suited for it. Too many applicants, in the recruiters' eyes, lacked such basic knowledge about the organization that they were applying to. Of equal value are the (non-assessed) personality inventories; company culture fit indicators, and job knowledge questionnaires. You can complete these and receive immediate feedback, before making a formal application, to determine how closely you fit the organization. Those who consider the company culture and procedures to be consistent with the way they like to operate, should ensure that they communicate this clearly during their selection process. The companies hope that non-matching candidates will self-select themselves out, thereby saving them time and money.

60

SELECTORS' AIMS AND CANDIDATES' ATTRIBUTES

For a long time, there has been broad agreement as to what selectors look for in candidates (Hakel and Schuh, 1971). They are seeking *winners* – people who are intelligent, assertive, knowledgeable, creative, optimistic, positive, enthusiastic and confident. They want to weed out *losers* – those who are hesitant, negative, unrealistic, self-deprecating, disorganized; who talk about failure and who blame others. More generally, they want someone who can make a quick contribution to the organization, or has the potential to do so. Selectors ask themselves four basic questions. Can the candidate do the job? Do they fit the company image? Will they disrupt or complement the department? Are they familiar with information technology? A variety of selection methods will be used to decide whether the candidate possesses the desirable characteristics. What exactly are these? Different organizations have a relatively consistent set of selection criteria against which they select new staff. About 80 per cent of these will be the same for all companies, with the remaining 20 per cent being unique.

While Dulewicz (1989) and Cockerill (1989) have their own lists of desirable, applicant qualities, we shall use Yate's (2001) list as the basis of our own. He identifies a number of areas, traits or profile keys, which have been added to (see Table 4.1). The first cluster gives an indication of what a person would be like to work with and their attitude towards themselves. The second cluster informs selectors whether a candidate is inclined to be a loyal, dependable person who respects an organization and its members. The third cluster ensures that new recruits will choose the most profitable options and not waste company resources. The fourth cluster relates to specific skills. The significance of the list is that your possession of these traits should be signalled in your application and confirmed in your replies to the questions that you will be asked during your interview.

Anderson (2001) argues that there has been a shift away from the skills a person may bring to a job, and a greater focus on recruiting applicants who demonstrate an ability to learn, to adapt to change (flexibility) and to commit to an employer. The importance ranking of these KSAs (knowledge, skills and abilities), will obviously vary with employers. However, a survey of forty-six different campus recruiters placed motivation, communication, people and time management skills at the top of their list (Chacko *et al.*, 1999). To this list of skills, knowledge and abilities, one can add the 'Big Five' personality trait clusters of Extroversion (sociable, active, energetic); Agreeableness (co-operative, considerate trusting); Conscientiousness (dependable, organized, persistent); Emotional stability (calm, secure, unemotional) and Opennes to experience (imaginative, intellectual, artistically sensitive). These will be discussed later in this chapter. Companies also want to ensure that the personalities, attitudes and values of graduates match those of the employing company.

Table 4.1 List of desirable interviewee traits

Personal profile keys (the kind of person you are). Answers to these tell the interviewer how you feel about yourself, your chosen career, what you are like to work with.

1	Drive	Goal-oriented. A desire to get things done.
2	Motivation	Enthusiast and willing to ask questions. Motivated, accepts added challenges, doing that little bit extra on the job.
3	Communication skills	Able to talk and write effectively to all levels.
4	Chemistry	Someone who is not rattled, is confident without being self-important, gets along with others, a team player.
5	Energy	Puts effort into little things as well as important ones.
6	Determination	Doesn't back off when a problem or situation gets tough.
7	Confidence	Friendly, honest and open. Maintains poise when dealing with all levels in the company.
8	Flexibility	Ability to quickly adapt and accept different roles and environments.

Professional profile keys. Companies seek employees who respect their profession and employer, and see people who do this as loyal, reliable and trustworthy.

9	Reliability	Follows up on themselves, does not rely on others that the job is well done, while keeping management informed.
10	Honesty and integrity	Takes responsibility for their actions, both good and bad. Makes decisions for the company's and not personal benefit.
11	Pride	In a job well done. Does to the best of their ability, and pays attention to detail.
12	Dedication	Does whatever it takes in time and effort to see a project through to completion by the deadline.
13	Analytical skills	Weighs pros and cons. Does not jump at the first solution that appears. Assesses short- and long-term implications.
14	Listening skills	Listens and understands, as opposed to waiting for your turn to speak.

Business or achievement profile keys (these will be achievement traits if you have been unable to do any of the first three below because, for example, you are a recent graduate.) These show that you are always on the look-out for opportunities to contribute.

15	Money saved	How you saved money by your thoughts and efficiency for the company.
16	Time saved	How your efforts saved your company time, thus freeing up resources.

Table 4.1 *continued*

17 Money earned	How you generated revenue for the company.
18 Efficiency	They avoid wasting time, effort, money or resources. Can provide examples of how their ideas or actions have saved money.
19 Economy	If there are several solutions, they implement the best value one.
20 Procedures	Follows procedures which are designed to keep company profitable. Works with their boss and keeps her informed. Called 'prepared to take direction'.
21 Profit	Is not ashamed or embarrassed about the company making profits. After all, they secure the employment of staff and their contribution to profit is a measure of their performance, and readiness for promotion.
Technical profile keys	
22 IT skills	Ability to use standard business hardware such as laptop and mobile, and familiarity with word processing, spreadsheet and presentations software.
23 Foreign language	Facility in one or more language other than English. Specify competency in speech, writing, reading or a combination. Indicate level of competency: beginner, adequate or fluent.

Source: Based on Yate (2001), *Great Answers to Tough Interview Questions*, London: Kogan Page, amended with Anderson, 2001

APPLICATION FORM AND CURRICULUM VITAE

Anderson (2001) pointed out the rapid technological developments taking place in this area. Online applications are becoming increasingly common, and are used alongside or instead of, traditional paper ones. In some cases, web-based forms give candidates the chance to assess themselves against the demands of a role, and receive immediate feedback on their suitability (Yapp, 2003). There is also a *talking CV*, which provides applicants with the opportunity to present themselves and their achievements in a different way. It allows recruiters to see and hear prospective candidates ahead of the interview, as they answer pre-set, structured interview questions. In recent years, graduates have also been able to file their details on company websites. These are then scored by software that evaluates applicants and assesses their answers to multiple-choice questions. It looks for patterns of words and then matches them against pre-specified criteria. Some sought-after words include initiative, proactive, enthusiasm and leading. These computer systems are capable of giving you an instant decision. However, because

63

candidates have been upset about getting an immediate rejection, an element of human judgement has been built in, and the rejection decision has been delayed by a week to make rejected applicants feel better (Heriot and Wingrove, 1984).

These and similar technological developments represent changes in the way in which applicants now communicate information about themselves to prospective employers. However, they do not represent fundamental changes in the purpose of the (curriculum vitae) CV/application form itself. The aim of your job application form is to secure an interview, or get to the next stage of the process, it is not to be offered the job. It is therefore crucial that you understand how a selector organizes and interprets the information about you. Many companies receive hundreds of job applications to interview a dozen or so candidates for three or four posts. This is why they frequently sub-contract this first, time-consuming stage to an outside recruitment agency. A major UK bank outsourced its graduate recruitment programme to shift the burden of sifting through hundreds of CVs. In this organization, graduate applications are first screened online to see if they have the basic qualifications. Successful candidates are then telephone interviewed, and are then given skill tests at an assessment centre, based on the company's key required competencies (*Personnel Today*, 2001). The type of selection methods and the order in which they are used varies between companies.

When applying for any job therefore, check whether this first stage is being handled by a recruitment agency or by the employing company itself. This is usually indicated by the return address for your completed application form. Search and recruitment consultants look for people on behalf of clients in exchange for a commission or fee, which is often linked to whether the eventual appointee stays in the job for a certain period. For this reason, the consultant will always play safe, having no incentive to find a brilliant candidate, but every motivation to find a steady hand who will stick it out long enough to ensure the payment of their fee. Hence, anyone who has even a slightly unconventional background, sets the consultant reaching for the rejection letter, while the undemandingly conventional person gets to the next stage of the selection process. Knowing this, you should prepare your application or CV accordingly.

Another important interpretative phenomenon is called the *primacy effect* (Aronson, 1992). Selectors form impressions from the early information that they receive. Information presented at the beginning of your CV affects how later information is interpreted. If the selector first reads positive information about you at the start of your application form, for example, that you are intelligent, industrious and somewhat impulsive, then later, more negative data about you, for example, that you are envious and critical, will have less impact. The opposite is also true (Asch, 1946). How does the primacy affect work? The 'interpretive set' explanation of this psychological phenomenon states that the first items read, serve to create an initial impression that is then used to interpret subsequent information, either through the discounting of incongruent facts (if you are intelligent why should you be envious?), or by subtle changes in the interpretation of the meanings that they give to words and facts written further down the application form (being critical is positive if you are intelligent, but negative if you are stubborn).

A positive primacy effect can be created with a CV where you decide about how best to sequence the information and how to present it to the reader. First, a standard application form may force you to put negative information about yourself at the beginning. If this is the case, you can attach a covering letter or a one-page summary to the front of your application form, which presents your positive points. You will thus get the selector to read this before the standard application form. Second, ensure that your application form is neatly typed, with correct grammar and punctuation. Remember that if you make an error in a document that is so important for your own future, the selectors will ask themselves, what errors will you tolerate in a business document that is important for the company's future? By paying attention to these two matters, you can create the necessary, positive primacy effect.

The majority of company recruiters have little time, and only rarely have been trained to interview effectively. Many will find the process as uncomfortable as you do. To save time, they use the application form to screen applicants out, as much as to select them in. You must therefore be all things to all men (and women!), while presenting them with a reason to interview you. Your completed application form is the first point of contact with your potential employer. Use the list of desirable profile keys listed in Table 4.1, to guide your selection of what items to include. If you have gaps, take steps now to fill them by joining or starting your own university clubs, learning a foreign language, developing computing skills, and generally doing those things that will carry weight on your application form. Inside the company, your form will be read first by the human resources or personnel department. It should contain only a limited amount of specialist information; be easy to read and understand; and should cast you in the light of a problem solver.

All organizations have problems, and they hire people to solve them. Additionally, commercial organizations are in business to earn profits, and they are looking for people who can reduce costs and save time (Yate, 2001). Avoid modesty and remember that your next employer is interested in what you can do for them, and in what makes you different from the other candidates. This is communicated in two ways. First, by describing the skills and knowledge that you bring with you to the job. So, list not only your previous and current job titles, but also mention what skills and knowledge you used to perform these duties. Hence, new graduates should replace their natural producer-approach ('I did computing at university'), with a customer-benefits orientation ('If appointed, I could immediately contribute to logistics work, because of my experience of spreadsheets that I gained at university'). Second, communicate

65

your achievements, and do this by using an active rather than a passive voice. Experience is passive, but achievements are active. Instead of saying, 'responsible for a diversification of squash club activities and a membership increase', write instead, 'I developed and implemented several measures to increase squash club activities and raised the club's membership'. Attempt to estimate the value of your achievements to your employer. If you increased market share by 5 per cent (achievement), the extra profit may have been £20,000 (benefit to company). In this way, you are stressing the benefits of your employment to the company. Achievements are likely to fall in the areas of sales (cash volume achieved); management and administration (time saved); and production and technical (production increased, costs reduced).

Some desirable words and phrases were discussed in the previous chapter on verbal influencing. We can add to these when discussing language in the context of the selection process. There are certain key words which selectors want to see written on a job application form, and which interviewers want to hear included in your answers to their questions. These were listed by Fitzwater (2001) and are all action verbs. They are shown in Table 4.2

Completed application forms inevitably create stereotypes in the minds of selectors. Craft your form to ensure that it projects the appropriate image for you. Different jobs will require different images. For example, the highly individualistic, competitive, go-getter, achievement-oriented, profit-driven person may be appropriate for the salesperson who works alone. In contrast, the effective team leader image will need to stress your ability to work with, and through people, to achieve company goals, client needs and subordinates' aspirations. Think what information you would include and exclude about yourself in preparing the first stereotype, and then the second. Get someone who does not know you well to read the form and comment on the image that its content conveys to them about you. Then alter or fine tune it, to meet your requirements. Most people fill in job application forms quite unaware of the image that their

Table 4.2 *Action verbs*

Analysed	Designed	Implemented	Provided
Challenged	Developed	Improved	Redesigned
Controlled	Directed	Increased	Reduced
Co-ordinated	Established	Managed	Restructured
Created	Exercised	Orchestrated	Strategized
Delivered	Expanded	Organized	Supervised
Demonstrated	Facilitated	Produced	Targeted

Source: From Fitzwater 2001: 31

words create in the minds of selectors. They are then surprised and disappointed that they are misjudged.

Research by Bright and Hutton (2000) concluded that the inclusion of competency statements in your CV or résumé, can significantly improve your perceived suitability for a job, and hence raise your chances of being shortlisted for an interview. A competency statement is a brief, written account that describes your knowledge, skills or abilities. Each will be related to some of Yate's profile keys mentioned earlier. Competency statements can take the following form, as illustrated by Bright and Hutton (2000: 44)

- *Highly motivated.* I have a proven track record of achievement, both within university and outside university, through extra-curricular activities. I have won numerous awards through my academic career but have still managed to maintain a balance with social activities.
- *Organizational skills.* As a person who is involved in many different activities, I have developed excellent organizational skills to ensure that I plan my time effectively. This enables me to achieve maximum output in minimum time, as well as handle a number of activities simultaneously.
- *Responsible.* As a person who has always been involved in a range of activities, I have developed a responsible and mature approach to any task I undertake, or situation that I am presented with. I believe that these assets will stand me in good stead for any future positions that I undertake.

The researchers found that even linking such statements to address desired job competences in a general way improved candidates' chances of being shortlisted. It did not matter how many statements were included (between two and six), and including more did not create a negative impression of the candidate. Nor did it matter where on the CV they appeared. As a written, impression management technique, the authors were unclear why competency statements were as influential as they were. It could be the provision of extra information to the selector relating to particular aspects of the job, or it might be the presence of the statement itself, which enhanced the global impression of the candidate given to the reader. Either way, the advice is to include such statements in your CV or application form. Many young graduates applicants need to overcome their natural reticence or hesitancy to make their achievements known to selectors. It is not a question of being boastful, as selectors want to know what candidates can do for the company.

In the case of a CV, update it regularly, eliminating material that is excessively old, or which has been superseded by something better. Views about its length vary. Some selectors recommend limiting your CV to no more than two typed pages. Others, who need reading glasses, do not like the information to

67

be too small, and difficult to read. Perhaps the rule is to make it as short as circumstances permit. If you have a PC, you can customize each one to the specific job that you are applying for. Using a standard, laser-printed general version, and attaching a personalized covering letter, highlighting those parts of your CV to the reader, which are particularly relevant for the job being sought is only a second best alternative. Feldman and Klich (1991) recommended constructing your CV so that your current job goal is not only consistent with past educational and work experiences, but is also seen as the logical next step in your career. Make it appear that there is some rhyme or reason for what you want to do. This is likely to be a total fiction since in reality, people's needs, abilities, interests and opportunities change. However, as far as the CV is concerned, any wild swings of interests should be suppressed, and the consistency between past decisions, current concerns and future goals need to be constructed. If you have a degree in languages and are applying for a job in a multinational firm, explain that your language focus represents a latent interest in international business.

The CV/application is usually the first, but may be the second document that a recruiter receives from you. It therefore creates a first impression. The first document may be your visiting card. Final year students and graduates attending company presentations, university milk round events and graduate fairs, are now advised to have cards printed, ready to distribute at these events. Both the cards and your CV are likely to contain your email address. In her study of first impressions on the internet, Wallace (1999) examined the information that your email address conveys about you and the impression it creates to others. She offered a number of fictitious examples:

tufdud888@aol.com
FoxyLady@flash.net
rgoldman6@microsoft.com

She suggests that *tufdud*'s objectivity about gender issues in the workplace might be questioned by a recruiter, and that one might be more inclined to follow advice given by *rgoldman* than by *FoxyLady*. Wallace reported the experience of a friend who chose *LoveChick* as a joke when she first got her account, but after she had created and expanded her desktop publishing business, she had constantly to explain and apologize to her customers. When purchasing a personal account, and if you have a choice of name to the left of the @, give some thought to what impression your email name will have on those whom you are seeking to influence.

Finally, one can note that Anderson's (2001) research on company selectors revealed that application form questions were also designed to measure the organizational fit mentioned earlier. Questions such as 'What scheme are you applying for?' and 'What steps have you taken to clarify your thinking?', are specifically designed to ensure that only committed applicants apply. The form itself there-fore provides applicants with an insight into the type of candidate the company is looking for. In the form, questions are phrased in a number of different ways to check the truthfulness of the applicant's personality characteristics. These include how geographically mobile an applicant is. Open questions also allow candidates to illustrate the behavioural competences that they possess. At the first stage of screening, selectors considered the candidate in terms of degree quality. It was at the second screening stage that a candidate's degree of organizational fit was assessed. Fit was considered so important, that several application forms have been redesigned to be able to measure it more accurately. The general point is the importance of ensuring that every application form or CV that you send out is 'hand-crafted' and customized to the specific company being applied to. Thus, if time is short, it is better to apply to fewer companies, giving great attention to each application, than to send out a large number of only generally applicable forms.

REFEREES AND REFERENCES

Anderson and Shackleton (1994) reported that 96 per cent of employers used references in the selection process. Research by IRS Employment Review showed that three-quarters of them checked references as part of their recruitment process, and acted upon them. The continued emphasis on reference checking is due to more candidates lying or exaggerating their achievements or experience on CVs. Job seekers may be surprised by the weight that employers still place on references. They are still an integral part of the modern selection process. Reference checking typically occurred in the final stages of the recruitment process. A Chartered Institute of Personnel and Development survey found that employers rated reference checking to be the most important part of the selection process after interviews and CV/application forms (Nelson, 2002).

With a reference, you are requested to identify referees willing to vouch for your character and past technical performance. While most references will be written, some will be solicited by telephone to confirm data supplied on the application form, and to gather new data on the candidate's suitability. Employers wrongly believe that references are reliable predictors of future job performance. It is unlikely that the candidate will knowingly identify a referee who will point out areas of weakness. Whoever the referee is, they tend to be lenient and always give a good report. The most reliable information in a reference relates to general intelligence, and the least reliable to personality. Whatever is included in a refer-ence is necessarily subjective, and is thus of limited value to the new employer.

Commentators recommend not giving the names of referees unless specifically asked to do so, either on the application form or CV. The argument is that you want to control what information is first read about you. Some selectors seek references early in the selection process, using referees' reports as data with which to shortlist candidates. Others use a referee's report after an interview, but before a job offer is made, in order to support a selection decision already made, rather than determine such a decision. In the case of new graduates, with little or no track record in a job, referee reports are likely to be sought early in the process. Apart from obvious referees whose absence would raise suspicion (e.g. university tutor, previous employer), you have the choice of who to nominate.

Why is a good reference important and what does it look like? Fritz Heider (1958) studied how we explain the behaviour of those around us. He concluded that people attributed others' behaviour, either to *internal* causes (a person's disposition), or to *external* causes (something in that person's situation). For example, an interviewer might wonder whether a graduate's class of degree was due to a lack of personal motivation or ability (an internal, dispositional attribution), or to physical or social circumstances (an external, situational attribution). If the interviewer reads your referee's report about you, how is she likely to interpret your past performance that is set out in the application form? Perception theory, especially the concepts of stereotyping and halo effect, together with primacy effect, would lead us to guess that a favourable referee's report about you, read by the interviewer prior to your meeting, would be most beneficial. That is indeed the case. Tucker and Rowe (1979) studied the effect of favourable and unfavourable referees' letters. When a reference was favourable, the interviewer attributed failures in the candidate's past to external causes, and his successes to internal causes. Similarly, when the reference letter was unfavourable, a candidate's successes where attributed to external causes such as luck, while their failures were attributed internally to their personal characteristics. An interviewer who begins with a favourable expectation about you, gained from a positive letter of reference, is therefore more inclined to give you the benefit of the doubt, and not hold you personally responsible for any of your failures or shortcomings. For this reason, it is important to get your referee to write you a good reference.

In general, your referee will be trying to help you for several reasons. First, as a reward for good service in the past (a job reference by a professor for a student who has worked hard (Tedeschi and Norman 1985)). Second, it may be to protect the image of his organization. Would they write, 'this man is a fool, and he studied at my university?' (Cialdini and Richardson, 1980). A good university or company cannot admit to having let in an idiot. Third, to protect the referee's own image as the teacher or manager, to those outside who might know or hear about him (Gioia and Sims, 1985). Finally, the referee may be seeking to place a subordinate or acquaintance in a strategic position so that he can help him later (Mintzberg, 1983, 1985). Most letters of reference therefore, have a highly positive tone (Paunonen *et al.*, 1987).

70

Table 4.3 *Features of an effective letter of reference*

Entitlings	Referee emphasizes your responsibility for positive results ('She was responsible for').
Enhancements	Maximizing the desirability of the successes ('Her ideas led to cost reductions of').
Burying	Less successful events, if not buried, should be explained by reference to external causes and justifications ('The recession just hit us'). Readers seem to buy this excuse.
Explaining	Average or below average performance can be explained by the context ('He has great potential which the course structure prevented him from displaying').
Justification	'He performed badly, but most people in their first management job do not do particularly well' (Schlenker, 1980).
Scarcity	Emphasize the scarce qualities of the candidate ('Her departure would be a loss for her current employer, but a gain for the new one').
Vignettes	The referee can construct coherent vignettes to convey a story to give meaning to events ('Mr Brown reminds me of a bull terrier always ferreting out key facts'; or put people into categories: 'She is one of those people who persevere after disappointment, and fight through to success' (Abelson, 1976)).
Length	Longer reference letters are more related to positive attitudes in situations, in cases where length is unrestricted (Mehrabian, 1965; Wiens *et al.*, 1969).
Factual	Anything that looks like a fact, carries a great deal of weight – time in a post; cost savings achieved; grade in a course; attendance record.

Source: Muchinsky, 1979

Courtesy demands that you contact your selected referee, to ask their permission to be contacted. Doing this gives you the opportunity to tell them about the job, and explain how they can write you a good reference. Your reference writer cannot see the reader, but tries to provide what they believe the latter wants (Baxter *et al.*, 1981; Knouse, 1983, 1989). Even if your referee is trying to help you, they may not know the best way to do this. Hence, your referees need to employ specific impression management tactics in their writing. Request them to follow the guidelines detailed in Table 4.3 when preparing your letter of reference.

PSYCHOMETRIC TESTS

The psychometric (or psychological) test is a selection method, which is likely to be encountered by new graduates applying to major, international corporations. Saville and Holdsworth, a human resources group estimate that 56 per cent of

UK employers, with more than 750 employees use personality tests, and an even larger percentage use ability tests (Donkin, 2003). It appears that use of such tests is generally concentrated in the top named, large corporations who recruit graduates. A psychometric test measures the less tangible attributes or aspects of mental behaviour. Such tests can be taken at different times during the selection process. For example, some are to be completed along with the job application form; some are taken after submission of the application form, but before attendance at the interview; while some are taken after an individual interview, but before a panel interview. The most commonly used psychometric tests assess candidates' abilities (numerical and verbal), and their personality. There are many short books which explain the purpose of psychometric tests, give examples of the type of questions that you will be asked and which explain how assessors interpret the results obtained (Tolley and Thomas, 2000; Smith, 2003; Bryson, 2002; Barrett, 2002; Al-Jajjoka, 2001; Parkinson, 2000).

More and more companies are using psychological testing to supplement the traditional interview, especially when appointing young graduates with no employment track record. So why do they use such tests? The official line is that since the cost of recruiting the wrong person can have an impact on profits, employers are wary of taking applicants' CVs information at face value. In their view, psychometric tests provide an unbiased and objective way of filtering out unsuitable candidates, and helping to predict how well individuals will do their job and fit into the team. Companies believe that such tests provide an objective way of assessing candidates, and give them an insight into the skills that cannot be revealed through the interview.

There is no strong demonstrated link between people's personalities, as measured by a psychometric test, and the behaviours that an employer considers to be essential for effective job performance. The relationship between an individual's test score and how they are likely to perform in the actual job is usually impossible to gauge since company criteria for measuring an employee's performance in a job are usually ambiguous. Ideally, companies would like a foolproof test of character that would save them time and money. Faced with hundreds of applications for every job, especially the most desirable ones, employers are less interested in whether testing works, and rather more in whether tests can provide a quick, cheap method of whittling down the pile. An additional bonus is that if recruiters make a bad selection decision, they can blame the test.

If psychometric testing is therefore an elaborate 'game', should candidates practise or even cheat? Job applicants should beware of the spurious scientificity of psychometric tests. Companies who produce tests, as well as organizations that use them, both have a vested interest in portraying the psychometric test as being akin to a blood test. In reality, the reverse is true. Hard work, determination and systematic preparation may not change the result of your blood test, but can improve your psychometric test score. These tests are only objective when compared to the other, more subjective techniques which form the stable of selection methods. As Byron observes, being three times more reliable than an unreliable interview is no great recommendation.

When playing for high stakes of getting a peculiarly sought-after job, and also knowing that such tests are used primarily to screen applicants out, rather than select them in, lying may be considered as a logical strategy by some candidates. In this case, it means portraying a personality that you feel the company is seeking, rather than your own. To combat such lying, test devisers structure the tests so that a comparison is made, not between a candidate's need for control against some outside norm, but against some other trait, such as how sociable they are. If the results on these two dimensions are in conflict, then this may indicate the possibility of lying (or it may indicate a candidate's lack of self-awareness!).

Numerical, verbal and abstract ability tests

Numerical ability tests assess how you deal with information which is presented in a numerical form; how you use numbers; and whether you can work out the relationships between them. They require you to perform basic arithmetical procedures without a calculator. The advice here is to practise your mental arithmetic before, and estimate numbers, rounding them up and down. Numerical reasoning tests, like their verbal counterparts, provide you with a block of information, such as a table of statistics, and then ask you a set of questions about it. Your knowledge of percentages, ratios, fractions and averages is being tested here, as well as your interpretation of pie charts and line graphs. The idea of a *numerical* test frightens even graduates. Remember, however, that the maths required to pass this test is only GCSE or Scottish Standard Grade level.

Verbal reasoning ability tests assess how you approach information presented in a written manner, and how you use it to reason with. Abstract ability tests are concerned with how well you can analyse a problem presented in a visual (non-verbal) manner and logically work out an answer. A widely used test to measure these three abilities is the Graduate and Management Assessment (GMA) battery. Ability tests assess whether you can discover similarities between things, and see which do not fit. For verbal ability tests, you should brush up on your grammar and spelling. Verbal aptitude tests come in the form of 'A is to B as C is to?'. Verbal critical reasoning tests give you a short passage of information on a topic, which is followed by a series of statements. For each you have to decide whether, on the basis of the information in the passage, each statement is true, false or not assessable. Focus on the information in the passage, do not let your personal views interfere with your logic, especially when the passage contains emotive material.

Research has found that practice improves scores (Nevo, 1976). A minimum of 12 hours is recommended on material that is similar to that to be used in the

73

real test. This should be done first, in an informal relaxed manner, and then again, under timed conditions. At least three, full mock tests should be completed. The results of such coaching suggest most people can improve their scores dramatically, with those who have not previously done tests, actually doubling their performance. Improvements for all are gained quickly, after which they flatten out. To get in the correct frame of mind for such tests, Anderson (2001) recommends adding up shopping lists in your head; doing crosswords, puzzle books, even jigsaws; reading a good-quality broadsheet newspaper like *The Times*, the *Guardian*, the *Daily Telegraph* or the *Financial Times*, to hone your analytical skills.

Irrespective of what type of test you are sitting, it is essential to be in the correct frame of mind. Really wanting the job and being motivated to try hard is essential. Confidence and a determination to do justice to your own ability is also required. Simple, commonsense techniques should be applied during the test. Check precisely how you are required to respond to the test questions, so as not to give the impression that you are unwilling to learn, or incapable of following instructions. Do not be put off by the length of the test. Most tests are not designed to be completed in the time available. At the test itself, work quickly but accurately. Neither go flat out and get all the answers wrong, nor spend too much time on a particular question. You have to trade off accuracy against coverage of material. It is better to move on to another question, and come back to unanswered ones if time permits. Do not panic in the exam room, as assessors will treat this as a sign of your inability to work under pressure.

As you progress through the test booklet, you will find the questions become harder or at least more complicated. Do not spend too much time on easy questions, and in consequence fail to double-check the more complicated ones. Many questions come in the form of multiple choices with between three and six options. If you are up against the clock, and have eliminated most of the answers, then it makes sense to make an informed guess. Before you do this however, you should ask at the start if you will lose marks for wrong answers. If you do, then avoid guessing. Some companies only mark and grade you on those questions which you have attempted, and ignore those which you have not answered. Of course, the test administrator may not be willing or able to tell you.

Able tests

In recent years, tests of numerical and verbal skills have been replaced or comple-mented by a new type of test which measures a candidate's ability to do the job in question – the so-called *able test*. They have been introduced partly because some candidates have had experience of completing traditional ability tests, and thus gain an advantage over other, equally competent, ones, who have not had the same exposure to them. The ability test is thus seen as being fairer. The test is also business based, and thus gives the applicants who complete it, a feel for the workplace that they might be joining. The new test focuses on an applicant's ability to learn. Each test simulates a particular type of work, using real life tasks and role play activities. Able tests are of different types. The critical appraisal version tests a candidate's ability to learn new material in a short space of time; tests their ability to understand numbers and concepts and gets them to apply the new knowledge that they have just learned. Thus it tests a combination of comprehension, numerical understanding and judgement. Candidates have to learn rules, sift information and make decisions in progressively ever more complex situations. As they work through the exercises, they have to learn and apply new skills and knowledge (Willis, 1997).

Rarely are practice booklets supplied for able tests, but candidates are given broad guidance of what to expect. Recruiters also recommend that candidates read the quality press mentioned earlier, to get themselves in the correct frame of mind for these tests. Able tests are more difficult than traditional ones, and it is rare to achieve a high mark in them. Many candidates will not immediately understand the test, because it is not obvious what is being asked for. Though the answers are not evident, an understanding usually dawns upon candidates as they proceed, and the majority complete them and do quite well. If you do one of these tests, you should not feel disheartened if you do not immediately know how to tackle the questions. Instead, relax, and read all the information for each question. As normal, work quickly, passing over questions which you cannot answer, returning to them later. It seems that if a candidate fails this type of test, they are automatically eliminated.

Personality tests

Unlike ability tests, personality tests are not strictly timed, and there are no right or wrong answers. There are many different ones used with names like the FIRO-B, Myers-Briggs Type Indicator, the Occupational Personality Question-naire (OPQ), PA Preference Inventory. Psychologists have decided that five major dimensions account for all behaviour. These are shown below. Different selection techniques will each focus on a different subset of these five trait clusters. These psychological tests attempt to measure where you are placed on these five main scales.

1 *Extrovert–introvert*. Extroverts are energetic, sociable, emotional and impulsive. Introverts are quiet, restrained and more considered in their outlook.
2 *Confident–anxious*. Confident individuals are comfortable with themselves, relaxed and tend to be optimistic. They may also be assertive and usually stick to their point of view in an argument. Anxious people (in these

75

terms) are cautious and tense, tend to be pessimistic and have a rather conservative outlook.

3 *Structured–non-structured.* Structured individuals are precise and formal. They tend to be self-controlled and do not like ambiguity or lack of organization. Non-structured people are informal and casual, tend to be tolerant of others and have a relaxed manner.

4 *Tough minded–tender minded.* Tough-minded characters are assertive, relatively insensitive and focus on the task at hand. They prefer to work with tough-minded people and can have an outspoken, sometimes dictatorial style. Tender-minded people tend to have a warm, friendly and benevolent outlook. They are sensitive to other people's feelings and more likely to listen than to dictate.

5 *Conformist–non-conformist.* Conformists are middle of the road, down-to-earth moderates. They tend to take a conventional and practical approach to things. Non-conformists are concerned with expressing themselves in an individual way and don't like rules, regulations or structure.

Candidates' possession of these Big Five traits is assessed not only through the personality test, but also at the interview and in the assessment centre. It is beneficial to make your personality sound as natural as possible, and selectors are interested in candidates displaying the trait clusters described above. However, it is important not to stray too far from the truth, as this can cause you trouble later if you are offered the job. Studies have been done concerning the Big Five trait clusters in job interviews (Caldwell and Burger, 1998; van Dam, 2003). These show that Extroversion was the most identifiable in such interviews, and was the one best predictor of whether a person was offered a job.

In these tests, candidates are advised to avoid marking too many extreme scores on scaled questions (especially on a 1–7 range), as this will make them seem impulsive. Similarly, 'maybe' answers should be avoided since they may show indecisiveness. That is why these questionnaires have built-it check questions to spot inconsistency. Job applicants are also generally aware of the characteristics that the employer is seeking. If applying for the job of a policeman, they consciously answer the questions the way that a policeman might. This can occur unconsciously, when you think long and hard about your desired job of a teacher or marketing person. When it is not clear what the employer desires, honesty may be the best strategy since the optimum combination of characteristics sought will be unknown. Is it possible to cheat on a personality test? A candidate may inadvertently provide inaccurate information about themselves because of the known huge gulf between what people say about themselves and their true characteristics (self-deception). They may not know themselves well enough to answer questions about their personality accurately (Arthur, Woehr and Graziano, 2001).

USE OF TESTS BY COMPANIES

Having scored your ability or personality test, the assessor uses it in any number of ways. Typically, the assessor compares your score to an established norm. This lets them judge whether, compared to others, your numerical and problem-solving ability is high or low; and in the case of the personality test, whether you are more or less extroverted, confident, structured, than other applicants. Companies use these test results in two ways. First, as a complement to the application form, to eliminate unsuitable applicants from the interview (known as the disqualification test). Second, to provide supplementary data to that obtained from the interview in the making of the final decision. In psychometric testing, personality tests are given less weight than ability tests. People with different personalities can do the same job equally well, and the best person to do a current job, may be different from anyone who has done it before. You should be aware however, that different companies have different policies. For example, one superstore chain, which uses numerical ability tests to select non-managerial staff, only measures them on the questions that they answer in the test. They are thus interested in the quality and not the quantity of the responses. Also, in a personality test, only 12 of the 60 questions may be assessed. In another organization, the process may be different. Test scores are also used to provide the basis for probing questions at the first interview.

So, does doing well in a psychometric test matter? The weighting placed on psychometric test scores by selectors differs widely. If you are required to complete a test early in the selection process, then you can assume that the company places importance on it. If you take the test late, such as the final assessment centre, then it is not considered crucial. The company will have already spent money on flying you down and paying for your accommodation. If it was that important, they would have tested you earlier on. In one study, only 4 per cent of responding companies rated such tests as 'very important' to the final selection process. This contrasts with a 71 per cent weighting given to a candidate's interview performance (Ramsey, 1994).

The psychology of perception tells us that, if the results of these tests are available to interviewers before the interview, those who do well in the tests will possess a positive halo or primacy effect in the eyes of the interviewers, and vice versa. Different companies place different emphases on the results of psychometric tests, and a good interview performance will always outshine a poor or average test performance or application form, especially if the interviewer likes you. However, it makes sense to perform as best you can, as your application form and your test score are what get you to the next stage in the selection process. Books on how to complete such tests recommend familiarizing yourself with the different types of test, the questions that they contain; and practising them beforehand. Clearly, preparing for these makes sense. Such practice and revision will calm you, and help you to perform well. Websites run by test providers such as the Saville and Holdsworth Limited Direct for Students, provide examples of test items for verbal, numerical, diagrammatic and personality test inventory items. In addition, they provide complete, timed practice tests for potential tests takers. Information on these is available from the web or university careers and placements offices. Anderson (2001) says that candidates should not feel downhearted if they are rejected on the basis of a test. Many tests reward conformity behaviour and able (ability) tests are often looking for a single skill, for example, accuracy under pressure, rather than more generalized competencies.

In recent years, psychometric test publishers have provided computer delivery of existing, manually administered tests (Bartram, 1999). However, new tests are being developed to assess a candidate's potential for acquiring key skills. These are being designed for use on computers and will have no pencil-and-paper equivalent. These tests do not have a fixed sequence of questions. Instead, they are tailored to the candidate's performance. If he or she is doing well, the questions become harder, and vice versa, until the candidate reaches their limit. Another development is computer-assisted telephone testing which uses interactive voice technology. This allows candidates to 'dial a test', and have the questions spoken to them. They respond using their keypad. This allows recruiters to process thousands of applications through this screening system that saves them much time and money. It seems that today's applicants need to find out more about the system currently being used, and prepare adequately for it. The problem for the company is ensuring the authenticity of the test taker at the other end of the telephone or computer.

Chapter 5

Influencing your job appointment II

Don't open your mouth until you've put your brain in gear.

INTRODUCTION

Being invited to an interview normally means that you have outperformed the other applicants, and have surmounted the first hurdle in the selection process. Your aim at the interview is either to be offered the job or to secure a place on either the second and final round of interviews, or an invitation to participate in an assessment centre. There are a number of general principles that apply to successful performance at all interviews, and a discussion of these forms the bulk of the contents of this chapter. Recent developments in technology have ushered in the era of *distance interviewing*. Thus, you may be interviewed either over the telephone, or by means of a videoconferencing system. The general question-answering principles will apply equally to these types of interviews, but with some modifications. You should be aware however, that while the face-to-face interview is located towards the end of the selection process, the telephone interview is placed towards the start. Both types of distance interviewing will be dealt with towards the end of this chapter.

PURPOSE OF INTERVIEWS

The telephone interview acts like the application form/CV form, in that it is a means of trying to select you out. In most of the other types of interview, the selectors are looking at your positive points, seeking reasons to offer you the job. Although Nelson and Wedderburn (1988) rate the interview used alone, as only 2–5 per cent better than random selection, the interview remains the most popular staff selection method, and is believed by managers in organizations to be the most effective method of selecting staff according to an IRS Employment Review survey of 100 UK firms (*Personnel Today*, 2002). It is used by between 88–100 per cent of companies (Robertson and Makin, 1986;

Shackleton and Newell, 1991). Interviewers are seeking to check candidates' possession of the profile keys mentioned previously and also, it seems, their possession of two of the 'Big Five' traits of Extroversion and Agreeableness (Lievans *et al.*, 2001). Either personnel experts, or line managers, and often both will conduct the interviews.

Despite the ubiquity of the interview, every interviewer faces some major problems (Schmitt, 1976). First, they need far more expertise and time to judge the potential of a young, inexperienced candidate, than that of an experienced person (Keenan, 1997). For example, it has been shown that interviewers are unable to assess accurately candidates' key personality traits such as their conscientiousness and emotional stability, which might best predict later job success (Barrick *et al.*, 2000). This means that candidates can easily project an image of themselves as dependable, hard working and persistent (high on Conscientiousness) and calm, stable and confident (high in Emotional Stability). A second difficulty is that job selection criteria such as *drive*, frequently refer to attributes that are either difficult to assess objectively, or which are of questionable relevance to job performance (Thomas, 2003). Third, organizations do not have a very clear picture of the ideal candidate. They know what they do not want, but beyond that, of the candidates that meet the minimum conditions, they realize that more than one type of person could do most jobs.

In most organizations, hiring the wrong person is seen as the interviewer's fault, and it reflects badly on their abilities. Despite its unsuitability for assessing candidates for managerial posts, interviewing is most frequently used to assess non-cognitive attributes. Final decisions on appointment lie with the line manager and not the personnel specialist. Managers hire people who they feel will 'fit' into the company culture (Fombrun, 1983; Rynes and Gerhart, 1990), who will form a homogeneous constituency, and who can help them to build a power base (Fletcher, 1979, 1990). Thus, assessors are looking for clues that a candidate will not only be capable in the job, but will also fit into the organization. Parsons and Cable (1999) even suggest that a candidate's *acceptability* (to other staff and the company as a whole), is more important that their *capability* (to do their job well). All interviewers ask themselves the question, 'Would I like to work with this person?'. This situation provides ample scope for influencing.

Whatever the type of interview, there are some basic points that all interviewees need to attend to. First, you need to prepare for it, and show the selectors that you have prepared. This single act, distinguishes the bulk of successful interview candidates from the rejects. This involves communicating that you have visited the company website; read the corporate brochure, annual report and accounts; reviewed the job specification and sought further information about the post being applied for; and that you have regularly monitored the financial press for company- or industry-relevant developments. All this can be done through your answers to their questions, and by the questions that you yourself ask your interviewer at the end of the interview. It enables you to justify your choices, and explain why you want the job. Anderson (2001) recommends using this preparation to develop points of view on company matters (although not hostile to the company), and questions to ask the interviewers. This impresses them. Basics also include being punctual; dressing smartly and professionally; smiling and giving a confident handshake; maintaining eye contact with the interviewer; maintaining open body posture throughout the interview; being friendly and appearing enthusiastic; and being as relaxed as you can be under the circumstances.

There are three essential impressions to convey during the actual interview. First that you are capable of doing the job, that you truly desire the job, and that you are circumspect and can behave in ways that will not embarrass yourself, your boss or company (Feldman and Klich, 1991). To create these impressions, you can use both ingratiation and self-promotion tactics (Baron, 1986). You can make self-enhancing statements to draw attention to your competence and likeability; conform to the interviewer's opinion on various job-related issues (although look out for the question where they are deliberately being provocative and expect you to argue back); glorify your past achievements, taking credit for visibly successful projects; and overstate your willingness to contribute to your employer's success. Whiddet and Kandola (2000) suggest that although new graduates may not yet have the experience or competencies desired by an employer, they can give examples of their competencies by describing situations at university where they have used the desired skills. Recruiters complain that poor interviewees either do not give, or else give poor, non-specific examples of their past behaviours or experience. For example, interviewees might comment that they had been part of a team in the past, but fail to explain their role in it, or their contribution to that team effort or outcome. This does not allow interviewers to judge candidates' possession of core competences, and leads to their rejection. Selectors are less interested in relevant past work experience (barmaid or financial company summer intern), and more in your ability to explain your role, the challenges you faced, how you overcame them, and your understanding of the importance of teamworking and the dynamics of work.

An assertive interviewee style will be more effective than a passive one. Such behaviour includes asking the interviewer questions, arguing a point and taking the initiative in raising topics for discussion (Dipboye and Wiley, 1977). McFarland et al. (2002) distinguished between 'soft' and 'hard' influencing tactics at selection interviews. They found that the use of soft tactics (rational persuasion, inspirational appeals, personal appeals, consultation and ingratiation) positively affected interviewer's ratings of the candidate's possession of interpersonal, problem-solving and analytical skills. There was no similar effect with the use of hard tactics (pressure, upward appeals and punitive threats). Ramsay et al. (1997) summarize the behaviours demonstrated by successful interviewees, as revealed

81

by past studies. Verbal ones include the use of positive and concrete language; support for the claims they make; and statements of identification with prospective employers. Non-verbal ones include avoiding long delays in responding to questions; run-on responses and hesitations. Candidates who use an assertive response style receive more positive ratings. Despite the fact that the interviewer is in control of the interaction during an interview, generally candidates are evaluated more positively if they display the skill of social control. For example, they need to show some dominance at appropriate points, particularly when the interviewer has not allowed them to reveal relevant information (profile keys) about themselves. Research studies reveal that interviewers expect successful candidates to demonstrate interview presentation skills. These include verbal and non-verbal presentation of job-related information; describing their skills and experience in a positive way; showing evidence of interview preparation; and demonstrating the relevance of the particular job being applied for, to their future career goals. Interviewers also expect applicants to show interpersonal skills, self-confidence and to take an active role within the interview.

An earlier chapter examined the effect of non-verbal behaviour on influencing. Within the interview situation, non-verbal behaviours can count for more than 80 per cent of an applicant's rating. In an experiment, 52 recruiters were shown videos of two groups of candidates who had been briefed to give exactly the same verbal responses. However, half had been instructed to exhibit maximum eye contact, high energy, head moving, smiling, and similar behaviour. The other group had been asked to do the opposite. Of the 26 specialists who saw the high non-verbal behaviour group, 23 would have invited the candidate back for a second interview. None of those seeing the low eye contact, low energy candidates recommended a second interview. Interviewers draw inferences about a candidate's personality, in this case their extroversion level, from their non-verbal behaviour (Caldwell and Burger, 1998). The conclusion is that an otherwise inferior interviewee who is trained, or trains themselves, to 'act appropriately' at an interview may be appraised more highly than a more competent applicant who lacks non-verbal interviewing skills (McGovern and Tinsley, 1978; Rasmussen, 1984; Gifford et al., 1985; Fleishmann, 1991). Life is not fair!

INTERVIEWER BIASES

Anderson and Shackleton (1994) list nine psychological characteristics that bias interviewers for or against you. The *primacy affect* has already been mentioned in connection with the application form and CV. The contents of your application form, letters of reference and psychometric test scores (if available prior to the interviewers) form this effect. You may be able to turn it to your advantage, since interviewers' judgements made about a candidate at the start of the interview, colour assessments made later. Fiske and Taylor (1991) argue that people are bombarded with cues from strangers that they are seeing and talking to for the first time, and they use shortcuts, and rely on just a few of these. They are cognitive misers. They tend to overuse some of these cues, which serve them as rules-of-thumb. One such rule is the warmth or coldness of an individual. Using their social thermometers, interviewers can quickly assess an applicants' warmth or coldness, and they need only a little more information, to quickly form that first impression of them. Although research challenges the long-standing and popular view that accept–reject appointment decisions are made in the first few minutes (or even seconds!) of an interview, interviewers do tend to remember what happened at the start and end of the interview (primacy–recency effect), but are somewhat vague about the middle unless they are taking notes. This argues for a good starting and ending performance by the candidate.

The primacy effect becomes transformed into the *expectancy effect*, where the interviewer forms an expectancy of the candidate from their application form and initial verbal and non-verbal behaviour. Together, these early impressions strongly affect the final appointment decision. The *contrast effect* tells us that inter- viewers' decisions are affected by those whom they have seen before you, and that they pay particular attention to any information (good or bad) that is unusual or out of the ordinary. The *personal liking bias* reminds us that interviewers select candidates whom they like, and allow their ratings of a candidate's ability to be influenced by such personal liking (Anderson, 1992). The interviewer's *confir- matory information-seeking bias* may lead them to actively look for evidence to support their initial impressions, and thereby to avoid contradictory evidence. These stored patterns in the brain may be positive or negative. In addition, interviewers possess *notions of stereotypical and prototypical* ideal job holders, and they seek to match candidates to these notions. It is not often clear how, as an interviewee, you can discover these. In such circumstances, you should use self-justification. Let us examine some of these biases in a little more detail.

The *halo–horns effect* refers to the interviewers' tendency to identify a single, distinguishing feature of a candidate (dress, height, achievement, handshake), which may be positive (halo) or negative (horn), and to allow it to affect their other judgements about the person. The explanation of this phenomenon is to be found in attribution theory, which tells us that people take personal respon- sibility for outcomes which are successful, while tending to attribute failure to external causes over which they have no control (Zuckerman, 1979). Such self- justification enables them to maintain self-esteem, and therefore their self-image. All threats to self-esteem are countered vigorously. A common mechanism for doing this is a 'belief in a just world' (Lerner, 1977). This leads us to assume that we have, in some way, deserved our rank, or our income, or our good health. Similarly, we assume that others are less fortunate because they deserve to be ('People get what they deserve'). The effect of this is that, unless you use self-justification, you will be blamed for your failures.

83

This is also the well-known *negativity effect* which states that negative information about a person, is given a disproportionate amount of weight by interviewers, in comparison to positive information (Carlson, 1971; Constantin, 1976; Kellerman, 1984, 1989). Job interviewers weigh negative information more heavily than positive information in forming impressions of others or in making decisions (Hamilton and Zanna, 1972; Peeters, 1971). This finding is a counter to the *Pollyanna effect* which says that, in the absence of any relevant information about a situation or a person, one proceeds as if the reality was good rather than bad. For this reason, avoid providing any negative information about yourself, and justify any that gets out. If asked what you consider to be your main weakness, couch it as a strength (e.g. obsessed about meeting deadlines, attention to detail, highest quality, expect others to perform to same high standards, etc.). In a similar way, once inside the company, it is better to minimize the number of your enemies or opponents, rather than maximize the number of allies.

We know that interviewers prefer candidates who are similar to themselves in biographical background, personality and attitudes. This phenomenon is technically referred to as *homophily*, but is more commonly known as the *clone syndrome*, the *similar-to-me effect* and the *in-group bias*. It has been extensively documented (Baskett, 1973; Miller *et al.*, 1966; Beer *et al.*, 1984; Ferris *et al.*, 1989; Frank and Hackman, 1975; Franklin, 1975; Golightly *et al.*, 1972; Nahemon and Lawton, 1975; Salancik and Pfeffer, 1978; Tajfel *et al.*, 1971). All of these different labels refer to the same unconscious preference of self over others. We like people like ourselves. It is natural for people to search out those who are similar to them in outlook on life, work habits, social concerns and intellectual pursuits, and in whose company they feel congenial and relaxed. People tend to cluster by race, ethnic background, age range, gender, level of education, social status and professional group.

Moreover, both within and outside the interview situation, individuals are more prone to be influenced by people who are similar to them, than those who are different. On learning that a candidate has something in common with the interviewer, he or she becomes endowed with the same values as the interviewer, and everyone else becomes an out-group member. One person's thoughts are attracted to another person's thoughts with a force directly proportionate to the similarity of their experiences. Similarity contributes to attraction. It has been found that listeners judged speakers who had speech rates similar to their own as more socially attractive and competent than those whose rates they perceived to be either faster or slower (Feldstein *et al.*, 2001). Job applicants who had leadership styles similar to the selector's were appointed more often (Eagleson *et al.*, 2000). The greater the perceived similarity between yourself and the interviewer, the more they will interpret your behaviour as reflecting attitudes that are similar to their own. In an interview situation, it has been found that positive, non-verbal cues such as smiling and making eye contact, encouraged perceptions of interviewer–candidate similarity (and therefore increased liking) coupled with verbal self-promotion (Kristof-Brown *et al.*, 2002).

The more a candidate is perceived as similar to the interviewer, the more suitable, knowledgeable and competent he or she is judged to be (Rand and Wexley, 1976). If the interviewer is confident in herself, it is natural for her to look for equally superior characteristics in candidates. If she wants to work in a congenial office atmosphere, the easiest way to achieve this is to select employees who will form a homogeneous group. It takes great maturity and patience to adjust to the behaviour of people who are very different to us. In general we do not bother. Instead, we just hire people who are similar to us, and whom we like. Ferris *et al.* (1991) argue that because most interviewers consider themselves to be successful employees, they use themselves as benchmarks for what constitutes an ideal employee. For example, if the candidate can 'get along' with the interviewer, then he or she is expected to able to get along with other company personnel. Thus, influencing your interviewer may ultimately reflect how closely you can manage to resemble them in terms of *attitude similarity* (Peters and Terborg, 1975; Ross and Ferris, 1981; Schmitt, 1976); *appearance similarity* (Allen, 1983; Molloy, 1975); and *personality similarity* (Paunonen *et al.*, 1987). It is for this reason that salespeople try to appear as similar to their prospective customers as quickly as possible (Gilmore and Ferris, 1989a, 1989b: Moine, 1982).

INTERVIEW MECHANICS

How are the aforementioned impressions created and communicated to the interviewer? The interview can be considered as consisting of three phases. The beginning is initiated when the interviewee and interviewer meet each other (Sterrett, 1978). Each sees the other, smiles to some extent, tilts their head and gives a verbal greeting. The interviewer starts to size up the candidate as he or she enters the room. Some interviewers observe how the candidate closes the door, and advances across the room, before they initiate the greeting. Others hesitate a moment before offering a chair, so as to observe the candidate's reaction. Interviewers pay a great deal of attention to the first impression, especially when recruiting graduates with little previous, relevant work experience. Raffler-Engel (1983) found that 26 of the 35 interviewers that she studied, seldom changed their minds about a candidate's personality after the first two minutes had passed.

The middle of the interview allows for kinetic synchrony, posture shifts to accompany changes in conversational topics, speech-accompanying and speech-substituting gesticulation; synchronization of speech tempo, and for chronemics (the timing of the intervals between questions and answers). All these provide clues to the interviewer about the candidate's personality. The candidate is expected to express herself clearly and concisely, and her gesticulation is evaluated

85

in terms of whether it helps or hinders the communication of their message. The prediction of a candidate's ability to get along with people in the company is assessed partly through their ability to handle the flow of the conversation in the interview, and partly by how well they perceive the paralinguistic and non-verbal cues to take the speaking turn in the conversation, or to relinquish it. The interviewee wants to avoid showing his nervousness, or lowering his bargaining power by appearing over eager. The end of an interview is signalled by the interviewer asking the interviewee, if they have any questions. Also, the interviewer may signal the conclusion by standing up. When he wants the candidate to accept the job offer, she will often walk up with them to the door, and even beyond.

The questions that you will be asked at an interview will concern the facts of your past employment or education, or your attitude towards the challenge involved in the job that you are seeking. However, the *way* you answer the questions is as important as the *substance* of what you say. This is because the way that you answer tells them the kind of person you are. Actually being able to do the job is only a relatively minor aspect of the decision, since all the other applicants could probably do that job just as well as you. It is other things that distinguish the successful from the unsuccessful. In many companies, people are promoted who have fewer skills, less professionalism and less dedication than others who have been passed over. The successful ones have been able to project the different profile keys. Therefore, at the interview, you should treat the questions as opportunities to do the same.

TYPES OF QUESTIONS

Bookshop shelves are creaking under the weight of works describing how to answer questions effectively at job interviews (e.g. Yate, 2001). One thing that might distinguish successful from unsuccessful candidates is that the former make the effort to buy, read, absorb, and use this information. Interview questions are targeted at six areas. Fitzwater (2001) suggests that the reason why interviewees often ask for a question to be repeated, is that they are unable to classify an interviewer's question correctly, and hesitate in their response. His list is summarized by the acronym, MATTER, which aids your memory. The six reasons are shown in Table 5.1.

Since interviewers use completed application forms to frame questions, they recommend that candidates should use theirs to plan answers to questions that they are likely to be asked. Better still, they should arrange a mock interview for themselves with a career advisor. A real company interview for your dream job, is not the place to start acquiring basic interviewee skills. Obvious questions include reasons for your choice of school subjects, degree, career, challenges faced, extra-curricular activities, and so on. All of these will be detailed in your application form or CV.

Table 5.1 *Reasons for interviewer questions*

Motivation	Discovering what excites you about your work or keeps you satisfied.
Ambition	Assessing whether or not you are likely to progress within the company if hired.
Technical	Finding out what skills and knowledge you possess.
Theoretical	Determining your creativity, attitude, on-the-spot thinking. These start, 'Let's suppose . . .', 'Let's imagine . . .'.
Energy	Your level of 'get up and go' towards achieving organizational goals.
Relationships	Your ability to fit into the company and work with others.

Source: Based on Fitzwater 2001: 46–7

Patterned behaviour description questions

According to Anderson (2001), these types of questions form the basis of the structured interview which is the most commonly used one in the UK. They are based on the assumption that past behaviour predicts future behaviour. The questions cover the main areas of a graduate's experience: academic performance, project work, work experience and extra-curricular activities. An interviewer has a comprehensive list of questions to explore each area. Interviewers use a funnelling-down approach to questioning. They begin with some basic questions, and then focus down on specifics to achieve a fuller understanding of each candidate. Interviewers are trying to spot *dissemblers*. These are candidates who are attempting to disguise their real personalities. How successful interviewers are depends on how well trained and skilled they are at spotting liars or, at least, those trying to be something that they are not, in terms of their personality, values and attitudes (Anderson, 2001).

Situational questions

This is like a verbal role-play. The candidate is presented with a scenario and asked how they would handle it. All applicants are asked the same questions, and it is assumed that that their actual behaviour in that situation would correspond to what they say in the interview. It is unlikely that graduate recruitment interview will consist entirely of such situational or hypothetical questions, because of applicants' limited job experience. This makes them ignorant of the key parameters and contextual factors that need to be considered. However, and more commonly, a situational question ('What would you do?'), may be included within their traditional interview, to see if a candidate can 'think on their feet'. It therefore tests your initiative, ability to analyse a situation and to debate a course of action effectively. For example, 'What would you do if one of our major food products on the supermarket shelves, had been found to have been contaminated?'.

Competency-based questions

These type of questions seek to assess what skills you possess. The interviewer may ask you a series of seven questions, attempting to elicit information about a situation and how you acted within it. Whiddett and Hollyforde (1999: 71) list such questions:

1 Have you been in a situation where you have had to influence the thinking of another person?
2 Describe the situation.
3 What was your role?
4 What did you do?
5 Describe how you presented your views.
6 What was the outcome?
7 Would you do anything differently in future?

The interviewer may not be so directive, but will still want you to think of a situation in your past which, for example, required you to take a leadership role or a team role, and seeks to know what happened. The interviewer expects you to answer using a simplified version of the previous sequence, which is referred to as the STAR approach. This stands for situation, task, action and result. Describe a situation in which you have been involved; describe the task you were performing; explain what action you took and why; and then finally describe and assess the result achieved. One student, who had been telephone-interviewed by an accounts manager from one of the main supermarket chains, received feedback on her performance. She was informed that her interview had been designed to investigate four main competencies that were important for a successful career with the company. These were accountability for results; commercial decisiveness; development and learning; and influencing. She was informed that although she had scored well in the last of these, her marks in the other two areas were too low. In particular, in commercial decisiveness, which examined how she would make a decision and follow it through, based on the given facts,

Bretz et al. (1993) were surprised at the extent to which recruiters looked for specific illustrations of demonstrated achievement, particularly work achievement, specific coursework, leadership activities (mostly assessed by extra-curricular, student society office-holding and team sports) and the class of university degree. For the top companies, an upper second (2.1) is the minimum requirement, and anyone with anything less need not bother to apply. Beyond that, they tend to favour applicants with previous work experience over those who focus more seriously on full-time, university studies. The successful applicants were those who were able to persuade recruiters that their previous experiences were relevant to the present vacancies; that their 'talk' was supported by previous actions; and that the pattern of their previous activities added up to some sort of overall focus or coherent career plan. The researchers concluded that to be successful, job search strategies are best developed long before interviewing begins. Their findings also confirm the value of the many, popular 'how to' manuals, dealing with how to make the most of the credentials you already have. Specifically, they recommended conducting accurate self-assessments of strengths and weaknesses; and practising explanations of how previous experiences link to one another and to the desired position.

By being aware of which key skills the organization values most, you can highlight your possession of these (Parsons and Cable, 1999). Plan what you are going to say at the interview, so that when you open your mouth to speak, you are really ready to do it well (Woodall, 1987). In one retail company group, 70 per cent of applicants are rejected because of an inability to speak English properly ('There's many reasons I want this job'). In your mind you should know the twenty-three profile keys you want to hit. Most candidates produce impromptu responses which are unprepared and off-hand. While the interviewer does not expect to receive rehearsed answers produced parrot-fashion, she does expect that you will have thought about possible questions, and are capable of answering the majority of them well. For most of the answers, you will have prepared suitable replies, consisting of vignettes, incidents, and events from your past, work, family and college life, which illustrate your possession of the desirable traits.

MANAGING QUESTIONS

What if you have not prepared your answers? Failing to prepare is, quite simply, preparing to fail! However, even the best candidate has to think on their feet. In this crisis situation, you need to maintain your credibility with the interviewer, appear professional and in control, sound assertive and generally project the best impression you can while constructing an answer to the difficult question. Woodall distinguished three different types of interview questions – easy, difficult and impossible – and suggested ways of dealing with each.

Easy questions

When answering easy questions, candidates often blurt out the first thing that comes to mind, and almost immediately regret it. Their regret is not that they gave a bad answer, but that they could have given a much better answer. To

89

avoid this, give the questioner a response, rather than an answer. When asked a question, most candidates give a reply which is either too short (leaving the interviewer to interrogate them to elicit all the needed information), or which is too long (a mini-speech). Neither is what is required. Instead, provide a *response*. This is defined as a short answer, plus one *support*. A support is one piece of free information, as described in an earlier chapter's section on starting conversations. It may be a reason, a fact, a statistic, a justification, quotation or an opinion. The trick is to mention just one supporting item, whatever it is. For example,

> Q: Have you taught youngsters before?
> A: Yes (Support: at a summer camp in the USA).

Limit yourself to one support, but insert a clue that you have more information available should the questioner want it. This allows the interviewer to control the exchange, since they will be asking the questions. In this way you are being interviewer oriented. Your clue words are *'main'*, *'primary'*, *'most'*, *'essential'* and *'major'*. They are inserted thus:

- The *main* reason for the decision was . . .
- The *primary* objective was . . .
- The *most essential* element was . . .
- The *major* difficulty was . . .

This allows the interviewer to follow up in greater depth, the most interesting responses ('What were some of the other reasons for the decision?'), while allowing her to pass over those of little or no concern. This technique avoids boring the interviewer or losing their attention. The shorter response allows both parties to contribute to, and participate in the conversation, and play an equal part in keeping it going. A response allows you to decide on the nature of the answer to give. When replying, you may wish to give an incomplete answer, provide only part of the information requested, or supply more appropriate information. Since you hold the information, you decide how to answer using it. Rapport is thus built by allowing confidence to grow and trust to be established. In addition, providing a response maintains your credibility, poise and professional demeanour. The interviewer is in control, and your relationship stays positive. Intersperse the response technique with your other, longer answers.

Difficult questions

Successful question answering involves creating thinking time for yourself. Too many interviewees put their mouths into motion, before their brains are in gear. You can use a three-step strategy to give yourself time. First, put all your attention on the interviewer and listen carefully to their question. Make sure that you understand both it, and the questioner's reason for asking it. Then reflect on the question. Finally, give your answer. By first listening closely to the interviewer, you understand the intent of their question. Too often, interviewees are distracted, and use this listening time to start formulating their answers. It is only by concentrating closely on the question being asked, that you can decide whether you understand it, or whether you want the questioner to clarify it for you. Do not jump into the middle of an interviewer's question. Not only is this rude and annoying, it can be disastrous if you answer the wrong question. So let the interviewer finish and ensure that you have grasped the point of their question.

The second step, that of reflecting on the question, is the one that most people are least used to, and least comfortable with. Still, your brain only needs a second or two to organize itself, and the interviewer does not expect you to open your mouth the moment she closes hers. Indeed, an immediate response can suggest to them that you are 'shooting from the hip'. A short silence projects an impression of thoughtfulness (a positive attribute) and avoids recourse to irritating fillers such as, 'uh', 'eh', 'well', 'you know' and 'and-uh'. If you need more than a few seconds of thinking time, there are a few techniques that you can use while maintaining a positive image of yourself. If the interviewer asks a difficult question, she will know herself that it is difficult. For example, a 'what-would-you-do-if' question. So acknowledge the question ('that's a good question' or 'that's a complex question'), and ask for time to think about it, either verbally ('may I have a moment to think through my answer?'), or non-verbally (available gestures include the nod, a slight lift of the hand, or a smile, but not a grimace!). In both cases the purpose is to signal the message, 'I think your question is a good one, and I'm going to give you a well thought out answer.' Use this silent period to reflect on the question. Check what information you can draw on, and which of the profile keys you can hit with your answer. Consider whether you want to reformulate the question, and how you intend to structure your answer. The third and final step in your answer is the reply. As you do so, ensure through the observation of your interviewer's face, that the points that you are making are being received. End your communication by stopping crisply! At all costs avoid ending on an apology or an excuse ('That's all I know about the situation' or 'I'm not sure if I've answered your question').

Giving a bad answer to a question undermines your presentation, loses you credibility and arouses suspicion. As the interviewer is in control, she has the power to ask her questions in her own way, and at her own speed. Although some questions can be anticipated, others may come as a surprise. The question may be intended to gain information, to make you look foolish, or check whether you can withstand pressure. Most young graduates have been programmed to accept that those in positions of power, like their university lecturers or company interviewers, have the right to ask questions, and that they, as interviewees, are powerless, and are obliged to answer them meekly. In their keenness to find an answer, interviewees never challenge the validity of the questioning process, the questioner or even the question itself. If you can break through this mind-set, think and act as a potential corporate asset that they would be privileged to have work for them, and see the interview as a two-way information gathering exercise (do you really want to work for them?), your approach can become radically different. You can become more powerful at the interview, and gain control by asking questions yourself, thereby making the interviewer powerless to some extent by having to answer them. It is always legitimate to ask a question of your own in response to an interviewer's question. In the case of a difficult question, it is a valuable aid, when you are clarifying what the interviewer wants to know from you. Since you want to supply them with relevant information, you will seek to refine and narrow their question.

One tactic that can give you more thinking time, without becoming defensive, is to *ask the interviewer to repeat the question*. Even when they have prepared their questions, interviewers do not always spend time planning how to ask them, and may do so badly. This can give you a problem in producing a polished answer. If you ask for the question to be repeated, the interviewer gets another chance to hear their own question, and to sound knowledgeable in front of you. Usually they will say, 'What I was trying to get at was'. In most cases, you will get a better question to answer, since their restatement is likely to be shorter, more specific and more focused. If it comes out in exactly the same way as before, only more emphatic, then you know that the interviewer is trying to pin you down. A second tactic is to *repeat the question yourself*, either as a question, or as part of your response. While your mouth and vocal chords are working, your brain has time to produce a reply. If you are repeating the question yourself, add some non-verbal gestures and intonation (e.g. raised eyebrows, stress on a word, '*Why* did it take so long?'). If you are incorporating the interviewer's question into your answer ('You ask, why it took so long? The short answer is'), remember that most people like to hear their words spoken back to them. Hence a repetition of their question, provided that it is done sparingly, will not elicit a negative reaction. It also allows you to clarify the question, thereby ensuring that you have understood it, and gives the interviewer the opportunity to re-state or re-phrase it, if you have misunderstood it.

Third, you can *get yourself a better question* to answer by changing the one that you have been asked. This is an acceptable strategy provided that your interviewer does not object. Some questions are virtually unanswerable because they are too long, vague, complicated, obscure or multi-dimensional. The interviewer may be unprepared, bad at the task, or may just want to show off. Rather than having a shot at an answer, with a high chance of getting it wrong, you can use one of the following techniques. *Re-phrase* the question while repeating it. This gives you the opportunity to eliminate any provocation or bias contained within it (Q: 'Why did you avoid team games at university?', A: 'You're wanting to know which sports I participated in?'). Alternatively, you might *amend* the question, departing a little further from the question asked, while still remaining in the legitimate area of interviewer interest (Q: 'Why did you avoid team games at university?', A: 'You want to know about my non-academic interests and activities while at university?'). Since you are moving further away from the specific content of the question, the interviewer may bring you back to the specific focus. However, there is no harm in trying. You might turn the question around by making it *bigger*, by expanding the context in which the question is asked, while still maintaining contact with it ('actually it affected the whole student union and not just the theatre club'). Or you can make it *smaller*, by focusing it down ('I can't speak for the entire student union, but in terms of the theatre club'). If all else fails, be honest and admit that you do not know. This can be a safer alternative to flannelling badly.

You can *clarify* any key words or phrases in the question by either offering a choice ('By educational career do you mean school or university?'), or asking for a definition ('You ask if this is ethical. Can you tell me what you mean by ethical in this context?'). When discussing abstract concepts or theories, it is important that both of you are speaking about the same thing. While they define it, you gain a clearer understanding of how their enquiry is focused, as well as time, to prepare an answer. If the interviewer cannot define it, then she will have to withdraw it, indicating perhaps that she was trying to put you on the spot. As the interviewee, you have the choice of clarifying a question or defining a concept yourself. You can *redirect* the question either by commenting on how it is asked ('Why are you so concerned about this issue?'), or redirecting back to the interviewer ('Tell me, why did you ask that question?'). At an individual interview, the only place to redirect a question is back to the interviewer ('You asked me where do I see myself in five years time. Before, I answer that, I'd like to know what this company's career development policy is'). In a board interview, you may be able to redirect it to another panel member. You might comment on the question itself ('Good question'), or on the process ('I think you have hit a controversial issue here'). Finally, you can *contextualize* your answer if there is a danger that it might give a negative impression of you. Insert an explanation between the question and your response, thereby producing a cushioned reply. Compare the two responses to the same question below:

Q: Why were you with International Motors for only six months?
A: I was made redundant.

93

Q:	Why were you with International Motors for only six months?
Explanation:	The company was contracting its European operations, and closed down its entire British facility, and as a result,
A:	I was made redundant.

Your explanation-plus-answer has to have some substance, however minimal, hence it requires more thought and planning than an easy question. All these tactics should only be used in emergencies. Simple questions should be answered straight away.

Impossible questions

An interviewer may ask a question which is inappropriate, or may involve revealing personal or confidential information. So, while you could answer it, you prefer not to. However, you want to do this while retaining your poise and credibility, and maintaining a good relationship with the interviewer. The skill here is to answer indirectly or refuse to commit yourself. It is possible to say outright that the requested information is confidential or, in your view, personal, private, irrelevant to the job being applied for, or illegal under discrimination legislation. Such a response carries the danger of damaging the rapport built up. It is more appropriate to be indirect in your response, and there are four techniques that you could use.

You might *respond only to one aspect of the question*. Any difficult question will have a number of aspects to it. You can choose just one of these, ignore the remainder, and construct your answer around that one. Having done so, there is a good chance that you will have satisfied the interviewer. People ask questions for reasons other than to elicit information. They may want to hear you talk, assess your confidence, observe your body language, and so on. A complicated question that produces a solid answer to one aspect of it, delivered with confidence, can meet the requirements. If it does not, and the interviewer reminds you of the missing answer, you will have had time to think over that part of the question, and perhaps ask for it to be re-phrased.

A second strategy is to *re-focus the question*. A question that asks about confidential information can be re-focused onto less restricted or more general issues. Take one word or phrase from the question (not the main topic one), and build a strongly supported answer around it. For example, Q: 'Success in management requires accumulating different kinds of experiences in different parts of the company. Do you feel that your *domestic situation* will be an impediment to your moving?'. A: 'I agree that diverse *management experience* is important, exactly how one gains that depends on circumstances, and there are several different ways of getting that management experience. For example'. Here the interviewer's question focused on the candidate's domestic circumstances, which the latter did not wish to discuss. By taking the phrase, 'management experience' from the question, the interviewee has re-focused her response by adding a support – different ways of gaining experience.

Another option is to *discuss the question instead of answering it*. Some apparently difficult questions are really easy, and seek only general, easily supplied, information from the interviewee. For example, a graduate who studied both management and French may be asked why he did not specialize in the former. In replying, he may explain the content of each course, the different teaching methods used, the challenges of each subject and the similarities and differences. In this case, the question was one which was designed to be discussed and not answered. A better question from the interviewer to achieve the same objective might have been, 'Compare and contrast the two main subjects that you studied at university'.

Finally, you could use *bridging* to make a transition from an inappropriate question to an appropriate answer. Successful bridging is high-level re-focusing. It requires extreme skill on your part since you need to make a seamless transition between the question and the answer, and do so without the help of a focus word in the question to help you along. The technique itself is straightforward. You agree that the questioner's point is valid, true or of concern. Then you move on quickly (bridge) to something else that you want to talk about. Your interviewer will not even recognize a well-built bridge, but a bad bridge is easy to spot (Reardon, 1991). To construct a bridge, acknowledge briefly what the speaker says, and move on quickly from there:

Q: You've had no experience of spreadsheet analysis, but this marketing post does involve financial budgeting.

A: That's correct. To date, I've not had the opportunity to familiarize myself with that particular software. However, my experience of product launches and of using market research oriented statistical packages convinces me that I can get up to speed on this quickly.

Q: The people that we have appointed to this team in the past have all had a technical background. You don't have that experience.

A: You're correct in saying that I don't have the technical background – however, successfully leading a team also involves familiarity with budgets, communicating an idea of what is possible to the team members, and some understanding of what makes people tick. These are qualities that I do possess.

Positive words

Woodall (1987) noted that some of the questions that you are asked will appear to be only answerable indirectly. This may be because the interviewer phrases them in a negative way. Negative questions include:

- Why didn't you use a spreadsheet?
- Why wouldn't you like to work in sales?
- Why shouldn't you study for the professional qualification?
- Why can't you finish this report by lunchtime?

However, it is a mistake to respond in a similar manner, either by using negative words or with a negative tone. Instead, respond positively to their negative question. *Don't, can't, wouldn't* and *shouldn't* are negative words. The natural response of the naive interviewee is to answer aggressively, using a similar tone and manner as the questioner. However, the effective interviewee turns both the question and her response into a positive encounter which not only defuses any anger, but also restores goodwill to the conversation. This is achieved by first repeating the question as part of your answer, and then changing the negative concept, for example, *didn't use*, into a neutral one, such as, *use of*.

Q: Why *didn't you* use a spreadsheet?

A: Your question about my *use of* a spreadsheet is a valid one. My decision was made on the basis of the complexity of the task that you gave me.

Q: Why *wouldn't you* like to work in sales?

A: I'm glad that you have *considered my working* in the sales department. Whether this would be the most suitable experience for me at this time depends on the nature of the re-organization.

Q: Why *shouldn't* you study for a professional qualification?

A: I appreciate *your interest in my studies*. However, studying at home, while at the same time fulfilling my work commitments would put a severe strain on me at the moment.

Q: Why *can't* you finish this report by lunchtime?

A: The lunchtime *deadline* is as important to me as it is to you. To achieve it, I need the data from Sales before 10 o'clock today.

In each case, there is an element of re-focusing on the part of the interviewee. The four questions could all have been phrased positively, but were not. Those who ask questions in a negative way have either been disappointed, are feeling hostile, or want to see how you will react under some pressure. In all cases, the basic technique is to avoid increasing their hostility or disappointment by not going along with either their negative tone or their negative words. These are all legitimate ways of responding to questions which are inappropriate, or which are impossible to answer. Your answers should be uttered with confidence, since delivery here is as important as content.

Concluding the interview

There is often a potentially awkward period at the end of the interview, before you leave, when the interviewer asks if you have any questions, or if there is anything that you want to say. All candidates are advised against the, 'no-questions-thank-you response'. Here you have the chance to ask a few, carefully chosen questions. If you were the interviewer who asked if the candidate had any questions, what would each of the following questions tell you about that candidate's personality, ambition and motivation?

Specific job questions:

- Why is the job available?
- To whom would I report?
- Where is the job located?
- What is the job's relationship to other departments?
- How do the job and the department relate to corporate aims?

Personal interest and career questions:

- What type of training does the job require, when will it be provided?
- What are the chances of growth in the job?
- Where are the growth opportunities in the company?
- Where does the job lead?
- How regularly does performance appraisal occur?

General interest and company knowledge:

- Who will be the company's competitors in the next few years?
- Do you expect to diversify into new markets/product areas?

However, you could do even better. What you make of this end-of-interview opportunity depends on how well you have done your homework. Researching the company in advance, gives you an advantage. It shows that you are willing to learn, and willing to put in effort to get a job done. It shows that you respect the company, and by inference, the interviewer. Most importantly, it allows you to tailor your final questions. Without preparation, you cannot match your skills and ambitions to company circumstances on the application form, relate your answers to questions during the interview, or ask sensible questions of your own about what the company can offer you at the end of the interview. Often, such preparation will be enough to distinguish you from other candidates who have not done this research. Compare the following questions with the earlier first three.

97

- I read in the *Financial Times* that your company is expanding into Europe. Is this job a result of that expansion?
- The *Economist* had an article about the extensive use of project teams and matrix structures in your organization/industry. To whom would I be reporting in this job?
- I have found that your company has three plants in Britain, and five on the continent. Where is this job located?

This stage in the interview also gives you the very important opportunity to hit any of the remaining profile keys that you may have been unable to communicate earlier. The way to do this is to state that, 'I haven't had the opportunity to tell you about X, Y and Z'. In the majority of interviews, the questioner will be left with an overall impression of you as a candidate, rather than with a list of the specific information that you have provided them with. This impression of you will be based heavily on their initial perception of you (primacy effect), the last impression of you (recency effect), and to a lesser extent on how you answered their questions in between (Asch, 1946; Luchins, 1957b). In this middle phase, what is most important, is not so much what you say, but how you say it. Mediocre responses given with superb delivery are likely to have a greater positive impact on the interviewer than good responses given poorly. Responding from a position of strength and credibility gives you a springboard for confident speech. If there are a number of people on a panel, or a series of interviews, the most important person to influence is the person to whom you would be reporting. Gill (1980) found that these people take the final appointment decision. Since these line managers are advised, but not constrained by personnel staff, it appears that, 'at the wire', candidate acceptability is more important than candidate suitability (Knights and Raffo, 1990).

DISTANCE INTERVIEWS

With the developments in technology, rise in travel expenses and globally based recruitment, it is possible, and increasingly likely, that you will be interviewed over the telephone or through a videoconferencing system.

Telephone interviews

These occur at an early stage in the selection process, and are often conducted by a recruitment agency on behalf of the company that the candidate applies to. They are used to screen out applicants. Job applicants are not comfortable doing them, and they prefer face-to-face interviews. Selectors are confident that they elicit enough information about a candidate to make a valid judgement about whether they want them to progress to the next stage in the selection process.

They listen for verbal signals from the candidates that indicate their experience, leadership and motivational skills. Hesitations should be avoided as they are interpreted as conveying untrustworthiness and a lack of power.

Selectors stated that their decisions were based only on the answers given by the candidates, and that they did not make judgements based on the communication skills or the accent of a candidate. This was because, in their view, a telephone conversation did not permit a free flow of conversation and was thus not a reliable indicator of a candidate's communication skills (Anderson, 2001). Telephone interviews are administered in a similar manner as face-to-face ones. They focus on the competencies possessed by the candidate, the interviewers follow a tight script, and always ask all the interviewees the same questions. These interviews tend to be shorter, typically 20 minutes. Here is a list of telephone interview questions asked by a major UK financial services company:

1   Describe your typical day
2   How many hours a week do you work?
3   Do you have any beliefs that you would not be willing to change?
4   How would you describe this time in your life?
5   Mrs Brown phones to say her daughter is ill and won't be into work. What do you do?
6   How would you encourage responsibility in your workers?
7   Are you dependable?
8   Have you ever orchestrated a project to its completion and what problems did you encounter?
9   How much administrative experience do you have?
10 On a scale of 1–10, how good would you rate yourself at administration?
11 Are you a good listener?
12 Do you agree with the statement that the customer is always right?
13 How productive are you?
14 How do you motivate someone who is not pulling their weight in a team?
15 How much difference does another, added good person, make to the company?
16 Are you more concerned about yourself or others?

Blackman (2002: 221–2) provided a similar list of questions used in structured telephone interviews:

1   If you were hired for this position, what would I see after a month of working with you, as your strongest work-related trait?
2   If you were hired for this position, what would I see after a month of working with you, as your weakest work-related trait?

3 How would your current or last employer describe you?

4 How would your peers describe you?

5 Think of your least effective manager/supervisor; tell me why he/she was ineffective.

6 Describe one strength of this manager.

7 Suppose that an individual came into the office and claimed to be a representative of the Disabled Students Office without presenting any identification. This individual then requests to pick up an exam for a disabled student to take to the Disabled Students Centre and refuses to leave until you present him/her with the test. At this point you notice that the office manager has taken a lunch break. How would you react to this individual? What course of action would you take?

8 Suppose you were employed in the psychology department office, and you were asked by the office manager to photocopy the exams for the course in which you were currently enrolled. What would you do?

9 If the office manager was to return a job that you completed in this office for you to redo, which of the following activities from the job description would it most likely be and why?

10 With regard to your previous job performance evaluations, what personality characteristic were your previous employers most likely to compliment?

11 Describe yourself to me.

All these questions are equally likely to be asked at a face-to-face interview, so there is nothing special or different about distance interview questions. Note the use of the situational or hypothetical ('What would you do?') questions in the lists. As before, your answers down the telephone need to hit the profile keys listed in the previous chapter. There are three ways of preparing for a telephone interview. First, intellectual preparation involves searching the company's website, and finding out what type of candidates make the grade in that company. For example, the website might stress 'working together', indicating the importance of team spirit in the organization. If they are looking for a combination of drive, initiative and ambition, this gives you a clue that they are looking for someone who will challenge the status quo.

Keeping this is mind, as you read the interview questions, consider which of Yate's profile keys you can incorporate into your practice answers, and how you might do it. During a typical half-hour telephone interview, you will have to hit one new trait or profile key, every three minutes. For this reason, use the above questions, to practise your answers. Get a relative or friend to ask the questions, while you respond. Use a cassette or minidisk recorder, to tape your answers and then replay and analyse them. Get feedback and make adjustments. Initially, your responses may sound artificial and lack spontaneity. Using positive words while achieving fluidity of delivery may take some time. In particular, practise talking about your past achievements confidently and without embarrassment.

Second, there is practical preparation. Organize the layout of your desk or table, where you will take the interview call. Select a comfortable seat, ideally one with a supporting back, allowing good body posture, thereby helping you to project your voice clearly. Fidgeting is a sign of insecurity and can be detected over the telephone. Design some prompt cards for yourself that refer to Yate's profile keys. On each card, briefly write down a description that supports your answer and enhances your credibility. Make a note of any specific words that you want to include in your telephone answers, and tick off the ones that you use, as you progress through the interview. Have your application/CV to hand for quick reference. Finally, consider your clothing. Although the telephone interviewer cannot assess your non-verbal communication, consider putting on the clothing that you would during a normal, face-to-face interview. Dressing the part can help you convey a professional and competent attitude, that matches your verbal message, and which can come over in your voice. How you feel, affects how you speak. Don't do the telephone interview in your pyjamas!

Third, there is psychological preparation that involves putting yourself into a positive state of mind and developing the confidence to succeed. Every interview is designed to test a candidate's mental control and discover how well they can work under pressure. Thus, you will need to influence yourself and control your own thoughts. You can begin by practising relaxation and doing breathing exercises. Libraries contain books on this topic. Listen to assertiveness and similar audiotapes that are designed to boost self-confidence and self-esteem. Adopt a strategy of self-talk which involves regularly telling yourself that nothing is impossible and that you can succeed. Finally, visualize the interview in your head. Imagine picking up the telephone, and answering the questions competently and smoothly. Picture yourself ticking your way through your list of traits; effectively illustrating each with relevant examples; and oozing competence and confidence. Imagine finishing off the interview effectively, and bidding the interviewer goodbye. Run this 'mental movie' through your head regularly before the real interview.

Much of the same previous advice applies equally to this form of interviewing. In particular, applicants should ensure that they communicate their possession of the twenty-three profile keys. However, this technology affects interviewers' judgements, and candidates need to be aware of this if they are to succeed. The main and obvious difference with this type of interview is that you are having to manage your impression using only verbal and para-verbal means. This is important because job-related personality characteristics are often communicated non-verbally. Candidates therefore need to take particular care to include competency-based buzzwords in their answers. Some of these verbs were mentioned earlier in this chapter, while nouns include 'initiative', 'teams', 'determination', 'challenge' and 'drive'. Remember: on the other end of the telephone, every time the interviewer identifies that you possess a particular competency, she ticks it on her evaluation card.

There is contradictory evidence as to how the telephone interview compares with the face-to-face version. Silvester *et al.* (2000) found that telephone interviewees received lower interviewer ratings than when interviewed face to face. Blackman (2002) also concluded that telephone interviewers gave harsher assessments than face-to-face interviewers. The possible explanations offered were broadly similar. They included the effect of the absence of non-verbal communication cues, which meant that candidates may have come over as 'cold and unfriendly', and this coloured interviewers' assessments of them. Interviewers may focus more on what is said and on the strength of their arguments, rather than on how it is said. It may have also been because candidates treated telephone interviews less seriously than face-to-face ones, or may have lacked practice in this form of interview. However, in Chapman and Rowe's (2001) study discussed below, distance interviewees were rated more highly than face-to-face ones. The implications of the research studies so far are that candidates should compensate for this by choosing carefully what words they use, and how they say them – perhaps by putting a 'smile in their voice'. They can prepare thoroughly and write down the points they want to include in their answers and have them to hand by the telephone. Finally, they can ask a friend or relative to telephone them with questions, to give them practice. Those applicants who have had a job in a call centre, are likely to have an advantage in this type of interview.

Video interviews

Videoconference interviews are also increasing in frequency. Employers can now use videoconference job interviewing (VJI) to 'visit' campuses electronically from geographically distance sites. One or more selectors interview the applicant remotely, using real-time video and audio communication. The applicant and the interviewers can see each other by looking at monitors which have a camera mounted on them, allowing an approximate face-to-face conversation to take place (Kroeck and Magnusen, 1997). This development is particularly useful for students attending the less prestigious universities which the top recruiting companies would not normally visit because of effort and expense. Unlike the telephone interview, video technology does allow the interviewer to view a candidate's non-verbal behaviour, but it only reveals some of it. The positioning of the equipment means that candidates are seen from the chest upwards only. Also, for technical reasons, it is difficult for the interviewer to know how much eye contact an interviewee is making. When being interviewed in this way, many candidates are apprehensive about this new technology and feel disadvantaged. This can evoke sympathy from the interviewer, who may be equally anxious.

In their study, Chapman and Rowe (2002) found that the interviewers felt that videoconferencing allowed them to evaluate candidates' communication skills, friendliness and support for arguments. However, the researchers found that selectors ranked those candidates they interviewed by videoconferencing higher than those they questioned face-to-face. They felt that this was because interviewers overcompensated for the videoconferencing situation. On the whole, the majority of interviewers preferred face-to-face interviewing, but nearly 90 per cent expected to use video interviewing because of its advantages. Job candidates should therefore increasingly expect and prepare to be interviewed by videoconference. In her investigation of company selectors and their search for organizational fit, Anderson (2001), confirmed the crucial role of the interview. On first laying eyes on the candidate, assessors asked, 'Does this person reflect what the organization wishes to stand for in the marketplace?'. They confirmed that how a person dressed and how professional they looked, was assessed. Their posture, friendliness, level of eye contact (all discussed in Chapter 2) were taken into account, and a poor initial impression did have a major impact on these interviewers' final decision.

ASSESSMENT CENTRES

An assessment centre is a process and not a place. It may however be carried out at a hotel or a company's residential training centre. It is a lengthy process that can often last two days. During this period, you and six to twelve other candidates, are exposed to a range of selection techniques. Reporting current trends in assessment centre content, Yapp (2003) observed that they were changing their focus to become more commercial. The group discussion, a standard feature in the past, was being increasingly replaced by individual exercises that identify the achievements and contributions of each candidate. Role-play activities are becoming more professional, with trained actors being hired to add realism and challenge. Business case studies are replacing another old assessment centre favourite, the in-tray exercise. Instead of shuffling papers and making tactical decisions for an hour or so, the cases test candidates' strategic and commercial skills. These may take the form of an exercise in which candidates receives a series of timed emails to which they must respond. It gives them a feel of what it is like to work in the organization. Books on 'how to succeed' at an assessment centre have begun to be available (Tolley and Wood, 2001).

Other common assessment centre events include a team exercise, individual presentations, and individual and panel interviews. The team exercises are particularly important. Assessors are looking at how you interact with others in a group situation; whether you display good interpersonal and leadership skills; and if you demonstrate the ability to work as part of a team. Exercises are also used to assess candidates' problem-solving approaches. The assessors consist mainly of personnel experts, but they may include company line managers. Some companies ask candidates to take psychometric tests during the assessment centre. Assessment centres are used by between 30 per cent and 60 per cent of the top companies. They are expensive to operate but are the most accurate section tool currently available. They represent another, and more objective way of assessing which of the main profile keys you possess.

Books on how to apply for a job, detail the objectives and content of assessment centres. They should be consulted to determine the nature and objective of the different activities. For example, individual exercises will test your time management and analytical ability, while group exercises focus on team membership, leadership and problem-solving. Once again, successful performance is based on thorough preparation. You will begin to be assessed from the moment you arrive, right through until the time you leave. This includes not only the formal tests, but also informal ones such as how you behave at the bar and at dinner. It is therefore also an endurance test during which you should keep your strength up, your head clear and your alcohol consumption limited. Use the opportunity to find out about the company from senior managers, and last year's graduate recruits. Above all, welcome the opportunity to take part and get involved. Anderson (2001) asked a number of selectors who used assessment centres to suggest hints on how candidates can perform well. Some of their suggestions are surprising, and must come from years of watching applicants perform well and badly in assessment centres. They are summarized below in Table 5.2.

The distinguishing feature of an assessment centre is that it focuses on candidate *behaviours*. Assessors are taught that, in the first phase, they should just observe the candidates, avoid any early judgements and record their observations in behavioural terms. It is only in the second phase that these noted behaviours should be assigned to dimensions (profile keys) and then evaluated. However, research studies show that, despite this aim, about 20 per cent of assessor notes contain not only behavioural statements, but also descriptions of applicants' personality traits (Lievens *et al.*, 2001). Knowing this, you can ensure that you demonstrate these traits to assessors. These researchers draw four conclusions from their study, which have implications for assessment centre candidates. First, they conclude that companies use centres to assess three of the Big Five personality traits: emotional stability, conscientiousness and openness to experience.

In contrast, the remaining two – agreeableness and extroversion – are less frequently written down. Candidates should therefore ensure that they demonstrate these first three traits to the assessors who will rate them positively. Second, assessors measure a broad range of personality aspects and use multiple exercises within the centre to do so. It was found that the in-basket exercise, when used, elicited positive conscientiousness descriptors; group discussion was characterized by extroversion markers; and the presentation exercise generated emotional stability trait descriptors. By knowing which personality aspects are expected by

Table 5.2 *Recruiters' hints for assessment centre candidates*

Before the centre
Think about your current interaction in teams and obtain feedback from your peers and team leaders, on how you currently behave in a team.

During the centre
You will need to absorb large amounts of information in a short space of time.
Read the briefings that you are given carefully so that you are aware of what you are being asked to do.
Try to enjoy yourself. A more relaxed candidate tends to perform better on the day.
Keep your eye on the time.
Don't get hung up on early mistakes. Assessors are looking for overall performance.

Specific skills to focus on
Ability to extract key points from large amounts of information.
Organizing your thoughts logically, e.g. structuring the presentation of your findings.
Ability both to respond quickly to issues raised, and to suggest possible solutions.

Teamwork: verbal communication skills
Look and sound as if you know what you are saying (conviction).
Be brief about what you are saying (conciseness).
Enthusiasm can help generate better ideas (energy).
Ensure you involve all team members, but do not embarrass those unwilling to speak.
Adjust your language to other group members, and avoid jargon if you are an expert.
Speak at an even pitch and pace. Take time to take a breather and collect your thoughts.

Teamwork: non-verbal communication skills
Maintain eye contact with other members without becoming intimidating.
Keep control over your hands, especially when nervous. Use them to support your verbal communication.
Avoid swinging in your chair when seated, or rocking in the chair.
Ensure that you come over as relaxed and approachable.

Influencing skills: needed to create an impact during the team exercises
Be open, listen to others' ideas, and build on them.
Show tact towards those with whom you disagree.
Express interest in the topic at hand and maintain active participation throughout.
Encourage others to elaborate their points when necessary.
Focus on the task, and do not get side-tracked.
Make your points clearly and concisely for maximum impact.

Facilitation skills: when taking the scribe role
Take a position at the flipchart with your pen with an open, welcoming stance.
Ensure your writing is legible.
Face your group when not writing.
Listen carefully to what is said and ensure your notes reflect this.
If asked to present your group's output, make your presentation clear and concise.

Source: Anderson, 2001

assessors for each exercise, you can demonstrate these particular traits while performing the exercise. Third, they found little difference in ratings between different assessors. This suggests that by doing research on the company and its assessment centre procedures beforehand, you can anticipate what will happen, and thereby increase your chances of success. If invited to an assessment centre, you should obtain as much information as possible (depending on what the organizers are willing to tell you), as to what will happen and what to expect. If you do not ask, you will not be told. Your enquiry itself can demonstrate positive aspects of yourself to the assessors.

Finally, all the graduate recruitment literature emphasizes the importance placed upon teamworking and of being a 'team player'. Anderson (2001) took advantage of asking her recruiters what, in their view, constituted effective team-working. Some of their answers, in terms of an individual's contribution to their team, are already included in Table 5.2. More generally, her respondents commented that good teamworking involved all team members:

- having enthusiasm;
- structuring the task;
- possessing good listening skills;
- being flexible in the roles that they adopted;
- respecting each other;
- being adaptable to the views or ideas expressed in the team;
- communicating effectively with one another by being clear and concise.

Some large companies are customizing their assessment centres, and giving candidates a sample of the kind of work that they will be doing if hired. British American Tobacco, for example, had a work sample test created that reflected its commercial activities. A fictitious company was created and the assessment centre candidates played the role of the management team, with the challenge of developing a product from the research, through to development and production, to marketing (Sheridan, 2000). In the case of Merrill Lynch, an assessment centre replicated the noise and activities of a trading floor. Candidates traded against each other, had to use IT screens for information, and were required to deal with phone requests. These customized assessment centres enable companies to offer candidates realistic job previews and allow them to be assessed more accurately. Assessment centres are very popular with selectors, if their companies can afford them. They commented that it allowed them to assess thoroughly not only whether the final stage candidates possessed the behavioural competences to do the job well, but also if there was a match between them as individuals, and the demands that would be made of them by the organization. During the assessment centre, they considered that the interviews and the group exercises, best revealed the presence or absence of organizational fit.

CONCLUSION

At this point in the chapter, you are probably wondering whether or not you should try to become the stereotypical employee and secure the job of your dreams. It useful therefore to conclude with Asleigh Anderson's comment, whose research findings have featured extensively in our discussion of job applications (Anderson, 2001). As a job-seeking graduate herself, she concluded that,

> Although some may dislike the advice, it is apparent that there is no point in acting a part in the selection process. If an attempt is made, the selection process has become so scientific and so extensive that a candidate who is lying will soon be caught out, and will quickly be eliminated. If, for some reason, this does not happen, and the candidate is offered a job and accepts it, he/she will soon realise that when being themselves, they are not suited to the role. The successful candidate will become unhappy in their position and will probably resign. Not being offered the job the first place, because you are not suited to the company, is less humiliating. Getting the job by acting a part and leaving after a few months because you are not suited to it, is far more painful and humiliating for the graduate. Especially since they will have a permanent, black mark on their CV so early in their professional career.

Other graduates, who have successfully 'faked the fit', have echoed her views. However if, after extensive personal investigation, you do truly believe that your chosen company is the one for you, and that you would fit into it like a glove, and would be happy and successful in it if given the chance, then you need to remember that you will be in competition with many other candidates who feel that they too are equally suited. Since the number of job offers will be limited, you need to communicate your greater suitability for the job to the company selectors. It is hoped that the advice contained in this and the previous chapter, can help you to do so.

Chapter 6

Impression management on the job

People may not always be what they appear to be, but what they appear to be, is always a significant part of what they are.

INTRODUCTION

The focus of this chapter is on the theory and techniques of impression management, and their application on the job (Giacalone and Rosenfeld, 1986, 1989; Gray, 2002). This area has been extensively researched by academics whose findings are summarized here. Impression management consists of two aspects. First, impression motivation which is the desire of individuals to generate specific impressions in others' minds in order to maximize their social and material outcomes, maintain self-esteem or cultivate a particular public identity. Second, impression construction, the process of choosing the kind of impression to create and deciding exactly what behaviours would be effective in transmitting such an image (Leary and Kowalski, 1990). Bertold Brecht said, 'It is not the play but the performance that is the real purpose of all one's efforts.' It is not enough to look the part, you have to act it as well. This not only assures your credibility with your audience, but is also a way to acquire power. Act powerful, and you will become powerful!

Most people attempt to control their images in social interactions to some extent (Baumeister, 1982; Wortman and Linsenmeier, 1977). They tailor their self-presentations to the social goals that they hope to achieve (Leary *et al.*, 1986). Impression management is the, 'conscious, intentional process of manipulating others' perceptions of us' (Chatman *et al.*, 1986; Tedeschi, 1981); 'behaviour aimed at influencing the perceptions of others concerning one's self' (Goffman, 1959); and 'behaviours used by individuals to control the impressions they make on others (Tedeschi *et al.*, 1985). Impression management sees social behaviour to be like an advertising campaign which individuals conduct on their own behalf, and in the course of which they seek to highlight their virtues while minimizing their deficiencies (Schlenker, 1980). We shall begin by making some general comments on starting a new job, and then consider some more specific techniques.

MANAGING YOUR IMPRESSION ON ENTRY

Your impression management begins when you walk into the office for the first time. Your new bosses and colleagues provide you with the opportunity to project your chosen image. First impressions are vital, and at the start, you hold the psychological advantage of fear and mystery. Use these and interact with new colleagues in a strict, slightly detached manner, avoiding over-friendliness. A cold eye and a critical look are preferable to being perceived as childishly enthusiastic ('puppy dog' syndrome). Distance lends enchantment, and enchantment creates power. Foster an air of mystery around yourself which will create interest. Restricting your availability will increase your value and respect more than being obliging and available.

Teach people to respect you by giving the impression that you are a busy and important person. Develop unpredictability. If you are predictable, you may be manipulated, others will learn which tunes you will dance to, and play them. When others are unsure of how you will react, they will treat you with respect, and will be less inclined to try to exploit you. Cultivate a moody impatience and work cleverly rather than necessarily hard. Task achievement is only partly important. As important is what you are seen to be doing. Later, whether as a new manager or a graduate trainee, you can relax your grip. This is easier than doing it the other way round.

An important decision, especially for women, is to decide what name to use when introducing yourself to new work colleagues for the first time. Typically at school and university, Deborahs, Margarets, Elizabeths, Angelas and Susannahs, will have become Debbies, Maggies, Lizzies, Angies and Susies. In work organizations such names are associated with pets and secretaries. Professional women with career aspirations therefore need to consider how they want to be addressed by those around them. The shortened form of a given name is the verbal equivalent of occupying the minimum physical space, as was described in the chapter on non-verbal influencing. Names like Deborah and Elizabeth, contain three and four syllables respectively. It takes longer to say them, and requires greater effort from the speaker. So, on joining a new organization, both men and women might usefully consider reverting to the full form of their first given name, using their second given name or selecting a new first name altogether. This last option does not involve any formal procedure, although the change of a surname does.

Establish your status early. Writers have stressed the importance of knocking on others' doors confidently, and entering. Knocking and waiting reduces your status. Having knocked and entered, walk up immediately to the person's desk, do not linger by their door. Nowadays, most people in companies will have

109

cubicles or just desks. Coming up close to the desk at which they are sitting will make you appear taller, and height is associated with increased status. Speak to them only when you are by them, since talking to them from the door, or at a distance, is a status-reducer. Finally, if someone knocks on your door, reverse this process to enhance your status and to lower theirs. Additionally, avoid shouting 'come in' immediately. Wait a moment to intimate that you are busy, and that your time is valuable.

Drummond (1991) recommended displaying your energy from the start, thus giving the impression of verve. Look energetic, speak briskly and move purposefully. In any organization, there is more to do than anyone has time. Most employees operate in a reactive mode, responding to demands at the time. Others use the extended work involvement career strategy. They create the impression that they are selflessly dedicated or self-sacrificing by, for example, arriving early for work and leaving late. Their aim is to make their bosses feel guilty about not giving them the desired reward or promotion. These approaches are equally inefficient and ineffective, both work-wise and career-wise. Gould and Penley's (1984) study reveals that career strategies that focus on work process, rather than work output or work performance, are ineffective.

The need to create a specific image is particularly important for a new employee entering an organization for the first time, or a recently promoted employee in a new role. Ibarra (1999) suggests that people adapt to new roles by experimenting with what she calls *provisional selves* that are potential but not fully elaborated professional identities. Why would you want to create a provisional self and how might you do it? Provisional selves are temporary solutions that are used to bridge the gap between current capacities and self-conceptions, and employees' views as to which attitudes and behaviours are expected of them in their new role. Thus they 'try on' different possible identities, as one would try on different clothes in a shop. These identities become clarified through experience and involve a three-step process.

The first step is observation, where a repertoire of possible selves is built. The new employee becomes aware of those around them, selects appropriate role models who display the role identity that they are trying to assume; and builds a store of tacit knowledge, attitudes and impression management techniques that they seek to copy to aid them in adapting to their new role. Building this repertoire involves *role prototyping* where the employee determines what constitutes a credible role performance, e.g. 'She makes people feel she really values them'. It also entails the individual *identity matching*, that is, comparing and contrasting role models with herself and deciding on the attractiveness of emulating their behaviour. The second step is experimentation, with the provisional self. One way of forging an effective self-image is through *imitation strategies*. This does not mean copying to 'become' their role model, but rather selectively choosing to replicate the styles and skills of several different role models and to blend them into a single, personal, effective image. The individual needs to ensure that the provisional self which has been created is authentic and true-to-self. In this way what one feels and communicates to others, does not appear false or manipulative. The final step is evaluation, which involves assessing and modifying possible selves. The use of impression management tactics is controlled, their effects are evaluated, and alternatives are considered. The employee compares his public persona with his own representation or who he 'really is' or wants to be, so as to achieve congruence between the two. The employee observes others' reactions to the impression that they are creating, which will endorse their behaviours or provide feedback on how to change.

MANAGING YOUR JOB TASKS

Although researchers have not shown that effective impression managers use their skills to perform their jobs any better (Viswesvaren et al., 2001), they have found useful principles which can be applied. When starting a new job, identify the tasks that it is in your interest to perform, and how to do them. Also, determine which tasks you should best avoid, and how to do them, if forced to. Every employee, however junior, has some degree of freedom of choice. Drummond recommended a five-step approach. First, review what you have been given and what you do. Control your job, and do not let it control you. Some tasks are more personally rewarding, while others will gain you visibility, power and success. Make three separate lists: those of tasks that you absolutely must do; those you are good at and enjoy doing; and those that would bring you and your work to the attention of those in power. Assess these three lists, and adjust your role accordingly. Second, review what you have achieved and how you did it. Focus on output performance and means, rather than activity. Whatever you do, make it count for you, and avoid just keeping busy. Ask yourself why you are doing this? How can you best do it? When can you do it best? How does task accomplishment contribute to your goal?

Third, do the work connected with a task or project that leads to control over it. As the work advances, others will need you increasingly, and they will be forced to involve you in the decisions associated with it. Doing the work makes them dependent on you, and their dependency on you gives you power. To avoid being exploited by others, direct your services towards those most likely to influence your promotion, or to those who you want to notice you. To undertake a task is to become responsible for it. Therefore, be careful what you commit yourself to. Assess each opportunity, and ask what might this become? What could it do for you? The best choices are ventures with long-term potential, involving the acquisition or use of specialist skills or knowledge, a reasonable prospect of a successful launch with a chance of some short-term pay-off. Choose those tasks or projects that are likely to be successfully accomplished, and avoid

111

those projects with a history of failure, or which are held in low esteem. If, despite all your careful selection and good work, you fail, review the list of ways of avoiding responsibility for that failure. These strategies are discussed later in the next chapter. In this way, you will prevent your career being blighted.

TAKING CHARGE

Accept additional responsibility. Look around to see who is likely to leave; where the problems exist; and what your boss is doing that you could be doing. Also, look for new in-company and external developments which are in the pipeline, and which could provide you with an escalator for your ambitions. Prepare to be ready to seize the opportunity when it comes. Learn about the various possible roles ahead of time, and ingratiate yourself with the existing post-holders. Let them know that you want to broaden your experience, but do it discreetly as overt ambition can stimulate hostility and resistance. When the chance arises, offer your services immediately (speed), or better still, just assume the role. Assuming leadership in work areas where there appears to be no leadership is a recognized career tactic. Your superiors are unlikely to remove you, as it is one less problem for them to worry about. Be careful however, as deputizing can increase or destroy your chances of being promoted to a post. After a time, filling-in exposes your negative as well as positive points. Goffman (1959) found that people prefer positively framed problems (the possibility of a successful appointment with an unknown candidate) to negatively framed ones (the certainty of appointing someone with known limitations). The more difficult and more different the new job is from your old one, the greater the risk in deputizing. Maybe better let your rival have it.

Seize the initiative. Avoid the 'wait and see' approach. Many people lose out because they are too slow. Do not allow yourself to be overtaken. Be first, then deliver. Control time by appearing reasonable, while knowing that the other party cannot meet the deadline imposed. This tactic is best used when the other party is least equipped to deal with it (Bacharch and Lawler, 1980). Be first to fill the vacuum, for example, suggest a date for the meeting. If you wait for someone to confer power on you, it may never happen. If you assume control, seldom will anyone stop you. It is always easier for your boss to say no than yes. If they give you the go-ahead, it means that they are taking responsibility for it, and may have to defend their agreement to their bosses, if something goes wrong. So, before they can confidently give you permission, they have to gain knowledge of your intentions, and assess them. This can be a long and time-consuming process. It is easier for them just to refuse your request, and save themselves all the trouble. Hence, apologize afterwards, rather than ask permission before. What is done cannot be undone. Power seekers can get what they want simply by asking. Power is there for the taking. You need to balance the costs against the benefits of speedy action. Your opponents might use it against you, but your superiors may see the rules as petty. If they knew what you were doing, they would have had to intervene, so they would prefer not to know. If you are found out, the worst thing that happens on the first occasion is that you will get a, 'Tut, tut, don't do it again'. Then you can act humble, apologize and either carry on or stop. There are a set of excuses and justifications that can be used if required, and these too are discussed later in this book.

Women's power bases, in contrast to men's, are perceived differently by non-verbal behaviour. When a female engages in a non-verbal behaviour that is incongruent with gender role expectations, such as direct eye contact, she is perceived as having a negative source of power and a high level of coerciveness. When she acts in a way that is congruent with her social role, but incongruent with the managerial role, she is perceived as having less power. This modifies the common advice to look people straight in the eye! Women face a trade off between their gender roles and their organizational role expectations. When fulfilling the latter, she may violate the former, and thereby be perceived negatively. Direct eye contact (congruent with the managerial role stereotype) leads to increased perceptions of coercive power. A relaxed facial expression (congruent with female gender stereotype) decreases participants' ratings on all six power bases (reward, coercive, legitimate, referent, expert and credibility). Finally, when a female is sitting back in a chair with her feet crossed, she is rated as having increased referent (that is, personal) power.

DEALING WITH REFUSALS

As a manager, how do you refuse an employee's request effectively? Your response can significantly affect the way they react to your answer and the perception that they have of you in the future. For example, how does a manager reject a subordinate's request for time off? Tate (1998) distinguishes a refusal continuum ranging from concession, to excuse, to justification to refusal. Concessional responses resemble apologies; excuses involve explanations, possibly beyond the control of the manager; justifications are explanations where the manager accepts causal responsibility; while certain types of refusals are point blank rejections. In Figure 6.1, the four types of responses are presented on a scale from mitigation through to aggravation. The responses at the concessional end of the scale reduce the friction caused by the action and are accepted as being most courteous to employees. Those in the refusal category increase the chances of friction, and are considered to be most threatening. How to respond most effectively appears to depend on whether you are a male or female manager.

Tate found that female managers both used more concessions than male ones, and provided more excuses to employees, although there were no differences in the use of justifications between the two sexes. The gender of the employee being

113

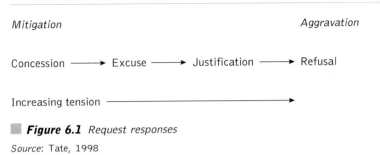

Mitigation   *Aggravation*

Concession ⟶ Excuse ⟶ Justification ⟶ Refusal

Increasing tension ⟶

Figure 6.1 *Request responses*
Source: Tate, 1998

talked to was found to influence the type of response made by a manager. Managers provided more mitigating responses to female employees than to male ones; and more aggravating responses to male than to female employees. This study confirmed previous research suggesting that female managers, by using mitigating responses more, showed greater compassion for employees, and used a more thoughtful interpersonal approach than did male managers. In contrast, women managers who deviated from social stereotypes by using more aggravating responses were less favourably evaluated. Male managers in contrast who chose to use more mitigating responses, were more favourably thought of. In both cases, it may be that socially undesirable deviations from the norms are evaluated more negatively than socially desirable deviations.

MANAGING YOUR REPUTATION

The first impression at work is so important that a bad start, whether through your own fault or someone else's, can wrong-foot you so much, that it is often easier to change jobs or even organizations, than to rebuild a negative image. If you have erred, failed, inconvenienced or disappointed anyone, and leaving your job is not an option, it is best to apologize and make restitution by overcompensating for your failure. Building reputation power starts the moment you join. Begin by studying your organizational and departmental chart. Developing a positive relationship with your head of department can help you to identify problems which you have the resources to solve. You need a few early 'wins', even if these are unspectacular. Such early successes provide a positive 'primacy effect', and build credibility with colleagues and subordinates which affect their subsequent perceptions of you. Your priority is to match your technical and interpersonal skills to the demands of the company. Cultivate co-operative relationships with key people, and begin building a credible track record. Position and expertise, along with reputation, are sources of power because of what they communicate to others about your ability to perform your job effectively (Kotter, 1985a). Your effective performance in turn, helps to build your formal authority and reputation as shown in Figure 6.2.

Position (formal authority)   +   Reputation   →   **Effective performance**

Figure 6.2 *Elements of effective performance*

In the long term however, you will not get credit for doing the mandatory or expected things well. Excellent performance in tasks that are routine may be valued, but will not add to your reputation power. Being known as a person who is reliable, predictable and gets things done, is necessary, but is not in itself sufficient. Your reputation in an organization will be determined by your performance on tasks that require discretion. Such tasks are more likely to be noticed. You can do something extraordinary by being the first in a new position, making organizational changes or by taking risks and succeeding. To be noticed, your impact should be short-term, have practical results and demonstrate your problem-solving ability, decisiveness and performance. Performing means being knowledgeable and capable of providing answers; drawing criticism away from your boss; accomplishing things that make your unit and boss look good; and reducing uncertainty.

A reputation for decisiveness is vital, but should you gamble on making a high-risk decision? Studies show that distortion of information concerning past decisions occurs routinely in organizations, and feedback from past choices does not correct the errors over time. Why not? First, history is ambiguous. At the moment a decision is made, it cannot be known if it is good or bad. Decision quality, when measured by results, can only be judged once the results of the decision are known. It is necessary to wait for a decision to be implemented, and its consequences clarified. This may take years. Since there are multiple determinants of outcomes, their cause–effect relations tend to be vague. There is no way of knowing if a 'correct' decision has been made, since this is a construct with almost no meaning in most circumstances. Moreover, decisions by themselves change nothing. You can make a decision, but it will not put itself into effect. The important aspect in organizational decisions is not the original choice, but what happens subsequently, and what actions are taken to make things work to plan.

We spend more time living with the consequences of our decisions than making them. We often rationalize, that is, match our attitudes and behaviour to our past actions and their consequences (Cialdini, 2001a; Festinger, 1957). Second, the length of time needed for a decision to have consequences means that the people who made it have either been promoted, or will have left the organization anyway. Third, decisions involve building up some collective responsibility, and this means that responsibility is shared, this makes it difficult to assign blame later to any one individual for what was a group decision. Organizations are

115

notorious for avoiding evaluation or looking backwards. They are incredibly non-introspective. It is for these reasons that government ministers who implement policies are happy to offer to resign if their policies fail to have the desired outcomes.

All in all, it is most unlikely that you will ever be asked to account for a past action or decision (Feldman and March, 1981). It is unlikely that you will be judged solely on the consequences of your own actions, and it is therefore safe to take decisions, even ones that turn out to be wrong. Being right is less important than being decisive, because gaining a reputation for decisiveness increases your power. You should be less concerned about the quality of your decision since, at the time you make it, you did not know how good it was anyway. You should be more concerned with adapting your new decisions and actions to the information you gain as events unfold.

People with favourable reputations get more interesting and challenging job assignments; receive more developmental opportunities; and are given more mentoring and coaching from senior managers. A reputation for having power, brings more power – 'to those that hath shall be given more'. Being influential will help you find allies and supporters; will give you more opportunity to exercise your influence; and will in turn, allow you to get things accomplished and enhance your reputation. It is a virtuous spiral (Berlew and Hall, 1966). If you get a reputation for being efficient and industrious, without limiting the credit received by those also involved, then others will want to work with and for you, while your bosses will want to take you with them as they move up. Your reputation creates opportunities to expand your competence and your sphere of influence.

In this context, fighting on the losing side can be a reputation killer, if not carefully handled. People like to think that the world is orderly and just. If you do suffer a reversal or accident, others will feel, unconsciously and perhaps unfairly, that you somehow deserved to fail, rather than viewing it as a random, luck-of-the-draw, uncontrollable event. The consequence is that those around you will devalue their perceptions of your capability and importance. Since you cannot win every issue, what do you do? If you promote an issue that you consider important but lose, extract yourself from it once it is clear that you will fail. Once the decision goes against you, do not fight on, but acknowledge your differences on the issue with the others, state the reasonable basis for your opinion, and then agree to go along with the different opinion of the majority. In this way, you get points for being both co-operative and a team player.

In contrast, any stubborn and continued resistance on your part will get you labelled as a loser, and others will resent your continued opposition. When involved with others' losing proposals, you should know when to, 'look away at the right moment' (Korda, 1976). Looking away means distancing yourself by not attending team meetings, not being seen with the losing team members, or by disclaiming involvement. Being repeatedly identified and remembered as being on the losing side will damage your reputation. You will be known by the company you keep, the issues with which you are associated, and by how these are decided (Lerner and Simmons, 1966). Although companies may stress teamworking and group decision-making and empowerment, this interest does not extend to group accountability. When the work is completed and the group achieves something, its members look for individual recognition and career progress. People are employed individually, and their contract with the company, real or implied, is as individuals. To hold a group accountable, an employment contract would have to be with the group, and companies simply do not do that.

MANAGING PROBLEMS

Another aspect of organizational performance is the management of problems. Drummond suggested that, since you will not be able to avoid them, you should manage, and not react to them. Identify only with problems that you can solve, and ideally, with those that you have already solved. Create a crisis and then solve it. Be careful how others define your problems. Prevent others setting you up for a failure, and then exploiting your weaknesses. You can re-define a problem that has emerged, or which you have been given, in any of the following ways suggested by Drummond (1991: 199):

1   'That is not the issue: what we need to concern ourselves with is . . .'
2   'Let's not go looking for problems where there are none.'
3   'I see no conflict between the two objectives. My problem is . . .'
4   'I wish that was the problem.'
5   'X is not my problem. My problem is . . .'
6   'That is the least of my worries.'
7   'If that is the worst thing that happens to us, we will have done well.'
8   'X isn't important, what matters is . . .'
9   'I agree that is a problem. However, a much bigger problem is . . .'
10 'X is only a thorn in our side, not a dagger in the heart . . .'

A problem shared is a problem dumped. If you can get someone to help you with your problem, with a bit of luck, you can make it their problem, and make them responsible for its solution. Ensure that others do not dump their problems onto you. To do this, ensure others understand your role, and be seen to be fulfilling it. Resist the temptation to do other peoples' jobs for them, even if you could do it better. If verbal counter-attacks are mounted, repel them by verbal parries of 'It won't work', 'Headquarters won't approve it'; 'We don't have the resources' or 'My option has the support of'. This strategy of suppression is likely to succeed because your statements seem highly plausible, and even

117

if challenged, require the challenger to use their time and effort to prove you wrong (e.g. they would have to show why it would not work; track down X and get their provisional approval, etc). The appeal of your favoured alternative can be enhanced by finding factual information to emphasize some aspect of it which others feel is important (e.g. quality, longevity). This is equivalent to tailoring your application form to match the job requirements. Alternatively, you can just keep repeating your point, over and over again. Although tedious, it does stop the other person scoring a point and gaining a concession from you.

YOU AS A NEW GROUP MEMBER

Before attending your first group meeting, familiarize yourself with the group's history and background. Analyse the minutes of past meetings going back a few months to determine how decisions are made, and who are the powerful members. Study the agenda and read any papers circulated beforehand. Clarify the issues you need to in advance. It is useful to arrive early, in order to get to know the other participants. Acknowledge people as they arrive in the room rather than slinking into a corner. If they are chatting before the formal start, get involved in their conversation. It will warm you up, and make you feel less nervous about contributing later. Many deals are made in the minutes just before the members sit down, and you need to be aware of any pre-meeting manoeuvring.

Arriving early also allows you to select an appropriate seat. As a new participant, check if there is any set seating arrangement, thus avoiding occupying someone's 'usual place'. Sit where you can be seen and heard by the chairperson and the other members. Hodgson and Hodgson (1992) reported research that showed that the person sitting to the right of the chairperson is more likely to get their attention than the person on the left. People with the most power and status locate themselves at the end of the table, nearest to the chairperson. By occupying a focal seating position, you will be perceived to share the power of that more influential member. Moreover, by being able to see everyone's face, you can spot both potential allies and opponents through their body language. In this position, everyone can see you, and you can catch everyone's eye, allowing you to signal when you want to speak. Such positioning encourages other people to listen to you more intensely.

There are some other points to consider. Where you sit in relation to others, affects your relationship with them. An across-the-table position suggests confrontation by raising the impact of your communication through increased direct eye contact. This is useful when you want to be aggressive or to dominate others. It increases the pressure on the other person by making your presence very direct and difficult to avoid. It is not the normal communication position. Ideally, you want to be opposite your greatest ally, and sit next to, or on the same side as the person whom you wish to influence. Side-by-side sitting denotes unity or at least neutrality between people. It is normal to 'side' with people of similar views. At least sit around the corner from them. For the same reason, you might get a supporter of yours to split up any hard-to-convince pairs, so that they do not sit side by side, and thus have the chance to confer and back each other up. Right angles is the normal relaxed position for communication. In a social situation, we naturally position ourselves in a circle. It provides good eye contact with a fixed distance, without becoming embarrassing or allowing anyone involved to dominate. When you move to a face-to-face position, you reduce the space between yourself and the other person, and increase the impact of your eye contact.

At your first meeting, either introduce yourself or get someone else to introduce you. State your name and job title, and briefly describe your work responsibilities. Find out who the other group members are. If the chairperson introduces the others, make an effort to remember their names and seating positions. Otherwise discover who they are informally. By knowing their names, you can use them at your first or second meeting ('Jean Brown's point about time, I feel is very valid'). If, for whatever reason, your membership of a group is controversial, ease yourself gently into your role in order to establish credibility and gain the trust of others. Prepare for the first meeting, but begin by just introducing yourself, and not saying anything. This will allow the other members to get used to your presence. During your next few attendances, ask one good question. After that, add some information to what is being discussed, and then participate normally.

Listen to what others say, ask questions and analyse their comments. You will lessen your power, if you remain disinterested and uninvolved, thereby creating distance. While no one may know what you are thinking, they may end up not caring either. Avoid directly opposing others' views initially. Instead, explore their position or views through your questions. This not only gives you information which can help you to design a solution to meet both sides' needs, but it can also increase others' feelings of being listened to, thereby making them more receptive to meeting your needs. Ask them for reasons to justify what they are saying, and use 'why' questions. With gentle pressure, you can make them appear extreme, while getting yourself perceived as reasonable by the other participants. Any aggressive personal attacks and criticism by you on others, will make you look like a petulant child. Not listening, or talking about irrelevancies, shows your insecurity and indicates how threatened you feel by others' opinions. Disagreeing with everyone and everything shows you to be destructive. Attend the meeting with the intention of adding something to it. This may be an informed opinion, an important fact, or a constructive suggestion. People who talk most in conversations with both friends and strangers, tend to be perceived as leaders. So, once the meeting starts, make an early contribution, since this makes it easier to contribute again later. The longer you leave it, the more difficult it becomes. Those people who contribute early to a discussion exert greater influence as it continues. Moreover, groups tend to close a discussion quickly on an issue as soon as a

119

feasible option is presented, even if it is not the best one. When making your input, lean forward and make it with enthusiasm and animation. Keep it short, and ensure that you speak at least once in every meeting, thus showing that you are listening, and also increasing your visibility. The quality and quantity of your contribution matter if you are to gain the meeting's attention.

If your status is low in the group, you can gain attention by asking a question, or inventing something to have clarified. In seeking clarification, information or advice, you will be asking the rest of the meeting to help you, and no one can consider that as presumptuous. You can make a powerful impression by preparing a specific and detailed idea for an important agenda item that interest you. For example, if the topic of cost-cutting appears on the agenda, come to the meeting with a three-point plan, supported with just enough detail, perhaps a statistic, to show that you have given the matter some thought beforehand. As most of the other members will not have prepared or will talk off the top of their heads, your contribution will stand out. You should anticipate controversial items since you will be most likely to be asked to speak when the group is divided on an issue. Prepare an impromptu speech, remembering that the best ones are written out in advance! You are your most impressive when others think that you are improvising. To avoid others stealing your idea at the meeting, or the group taking it over as their own, summarize it in outline form on one sheet of paper which has your name at the top. Make sufficient copies ready to distribute to all members. Present your idea, and if it dies, lay the papers face down in front of you. If it is passed or is positively received, pass out the papers to each member by saying, 'I've got the key points here written down. Let's build on this'. Your contribution should be minuted.

Speak with authority to the group, and avoid starting with disclaimers. Rather than beginning with, 'This may already have been discussed' or 'Maybe this won't work but', just make your point with a moderate voice tone and a relatively low pitch. Complement your powerful speech with expansive, non-verbal gestures. At the start, stake out your territory in a status-enhancing way, by spreading your papers in front of you. Subsequently, avoid fumbling with your papers, since the more disorganized you look, the more likely it is that you will be interrupted. While listening, women should not smile (unless something funny has been said) or bob their head. Instead, they should look alert by sitting straight and attend by maintaining eye contact with the speaker, even if the speaker is not looking at them.

IMPRESSION MANAGEMENT TACTICS

Impression management has been defined as a conscious or unconscious attempt to influence images during interaction. Impression management tactics involve presenting information about yourself so that you are perceived as competent, successful and worthy of additional rewards and promotions (Jones and Pittman, 1982; Iedema and Poppe, 1996; Bozeman and Kacmar, 1997; Mohamed *et al.*, 1999; Rosenfeld *et al.*, 2002). The first three tactics to be described here are 'acquisitive', in that they proactively promote you (basking, ingratiation and self-promotion), and the last four are 'defensive' tactics (problem management, excuse or blame management, falsification, information filtering), which are intended to protect your image should it be challenged.

Basking

Basking is a technique through which you enhance your reputation by claiming association with prestigious figures, institutions or achievements (Cialdini *et al.*, 1976). You bask in the reflected glory of others. It is the only tactic that is concerned with managing the information that you distribute that is not about yourself, but about the people and things with which you are connected (Cialdini and Richardson, 1980). You promote your favourable, and minimize your unfavourable associations in the eyes of observers. Some people feel that they can bask in the reflected glory of an associate's or subordinate's achievement, even when they are in no way responsible for it. Basking can be effective because of the effect of raw association – the tendency of observers to respond in a similar fashion to positively linked stimuli. Balance theory tells us that people exposed to even simple unit connections (e.g. a project, an office) will tend to see positively connected, close objects as similar, and negatively connected, distant objects as different (Heider, 1958).

Ensure that you do not have to give bad news, or be associated with bad news, as you will be evaluated negatively, despite the fact that you have in no way caused the bad news. Bearers of bad tidings still get slain, at least metaphorically. If you are visibly and negatively linked to a rival, manage the information you give in such a way that observers see the rival as having negative traits. The opposite is also true. Associate yourself with successful events, people and institutions (Manis *et al.*, 1974). The interviewer infers that if you have studied or worked at a prestigious university or company, then you must be good. When associating yourself with a person, ensure that they are seen in a favourable light in the organization. The rule of thumb is to be positively connected to favourable others, and negatively connected to unfavourable others. It sounds simple, but in practice is somewhat more complex.

Four basking behaviours affect your observers' perceptions of the nature or strength of your connection with another person. *Boasting* involves proclaiming a positive link to a favourable person. You should boast not about your own achievements, but about your link to someone else's accomplishments. When your boss secures a substantial budget increase, mention this, and tell others that you are a member of her department. *Burying* is disclaiming a positive link with

121

an unfavourable individual. If you are associated with such a person, distance yourself from their failure in the eyes of observers. Dissociate yourself from a failed or failing project team by seeking a transfer elsewhere (Snyder *et al.*, 1986). *Blaring* is producing a negative link to an unfavourable other. You ensure that you are perceived as distinct from the unfavourable individual. Trumpet your own negative connection to such a source, either by drawing attention to your negative connections, or by establishing new ones (Cooper and Jones, 1969). When a colleague publicly challenges your mutual boss on a topic, distance yourself from him on this matter, and on similar, subsequent issues. Finally, there is *blurring* where you disclaim a negative link to a favourable other. You obscure for observers the genuine negative connection that you have with someone who has been favourably evaluated by others. You can do this through an act of strategic omission, rather than commission. Describe a successful, recently promoted work colleague in terms that obscure the distinction between yourself and her. For example, when applying for her job, avoid mentioning the fact that she possesses a university degree while you do not.

There are another four basking behaviours that are designed to affect observers' perceptions of other people with whom you are connected. *Burnishing* involves enhancing the favourable features of a positively linked other. When there is a demonstrable positive link between you and some other person or thing, you can improve your public prestige by persuading observers of how favourable that person or thing is. For example, exaggerate the qualities of an employee that you have hired or promoted. *Boosting* is minimizing the unfavourable features of a person with whom you are positively linked. Minimize or ignore the failings of a person that you have personally been responsible for hiring, or tell others that your boss's behaviour was not as outrageous as they believed it to be. *Blasting* is exaggerating the unfavourable features of a person or group with whom you are negatively linked. As with burnishing, you exaggerate the unbecoming aspects of a rival. This is not amongst the tactics to be preferred because it can lead to scapegoating others that, in the eyes of observers, may provoke a negative reaction against you. Blasting is probably best performed in situations where being blamed is more detrimental to you that scapegoating another. It is best done by presenting observers with information in a form that they can use, to deduce the unfavourable actions of your rival. Finally, *belittling* concerns minimizing the favourable traits of a negatively linked other. By minimizing the worthy traits of a rival, you can enhance the positive view that others have of you. Giving lower than merited performance assessments to a rival for a senior job would be an example of this.

Self-promotion

It is not enough to do, or to have done your job well. You need to be seen to be doing it successfully (Rowntree, 1989). To do this, you need to gain visibility for yourself, and advertise your achievements to significant others in the organization. Self-promotion is associated with attributes considered as prerequisites for employment – confidence, competence and ambition. In the interview situation, self-promotion involves embellishing your achievements, exaggerating the recognition that you have received; and overstating your abilities (Giacalone and Rosenfeld, 1986). Never express any doubts about your ability to acquire quickly any skills needed (language, accounting, computing), even if you do not possess any of them yet. Point out any extra training, new methods or other steps that you have taken to improve your performance. Do not moan to your current or past boss about the difficulties you are facing, or blame the shortcomings of other people. In talking to others in the organization, be open and confident about your work. People are usually willing to believe what you tell them, provided that they do not have any blatant evidence to the contrary. So do not be unduly modest; do not hide your light under a bushel; and never ever run yourself down. By all means ask for help or advice from your colleagues, but do so as one who expects to be able to help them equally on other occasions.

Bosses are sometimes unable to pick up the signs of a subordinate's job or company commitment. If they lack such a clear view, then it is up to the employees themselves to convey to them the impression that they are indeed working hard and are committed. Drawing upon the work of Tepper (1995), Singh and Vinnicombe (2001) listed different sets of commitment-signalling strategies. The *manager-focused strategy* involves subordinates building up a good relationship with the boss, rather than focusing on the work, in the hope of influencing decisions to their benefit. Men were more prepared to do this than women. It involves the subordinate going directly to their boss, and stating that they are ready for a new challenge. You can go regularly to your supervisor with your work, and asking them questions about it, to show that you are doing it. You need to ensure that you always complete the work that you are given, and that you get noticed by exceeding what is expected of you. Singh, Kumra and Vinnicombe (2002) suggest a *self-focused strategy* which involves 'talking yourself up' and letting your influencee know what you are currently doing, or are capable of doing in the future. Surveys suggest that women are poor at this. Men in contrast seem willing to take personal credit for group work. Women's reluctance to engage in impression management to enhance their chances of promotion, has been confirmed elsewhere. They seem to know that they need to, but are unwilling to participate despite their knowledge, and instead pretend that their personal style and contribution at work will be sufficient to get themselves noticed and rewarded, when clearly it will not.

In connection with your boss, self-promotion aims to win you their respect and admiration in competition with the other staff who report to them. This is the means of achieving desirable work assignments, good appraisals and ultimately promotion to a more senior position in the company. Keep your boss up to date on your work progress, whether or not they have asked you for a report. If they request an update, treat it as an opportunity, and deal with it immediately. Send them a brief note recording the completion of all your major projects or objectives, ensuring that they notice all your successes and improvements. Offer them solutions, and not problems. Seek your boss's help in implementing the possible solutions that you have thought up. Generally, present yourself as the person who 'gets things done'. Modestly pass on to your boss any praise that you receive from elsewhere in the organization or outside it. Couch it in a way that enables them to interpret it as reflecting well on them and their department. Send a copy of any congratulatory note to him with a 'Thought you'd be interested in this' appended. If you are seeking promotion, remind your boss of this on every suitable opportunity. Show that you are not complacent by continuing to develop your skills and knowledge, thereby indicating your belief in constant self-improvement. Beyond your immediate boss, use self-promotion to cultivate champions and mentors around the organization. These will be people whom your boss respects, for whom you will have done work, and who are prepared to speak well on your behalf.

Is there a problem with self-promotion for women? Studies have shown that women who behave confidently and assertively are not as well received as men who engage in the same behaviours. Women suffer a backlash effect in which self-promotion enhances perceptions of their qualifications, but at the cost of social rejection. This may be because the women are seen as violating what society still sees as being their gender role. Rudman's (1998) study broadly confirms these earlier findings. She examined how self-promoting women were judged when they acted in either a self-promoting or a self-effacing manner. With respect to task aptitude, both male and female perceivers rated self-promoting subjects of both genders higher than their self-effacing counterparts. This is not surprising as a person who is told by another that they are good at something, and knows nothing to the contrary, is likely to believe it. It shows that self-promotion is a good way of getting strangers to believe that you are competent. Other findings included the fact that although male perceivers preferred self-promoting woman, they needed a substantial amount of self-promotion by a woman before considering her hireable. This suggests women have to present a very atypical, 'masculine' image of themselves to get appointed. Women selectors were less likely to find a self-promoting woman socially attractive. Rudland suggests that this was because the cultural perception of women to be modest may be more strongly defended by other women than by men. Since hiring decisions seem to be affected by the interviewer's gender, female applicants are advised to reduce the level of their self-promotion in the presence of female interviewers, and increase it substantially in the presence of a male ones.

124

Ingratiation

Apple-polishing, crawling and brown-nosing are all terms synonymous with ingratiation (Stires and Jones, 1969). Despite such condemnation, ingratiation remains a pervasive feature of organizational life and a tactic of political influence (Kipnis *et al.*, 1980). As an ingratiator, your objective is to appear professionally or socially attractive to the influencee, so as to gain power over them. The key to successful ingratiation is your personal attractiveness – being liked by them (Blackburn, 1981; Mechanic, 1962). Attractiveness is created by using a number of strategies. The first of these is *opinion conformity* with your boss. This can take the form of agreeing with your boss's opinions outwardly, even though you may disagree inwardly. As a technique it needs to be very carefully applied as it can backfire to your detriment, leaving you classed as a 'yes-man or woman' (Aronson, 1992). An alternative strategy is to begin by determining your boss's position on an issue, feigning a contrary position, before finally allowing your boss to convince you of her view (Jones and Wortman, 1973). You might praise your boss's major strengths, while criticizing her 'minor' weaknesses. Another ingratiation tactic is to agree with your boss's major ideas, but carefully disagree with her minor ones, thereby appearing to be both discriminating and independent.

Opinion-conformity is a powerful influencing and career enhancement tactic. All of us like those whose behaviour provides us with a maximum reward at minimum cost. Specifically, we like people whose beliefs and interests are similar to our own. People who conform to our views reward us by helping us to believe that our own opinions are correct (Byrne, 1969). Why should this be important? We are all motivated to be logical and accurate in our interpretations of our environment. Thus the agreement voiced by others reinforces and satisfies our need to be correct. Our desire to avoid people who disagree with us is stronger than our need to associate with those whose attitudes are similar to our own. This is because, if a person disagrees with us, it not only introduces the possibility that we may be wrong, but also we come to suspect that that individual's opinion on that issue is indicative of the kind of person we have in the past found to be unpleasant, immoral or stupid. Equally important is the fact that people are so sure of the link between attitude similarity and liking that, if they like someone, they will automatically assume that this person's attitudes are similar to their own. Thus causality works in both directions. We like people whose attitudes are similar to our own and, if we like someone, we attribute to them attitudes that are similar to ours (Granberg and King, 1980; Marks *et al.*, 1981; Rosenbaum, 1986; Sigall, 1970). Of course, people are influenced by other similarities as well (e.g. dress).

Second, the more skills, abilities or competencies a person possesses, the more we like them. Because of our need to be right, we stand more chance of being so if we surround ourselves with highly able, competent people. So you raise

125

your perceived competence by developing expertise in areas that are critical to your department's operations. On the other hand, competent people can make us feel uncomfortable, especially if they are unapproachable, distant or apparently super-human. So, if you are a highly competent person, provide some evidence of your fallibility occasionally, since this so-called, 'pratfall effect', increases your attractiveness still further, especially to males with moderate self-esteem (Aronson *et al.*, 1966). In contrast, females and low-esteem males are less impressed, but all types prefer competent people to mediocre ones (Deaux, 1972).

Those who are good-looking are liked, since they fulfil our needs for beauty and provide us with aesthetic rewards of beauty (Walster *et al.*, 1966a; Stewart, 1980; Kulka and Kessler, 1978; Stewart *et al.*, 1979). To good-looking individuals, we naturally assign favourable traits such as talent, kindness, honesty and intelligence. Most readers may be incredulous and appalled by such a suggestion. Nevertheless, attractiveness does play an important part in who likes whom, in both the long and the short term. Physically attractive people are assigned more desirable traits, irrespective of gender. There is a high degree of cultural agreement on the physical characteristics and concomitant personality traits of 'beautiful people' which come from socialization and media, and which teach the population cultural standards of beauty. These include regular features, small pert noses, big eyes, shapely lips, blemish-free complexions and slim athletic bodies. Attractive people are given the benefit of the doubt, and their misbehaviours are forgiven as aberrations. Physically attractive people affect us, and unless they do something unpleasant to us, we tend to like them better (Dion *et al.*, 1972; Snyder *et al.*, 1977). When we learn that others share our opinions, we believe that they will like us, if and when they get to know us. Then, when others like us, we tend to like them too. It operates as a self-fulfilling prophecy. Our beliefs, right or wrong, play a potent role in shaping reality (Condon and Crano, 1988; Secord and Backman, 1964; Curtis and Miller, 1986).

We like those who co-operate with us. Such people give us aid, listen to our ideas, make suggestions and share our load (Aronson and Osherow, 1980). We also like those who provide us with favours, since these can be considered as rewards (Jennings, 1959). We like those who 'contribute to our victory' more than those who do not, even if they had no intention of doing us a favour. We like those for whom we do favours. When we do someone a favour, we justify this action by convincing ourselves that the recipient of our favour is an attractive and likeable person. Otherwise, why would we be spending our time and effort on this person? In his novel, *War and Peace*, Tolstoy wrote, 'We do not love people so much for the good they have done us, as for the good we have done them'. Once someone has done you a favour, they will be more ready to do you another one, than a person who owes you a favour. This is provided that the effort they expended on your behalf has produced a successful outcome (Jecker and Landy, 1969; Lerner and Simmons, 1966).

We like people who flatter us. The tactic of flattery consists of complimenting people on their achievements, looks, group contributions or membership. Individuals like those who like them. We like to evaluate ourselves favourably, and look to others to reinforce our positive assessments of ourselves (Clore and Byrne, 1974). We like those who like us, and we evaluate them positively in return, since they raise our self-esteem (Aronson and Darwyn, 1965). We prefer balance, and will reciprocate their liking (Heider, 1958). We will come to like people who show that they like us. One-way liking is unbalancing so, to re-establish balance and to reduce their discomfort, the other person will come to like us. Flattery directed towards personal effectiveness ('You certainly succeeded there') is more effective than either flattery directed at a position ('You must be really clever to be head of marketing'); or the opinion-conformity mentioned earlier ('You've convinced me you're right') (Byrne, 1971; Tjosvold, 1978).

People like praise but do not like being manipulated, so it is best not to make your praise too lavish. As an influencer, you may be anxious about using flattery to increase another person's liking for you, and thus increase their willingness to accede to your requests. You may fear that your compliment will be taken as either insincere or instrumental, and may backfire on you. Pfeffer (1992) noted that there was a motivational bias towards a compliment being taken as sincere by its receiver. If your influencee believes your flattering remark, they will feel positive about themselves. If, in contrast, they treat it as instrumental, that is, as untrue and serving only as a means to an end, they will not feel so good about themselves. They will have to question your opinion of them ('What's wrong with me, that someone like you, feels that I can be taken in by flattery?'). Since your influencee will prefer to feel good rather than bad about themselves, they will want to see your compliment as sincere. Psychologically, therefore, you are on safe ground (Brehm, 1966).

Paying a compliment to the interviewer and organization, and showing respect by having prepared for the event, help to bolster the interviewer's self-esteem (Aronson and Linder, 1965). Compliments are a potent form of ingratiation, not only because people like to receive them, but because the norm of reciprocity leaves the other party with the obligation to return a compliment. Even if they do not like you, reciprocity demands they say something nice about you, back. Having done so, they then face the pressure of maintaining cognitive consistency (i.e. keeping their actions, opinions, values, attitudes and standards about you, consistent or congruent with each other). They will find it difficult to say nice things about you, which reciprocity forces them to do, while at the same time, not liking you. This is not because they are mean or petty, but because it will seem inconsistent to them to recognize some quality they like in you, without also liking you. Having said something positive about you in return, they are likely to adjust their impression of you from negative or neutral to positive, to fit the positive statement they were at first forced to make. This combination of

127

the reciprocity norm coupled with the effects of cognitive dissonance, means that paying compliments to those who may initially dislike you, leads them ultimately to develop a positive attitude towards you.

You can ingratiate yourself by making influencees feel important. Asking them for help and advice flatters them (Davies, 1991b). Do it in a manner that says, 'you are the expert', and which also expects them to supply the expertise. Do not grovel or be apologetic, but let them know that they are in a position to help you. If you cannot think of any help or advice that you want, you could ask them a question to which you already know the answer, feigning gratitude and interest. Alternatively, you can thank them for the help and advice that they have given you in the past, commenting on how useful it was, and perhaps requesting advice about something else. You can let them know you respect their expertise ('I'm well aware that you know a lot about'); or give them proposals or sugges-tions which they can alter. Instead of saying, 'I've put down on paper what I think we ought to do about this', say instead, 'I've put down a range of ways in which I think this problem can be solved. There are some gaps though, and I'd like you to look over it, and make whatever alterations are necessary, and tell me what you think'.

When you involve the other person, they start to get a sense of ownership of your idea. This is why, if you ask people to help you, their commitment to help-ing you engenders a feeling of personal investment in your success. For this reason, asking for favours gains their commitment to you, while your granting them favours, obligates them. Finally, you can give them a good press, telling oth-ers how helpful they have been to you, in a way that gets back to them. Additional ingratiation strategies include dressing like your boss; disclosing intimate infor-mation about yourself to your boss (if you have a high opinion of them); devel-oping interests similar to your boss; and taking an interest in your boss's personal life. Gould and Penley's (1984) study identified opinion-conformity and ingratia-tion to be the two techniques most positively associated with salary progress.

Ingratiation differs culturally and between the sexes (Applebaum and Hughes, 1998; Stratton et al., 1995). It is suggested that subtlety and moderation are the essence of effective ingratiation, since excess can lead to problems. What effect might the use of ingratiation and its rewarding, have on the influencee and on the influencer's co-workers? A study by Zellers and Kacmar's (1999) found that when a subordinate ingratiated a supervisor *and* was rewarded for it, his co-workers responded negatively. In contrast, co-workers did not view unsuccessful ingratiation attempts negatively. On successful occasions, co-workers perceived favouritism, experienced less satisfaction with the supervisor concerned, with their ingratiating co-worker, and with their job in general. This would create a detrimental effect on any team-oriented work environment. The ingratiating influ-encer therefore needs to be aware of the problems that are created for his manager and his manager's team.

128

BLAME MANAGEMENT AND EXCUSES

Blaming, that is, constructing plausible justifications and excuses for what you have done, is a fact of organizational life (Bell and Tetlock, 1989). News pro-gramme interviewers on the radio constantly ask their interviewees whom they blame for whatever problem is being discussed. It is important in preserving your self-image and the image that other company personnel have of you. Since you want to avoid being blamed when things go wrong, blame management, is an important skill. The people around you in the organization can be considered as 'naive scientists' who make causal inferences about what is going on, based on their own logical inference processes. Given a negative act, they attribute respon-sibility to its perpetrator on five different levels identified by Heider (1944, 1958). These are shown in Figure 6.3. The perpetrator's responsibility for the error increases from levels one through to four, and then reduces somewhat as level five is reached (Hamilton, 1978, 1980).

Let us take an example of the failure of a project team of which you were a member, to introduce a local area network computer system on time and to budget. The first and lowest level of failure responsibility is that of *association*. You are held responsible for any effect that is in any way connected with you, or that seems in any way to belong to you. The attribution of failure to you is minimal, no conspiracy is implied, and mere association is sufficient. In the non-work situation, parents are held responsible for the delinquent acts of their children. In the case example, you knew the person who led the project team that failed. In law, you might be held to have vicarious responsibility.

The second and greater level of responsibility is *causality*. Anything that is caused by you, is ascribed to you. Causation means that you were a necessary condition for the failure to happen, even though you could not have foreseen the outcome, however cautiously you might have proceeded. Here, you are being judged, not by your intentions, but by what you actually did. The team of which you were a member did indeed go over-budget and beyond the deadline. It

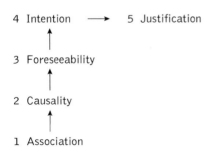

Figure 6.3 *Heider's levels of responsibility attribution*
Source: Heider 1944, 1958

miscalculated the figures and under-estimated the time required. You are the direct cause of the failure, but no assumptions are made about your foresight or intention. The legal equivalent is strict liability. The third and still greater level of responsibility is *foreseeability*. Here you are considered responsible, directly or indirectly, for any failure that you might have foreseen, even though it was not part of your goal, and was not therefore part of personal causation. For example, in the project, you were given an unrealistically short timeframe, and an unusually small budget with which to implement this type of programme, and you knew that these factors would cause problems. Attributions about your responsibility for the failure would be made at this level. The legal equivalent is negligence.

The fourth and most damning level of responsibility is *intention*. At this level, only what you intended, is perceived as having its source in you. You are held responsible for outcomes which were part of your goal in acting. For example, if you deliberately overspent and intentionally delayed holding meetings, you are fully responsible for the failure, and not just causally implicated in it. Legally, you would be charged with criminal responsibility. Heider's fifth level, that of *justification*, reduces responsibility somewhat. Your action, admittedly intentional, is attributed to internal or external causes, and thus observers may attribute less responsibility to you. For example, even if you ran over budget and over time on purpose, you might have done it to prevent something worse happening, for example, the computer system not actually working properly when finally installed. Or, that you were ordered to carry out the project under these time and budget constraints, by the managing director who disagreed with the whole programme and wanted it to fail. The legal equivalent is legal justification, excuses and mitigation (e.g. duress). All these judgements of your actions by observers are based on an assessment of whether, 'You could have done otherwise'. The practical implication of this hierarchy is that, should you find yourself at level four, you should attempt to provide your observers with information about yourself and your error, which would lead them to redefine your responsibility as being lower down the hierarchy (3, 2 or ideally 1) or, failing that, provide them with reasons to see you as a 'five'. As an effective blame-manager, you will seek to persuade others to accept your own attributional definition of the error situation.

But why would others want to blame you for the failure anyway? When a serious error is committed and a loss occurs, you may be blamed. The blamer may be doing this because they believe that such a major event could not have occurred by accident, and that it was avoidable. However, you can seek to dissuade them from acting this way. Through blaming you, they want to stress the difference between themselves and you. The more that you manage to project an impression of your similarity on them, the less they will blame you, because others will start to perceive you to be similar to them. They will only blame you if they can justify their blame by citing widely accepted criteria for blame assignment. So, in these circumstances, say to them, 'I did not intend or foresee the consequences, and I can prove it'. In doing this, you are stressing your lack of both foresight and intentionality. Research suggests that you will be blamed more for any resulting loss if you over-stepped your authority, than if you had remained within it. Additionally, if you happen to possess knowledge, skill or other resources that a group or company needs, and which are not easily replaced then, whatever the error with which you were involved, you will not be blamed since you are a valued team member. Finally, if you acted as part of a group, rather than autonomously, you will receive still less blame, because it is difficult to allocate blame to individuals in a group. In these circumstances, the blame moves up the hierarchy, and observers will blame your boss.

While the impression management tactic of *basking* concerns your relations with people, *excuses* relate to events. These are explanations in which you admit that the disruptive act was, bad, wrong or inappropriate, but you dissociate or distance yourself from it. Heider's hierarchy provides a framework for inventing these. For example, you could deny any personal responsibility for the problem ('I was only following orders'), or diminish the dimensions of the problem ('It's not really so bad'). Excuses attribute failure for poor performance to external causes. Since making excuses may be a frequent occurrence, it is useful to look at the different types available to choose from. *Anticipatory excuses* foresee a problem, and you activate them before the negative act actually occurs (Smith *et al.*, 1982). If the problem is an impeding project failure, you can announce it to all around. You say that, 'Due to circumstances, it looks as if the objective will not be attained'. If you are having to do something unpleasant, e.g. cut staff overtime, expenses or benefits, give the excuse before you do it, and the reasoning behind it. *Retrospective excuses* point out to others that your failure is uncharacteristic. The tactic is most effective when you have an existing, positive image and reputation. This can form the basis for subsequent good excuses. What you are doing psychologically, is disavowing, or splitting off a transient or circumscribed 'bad self', from the more enduring or encompassing 'good self'. You are saying that this is not the 'real me'. If you acquire a positive reputation, it is more likely to remain untarnished despite negative outcomes (Tetlock and Boettger, 1989).

The *linkage excuse* convinces others that you had nothing to do with the mistake. An absolute denial is frequently, although not always, the best choice. A weakening of the link between you and the act may be sufficient. Such weakening is achieved by sharing the blame with others – 'five other team members were involved' (Snyder *et al.*, 1983); by disavowing any intention to do harm – 'the computers crashed just as we were changing over to the new, more efficient system'; by claiming the harm was unforeseeable ('It was a freak accident'); or by implying the outcome was uncontrollable – 'The software was faulty, giving us no advance warning'. You could also try heavy-handed scapegoating or blaming, which is especially useful if the mistake or problem was unforeseeable or uncontrollable – 'the computer manufacturer did not inform us that the system had failed in other plants' (Weiner *et al.*, 1987). In some very specific circumstances, the best tactic is to admit to a lesser error, while denying the major one.

You can try a class of excuses called *justifications*. These are explanations in which you do take responsibility for the action, but deny that it has had the negative qualities that others attribute to it (Higgins and Snyder, 1989; Snyder and Higgins, 1988; Tedeschi and Riess, 1981). You can use justifications which assert the positive value of a foolish act, in the face of claims to the contrary – 'I dropped out of college to gain work experience' (Scott and Lyman, 1968). Justifications capitalize on the fact that some mistakes are more negative than others. You can use a favourable contrast to make your negative outcome look better than it is. Finally, *information filtering*, the so-called being economical with the truth, involves avoiding mentioning potentially unfavourable information, but not actually lying: e.g. mentioning only the exams taken and passed, but not those taken and failed (Schmitt, 1976). It can be used in a wide variety of circumstances, especially when it is clear that you are in the wrong. In such situations, you may be obliged to explain your failure. Drummond (1991) suggests a number of ways of getting yourself off the hook. Start by emphasizing that your plan was soundly conceived, drawing upon any of the ten justifications shown in Table 6.1 and concluding by reducing your listeners' tension by ending on more optimistic

Table 6.1 *Justifying your failure*

1 'What was right (or would not have been right) two years ago is very different from what is appropriate today.'

2 'When those changes were made, never at any time did I say the process was complete.'

3 'I have reconsidered my decision in the light of . . .'

4 'Had this been known at the time . . .'

5 'This could not have been predicted when the original decision was made.'

6 'What I said/meant was . . .'

7 'There was never any commitment to . . .'

8 'The original decision had to be taken quickly, much more quickly than I would have liked.'

9 'It was always recognized that this would be a temporary move.'

10 'Since then, new opportunities have increased, and it would be foolish to ignore them, even if it means revising earlier policies.'

Source: Drummond (1991), *Power: Creating It, Using It,* London: Kogan Page figures than first released. All government spokespeople are experts on excuses, and it is instructive to analyse the excuses that they give in the media after some problem occurs.

Blaming and excuses are facilitated by keeping written records which are a useful defensive strategy. It is not what you do, but what you can prove to have done, that counts. Whenever a disaster strikes that involves you in some way, it is helpful to have a copy of your letter warning somebody that this might happen. Your documents should always be composed of supporting documentary evidence with a future reader in mind. Remember that others will be composing their documents against you, and the last communication usually wins. So respond to others' memos (or lack of them) with your own. This puts the onus on someone else to do something and it absolves you from responsibility ('Since you did not phone to confirm, I assumed the meeting had been cancelled'). Documenting such writing is tiresome and time-consuming, but must be done for important issues where failure to have a written record can have serious personal consequences. Since documents are more difficult to retract or deny than speech, compose them with care and without emotion. Write a draft, and then sleep on it. Use the lawyer's criteria of how would it sound in court and, 'If in doubt, leave it out'.

COMPLAINING

There is one other impression management technique that needs to be mentioned, and that is complaining. Complaining is defined by Kowalski (2002) as the verbal expression of a subjective experience of dissatisfaction, distaste or unhappiness. It is done, in his view, because it helps you as the complainer to regulate the impression others form of you. It offers two ways of meeting such self-presentational goals. First, it allows you to convey to others information about your personal attributes. For example, because complaining implies that a person, product or service, is not up to your standard, it shows others that you are discriminating in your tastes. Second, it allows you to save face in front of others. For example, complaining about your tiredness provides you with an excuse for your poor performance. This is best done pre-emptively ('I don't think I'll do well in this exam, I haven't been able to sleep well this week'). Kowalski lists a number of other useful relational, interpersonal and financial-material benefits which are worth considering. Complaining about a person with whom you are dissatisfied may change your perception of that person, and produce a more positive affect for you. For example, by objectively examining your flatmate's annoying habit of smoking, may lead you to reframe their behaviour (they are stressed), thereby reducing your negative feelings towards that person. Finally, in line with the matching principle, which is a recurring theme throughout this book, if you complain about something that your influencee also dislikes, then they will be drawn into a closer relationship with them, in your capacity as the complainer-influencer. Whenever using impression management tactics, it is important to ensure that the desired image is conveyed, while an undesired image is avoided. Studies have now found that women use impression management strategies as much as men, but do not feel as comfortable in doing so, in order to demonstrate their commitment to their organization (Singh and Vinnicombe, 2001; Bolino and Turnley, 2003).

INFLUENCING YOUR APPRAISAL

Even after you have been appointed, your interviews will not end. Life is one long series of interviews. People are constantly sizing you up – before you have got the job, when you are being considered for promotion; at significant milestones, and during normal daily conversations. The next most important formal assessment is likely to be your appraisal interview. The types of staff appraisal vary considerably and some are no more than general chats. Despite the fact that it is often difficult for an organization to assess realistically how an employee performs in a job, both promotion and salary increases continue to be awarded to those who are rated highly in their staff appraisal (Gardner and Martinko, 1988; Giacalone, 1985; Liden and Mitchell, 1988; Ralston, 1985; Wayne and Ferris, 1990; Zalesny, 1990; Dulebohn and Ferris, 1999).

Despite what the human resources press claim, it appears that managers' primary concerns are to use the appraisal process to motivate and reward subordinates, and help them (the managers) to survive in the company. Managerial discretion and effectiveness, and not accuracy, are the watchwords. Research suggested that managers did not allow excessively accurate ratings to cause them problems, and used the appraisal process to their own advantage. The study found that political considerations were nearly always a part of the executive evaluation process. This was because executives had to live with their subordinates in a day-to-day relationship; because the formal appraisal resulted in a permanent written record; and because it impacted on the subordinate's career, advancement and salary. These, and other factors influence the political culture of every organization, and all act to inflate appraisal ratings.

The political dimension of appraisal, plus an organizational situation in which performance criteria are vague, ambiguous or subjectively evaluated, provide many opportunities for the skilled influencer. First, there will be much opportunity for you to engage in influencing behaviour in general, and politicking in particular. Try to influence the criteria against which you are judged, by selecting those that will favour you. Use company situations, techniques and your own talents, to interpret your experience for your appraiser at your annual appraisal. Second, managers tend to incorporate non-performance factors into the assessment of their staff (Hater and Bass, 1988). These include, 'liking'; 'perceived similarity of beliefs, values and attitudes'; and 'extent to which subordinates think and make decisions like the boss, and support the boss on important matters' (Ross and Ferris, 1981). You therefore have to pay attention to any salient cues regarding your manager's expectations, preferences and social approval, since these can become surrogate criteria. Third, in situations of ambiguity, appraisers will focus on employee behaviour, and not necessarily on the results that they have achieved (Ferris et al., 1989). Some companies even evaluate their staff on their efforts (Pfeffer, 1981). Wayne and Kacmar's (1991) study indicated that impression management skills improved performance rating in appraisals independently of actual performance.

You can use impression management to improve your appraisal rating. If your assessment includes a preliminary self-evaluation, rate yourself lower than you think, so as to appear excessively self-critical. This gains praise from your supervisor. This is because we impute characteristics of humility to this strategy, and egoism to inflated ratings. We are socialized to react more favourably to a humble person than to an arrogant one (Teel, 1978). There will always be a tendency for your boss to rate your performance more highly and thus upgrade your rating, in order to appear more successful herself (Sims et al., 1987; Greenberg, 1990). Some organizations attempt to replace appraisal vagueness and subjectivity, by assessing employees against pre-set goals or objectives in areas such as profit, turnover, machine down-time and so on. These are agreed and written down at the end of the previous year's appraisal interview. For appraisees, the problem with this is twofold. First, their performance may not be wholly or even mainly within their own control. Second, even if it is, it may be below that required. What prescriptions does research offer to best deal with these situations?

It reveals that employees who themselves set the highest goals with their managers receive the highest performance evaluations, irrespective of whether or not they have achieved the agreed goals! 'People tend to judge a man or a woman by their goals, by what they are trying to do, and not necessarily by how well they succeed.' What is happening here is that you are being evaluated on your intentions and values (which you can control), rather than on outcomes or even behaviours (which you cannot). Your personal work effort, as reflected in the type of objectives that you set, often becomes a substitute for your actual performance (Dossett and Greenberg, 1981; Ferris and Porac, 1984). The psychological explanation is that the mere setting of high goals creates an initial impression of the subordinate in the minds of the boss that the employee is doing the right things, and that they are ambitious, hard-working, energetic and effective performers. This is another version of the primacy effect in operation. Once that impression has been established, it remains there, despite later evidence that may show that these high aspirations have not been achieved. The effect is so powerful, that the performance ratings secured by high goal *non-achievers* are higher than ratings obtained by low or medium goal-achievers.

Should you take the initiative in specifying a performance goal as suggested, or wait for your boss to give you one? Research evidence is mixed here. There is an argument for taking the initiative and setting your own goals. Setting a specific, high performance goal communicates to your boss an impression of yourself as a person with ambition, who is willing to expend effort. When you suggest a relatively high goal, even if the goal finally agreed with your boss is lower, your boss will still rate you as more committed to goal attainment than someone who does not set their own goals, or who sets them lower. This will lead them to inflate your subsequent performance rating. A counter-view is that you should wait, and accept the goal assigned to you by your boss, rather than suggesting your own. The reasoning here is that accepting an assigned goal from your boss capitalizes on the fact that as human beings, we like people whose values and beliefs appear to be similar to our own (Byrne, 1971). In this situation, concur with your boss that the goal which she has chosen for you is an appropriate one, and avoid giving the impression that you will be wanting something from her later in return (Jones et al., 1963). Pay attention to what you are being assigned without objecting, as this is a form of your giving consent (Salancik, 1977a). Commit yourself to goal accomplishment. If you exert effort towards the goal, you will be viewed as more motivated than a subordinate who does not accept job challenges (Campion and Lord, 1982; Huber et al., 1985, 1988).

Irrespective of whether you choose your own goal or have it assigned to you by your boss, use ingratiation at the appraisal interview. Ask your boss for specific advice or instructions on ways of meeting your agreed objectives, even if you do not need such advice. By proffering you advice, your boss makes a commitment to the achievement of your goals, or at least to giving you a high performance rating. Subordinates who seek and follow the advice of their managers are viewed more positively than those who either do not ask for assistance, or who do not follow the advice given. As job objectives and appropriate job behaviours become more ambiguous, external legitimacy becomes more important than objective measurement. In the end however, 'nothing succeeds like success', and your actual performance will ultimately define your social identity within the organization, and will set the tone for your subsequent interactions.

If you have failed to achieve your objectives very badly, and there is little chance of changing your boss's perception of your performance, you should opt for a damage limitation strategy. Make it difficult for him to punish you for your failure, without feeling guilty about doing so. By using some of the excuses and justifications described earlier, your boss will attribute less responsibility to you personally, will be less personal in his criticism, and will generally treat you less harshly (Wood and Mitchell, 1981; Giacalone and Pollard, 1987). If you apologize, that is, show remorse after you have done something wrong, this also affects how hard he will be on you, irrespective of whether or not he thinks that you were responsible for your poor performance. Finally, you could make apologies in advance, or make self-deprecating statements that evoke sympathy from your boss (Goffman, 1971).

Another option is to replace measures of outcome with measures of process. A *measure of process* refers to your efforts or behaviours. Coming into work early, leaving late, being busy in between, are all measures of process. In contrast, measures of outcome refer to what you actually achieve in the job – the number of sales made, or the percentage of costs saved. The two are only vaguely related. Busy workers may achieve little, while less active ones can achieve goals. An important way in which process and objectives both differ from outcome is in terms of personal control. A successful outcome often depends on factors outside your control, while you can influence the choice of objectives and decide how busy you are going to look. In bad times, when your environment is unfavourable and hence when your outcome measures might suggest poor performance, you should opt for process measures. In contrast, in good times, choose the outcome measures when these are easier to achieve. However, in this latter case, ensure that you are only held accountable for the performance that is under your control.

Studies have shown that when women are less known to an evaluator, the perception of them is likely to be negative (Lott, 1992). However, the opposite is not true (Thomas, 1987). In appraisals, women were more frequently described as 'less competent, logical and mature'; and their performance was seen as meriting fewer recommendations and less praise. Studies suggest that women are less likely to overestimate their performance than their males colleagues, and tend to rate themselves lower than either men or their bosses (Fletcher, 1999). They give lower estimates of their performance or ability. This has been attributed to gender differences in self-presentation rather than self-confidence (Daubman and Sigall, 1997). It thus seems that female modesty is impeding female progress up the organization. Finally, how should you present yourself non-verbally at your appraisal? De Groot and Motowidlo (1999) confirm that the majority of effective non-verbal cues described in Chapter 2 are relevant to the appraisal situation. They list physical attractiveness, smiling, gazing in the interviewer's direction, using impressive hand movements, and leaning towards rather than away from the appraiser.

INFLUENCING YOUR PROMOTION

Promotional opportunities are scarce organizational rewards, which are highly valued by employees. They become the focus of acquisitional struggles, in which individuals use influencing tactics to improve their chances (Thomas, 2003). The traditional view that objective and rational criteria are used in promotion has been widely challenged (Coates and Pelligrin, 1957). While, officially, a company-wide appraisal system is there to identify and assess potential for promotion, few managers see it as being related to promotion. 'Managerial potential for career development [within the company] was evaluated by a process of social selection rather than any independent assessment of aptitudes, characteristics, skills or learning abilities' (Barlow, 1989). The ability to influence higher-level gatekeepers who controlled access to promotion was found to be a more effective means of being promoted than by getting a good appraisal.

A number of Machiavellian self-aggrandizement strategies can be used to create an image of yourself in the mind of your manager as a person who is valuable and promotable. One strategy is to job-hunt regularly and generate outside job offers. Despite what they say, most companies do not distribute pay on merit, since they do not want the trouble of defending pay decisions based on largely unobservable, and subjective criteria. Except at the very top, the pay difference between the average and outstanding performers is small. To gain a significant pay rise, you need to generate outside (lucrative) job offers which you do not accept, but which will provide independent evidence of your 'market value' to top management inside your company. You can then use that external evidence to justify your large, internal salary increase, and ask your organization to match what others have offered you. Senior managers who make assessments for selection, appraisal and promotion are reluctant to use their own internal judgement and standards about people whom they cannot observe on a daily basis throughout the entire week. Instead, unsure about their own ability to make such key decisions, they rely on external cues. In this situation, external visibility replaces internal competence as the criterion for career advancement and reward decisions. However, be prepared to have them call your bluff with respect to your alternative job offer.

Wayne *et al.* (1997) found that a manager's liking of and perceived similarity to their subordinate affected their assessment of the subordinate's interpersonal skills. Subordinates, who received the highest performance ratings in the appraisals, also rated highest on interpersonal skills possession by their bosses. Perceived similarity had the greatest effect on performance rating. Moreover, perceived similarity and interpersonal skills had the greatest effect on promotability which, itself, was associated with salary progression. Salary progression was found to be related to assessments of promotability rather than to performance ratings. The authors conclude that employee potential is more important than current performance.

Organizational hierarchy and culture play an important role. One study focused on the growing importance of 'flat' or 'organic' organizations which have fewer hierarchical ladder rungs (Davies, 1988). Within them, more emphasis was placed on group and team-based working. In teams and self-directed work groups, influencing one's peers was crucial. Church and Waclawski (1999) studied which supervisor behaviours in such teams were perceived to be the most effective. These became the criteria for the assessment of group members. The researchers found that superiors identified establishing good relations with upper-level executives; building supportive relationships rather than remaining distant

138

or impersonal; and knowing how to clarify an issue and keep focused on important things, to be the key ones. This study highlights the importance of self-awareness; of building good relationships with superiors and peers (especially cross-functionally); and of promoting an open and interactive working style with others, especially team members, if you want to be promoted.

On the organizational culture side, another study contrasted those companies that emphasized the importance of hierarchy, and a willingness to adhere to the authority of others (labelled 'high vertical collectivism'), with those which stressed personal equality and interdependence over merit and competition (labelled 'high horizontal collectivism'). It was found that in the former, candidates for promotion who resembled their managers in terms of perceiving, interpreting and responding to events, were more likely to be judged as potential effective leaders and promoted. In those that emphasized the latter culture, it was those employees who resembled their peers, who were judged to be most suitable for promotion to leadership posts (Schaubroek and Lam, 2002). The message is become aware of the company's culture and adapt yourself as required if you wish to be promoted.

Performance in organizations is socially defined, and hence it is difficult to attribute success to one person when they work in teams. Since so much work in an organization gets done through teams, being seen as a 'good team player' is an important selection criterion. However, *only* being seen as such, can be the kiss of death if you want to be upwardly mobile. Lasch (1979) reports the use of the technique of 'antagonistic co-operation'. This involves a person being unfailingly friendly with their co-workers, and co-operating smoothly with them on joint projects, while at the same time, collecting negative information about their personal lives or professional competence which could be used to their own career advantage later. Just how Machiavellian are you?

INFLUENCING YOUR BOSS

Being a good subordinate helps your promotion, but which behaviours lead a boss to judge their subordinates to be effective? Downs and Conrad (1982) identified what managers considered the most valued attributes of a subordinate. These are summarized in rank order in Table 6.2. The first percentage column refers to managers' assessments in the role as bosses, while the second column refers to their assessments of what they believed that their own bosses valued. A recent study suggested that, as an employee, you should come over to your boss as an innovator rather than as oriented to the status quo. However, it noted that those who critically challenged the existing situation without offering innovative alternatives experienced lower career success (Seibert et al., 2001). This suggests that speaking out and being critical in front of senior management can enhance your career, but only if you offer constructive ideas along with your criticisms.

139

Table 6.2 *Characteristics of effective subordinates*

Specific communication behaviour	Managers as superior (%)	Managers as subordinates (%)
1 *Communicates clearly*: articulate; explicit; uses illustrations; writes and speaks clearly.	16.0	12.0
2 *Provides feedback*: confirms understanding; responds freely; exposes feelings.	8.3	11.8
3 *Communication timely*: on time; prompt; current; up-to-date.	7.7	4.0
4 *Is brief*: succinct; gets to the point; concise; does not waste time.	7.7	7.0
5 *Listens carefully* and pays attention.	7.5	13.2
6 *Is factual and thorough*: researches topic; provides adequate detail; does not confuse inferences with observations; highlights critical information; does not filter bad news.	7.0	11.8
7 *Asks questions*: requests details; seeks clarification.	5.3	11.8
8 *Checks perception*: paraphrases; re-states discussions in own words; repeats back assignments.	4.8	4.2
9 *Volunteers substantive input*: acts as sounding board; provides new ideas and relations; recommends; willing to approach me; keeps channels open by volunteering upward communication; discusses plan of action; attempts to solve problems.	4.2	4.2
10 *Anticipates superior's needs*: gives me no surprises; informs me to prevent problems; does not bother me with trivia.	3.8	2.9
11 *Follows instructions*: takes guidance and direction; carries out orders; follows through.	3.7	3.8
12 *Initiates communication*: willing to start communication, no need to drag things out of him; eager to contribute ideas; seeks direction.	3.1	2.1
13 *Confronts*: verifies; candid; not afraid to disagree; expresses disagreement.	2.9	2.6
14 *Liaison*: relays to other shifts; is a link in indirect corporate communication; effective intermediary; uses proper channels.	1.5	2.0
15 *Organizes well*.	1.0	–
16 *Takes notes*: writes summaries that I initiate; keeps records.	0.5	–
17 *Prepares*: investigates and plans; prepares well; sets goals; defines problems; sets agendas.	0.2	0.7
18 *Follows structure*: uses chain of command.	0.1	0.7

Source: Downs and Conrad, 1982

Do you have to rely exclusively on yourself to communicate your potential to your boss, or can you use friends or colleagues to assist you? Self-presentation concerns the control and dissemination of self-relevant information. Additionally, there is the presentation of information concerning others, which can be called *recommendation*. This is equally important in the workplace for two reasons. First, recommending another person who will later benefit from it, will boost the recommender's own mood, self-esteem, sense of self-efficacy, and will gain them the beneficiary's thanks, admiration and respect. Second, this can result in the recommender's own image being enhanced by the beneficiary of his comments, or by some other individual. Hence, the recommender, and the beneficiary of their recommendation both gain. Schlenker and Britt (1999) studied whether friends would recognize each others' need to impress someone else, and whether they would provide them with the social support to do so. Translated to the workplace, the results suggest that friends and colleagues will indeed be prepared to impression manage for each other (recommend), to achieve desired outcomes. However, they have to be told what is needed and from whom. Additional findings were that those friends who used the impression management technique of basking (enhancing one's own reputation by associating with successful others), were also willing to promote their own friends to produce the same effect to help make their friends successful.

These findings reinforce the Dutch admiral's story, where two junior officers in the Dutch navy made a pact with each other that whenever one attended a naval social function, he would make a point of talking in glowing terms about the merits of the other, and vice versa. This pact was revealed by them on the day they were both promoted to the rank of admiral, and were the youngest naval personnel to achieve that position (Deal and Kennedy, 1982). They had influenced the perceptions of senior naval and civil personnel who were influential in decisions concerning promotions. Thus this was a case of 'believing was seeing' rather than 'seeing was believing'. The implication of this story and the earlier study, is that one needs a network of work colleagues who are favourably disposed to you; who are willing to 'talk you up' in front of strangers; who must be told what you want them to say; and to whom you should stress the importance of doing so.

IMPRESSION MANAGEMENT WARNING

Will your attempts at using impression management skills to portray a desirable image of yourself to others be successful, or will you inadvertently create an undesirable image? For example, while wanting to appear dedicated, might you unintentionally come across as superior and patronizing? Turnley and Bolino (2001) examined the effect of self-monitoring on success and failure in impression management. Self-monitoring encompasses both the ability to use impression

141

management and to execute successfully impression management strategies. A high self-monitor is someone who is aware of the image that they are conveying to others, and who is able to change perspectives, behaviours and attitudes to fit different situations. High self-monitors also manipulate information to portray positive images of them, and are attentive to others' behaviour in order to analyse their influencees effectively. In their study, the authors found that high self-monitors who used ingratiation, self-promotion and exemplification, had more chance of being judged to be likeable, competent and dedicated by other group members. However, low self-monitors were likely to be perceived as sycophantic, conceited and egoistic when they employed these same tactics, as shown in Table 6.3. The study reminds us that there are risks involved in using impression management tactics. However, these can be reduced by enhancing your self-monitoring skills which will provide you with greater control over the image that you wish to project.

Table 6.3 Representative, desired and undesired images through impression management

Impression management strategy	Representative behaviours	Desired image	Undesired image
Ingratiation	Flattery, favour-doing	Likeable	Sycophantic
Self-promotion	Performance claims, boasting	Competent	Conceited
Exemplification	Going beyond call of duty, appearing busy	Dedicated	Feels superior
Supplication	Asking for help, playing dumb	Needy	Lazy
Intimidation	Making threats, displaying anger	Intimidating	Bossy
Complaining	Expresses dissatisfaction	Discriminating, not responsible	Bad tempered, unco-operative

Source: From Turnley and Bolino (2001). Reprinted with kind permission of Lawrence Erlbaum Associates.

142

Chapter 7

Motivation and influencing

The secret of getting others to do as you want them to do, lies in your ability to penetrate and understand the hidden world of self-interest that each of us carries around within himself.

Theodore V. Houser

INTRODUCTION

The understanding of another person's needs is at the heart of every successful influencing activity. In the first chapter, we built upon Zuker's (1991) definition of influence as, 'the ability to affect another's attitudes, beliefs or behaviours – seen only in its effect – without using coercion or formal position, and in a way that makes influencees believe that they are acting in their own best interests'. It is the last part of this definition upon which this chapter will focus. People will do things for you, and feel good about it, provided they believe that they are acting in their own best interests and are achieving their personal goals. This is in fact a definition of motivation. Drzdeck *et al.* (1991) go as far as to define influencing as the discovery of another person's needs, wants and desires, and then the presentation of a solution which will satisfy those desires. Once you have identified these needs, and have shown your influencee how your suggestion or proposal can meet them, they will accede to your request and will support you, because they see themselves as acting in their *own* interests, and not yours. This perspective contrasts with the way many of us attempt to persuade another person. This is encapsulated in the phrase, 'would you do me a favour?'. To be an effective influencer, you need to show the influencee how, by agreeing to your request, they will be doing themselves a favour!

MOTIVATION NEEDS

Psychologists have conducted extensive studies of human motivation during the last fifty or so years. They agree that motivation is a decision-making process

143

through which an individual chooses desired outcomes and sets in motion behaviours appropriate to acquiring them. This is depicted in Figure 7.1. What they disagree agree about, is what is contained in the box labelled 'Needs' in that figure. Recent research has provided highly complex and sophisticated theories. By contrast, the influencer in the field requires a theory of motivation which is understandable, portable and practical, even if it lacks sophistication. Influencers are seeking only to 'nudge up the averages' of their successful influencing attempts, not get a doctorate in the subject.

Abraham Maslow developed one particularly usable theory of motivation in the 1940s. He identified five human needs, which he listed in the form of an ascending hierarchy. These are shown in Table 7.1. While succeeding motivation theories may have developed and extended Maslow's (1943) work, his five needs hierarchy theory is still suitable for the influencer. These various needs represent the *hot buttons* that influencers can push in order to gain the support of the influencee. The main task here is to ensure that you push the correct

Figure 7.1 *The cycle of motivation*

Table 7.1 *Maslow's hierarchy of needs*

Level	Need
1 Self-actualization needs:	For development of capability to the fullest potential.
2 Esteem needs:	For strength, achievement, adequacy, confidence, independence, and for reputation, prestige, recognition, attention, importance, appreciation, high self-evaluation based on capability, and respect from others.
3 Social or affiliational needs:	For relationships, affection, giving and receiving love, for feelings of belonging.
4 Safety or security needs:	Freedom from threat from the environment, for shelter, security, order, predictability and for an organized world.
5 Physiological needs:	For sunlight, sex, food, water and similar outcomes basic to human survival.

144

button. Maslow argued that a need became active, that is, a button became 'hot', only when a lower-level need had been satisfied. A starving person would have little concern for security (level 4) until they had satisfied their hunger need (level 5). Our needs engender behaviours which achieve goals, that fulfil our needs. Thus, a person with a need for esteem will study hard to gain a university qualification that will increase their own self-esteem and secure the esteem of others.

IDENTIFYING INFLUENCEES' NEEDS

Research suggests that managers are not as good at judging employees' motives as they think they are. People from all walks of life seem to misunderstand consistently what drives employee motivation (Morse, 2003). Accurately assessing an influencee's needs or motives is vital. Successful influencing takes account of not only what the influencee says, but also of their probable reason for saying it. People have hidden or unstated needs, wants and desires, which are their actual driving forces. Discovering these can be problematic since individuals may cover them up. There are several ways of discovering your influencee's needs. The first guiding principle is that all people, at all times, are seeking to meet their current primary need. By observing how they behave, what they devote their energies to and what they avoid doing, you can discover their current driving need. For example, the manager who delegates all tasks that she typically does alone to her subordinates and instead gets herself onto project teams, voluntarily attends meetings and socializes with colleagues after work, can be judged to be meeting her social or love needs. People move up and down Maslow's hierarchy constantly, and even a rumour of possible redundancies, may make this manager more concerned with her security needs than with her social needs. However, observing an individual and getting to know them, will make your task of assessment easier.

A second way is to deduce their needs from speaking to them about their life and work. Lord (2002) described one such study which sought to identify what motivated middle-aged to elderly engineers in order to persuade them not to retire. If observing or talking to them does not reveal peoples' needs, you can simply ask your influencee what their needs currently are. Ask them what they are looking for in a job, a car, a hobby, a home; or how they decided when they last bought a similar product or service. Get them to state their needs, requirements, priorities or general objectives. Use this information to craft your influencing strategy. This is important because the influencee will be attracted to those aspects of your idea which meet their current needs. Unless you know what these are, your proposal will not appeal to them, even though it may to you. Salespeople do this by asking prospective customers to describe the last time they bought a particular item, what they looked for and why. The prospect's ensuing description will highlight which needs they hold to be paramount. Of

145

course, since needs change, the salesperson has to check whether the same order of priority still operates or if it has changed, and in what way.

MEETING INFLUENCEES' NEEDS

Cohen and Bradford (1989, 1991) saw influencing as a process of give-and-take, in which people co-operated, giving certain things, in the expectation of receiving something of equal value in return eventually. Underpinning this notion is the law of reciprocity to which we shall return intermittently throughout the book. Reciprocity is the almost universal belief that people should be paid back for what they do. That one good or bad turn deserves another. Over time, such repeated exchanges should balance. This process is based on four precepts. First, that of mutual respect, where one must assume that the other person is competent. Second, openness, that talking truthfully to them, giving them the information they need, will help them to help you better, and vice versa. Third, trust, assuming that one party will not take any action that will hurt the other, thereby obviating the need to hold back on provision of information. Finally, there is the precept of mutual gain, that is, planning how both you and they can win. Unless this is done, your alliance will break up. Cohen and Bradford classified all transactions between people in organizations in terms of the exchange of five different *currencies*. They labelled these inspiration, task, position, relationship and personal.

Inspiration currencies

These provide a person with meaning for the work that they do, and are of three types. The *vision* currency gives the influencee the chance to become involved in a task that has great significance for the unit, organization, customer or society. The influencer describes an exciting vision of a company's or department's future, and explains how the influencee's co-operation will help achieve it. Steve Jobs at Apple Computer did not ask his people to design or build personal computers. Instead, he invited them to contribute to a revolution in how people communicated with others. By making your influencee believe in your vision, you can overcome their personal objections. This currency meets their self-actualization need to accept a reality beyond themselves, and their belonging need for participation in a grand scheme. The *excellence* currency is the opportunity to do something really well, and to have the chance to take pride in having accomplished important work of genuine excellence. It meets the self-actualization need for the fulfilment of potential. Finally, the *moral and ethical correctness* currency involves doing what is 'right' by a higher standard than efficiency. Your influencees may act for what they perceive to be ethical, moral or altruistic reasons. They will respond positively to your request if they feel that they are doing what

146

is 'right'. Their self-image leads them to prefer to be personally inconvenienced, than to do anything that they feel is inappropriate. By letting them feel good about themselves, virtue becomes its own reward. This contributes to their need for self-actualization.

Task currencies

These currencies focus on the ability to perform an assigned work task, and on the satisfactions that arise from such task completion. There are six of them. When resources are scarce or difficult to obtain, the offer of *new resources* in the form of budget increases, extra people, space or equipment will be a valued currency. It can meet an influencee's esteem need to complete their task, and thus obtain an accompanying sense of achievement. *Challenge and learning* currencies are gained through being given the opportunity to do tasks that increase skills and abilities. Working on a task that stretches a person is highly valued by those for whom the challenge is its own reward. To influence a subordinate, offer them membership of a problem-solving group or task team, or delegate challenging parts of your own job. This meets their self-actualization needs for intellectual stimulation and creativity.

The *assistance* currency relates to providing others with help with their existing projects or unwanted tasks. The influencee will value the chance to have the pressure taken off them, and will respond positively to anyone providing such relief. It meets both the belonging need of sharing and working with another, and the esteem need of achievement to get the task completed satisfactorily. *Task support* involves giving subtle or overt support. All new projects require the support of others since, by definition, they generate opposition. This currency involves behind-the-scenes promotion, putting in a good word with colleagues and those higher up. It is offering to be the 'friend at court', who makes a public stand on an issue in support of its proposer when they are under fire. It meets the safety need of protection. The *rapid response* currency is the offer of a quick response time by you to the influencee, on any matter. It will be valuable for an influencee to know that you will respond quickly to their request. Members of the organization who are in charge of much needed resources soon discover that helping someone to avoid a queue builds valuable credit that can be drawn on later. It is useful even if you do have spare capacity, in which case you simulate the impression of being overloaded. The guarantee of a rapid response meets the needs of security and safety. Finally, the *information* currency offers the influencee access to organizational as well as technical knowledge. The emphasis here is upon access. Since knowledge is power, some people value information that can shape the performance of their unit. Possessors of such information are more powerful, and are more highly regarded by others. It can thus contribute to meeting their esteem needs.

147

Position currencies

This set of currencies enhances the influencee's position in the organization, and thus their ability to accomplish tasks and advance their career. They are of five types. *Recognition* currencies relate to the acknowledgement of effort, achievement or ability. Many people will acquiesce to requests if they feel that their contributions will be recognized. To influence, spread your recognition currency around widely. Share credit and spread the glory to others. Recognition meets the esteem need. As a currency, *visibility to those higher up*, is the chance to be known by senior, significant others in the organization. It is especially valued by ambitious, fast-track individuals in large organizations. If you can give them the opportunity to perform for, or be recognized by senior, powerful people, they will value that. Gaining such visibility can be a deciding factor in their securing future opportunities, information or promotion. Task force members often fight for the privilege of presenting their findings to senior management. Visibility meets the esteem need for exerting leadership.

Reputation currency is frequently neglected. Having a good reputation as competent and committed, can pave the way for many opportunities, while a bad reputation shuts a person out, and makes it difficult for them to perform. Good reputation people get invited to important meetings, are consulted on new projects, and are important to have 'on your side'. Ability is only marginally related to reputation, especially in large organizations. In these, there are only few senior managers who possess any direct knowledge of anyone's actual capabilities. A reputation is used as a surrogate indicator of potential. It carries potent consequences. For this reason, if you can offer to promote the positive reputation of others, for example, of your own manager, colleague or subordinate, by speaking well of them in the company of powerful others, it will meet their esteem need for competence, and enhance their career progress.

Insiderness and importance currency concerns securing centrality in information exchange and presence when important decisions are being made. It meets the belonging need for affiliation. For some, being on the inside and 'in the know' (for example, knowing who is ahead, who is in trouble and what top management's latest concerns are) may be valued for its own sake, irrespective of what might be done with the information so obtained. The appeal of this sometimes trivial information is that it is unavailable to outsiders. For some, being invited to important events is a way of gaining insider status. If your influencee values such a currency, use your network to develop wide-ranging relationships that can supply you with information to give them their regular 'fix'. If they value the ability to be associated with certain tasks, you might arrange this. These people use information possession and involvement in important decisions as a way of defining their status in the company. Finally, the *contacts* currency is the opportunity to create a network of people with whom relationships are established, so that whenever a need arises, contacts can be approached to explore mutually helpful transactions. For some, the chance to meet others is in itself a sufficient reward for being helpful to others, and will meet their belonging need for membership. For others, being able to call upon people in an emergency, can meet their safety need for security.

Relationship currencies

These are currencies which strengthen the relationship with another person, rather than focus on the achievement of organizational tasks. They are of three types. First, *acceptance and inclusion* involves giving the influencee the feeling that they are close to you – a friend, that can be valued. This is the offer of friendship. These people will be most receptive to those who offer them warmth and liking. This meets an individual's safety need for stability, as well as their belonging need for affection from others. Second, the *understanding* currency relates to having one's concerns and problems listened to. A sympathetic ear for people who are isolated or unsupported by their boss is valued. Most people value the chance to talk about their problems, especially if you as the listener are not involved and are distanced from the problem. Sympathetic listening meets the individual's safety need to experience a feeling of personal comfort. Finally, the *personal support* currency relates to the emotional backing that you can give to the influencee. By giving the person that support while they are stressed, upset or vulnerable, perhaps in the form of a thoughtful gesture, a kind word, or a hand-on-shoulder, will be appreciated. Such expressions of concern, provided that they are not misconstrued, can meet people's belonging need for acceptance.

Personal currencies

This class of currencies meet esteem and safety needs which relate to either task or interpersonal activity. There are four types. The *gratitude* currency, thanking a person, is another form of recognition or show of support. Those who make a point of being helpful to others value it. For their efforts, they are seeking a statement of appreciation from the receiver of their help, expressed in terms of thanks or deference. As a currency, it can be devalued if overused. It meets the esteem need of recognition. The *ownership and involvement* currency refers to influence over important tasks. This goes beyond Insiderness and Importance mentioned earlier, in that it is not just about being there, but also about involvement in the chosen decision. This meets the esteem need to exert leadership. The *self-concept* currency affirms the influencee's values and identity. It is being given the chance to demonstrate who you are, by what you do and with whom. Someone will agree to your request because of their cherished values, sense of identity and feelings of self-worth. You allow the person to gain these emotional benefits. For example, a company executive seconded to a charity to help them organize their business, will value the opportunity to live these values and beliefs. This meets their esteem need of confidence in themselves through being permitted to act out their values and beliefs. Finally the *comfort* currency relates to avoiding trouble, embarrassment, public fuss or confrontation. Some people are less interested in advancement, and more in being allowed to get on with their job with minimum disturbance. Protecting such individuals from outside disturbances meets their safety need for comfort.

The relationship between Maslow's hierarchy of human needs and Bradford and Cohen's twenty-one currencies is shown in Table 7.2. It will be seen that the latter's currencies focus on the middle levels of the needs hierarchy. However, as this book goes on to demonstrate, the needs listed at the extremities can also provide a potent motivation to action. Lewicki and Litterer (1985) note that even having identified your influencee's real needs, and having offered them an appropriate currency, you cannot assume that they will recognize its appeal. Prus (1989) argued that, stripped of their context and applications, the currencies that you have available to give to others, have no inherent value. The meanings attributed to them by your influencee will reflect their perspective, their ongoing exchange with other influencers and their anticipated lines of action. Influencees already pursue particular ideas on their own which have inherent meaning for them, and which are defined within their own frame of reference. Thus, to promote your currency offer, you have to define it as more favourable to the influencee, by relating it to their situation. Sell its benefits – explain how it realizes their interests, or solves their problem or meets their needs. You may have to change your influencee's frame of reference by getting them to take a different viewpoint or make a new interpretation.

TYPES OF EXCHANGE

Cohen and Bradford suggest three predominant types of exchange from which you could choose when asking for beyond-routine favours. First, there is the *compliance for mutual benefit exchange*. This is the least costly to you as an influencer, since the action requested is also to the influencee's benefit. For example, you have an idea which will speed up production, but which will require Bill to change his procedures. Because Bill will also benefit from the increased output, he will agree to it gladly. This is the most preferable type of exchange. The second is the *compensation of costs exchange*. This involves asking the influencee to cover the costs incurred for compliance with your wishes. This exchange works best when you as the influencer have specific resources that can compensate the influencee directly for any costs involved: for example, asking someone to take on extra duties, and providing them with additional support staff. To do this, you must control the relevant resources. Third, there is the *equivalent payment*

Table 7.2 *Maslow's hierarchy of needs and Cohen and Bradford's currencies of exchange*

Needs (Maslow)	Currency (Cohen and Bradford)
1 Self-actualization	
Fulfilment of potential	Excellence
Doing things for the challenge they offer	Challenge/learning
Intellectual stimulation	Challenge/learning
Creativity	Challenge/learning
Aesthetics	
Justice	Moral/ethical correctness
Acceptance of a reality	Vision
2 Esteem	
Leadership	Visibility
Achievement	New resources
	Assistance
Recognition	Recognition
Confidence	Self-concept
Competence	Reputation
Intelligence	Information
3 Social or love	
Affiliation	Insiderness/importance
Sharing	Assistance
Affection	Acceptance/inclusion
Acceptance	Personal support
Participation	Vision
	Ownership/involvement
Membership	Contacts
4 Safety	
Security	Contacts
Safety	Rapid response
Protection	Task support
Comfort	Understanding
	Comfort
Stability	Acceptance/inclusion
Neatness	
5 Physiological	
Hunger	
Thirst	
Sleep	
Health	
Physical well-being	
Sex	

exchange. This method offers something to your influencee which is at least as valuable as what you are requesting of them. Essentially this is barter. Whether made on the spot or in the future, your payment must be perceived as equivalent in value to that which you request. An exchange will take place provided that you and the other party can agree upon equivalent value. That is, that what you give them is equivalent to what they give you.

You can also use these same exchanges negatively. For example, in the case of mutual benefit, you can tell the influencee how not complying with your request will lead to negative consequences, both for you and for them. In the second situation, while their compliance will earn them compensation, their refusal would lead them to incur future costs. In the third situation, instead of paying in kind, you can make it clear to them how you will repay their refusal now, with a comparable future refusal to co-operate with them in the future. While the threat of negative consequences is less friendly, it may be necessary in certain difficult situations. For example, you want your colleague to sack a worker. You can explain how his failure to do so will affect both him and you (negative mutual benefit); or you can threaten to complain to his boss (negative compensated cost); or you might threaten to assign his project low priority (negative payment in kind). However, this really is a last-ditch approach, and should be avoided except in the most extreme circumstances, since people are more receptive to positive rather than to negative stimuli. Cohen and Bradford suggest an eight-step approach to the influencee:

1 *Assume the other person is a potential ally*. Doing otherwise automatically makes them an adversary which prevents your gaining an accurate understanding of their needs, and leads to misperception, stereotyping and miscommunication.

2 *Clarify what you want from your influencee*. Ask for something definite and concrete that achieves your objective. Start by asking for essentials and not extras, the latter will come later as you gain their support. Know what you are willing to trade off in order to get the minimum you need.

3 *Diagnose your influencee's world by identifying* what is important to your ally in terms of their needs, goals and concerns. Consider what costs they would incur if they acceded to your request.

4 *Assess your available currencies relative to your influencee's needs*, both now and in the future. People typically underestimate the resources that they have at their disposal and believe that they have little to offer others.

5 *Diagnose your relationship with the influencee*. Is it positive or negative? Do you have the necessary trust and credibility or does it need building up?

6 *Find something valuable enough to offer your ally* to meet their need, so as to effect an exchange.

152

7 *Decide on the appropriate form of exchange.* Will it be compliance to mutual benefit, compensation for costs or equivalent payment? Decide whether it will be positive or negative.

8 *Make the exchange.* Your approach will depend on how attractive the currency you have to offer is, how badly you want what the influencee has to give, the organization's unwritten rules, how explicit people are allowed to be in expressing their requests and wants, your existing relationship with the influencee and your willingness to stick your neck out.

Asking the appropriate person

You need to actually ask what you want from your influencee. This action step can cause an influencer difficulties. Ross (1989) offered many useful tips for asking. He stressed the need to ask the right person. This is defined as the one with the means and the desire to assist you. Ask someone who can and wants to say yes; who has the power and the motivation to get it for you. Avoid those who want to help but cannot, or can but do not want to. Find out who is best qualified to give you what you need and persuade that person. Do not be afraid to ask the top people with power, position or authority in the organization. Since these people often ask for help themselves, they will be willing and motivated to help you out. If your chosen influencee is successful or prominent, you may wish to approach an intermediary to ask on your behalf. If that intermediary is a secretary, ask for her by name, explain your purpose, flatter her and get her on your side. Remember, you are helping her to do her job of protecting her boss's time, while bringing matters of concern to her boss's attention. Secretaries can convince their bosses that they ought to see you. Co-workers, friends, business associates can also act as intermediaries. List the people who might say yes. Ask who possesses what you need, and who has enough to give? Who would like to help a person like yourself? Who has the necessary skill and knowledge? Mentally rehearse asking the right person. Imagine calling them on the telephone or meeting them face to face. Mentally or out loud, before a mirror, state your situation, and ask for what you need. Rehearsal will help you overcome any nervousness or shyness.

Prepare a good case

If something is to happen, you need to ask for what you need. People can't read your mind. Let others know your needs, and request their help in meeting them. If you do not ask, nothing happens. When you get turned down, keep asking. Perseverance pays. If you do not get results the first time, try again. Successful people are those who have kept asking. Persistence pays because it impresses

153

people with the seriousness of your intent. When deciding how to ask, consider the merits of your situation, and plan how to get these across. Influencees will usually hesitate to help, if they feel that you are capable of getting what you want without them. You must therefore begin by explaining how their contribution is essential to your success.

To make a good case, put your best foot forward by telling them about your positive qualities, goals ambitions and objectives. State specifically and clearly what you need from them. Explain why you really need their help, and how it will make a difference to you. For example, if you want advice from a busy person, explain how their contribution will help you solve a problem or get ahead. Do not just say it but also offer evidence in the form of facts, figures or expert opinions. A clever request not only arouses curiosity, but also overcomes resistance or opposition. Try humour to disarm the approached person, especially when a bald request may evoke an angry or ill-considered response. Quick (1990) encouraged influencers to make their request interesting (so what is being said will be listened to); make it valuable (so that it appeals to the self-interest of influencee); and to make it easy (make it seen as do-able), and thus more likely to be done. Think of new and different ways of asking.

Ross highlighted three obstacles or blocks to asking for help. First, was fear of getting a 'no'. People fear being turned down, being rejected, so they prefer not to ask. So go around this block or push through it. If they say no, you are only as bad off as you would be, had you not asked at all. It they say yes, you have got what you wanted. This is possibly the most common and hardest block to overcome. A second common block is pride. A positive type of pride is a belief in yourself and confidence in your abilities. A negative type says that you are better than others. The latter gets in the way of asking for help. Such people feel that, being superior to others, they ought to be self-sufficient. For them to ask is to admit that they need other people, and thus they have to admit that others have power over them by having the power to help them. A third block is low self-esteem. Feeling unworthy of help. You have got to convince yourself that you have something to offer. To overcome these blocks, grit your teeth and ask anyway, or try to resolve these feelings that may prevent you from asking.

While you should request or invite, you should never demand or beg. Making demands of people is the least effective way of getting what you want. By asking the other person, you are showing respect for their right to say no. It gives the influencee a choice rather than an ultimatum. If the influencee accedes to your request, it allows them to feel good about it. This is because they have made a decision and not a concession, and both of you can feel that you have won. In contrast, making a demand makes it difficult for the other person to say yes or no. In practice, you are making a veiled threat, putting them on the spot, taking away their option to say no, and thus robbing them of their freedom of choice. Nobody likes to give in to demands, and if they do, they do so grudgingly and with resentment. Some requests are actually veiled threats ('But Bob, you've got to do this overtime — *so why don't you just order me?*' Demands can take the form of abusive behaviour, such as shouting, or threats, 'If you don't . . . I'll'. It is possible that you will receive a negative response to your request. In that case, you just ask someone else, who can provide you with what you want. Alternatively, accept their 'no' now, and try again later or at another time when circumstances might have changed. Some people beg or plead for what they want. Begging breeds contempt. Begging, though apparently different from demanding, is actually the opposite side of the same coin. When you beg or plead, you again circumvent the other person's right to say 'no', this time, through creating a sense of guilt. It rarely turns a no into a yes. It both demeans you and betrays your sense of insecurity. Whining to get what you want is another form of begging. Examples include, 'Why can't I get this?', or 'Why don't you ever do that?'. Such a powerless posture invites a negative response.

Showing respect

To different degrees, everyone wants esteem in the form of appreciation, courtesy and consideration. People want others to say or imply, 'I respect you, I think you are a worthwhile important human being'. Three key phrases convey respect — *please*, *thank you* and *I'm sorry*. *Please* is not just a word but a concept. It means that such and such would please me, if it is not an inconvenience to you. That is why saying 'please' properly, makes people more willing to say yes. The same notion of shared happiness and respect is also achieved through the phrase, 'Would you . . .'. So, always get across the idea of please, irrespective of what you are asking for. *Thank you* is not just a nice thing to say after you have been given something. It is also an influencing tool. There are four occasions on which to express thanks:

- when you are asking for something, but before you get an answer ('Thanking you in anticipation');
- after you receive an answer when it is yes;
- after you receive an answer when it is no;
- after you have benefited from a positive response.

In the first of these cases, it is courteous to thank people in advance. It gives potential givers a bit of appreciation, a foretaste of the gratitude that they will get when they say yes. It can also trigger a feeling of obligation and creates the need to give back ('She's already thanked me, I have to reciprocate'). In the second case, write thank you, when you have received a yes. It is surprising how many people fail to do this. Such thanks can set a positive scene for future, additional requests. In the third situation, say thank you even when you get a negative response. You can thank them for their time, for considering your request, or for their comments. It will make the other person feel better, and may even get you a yes-response in the future. For example, write a thank-you letter after not being offered a job after an interview. Here, you would thank the interviewer for their time, and the chance to learn more about their company. In your letter, take the opportunity to confirm your continued interest in being employed by the company, and in being considered for any other current or future vacancies. Remember, you have only been judged inappropriate for a specific job in competition with particular applicants. You have not been rejected as a human being. The interviewer has already invested time in you, and knows a lot about your capabilities. Most jobs are not publicly advertised. For this reason, a 'thank-you-have-you-got-anything-else' letter, can keep the door open to take advantage of other job opportunities. Such politeness is on the decline, and can help to mark you out in terms of tenacity and good manners. Finally, say thank you when you benefit from a yes. This shows the giver the tangible benefits to you of their positive response. For example, when receiving a grant to study, thank the charitable association after you have graduated, explaining what you learned and how your qualification has helped you in your career.

I'm sorry says that you have made a mistake and are admitting it. When you hurt someone apologize. Saying sorry is a powerful way of showing respect, and sometimes you may have to say sorry if you want people to come to your aid. If you need help because you have made a mistake, if you want assistance, admit your error first. People like to help those who are willing to reform. There are other ways of showing respect to the giver when communicating. Your neatness in your letters, dress and appearance do this. Putting on a happy face, communicating confidence with your body, respecting the other person's time, and not contradicting them are other ways. As you communicate with them, make them feel important. People seldom say yes to those that make them feel small. Build them up if you want them to be on your side. Finally, remember that whenever you ask for something, you take on an obligation. Living up to that obligation qualifies you to ask again and to receive again in the future. It shows that you respect yourself, and the person or the institution from whom you have accepted the obligation.

MOODS, GOALS AND DECISION-MAKING

Anecdotally, 'catching people in the right mood', has always been acknowledged as a key element in influencing success. Understanding how a person's mood can influence the decision-making process, can be a valuable aid to influencers. Research in the 1960s and 1970s suggested that messages become more persuasive through associations with good feelings. Salespeople who conduct business over a sumptuous lunch for their clients already know this. Good feelings enhance persuasion partly by enhancing positive thinking in the influencee who comes to view the world through rose-tinted glasses. In these circumstances, influencees have been found to make faster, more impulsive decisions. They rely less on systematic thinking and more on rules-of-thumb (heuristic cues). In contrast, unhappy people, ruminate more before acting and are less swayed by weak arguments. Thus the advice to influencers is to put your influencees in a good mood in the hope that they will feel good about your message without thinking about it too much. A more recent study by Barone *et al.* (2000) examined how a positive mood influenced consumers' evaluations of brand extensions. For example, the brand of a chocolate bar was extended to become an ice cream as well. The results confirm the earlier findings that a positive mood does indeed enhance favourable attitude.

Moving onto negative mood, the earliest studies considered the effect of fear. The question is how much fear is optimum. Studies suggest that the more the better, provided that they are accompanied by information as to how to avoid the danger. Staying with the negative, Raghunathan and Pham (1999) argued that different negative moods activated different personal goals in the influencee. They focused on the negative states of sadness and anxiety, since these are among the most common form of emotional distress. Each of the two states will have a different impact on decision-making, because the influencee obtains a different meaning from each of the states, and this affects the goals that they have. The situation that created the emotional state and the situation in which the decision is to be made, need not be connected. If your dog died in the morning, your mood can affect your decision to invest in a company in the afternoon. Beginning with sad emotions, say the authors, the individual experiences a loss or absence of reward. Feeling depressed or in despair often occurs as a result of a death or a relationship breakdown. Both are situations when something has been removed and hence is missing. Raghunathan and Pham found that sad individuals would take a higher risk if it offered a higher pay-off. The authors recommend that being offered rewards of substitution should influence sad people. This is consistent with the common act of buying a gift for yourself if you are feeling down. Turning now to anxiety, this emotional state is characterized by high uncertainty over an outcome, coupled with low control over a situation. For example, job selection situations are characterized by anxiety. Anxious individuals were found to prefer lower risk and lower pay-offs. To influence them, say the writers, offer them a reduction of uncertainty, or increase in risk avoidance in decision-making.

Chapter 8

Personality and influencing

Everyone is like all others, some others, and no one else.

INTRODUCTION

In day-to-day interaction with others, whether at home or in the office, it is most unlikely that you will seek to influence the different people that you encounter in exactly the same way. At home, you will take one approach with your mother and another with your boyfriend; whereas at work, your tactic with your manager will be different from the one that you use with your colleague. In the latter case, the reason for the difference is only partly due to seniority, one of them being your boss, the other being a fellow employee. You also probably modify your approach because you perceive your mother, boyfriend, boss and colleague to be different kinds of people. We are all amateur psychologists, and the most successful influencers are able to assess accurately their target influencees, and adapt their influencing messages to suit them.

Such adjustments lead to the creation of influencer–influencee rapport. Earlier in the book, the concept of *rapport* was introduced and defined as the process of establishing and maintaining a relationship of mutual trust and understanding with another person, and the ability to generate responses from them. Establishing rapport involves sharing and trading particular behaviours. One can be in or out of rapport when interacting with another person. The conversation of people who are in rapport flows, and both their body movements and their words become synchronized with each other. It is possible to create rapport by matching and mirroring what the other person says, how they say it, and how they present information. Once rapport is established, the other person is put at their ease, and their trust in you rises. The recommendation to match the influencee so as to create rapport is itself based on the even broader notion of *liking*. This says that we like people like ourselves and, in consequence, will be more willing to comply with their requests.

The earlier chapters on influencing and verbal and non-verbal behaviour both stressed the importance of matching. Specifically, match the dress, posture and speaking style of your influencee, since this creates rapport between you. This chapter develops the same theme, by suggesting that the influencee's preferences that you will be seeking to match, are all broadly consistent with each other. Some authors, like Beauvais *et al.* (1999) take a characteristics or personal qualities approach to distinguishing people's personalities. They introduced the notion of the self-concept, saying that individuals possessed three general sets of attributes about their perceived self–traits, competencies and values. *Traits* are broad reaction tendencies, and can show relatively permanent behaviour patterns. For example, 'caring', 'generous' and 'sociable' are all traits that describe a person's nature. *Competencies* are the skills, abilities, talents and knowledge that an individual possesses. *Values* are the concepts and beliefs that describe end states that are general, and which guide their evaluation of behaviours and events. They are displayed through what a person says and does. By taking notice of a person's influencee's competencies and values, the influencer can organize their communication attempts effectively.

However, the personality characteristics approach is both problematic and overly complex. If instead, we begin by focusing primarily on the personality type that an individual fits, we can then relate this to their characteristics and to their motivational needs. Four basic personality types are distinguished, and the characteristics of each are described. Under normal conditions, people belonging to each personality type will also possess a relatively stable set of motivational needs. These were introduced in the previous chapter. Knowledge of both an influencee's preferences, in terms of the way they like to be communicated with, and of their primary motivational needs, will allow us to tailor our approach, establish rapport quickly, and thus become more influential.

PERSONALITY AND CLASSIFICATION

Not only do we know that people are different, but we also know that they are predictably different. Indeed, we spend a great deal of our time classifying them into broad types, and explaining the differences between the types. Every popular newspaper contains an astrological section which implies that Capricorns behave in one way and that Scorpios act in another. The twelve signs of the Zodiac represent one attempt at classifying people into personality types based on the time of the year in which they were born. How accurate or useful are they? Historically, many attempts have been made to classify people according to their personalities. The Greek physician, Hippocrates, offered the temperaments model of personality. He believed that there were four basic personalities or temperaments – melancholic, choleric, sanguine and phlegmatic. In his view, each was determined by the amount and type of bile and phlegm that people possessed in their bodies.

While Hippocrates' biologically based classification has now been superseded, he was amongst the first people to recognize that people possessed a set of stable

159

characteristics; that these were responsible for differences in their behaviour; and that such characteristics could form the basis of a personality classification system. Management consultants and trainers have also written about this and run courses on how to deal with 'difficult people'. A recent contribution by Dalton (2000), distinguishes eight classic behavioural types to be found in the workplace which he labelled Commander, Drifter, Pleaser, Performer, Avoider, Analytical and Achiever. Once their personality and typical behaviours have been described, their motivations are identified, and suggestions made as to how best they are to be dealt with. Two, similarly focused articles, one by Goleman (2000) and another by Lippitt (1999), distinguish types of leaders, each of whom is seen as having their own decision-making priorities. By recognizing which type of boss you had, it is claimed, you can adjust your influencing tactics suitably. Lippitt's six types are summarized in Table 8.1.

An entire sub-field of psychology has now developed called personality theory devoted to distinguishing different personality types and traits. It is a controversial field with writers holding different views about the nature and development of personality. For example, behaviourist psychologists such as B.F. Skinner, believe that personality forms through the process of trial and error learning. That is to say, human beings repeat behaviours that achieve their aims, and eliminate those which do not. The repeated success of a particular behaviour leads to it being incorporated into our behavioural pattern, and thereby becomes part of our personality. In contrast, other psychologists like Sigmund Freud and the psychodynamic school, believe that a person's personality is formed by the unconscious conflicts that arise from anxiety. As far as the influencer is concerned, the source and nature of a person's personality is less important than being able to broadly classify it, at the time of the influencing attempt. In order to be able

Table 8.1 Personality types of leaders

Type of leader	Decision-making priorities
Inventor	Developing new ideas, products and services
Catalyst	Gaining market share and winning customers
Developer	Building infrastructure, creating systems and processes for high performance
Performer	Improving processes and procedures for effective use of resources
Protector	Developing a committed workforce. Building capabilities and supporting culture capabilities and values
Challenger	Identifying strategic options and positioning the organization for the future

Source: From Lippitt (1999)

160

to use personality theory to assist influencing, it is necessary to assume that every person's personality is, generally speaking, stable, and that such stability forms the basis of a set of consistent behaviour preferences and actions which an individual will demonstrate in a variety of different situations.

DISTINGUISHING BETWEEN PERSONALITY TYPES

If you are to select a particular influencing approach on the basis of your target influencee's personality, then the personality framework employed has to be both easy to understand and simple to use. You need to be able to divide people into a very limited number of personality types or classes, based on the personality traits that they possess. In modern times, Carl Gustav Jung was the first to observe that people's behaviour, rather than being individually unique, fitted into patterns, and that many of the seemingly random differences in human behaviour were actually ordered and consistent.

According to Jung, people differed in terms of their psychological attitudes and functions, and could be divided on the basis of *perception* preferences and *judgement* preferences (Jung, 1926). Depending on the choices made, an individual would be classified into one of four types which Jung labelled Intuitor, Thinker, Feeler and Sensor. We shall examine each of these in more detail shortly. From Jung's theory, the mother and daughter team of Katherine Cook Briggs and Isobel Briggs Myers (Myers, 1962, 1976; Myers and McCaulley, 1985) developed the Myers–Briggs type indicator (MBTI), a still popular personality assessment, which continues to be widely used in the selection process. Virtually all subsequent personality-type classifications, right up to the present day, utilize Jung's original dimensions to a large degree. More recently, Hans Eysenck identified two dimensions of personality based on trait clusters. The first of these he labelled *extroversion-introversion*, and the second he called *neuroticism* (stable and unstable). As people varied along each of his two dimensions, they could be fitted into one of his four personality types. Each type was defined using a cluster of adjectives such as touchy, restless, aggressive and excitable (Eysenck, 1960). Hippocrates, Jung and Eysenck have together provided us with a four-cell framework that can help influencers be more successful. Their models are integrated and summarized in Figure 8.1.

It is obvious that any attempt to reduce personality into only four categories inevitably ignores the subtlety of human differences. On the other hand, anything more complex is unusable by an influencer. For this reason, in using these four personality stereotypes, one is inevitably trading accuracy off against ease of use. The framework does allow you to classify the individual whom you may wish to influence in a simple way using your observation of their behaviour and the examination of their created work or home environment. Such information can then be immediately put into practice. Let us now briefly consider Jung's

161

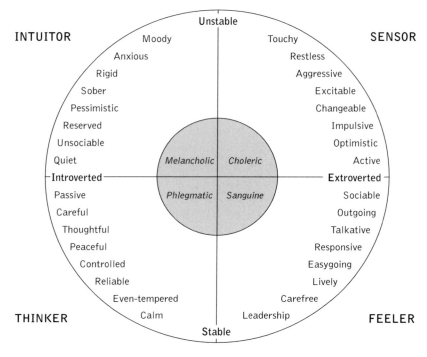

Figure 8.1 *Hippocrates', Jung's and Eysenck's personality-type classifications*

classification of personality in a little more detail before discussing how it might be applied in practice.

PERCEPTION DIMENSION: SENSING OR INTUITING?

The first preference dimension used by Jung referred to how an individual gathered information about their world. It is depicted in the first row of Table 8.2. Was it in a sensing or in an intuitive way? This perceptual dimension of sensing versus intuiting concerns the way in which an individual becomes aware of facts, ideas and events. The person who has a preference for perceiving through *sensing*, becomes aware of things through all of their five senses. To ascertain if your influencee has a sensing preference, see how they deal with others. Sensing people are relaxed and warm in their dealings with others. They are self-disclosing, showing and sharing their feelings freely. In conversations, they will often stray from their subject. They give their opinions, and are easy to get to know in business, or in unfamiliar social situations. They are flexible about how their time is used by others, and feel cramped by schedules. They have flexible expectations about people and situations, and prefer to work in teams. They frequently initiate and accept physical contact, enjoy listening to discussions about personal feelings, and are responsive to dreams and concepts. As open, sensing individuals, they will welcome you with a friendly handshake, have animated facial expressions when speaking and listening and will show a great deal of enthusiasm. They are more likely to give you non-verbal feedback. They tell stories and anecdotes, with a great deal of inflection in their voice. Their gestures are spontaneous and often dramatic.

In contrast, the individual who prefers to perceive through their *intuition*, does so through a subconscious process in which ideas or hunches comes to them, 'out of the blue', suggesting possibilities to them. Their intuitive process is future oriented, and concerned with inspiring others to innovate. In their dealings with others, intuiting people are guarded, and keep their feelings private. Behaviourally, they are task oriented, focus their conversations on the issues, and decide

Table 8.2 *Summary of personality-type labels equivalent to Jung's original classification*

Author(s)	Equivalent personality-type labels			
Jung (1924)	Intuitor ST	Thinker SF	Feeler NF	Sensor NT
Alessandra *et al.* (1994)	Thinker	Relater	Socializer	Director
Morgan (1988)	Detail seeker	Harmony seeker	Excitement seeker	Results seeker
Klein (1988)	Technical	Sympathetic	Expressive	Bold
Bolton and Bolton (1984)	Analytical	Amiable	Expressive	Driver
Atkins (1982)	Conserving-holding	Supporting-giving	Adapting-dealing	Controlling-taking
Merrill and Reid (1981)	Analytical	Amiable	Expressive	Driver
Hunsaker and Alessandra (1980)	Analytical	Amiable	Expressive	Driver
DeVille (1979)	Comprehender	Supporter	Entertainer	Supporter
Greier (1977)	Compliance	Steadiness	Influence	Dominance
Lefton (1977)	Q2: Submissive-hostile	Q3: Submissive-warm	Q4: Dominant-warm	Q1: Dominant-hostile
Hippocrates and Galen (AD2)	Melancholic	Phlegmatic	Sanguine	Choleric

163

on the basis of objective, factual evidence. They respond most to realities and actual experiences, rather than to abstract ideas or visions. They are formal and proper, stick to the agenda, stay on the subject and prefer to follow established schedules. They are reserved in expressing their opinions, and it takes time for them to get to know others in business or in unfamiliar social situations. They are disciplined about how their time is used by others, and prefer to work alone. They have fixed expectations about people and situations. They tell and enjoy listening to goal-related stories and anecdotes, but are likely to be expressionless when speaking or listening. They have little inflection in their voices, with few voice pitch variations. They are unlikely to give you any non-verbal feedback.

JUDGEMENT DIMENSION: FEELING OR THINKING?

Jung's second preference dimension related to how, after having perceived, the individual makes judgements about the information acquired. It is displayed on the first row of Table 8.2. Do they use thinking or feeling? *Thinking* is the logical and analytical process which involves searching for the impersonal truth. Principles are more important than people here. Those with a preference for thinking can have difficulty adapting to situations that cannot be understood intellectually. They are relatively unemotional, uninterested in people's feelings and may hurt others without knowing it. They like analysing and putting things into logical order, and can get along without harmony with others. They need to be treated fairly and are able to reprimand or fire others when necessary, thus appearing hard-hearted. Behaviourally, a person with a thinking preference makes empathic statements like, 'That's right' and 'I'm sure'. They emphasize points through their confident voice tone and assertive body language. Their questions tend to be rhetorical, emphasizing points or challenging information. They express their opinions easily. They are direct, impatient, competitive, confronting and controlling, and will maintain their position when disagreeing. They bend or break established rules. They are more likely to introduce themselves to others at a social gathering with a firm handshake. Their voice is loud, their speech pattern is fast, and they use gestures to emphasize points.

Alternatively, people may make judgements using *feeling*. This is a personal subjective process which seeks a 'good versus bad' and a 'like versus dislike' judgement. Whereas thinking uses objective criteria, feeling is based on personal mental evaluations. This internal process should be distinguished from another, that of emotion. An internal, mental evaluation is not an emotional reaction. Behaviourally, this type of person approaches risky decisions and change slowly and cautiously. Individuals with this preference are infrequent contributors to group conversations, and use gestures and voice intonation sparingly when emphasizing points. They tend to make qualified statements such as, 'According to my sources', or 'I tend to think that'. They use questions for clarification and support.

164

They reserve the expression of their opinions, and are patient and co-operative with others showing a high degree of diplomacy and collaboration. When not in agreement with others, they are likely to go along with the majority. At social gatherings, they are reserved and are likely to wait for others to introduce themselves, greeting them with a gentle handshake.

FOUR PERSONALITY TYPES

For the influencer, Jung's four-type personality classification model is a valuable tool, but the labels that he uses for each personality type are obscure and confusing. They lack the immediately clarity that can differentiate types of people. For example, Jung applied the label, 'Thinker', to a cluster of personality traits, which most people would associate with a set of somewhat impulsive behaviours. What influencers actually need is a set of labels that memorably and succinctly denote the essential features of each of Jung's personality types. For this reason, instructors have retained Jung's original framework, but relabelled his types, producing their own set of more descriptive terms to refer to each one. Table 8.2 lists some of the different labels that you will encounter in the personality and management literature. New, four-cell personality classifications are being published every day. While each set of labels may differ, they all refer to the same four personality designations.

To illustrate how Jung's personality framework can be used in influencing, this chapter will adopt Alessandra *et al.*'s (1994) personality-type labelling system. These authors' labels have been found to pass the test of memorability, and have been used extensively and successfully by many students. Each of the four personality types is summarized in the section that follows, and each is indicated by Jung's label in brackets. Meanwhile, Table 8.3 offers a pen-picture of each type.

Thinkers (ST)

Thinkers like their work environment to remain the same, dislike change and too much personal attention. They will do a precise job, provided that they receive adequate information. They measure their achievements in terms of the level of precision and accuracy attained, and the amount of progress made. For them, their task is a priority, and they progress towards it at a slow, steady and methodical pace, focusing on details and examining the facts. The process of getting to an answer is as important as the answer itself, sometimes even more! Thinkers seek great amounts of factual data; ask specific questions of those who produce it; and quiz them about how they arrived at their conclusions.

They place great weight on being correct. For this reason, they invest time in developing systems and procedures which can produce correct answers. You can identify a Thinker by their serious, orderly and structured approach to things.

165

Table 8.3 *Summary of four behavioural personality styles*

Relater
A Relater is open and indirect with a steady performance. Fears confrontation. Seeks attention and needs to know how things will affect them. Likes you to be pleasant and wants to be liked. Decisions are considered.

Socializer
A Socializer is open and direct; who influences others. Fears loss of prestige. Seeks recognition and needs to know how things will enhance their status. Likes you to be stimulating and wants to be admired. Decisions are made spontaneously.

Thinker
A Thinker is self-contained and indirect with a compliance performance. Fears embarrassment. Seeks accuracy. Thinkers need to know how they justify things logically. Likes you to be precise and wants to be correct. Their decisions are deliberate.

Director
A Director is self-contained and direct with a dominant performance. Fears loss of control. Seeks productivity and needs to know what things do, by when and what it costs. Likes you to be to the point and wants to be in charge. Directors are very decisive.

Source: Alessandra *et al.*, 1994

They persist at a task in an effort to attain perfection. They possess problem-solving skills which are exercised in relation to the data collected. When making a decision, Thinkers are cautious. They set high performance standards for themselves, and are critical of both themselves and others if these are not met. In their interactions with others, Thinkers are slow and cautious. They would prefer to work alone, and dislike having to be involved with others. They like organizational structures, follow any rules or standards set, and comply with authority.

When you visit a Thinker, dress conservatively and professionally. Shake hands only if they offer you theirs. During your meeting avoid being over-friendly, and respect their need for personal space. Be formal, logical and businesslike in your approach, and adopt a slow and deliberate speaking style. Because Thinkers seek security, standard ways of working and reassurance, you will want to present your proposal in such a way that they will be able to justify it logically, both to themselves and to others. You should ensure that they understand how your idea will work in practice; and how it can maintain and enhance their credibility with others. Overall, they need to feel that they have made a thorough analysis of the situation and have come to an accurate decision. During the discussion, support their thoughts about your idea, and allay their fears about being embarrassed by others in accepting your proposal.

You already know that Thinkers tend to be serious, rigid, excessively cautious and slow to make decisions. Expect them therefore to ask you questions about details, and to be prudent and deliberative. For these reasons come well prepared and organized. Be exact, specific and detailed in your responses, focusing on each step in your argument. Present both the pros and cons of an issue, thereby showing how thoroughly you have researched it. Where appropriate, provide data and proof of your assertions, and avoid any surprises or unpredictability. Thinkers will want as much information from you as possible, and will not be in a hurry to make a decision, so do not rush them. Once they have compared and analysed all their options they will make a decision.

Relaters (SF)

Relaters measure their personal worth by the attention that they receive from others. They are slow and relaxed in their movements, placing emphasis on relationships, and focusing on building trust and getting acquainted. Since they seek guarantees and reassurance from those they meet, they will be irritated by pushy and aggressive behaviour. They like to support others and rely on close relationships. Relaters actively listen to others, are warm and accepting, and hence quickly gain the support of those around them. They work methodically and cohesively with colleagues, coming over as steady, agreeable and calm people who are prepared to share their feelings and emotions. They prefer informality, like to be on first name terms with others, and are loyal employees. They make decisions only after thorough consideration, avoiding interpersonal conflict wherever possible. With their good counselling and listening skills they make excellent social workers.

Since Relaters seek security and your appreciation, they want little change, and will prefer the application of the traditional ways of doing things which do not interfere with their home life. So if your idea is likely to have major repercussions, introduce it carefully to avoid a negative reaction. Relaters do not like taking the initiative, although they will listen to your new ideas patiently. Their anxiety about making a wrong decision is that it might expose them to the criticism of others, thereby destroying the harmony that they value so much. Hence, you should frame your proposal to take account of their concerns. For example, imply to them that, by agreeing to your suggestion, they will be maintaining or strengthening their relationships with others; or that their personal circumstances will benefit from adopting your recommendation. Explain how the acceptance of your idea will demonstrate their conformity and fellowship with and loyalty to others; and how these people will, in turn, come to like them more. During your meeting with a Relater (which will be at your request), you should initiate the handshake; use a slow and easy talking style; avoid confrontation by giving them your full attention. Be warm, likeable, friendly and informal, and use positive language throughout your meeting. Acknowledge and support their feelings about your proposal, and offer reassurance and guarantees. Whenever

167

appropriate, invite them to contribute, so as to meet their need for involvement and helping. Above all, avoid impatience. Do not be over-demanding or attempt to press them for a decision. Instead give them time to consider your proposal.

Socializers (NF)

Socializers measure their personal status by the amount of acknowledgement and recognition that they receive from others. They are fast-paced in their manner and place an emphasis upon relationships. They seek out person-to-person situations and like to join in with what others are doing (provided that it is not boring!). They are flexible, emotional, friendly and playful. Socializers act spontaneously from intuition. They jump from one activity to another, have little concern for time, and 'shoot from the hip' (not always successfully). They are excellent at parties since they are stimulating, talkative, gregarious and often voice dramatic opinions. Some people would call them dreamers but they see themselves as visionaries. Their constant enthusiasm and optimism enhances their innate persuasive skills. In leadership roles, they may be called charismatic. Socializers want to express their views and gain public recognition. They dislike having their freedoms restricted and want others to deal with the details to save them the effort. They are disorganized as individuals, do not attend to details, are impractical and tend to jump to conclusions prematurely. Having fun and helping people are their main ambitions. They like being spontaneous and involved.

Try to dress like the Socializer, who may be attired formally or informally. During your face-to-face meeting, be friendly and maintain a fast and spontaneous talking pace. Be lively, stimulating and energetic since Socializers get bored easily. You should frame your proposal to imply that by agreeing to it, the Socializer will enhance their own status. Moreover, they will remain in step with others whose approval they desire, thus gaining their recognition. Be bold in presenting your ideas, highlighting those aspects of them which are original and imaginative, even if other parts remain mundane and routine. Provide examples and testimonials for your proposal; support and build on any suggestions that the Socializer offers. Most importantly, give them time to talk, and stimulate and excite them with your ideas. Link these to the Socializer's own goals and ambitions. Push them to make a decision on the spot, ideally when they are at their most enthusiastic.

Directors (NT)

Directors measure their personal success in terms of tangible results. They stress dominance, and work to modify the world around them so as to achieve their desired goals. Directors place a priority on getting the task done. Being in control is not only a specialty of theirs, but they also rely on it for their personal sense of security. For this reason, they will prefer that you offer them a range of solutions to allow them to choose their preferred option. This focus on results and control leads Directors to consider suggestions in terms of their likely benefits and risks, and when the former are likely to accrue. Directors become irritated with emotional issues, especially if they feel that these are impeding progress towards their objectives. As individuals, they are independent and strong willed. In pursuing their goals, they are decisive, cool, calculating and competitive. Directors enjoy a challenge, and welcome an opportunity to take authority since this will give them freedom to manage themselves and others. Because of their natures, they tend to dominate, to be impatient with slower paced people, and have a low tolerance for the feelings, attitudes and advice of others. Being so independent, they work best by themselves, and are thus not good team players.

Directors use facts and intuition to make decisions. They are the entrepreneurs who enjoy taking risks and competing. They have a preference for action, are purposeful listeners, and like to be in control. Arrive smartly dressed for your meeting, and during it, use a fast and decisive speaking style. Be assertive, well briefed and succinct. Frame your proposal so as to imply that by agreeing to your proposal, the Director will achieve the measurable results that they seek; and will maintain and enhance their control over the issues and processes discussed. Come with a one page summary of your proposal together with back-up material, should it be required. Avoid using qualifiers in presenting your idea (e.g. 'perhaps' or 'might'). Keep things professional and businesslike throughout your encounter, and avoid any hint of indecision or inefficiency. Stick to the facts, focus on bottom-line results and benefits to them and push them to a decision on the spot.

IDENTIFYING PERSONALITY TYPE BY WORK ENVIRONMENTS

The primary way of identifying each personality type is to assess what is important to them, what they say, and what they do and avoid doing. More information is available to you in a situation where you have access to their work area, and can inspect their possessions. This is provided, of course, that the choices in the person's workspace has been made by them and not by others. In some companies, the colour scheme, choice of wallpaper, carpets and work furniture, are all centrally determined, leaving the employee with very little opportunity to customize it to their own taste. Indeed, some organizations even have a 'clean desk policy' which forbids piles of clutter, and dictates that only a limited number of documents are worked on at any one time. Such a degree of direction however, is unusual. Even in most standardized work environment – office, cubicle or desk – the human need to individualize their workspace breaks through, and this can provide you with valuable information about the personality of the person.

169

For this reason, ascertain at the start what choice your influencee had in determining their office space. This can easily be done as part of an opening compliment when you say, 'This is a very nice place. Did you choose the colour scheme and furniture layout yourself, or does it come with the job?'. Once you get the reply, focus only on those aspects of their environment that have been chosen by them. Notice what is included, what is absent, what furniture there is and how it is arranged. The reason for this is that a chosen office layout and content can be an external, physical representation of its occupant's internal personality, helping you to decide which of the four personality types you are dealing with.

For example, we have already noted that Thinkers place great stress on accuracy, precision and progress. They like their efficiency to be noticed by others. That is why their offices are neat and tidy. If their desks contain materials, these will be placed in order, awaiting action. Thinkers' walls contain charts and graphs which relate to the job, and frequently indicate progress. White boards contain lists of 'to do' reminders, while exhibits and pictures reflect 'have done' achievements, all of which relate to the task rather than to the individual. The decor and equipment in the room are functional. Colour schemes, desks, PCs, filing cabinets, etc., are chosen purely on the basis of being the best available to get the job done. The seating arrangements in Thinkers' rooms stress formality and non-contact. Thinkers would prefer you to discuss your business without engaging in social small talk, either before or after, hence a coffee table is unnecessary. If your Thinker has an office, their desk will separate you from them, providing a barrier behind which they will remain.

Relaters, in contrast, measure their personal worth by the amount of attention that they receive. They also emphasize steadiness and co-operation with others in order to carry out the task. In consequence, their offices will contain materials which tell any visitor how much they are liked. Their desks and cubicles will contain photographs of friends and relations, as well as personal items received as gifts. The walls will have on them photographs of formal or informal groups of which the Relater is a member. The office itself will be friendly, and open, without excessive amounts of furniture. Within it, the visitor will feel relaxed, partly due to the seating arrangement which avoids having the desk as a barrier.

Socializers like to shape their environment by incorporating others in coalitions through which they will get the job done. They measure their self-esteem by the amount of applause, acknowledgement and recognition that they receive from others. They like to be noticed, and their workspace will reflect that need. For example, their desk, far from being 'clean', will be disorganized, with papers and notes piled on top of each other. Such clutter is however, deceptive since when enquiring about a document, a Socializer will wade through their mountain of paper, and locate the item without difficulty. On their walls will be personal achievement awards and photographs. University degrees, membership of select societies, even confirmations of completing mini-marathons! Alongside these will be personal motivational slogan posters such as, 'Do It Now!' and 'The Customer is Our Final Quality Controller'. The room's decor is open and friendly, emphasizing contact and activity. If an office is large enough, a coffee table with low-slung chairs will be positioned away from the desk, allowing Socializers to interact informally with their visitors.

Directors seek respect from others while tending to dominate them. They measure themselves in terms of their achievements, which they want others to be aware of. They therefore design their workspaces accordingly. Their desks will contain many papers, separated into piles which reflect a number of different projects or 'deals' being worked in parallel. The walls contain calenders which track progress, as well as depicting achievements in the form of photographs, certificates and framed magazine or newspaper articles containing the Director's

Table 8.4 *Summary of personality-type characteristics and preferences based on Jung's (1924) and Alessandra et al.'s (1994) frameworks*

Author	Personality-type characteristics			
Jung	Intuitor ST	Thinker SF	Feeler NF	Sensor NT
Alessandra	Thinker	Relater	Socializer	Director
They prefer	Sensing and thinking	Sensing and feeling	Intuition and feeling	Intuition and thinking
They focus their attention on	Facts	Facts	Possibilities	Possibilities
They handle these with	Impersonal analysis	Personal warmth	Personal warmth	Impersonal analysis
Thus they tend to be	Practical and matter-of-fact	Sociable and friendly	Enthusiastic and insightful	Intellectually ingenious
They focus on	Production Construction Accounting	Sales Service Customer relations	Research Teaching Preaching	Research Science Invention
	Economics	Welfare work	Writing	Securities analysis
	Law Surgery	Nursing General practice	Psychology Psychiatry	Management Cardiology
Focus on	Business Technical Theoretical Practical Sceptical Down-to-earth	People Social	Language Creative Religious Imaginative Subjective Human	Science Intellectual Economic

photographs or write-ups. The colours of the decor, blues and greys, convey control and power. Theirs is not a cubicle or office which is friendly, or one in which you feel relaxed. The seating is formal and non-contact. The desk will separate you from a Director. It is likely to be a large one, and you will notice that the Director's chair is higher and grander than yours. We can conclude this section by contrasting in Table 8.4, the main differences between the four personality types described.

MOTIVATIONAL NEEDS AND PERSONALITY TYPES

This behavioural-style model of personality is based on the assumption of stability in an individual's personality features, and their preference to behave in one particular, way in a variety of different situations. Table 8.2 described two independent dimensions, perceiving and judgement, and it is possible for an individual to be high on one and low on the other, or vice-versa. However, at the margins, a person may be a Socializer-nearly-Director, or Thinker-nearly-Relater. Your greatest likelihood of influencing success will come when your influencee is located at the extreme edge of their particular type cell, and when they are clearly a Thinker, Socializer or whatever. When this is the case, you can reasonably surmise that, all other things being equal, each personality type will possess specific needs. Maslow's list of motivational needs was introduced in the previous chapter, and is shown in Table 7.1.

Table 8.5 suggests that Thinkers will place importance on the need to be right. It is this which gives them their high security rating. It is not only the security of continued employment or a pension, but also the security of knowing that they have made the correct decision in the right way. Such rightness, in turn, impacts on their self-esteem, a fourth level need. Socializers have a need for the respect of fellow workers and to participate in doing something worthwhile. They like others to applaud and recognize their achievements, and are therefore likely to have social and affiliational needs, the esteem of others need, and additionally, self-actualization. Since Relaters have a need for the attention of others, they use this to assess their personal worth. Their primary motivational needs are likely to be in the social and love area, as well as seeking the esteem of others. They like to feel that they belong, and will seek out opportunities to be included in group and team activities. They welcome the chance of promotion, and like job security and a safe working environment. Finally, Directors will place great stress on self-actualization, self-esteem and the esteem of others. They learn new information and skills in order to remain autonomous. They are full of projects, proposals and ideas with which they want to experiment. However, things will not always be equal when, for example, your influencee is made redundant. In such circumstances, individuals from all four personality types will be focusing on their physiological needs. It is therefore useful to consider personality-type assessment as a snapshot, correct at the time the camera shutter

Table 8.5 *Personality type and primary motivational needs*

Personality type	Physiological	Safety	Social	Esteem	Self-actualization
Thinker	Low	High	Low	Medium	High
Relater	Low	Medium	High	Medium	Medium
Socializer	Low	Low	High	High	Medium
Director	Low	Low	Medium	High	High

was pressed, but capable of becoming out of date later. For the short period after the photo has been taken, your knowledge of the influencee's personality type and associated motivational needs can help you to influence them.

APPLYING THE PERSONALITY-TYPE MODEL

Let us now pull the various sections of this chapter together, and consider how to put this information into practice. The application of personality-types framework to the task of influencing involves three stages. The first of these is determining which personality type you are. At the start of the book, the impression management model of Awareness–Flexibility–Control was introduced. In the context of personality assessment, *awareness* refers to assessing whether you, yourself, are a Thinker, Relater, Socializer or Director. This can be done through a reading of the four description profiles described earlier; by analysing your workspace or room at home; or by completing any one of the Jungian-based personality questionnaires listed in Table 8.2.

The second stage involves deciding the personality type of your influencee. Giving them a questionnaire to fill in is rarely an option. Instead, you will have to observe their verbal and non-verbal behaviour, and assess their workspace, if appropriate. People whom you meet on a daily basis are easier to classify than strangers. On the other hand, car sales staff have to make rapid assessments of hundreds of prospects who enter their showrooms, and whom they meet on a one-off basis. Their assessments will be based on information such as the customer's current motorcar, dress, manner, occupation and address. If these professional influencers can make a classification in under five minutes, you should be able to do the same with some practice. As you pick up diverse clues, check that they correlate. In this way, your initial assessments can be checked with information acquired later on.

Once you have raised your awareness of your own personality type and determined that of your influencee, you are then able to proceed to the third stage, actually doing the face-to-face influencing. This will require behavioural *flexibility*,

173

another feature of our impression management model mentioned earlier. Here you temporarily adjust your natural behavioural style, in order to match that of your influencee, so that they can feel more comfortable with you. By taking into account your influencee's preferred communication style, talking with them in the way they like to be talked to, you can increase your chance of a successful influencing outcome. Throughout your meeting, you will have to choose consciously what to say and do. You will thus have to monitor your behaviour while interacting with the influencee, speeding up or slowing down your rate of speech as required; emphasizing details or omitting them, and so on. What you are in fact doing here is customizing the content and presentation of your proposal to fit the preferences of your influencee. Let us take two examples of how you might exercise flexibility and control (Bringhurst, 2001).

If you have established that you are a Thinker personality type, and that your influencee is a Socializer, you will need to be more open and direct than you naturally are, when talking to them. To increase your openness, you will need to pay your influencee a personal compliment, and engage in small talk before discussing the issue at hand, even if you find this difficult. During your discussion, you will have to force yourself to share both your own feelings about the matter, as well as responding to theirs. Verbally, your language will be friendly, irrespective of how annoyed or exasperated you may feel. Non-verbally, you will need to maintain a relaxed posture by leaning back with arms uncrossed, even though this may not be your usual seating position. Do not hurry a discussion with the Socializer, even though inside you may be anxious to get on. Support their ideas or hopes, without argument. Push yourself to be entertaining and fast moving, and have examples to hand showing how other people have done the same things that you are suggesting with success. To gain the Socializer's agreement and motivate them, offer them incentives and testimonials.

If later that same day, you need to influence a Director personality type, as a Thinker, you will not need to change your normal level of openness, but you will have to increase your directness. To do this, adapt your speech delivery style by initiating the conversation and speaking faster than you normally do. Your increased speed of delivery should be accompanied by a clear belief in your proposal. Use direct statements even though you typically prefer questions, and make recommendations even though you may feel happier with making requests for opinions. Face any conflict that you encounter with them openly, and do not be afraid to challenge or disagree with the Director. If you do so, argue about the facts, and not about personal feelings. Give recognition to their ideas, rather than to them. Keep your relationship businesslike, and throughout your meeting be precise, efficient and well organized. What these two brief examples particularly stress, is the importance of adjusting your natural, habitual approach to match the preferences of your influencee, for the period of time that you are interacting with them.

Chapter 9

Influencing
decision-making

Joe Pine (vituperative US TV chatshow host and amputee):   I guess your long
hair makes you a girl.

Frank Zappa (1970s pop star):   I guess your wooden leg makes you a table.

Cialdini (2001a: 234)

INTRODUCTION

This chapter deals with incorrectly generalizing from one piece of information,
and considers how influencers can exploit this phenomenon in decision-making.
It was mentioned at the start of this book that psychologists have distinguished
between two general approaches to influencing, which they label central route
and peripheral route. Central route persuasion occurs when interested influencees
focus on the arguments that you present, mentally construct their own arguments and counter-arguments, before reaching a decision. For these analytical
influencees, it is the arguments that you present that are persuasive, as these
encourage your listeners to think (Petty and Cacioppo, 1986; Eagely and Chaiken,
1992). Computer advertisements use central route influencing. They describe
product features and rarely have film or pop stars advertising their products. In
contrast, peripheral route persuasion occurs when people are influenced by incidental cues, such as a speaker's attractive face or the way the message is presented.
This approach to influencing is likely to be most effective on mundane issues
which do not trigger people's thinking, and with image-conscious people who
care less about being right or wrong and are more interested in the impression
that they are making. For example, advertisements for face cream do not contain
much information about the product's features, but associate it with successful
and beautiful women. This is because potential buyers will respond more to such
peripheral cues. However, even analytical people sometimes form tentative opinions through attending only to selected cues and simple heuristics which expose
them to biases (Myers, 1993). It is the biases associated with this peripheral route
to influencing that we shall examine in this chapter.

Research from social psychology (Cialdini, 2001a, 2001b; Cialdini and Ascani, 1976) and prospect theory (Kahneman and Tversky, 2000) has revealed how people typically make decisions using their intuitive judgement. By comparing rational with intuitive decision-making, the biases inherent in the process have been revealed. These biases, which operate at the subconscious and hence undetectable level, have a powerful and immediate impact on individuals' choices and actions. They are activated by a number of heuristics which influencers can use their knowledge of, to activate their associated biases, and thus lead influencees to willingly but unknowingly, comply with their requests. A heuristic is a simple and approximate rule, guiding procedure, shortcut or strategy that is used to solve a problem. Three types are particularly important (Gilovich, 2002).

The first of these is the *representative heuristic* where people come to judge things on the basis of how well they represent or match, particular prototypes. People tend to treat events as being representative of some well-known class or pattern. This gives them a sense of familiarity with an event, and thus the confidence that they have diagnosed it accurately. It leads them to 'see' patterns in data even when there are none. This heuristic uses the similarity of one object to another to infer that the first object acts like the second, and this can lead people to ignore other relevant information (Tversky and Kahneman, 1974). For example, using price or packaging to infer the quality of a good or service; assessing the likelihood of an event's occurrence by the similarity of that occurrence to their stereotype of similar occurrences; or predicting the success of a new product on the basis of its similarity to past successful and unsuccessful products.

In the interview situation, a candidate is analysed by the recruiter who uses the representative heuristic. The heuristic comparison is based on the interviewer's previous experiences rather than logical analysis of candidates' abilities. Showing evidence of one trait from a desired category of traits, will lead the interviewer to believe that you possess all the other traits in that category, beside the one that you have made visible. You can use the representative heuristic yourself to help others to form positive impressions and to make favourable judgements about you. Attractive people are seen as more successful, sensitive, warmer and of better character than less attractive people. People of high social stature, (often inferred by dress and mannerisms), are respected and held in high esteem. Thus 'dressing for success', wearing the right clothes to create the right image, or enhancing your appearance with cosmetics, are all based on the representative heuristic (Kahneman and Tversky, 1973; Shafir et al. 1990; Tversky and Kahneman, 1983).

Second, there is the *attitude heuristic* which is a special type of belief that describes the evaluative properties of an object. An attitude is a stored evaluation (good or bad) of an object or person (pay rises are good, deficits are bad). People use attitudes to solve their problems. They assign objects, including people, to a favourable class (where they are praised, cherished and protected), or to an unfavourable class (where they are avoided, blamed, neglected and harmed). People use attitudes to make sense of their social world. In practice, the halo effect is the most pronounced outcome of the attitude heuristic. It is a general bias for a liked individual, for example, a job candidate, who is expected to possess positive traits which act like an angel's halo. They have the effect of discounting any negative information about the person, while overvaluing positive facts about them (Pratkanis, 1988).

Third, people use the *availability heuristic* to estimate the likelihood of an event by assessing how readily instances of it come to mind. An event that is vivid, evokes emotions, is easily imagined, and is specific, will be more 'available' in your memory, than one that is bland, stirs no emotions, is difficult to imagine and is vague. This is a useful heuristic because more frequently occurring events are more easily revealed in our minds than less frequently occurring ones. However, the availability of information in our minds is determined equally by imagination and vividness, which are factors that are not related to the objective frequency of judged events (Tversky and Kahneman, 1973: Taylor and Thompson, 1982).

USE OF HEURISTICS

There are three fundamental reasons why we use heuristics, and in turn become exposed to their biases. First, human beings experience information overload. Modern life is fast, complex and changing. We lack the time, energy and capacity to investigate all aspects of it. We are also lazy and wish to avoid the trouble of detailed problem analysis. We all use shortcuts when making a decision. Typically, we use a single, highly representative piece of the total information available, which is usually reliable. However, when we do so, we are gambling. For example, we gamble that the higher priced tomatoes are better than the cheaper ones. When interviewing people, we gamble that the content and style of their speech is an accurate indicator of the quality of their future job performance. The rule of thumb and stereotype described here are based on one or a few key features. When we recognize these key features to be present in a situation or person, we frequently respond without further thought.

A second reason why these biases can occur is societal organization. For society to work and develop, its members need to hold certain views and attitudes in common. The possession of these is so important, that they are taught to each of us during our socialization and education processes. These biases thus become a part of ourselves. Third, we each have a desire to be influenced. We often want to be persuaded because it eliminates the need for difficult decisions and places the responsibility for failure on others. Each of these reasons alone, would produce a powerful force for compliance, together they are virtually irresistible. Our shortcuts usually work to our advantage, but we can be duped into using

177

them at the wrong times. People will respond mechanically to a piece of information, rather than make a more considered response. Our use of shortcuts produces responses that are so obvious, so natural and so correct, that we cannot conceive that they could be wrong (Shiffrin and Schneider, 1977).

People are most likely to take shortcuts and commit errors when a decision has to be made under conditions of uncertainty. Specifically, when they do not have time to think carefully about an issue; when they are so overloaded with information that it becomes impossible for them to process the information fully; when the issue at stake is not very important; or when little other knowledge or information is available. While these conditions may occur opportunistically, they can also be consciously created by you, so as to increase your chances of successful influencing. How you frame your information determines whether you trigger a bias in your listener (Frisch, 1993). For influencing purposes, what is important is knowing about the different types of bias which the use of heuristics elicits. The remainder of this chapter will detail these biases. Although frequently related and overlapping, for clarity of presentation, each bias will be described separately, beginning with those revealed by social psychological research.

Contrast bias

This bias of human perception affects the way that we see the difference between two things that are presented one after another. If the second item is fairly different from the first, we will tend to see it as more different than it actually is. If you lift a light object first, and then a heavy object, the latter will appear heavier than it actually is. When your enter a shop and want to buy a number of items, the sales staff are trained to sell you the most costly item first. Once you have bought it, the second item, will not appear as expensive in comparison. To apply the contrast bias yourself, you need to present the follow-up options independently of each other. For example, in a selling situation, each smaller price will seem petty when compared to the already agreed much larger price. This influence tactic is almost undetectable. Your influencee will not be aware that a situation has been structured in your favour. The bias applies to a wide range of issues (Kenrick and Gutierres, 1980). When persuading a group to adopt your proposal for a new computer system, if you are worried about its being rejected on cost, you can contrast what you are proposing to spend, for example, £25,000 with the company's past and much higher capital investments. Alternatively, seek to position your proposal on an agenda to have it discussed after the group has approved a much larger project, ideally one costing several millions of pounds. Using these contrasts, your own sum will appear small and insignificant in comparison. Be vigilant, however, to ensure that a contrast is not made to your detriment.

178

The contrast bias is also known as the *insufficient anchor adjustment bias*. It states that people find that starting from somewhere is easier than starting from nowhere. When individuals make estimates for values based on an initial value derived from past events, for example, the cost of a building, they typically make insufficient adjustments, upwards or downwards from that initial anchor, so as to reflect other significant factors when establishing a final figure, (e.g. inflation, cost of materials). In all cases, the final figures are biased towards the initial figure, even if it is irrelevant. Different starting points therefore yield different answers. Companies ask job applicants their current salaries to find a value from which they can anchor an adjustment. When asking for a quotation for a job, you can suggest a 'figure that you are thinking of' which can anchor the bidder to give a much lower estimate than they might have provided independently. Alternatively, if asked what your fee is, select a high figure (Slovic and Lichtenstein, 1971; Tversky and Kahneman, 1973, 1974).

Reciprocation bias

A basic norm in society is reciprocation. This says that one person must try to repay in kind in the future, what another has provided in the present (Gouldner, 1960). We are socialized from childhood to abide by the reciprocation rule or suffer social disapproval and a feeling of personal guilt. Such reciprocation leads to concession-making, and allows different individuals' initial, incompatible demands, to become compromised, so that they finally work together towards common goals. The reciprocation norm not only stabilizes relationships between individuals, but also acts as a start-up mechanism, making people free to make the first concession, confident in the knowledge that they will receive back in the future, what they have given in the past.

There is a triple obligation – to give, to receive and to repay. First, by doing someone a favour, you obligate them to return it. Second, there is an obligation to receive a favour. It is rude to reject it. This reduces our ability to choose whom we become obligated to. It is not important whether you wanted the favour, or liked the person who did it for you. Indeed, you will feel obliged to reciprocate an unwanted favour from a person whom you actively dislike. While the reciprocity rule was developed to promote equal exchanges, it can be used to bring about unequal ones. For example, in a one-to-one situation, you can do someone a small favour, and ask for a much larger one in return. In these circumstances you can still make the influencee feel sufficiently indebted to grant you your wish. This is because we dislike being obligated. To eliminate the burden, we will agree to perform a larger favour than the one received, just to relieve ourselves of the obligation. In a group situation, the person who does not reciprocate, is disliked by the group (e.g. not buying your round of drinks). Individuals will often agree to an unequal exchange in order to avoid group disapproval.

179

In such circumstances, the psychological costs outweigh the material ones (Greenberg and Shapiro, 1971; Riley and Eckenrode, 1986).

An obvious yet effective way of taking advantage of the reciprocation bias is to give something to your influencee before asking them for a favour. To make it less obvious, it is useful to institute a time delay between the two actions (Beaman *et al.*, 1988). A second and more subtle approach is to apply the *reject-and-retreat technique*. For example, in a money-borrowing situation, you ask for a loan of £20, an extreme request which you feel sure will be rejected. The initial request will be refused. This is why it is also known as the *door-in-the face* technique When the refusal comes, you ask them for the £10 that you wanted all along. By reducing your request by half, first big, then smaller, you are defining the interaction situation as one involving bargaining and negotiation. In such situations, a concession on one side is typically reciprocated with a concession by the other side. Your second request does not have to be small in absolute terms, only smaller than the initial one. It represents a concession on your part, obliging the receiver to reciprocate, provided of course that they clearly see it as the concession that it is (Cialdini *et al.*, 1975).

Reciprocation incorporates the contrast bias in that, the second request appears to be smaller when contrasted with the first (Miller *et al.*, 1976, Miller, 2002; Wade-Benzoni, 2002). In terms of sequencing, you cannot lose. If you first make a large request and get it, you will receive perhaps twice what you had hoped for. If on the other hand you are turned down, you can retreat to your second request, and place a concessionary obligation on your influencee. Either way you benefit. Reciprocation spurs people on to agree to your request, and motivates them to actually implement it. A study has extended our knowledge in this area. It found that the more precise and unusual the request is, the fewer people are able to resist it. In this experiment, students posing as beggars received small change from passers-by, in 44 per cent of occasions that they asked directly for it, without specifying a sum. If they asked for a precise sum that was a single coin (25 cents), they received it 64 per cent of the time. When they asked for an apparently arbitrary amount (37 cents), they were given it 75 per cent of the time (*Economist*, 2002).

An associated approach to gaining compliance is called the *that's not all technique*. Following an initial request, but before the influencee can say yes or no, you add something that sweetens the deal. This can be some small, extra incentive. For example, by either reducing the price slightly, or keeping the price the same but adding some extra feature or item to the package. As before, the extra, added at the very end, is viewed as a concession, and the influencee feels obligated to make a concession themselves This increases the probability of their complying. So the recommendation is to keep a little something back when making your initial pitch to the influencee, and then, just before they have the chance to decide how to respond, throw it in at the very last moment (Baron and Byrne, 2000).

180

The reciprocity bias in its various forms places great emphasis on the concepts of responsibility and satisfaction. If not viewed as a trick, your influencee will return your favour or concession, and in so doing, will feel a greater responsibility for, and satisfaction with, the final arrangement (Benton *et al.*, 1972). Being so satisfied in the present, they are more likely to agree to similar arrangements in the future. In this way, you are able to prompt your influencees to agree to future requests. Moreover, a person who feels responsible for the terms of a contract is more likely to live up to that contract. That is why modern staff appraisal systems get appraisees to set their own performance objectives, even to the point of writing out their goals or objectives themselves, to be discussed and agreed with their bosses. We shall return to this phenomenon when discussing the next bias.

Commitment and consistency bias

Commitment is a state of being in which individuals become bound to their actions, and through these, to their beliefs. Commitment sustains action in the face of difficulties. In these circumstances it is behaviour which is being committed. It represents a visible indicator of what we are and what we intend doing. This perspective stands in contrast with the belief which holds that behavioural change is preceded by attitude change. That is to say, we first change our attitude and then, and in consequence, we change our behaviour. Here it is argued that behavioural change precedes attitude change. After taking an action, people will adjust their attitude to make it consistent with their behaviour. Our behaviour leads to expectations about what we will do in the future. These expectations then surround our behaviour and constrain us to act within it. Commitments thus mould our attitudes and maintain our behaviour, even in the absence of positive reinforcements or tangible rewards (Salancik, 1977a). Human beings have an obsessive desire to be, and to be seen to be, consistent with what they have already done and said. Once we make a choice or take a stand, we will encounter personal and interpersonal pressures to behave consistently with that earlier commitment (Festinger, 1957; Heider, 1946; Kanter, 1968; Newcomb, 1953). Outsiders will also survey our behaviours. For example, politicians spend hours explaining that their current actions are not U-turns, but that they are consistent with past decisions and existing policy guidelines.

Thus commitment and consistency is a powerful bias with which to influence others. How does it work? At the individual level, by making a commitment, influencees change the image they have of themselves. The psychological mechanism involved is self-perception. We are aware of the fact that we look at other people's past actions as evidence with which to determine their current beliefs and values. What we are less aware of is that we do the same to ourselves. We use information about ourselves as evidence when deciding what we are like.

181

We look at our past actions as a guide to our attitudes and beliefs. It is a primary source of information for us about ourselves! Moreover, we change our attitude to match our committing behaviour (Bem, 1972). Perceptions of causality are dependent on the circumstances in which the behaviour takes place. If the behaviour is carried out in a situation in which the individual is free to do what she chooses, she will infer that she caused her own behaviour. This perception of self-motivated behaviour will then bring about a change in the individual's concept of self. Within this context, making a commitment, even a small one, produces inner change. That change is not just specific to the situation where it first occurred, but will cover a whole range of related situations. In addition, the effects of the change are lasting. Once people have been induced to shift their self-image (e.g. to be generous), they will be generous in a variety of other circumstances where their compliance may also be desired. They are likely to continue their generous behaviour for as long as their new self-image holds.

Being consistent makes life easy, predictable and integrated for people (Conway and Ross, 1984; Goethals and Reckman, 1973). Having once decided about something, consistency means we do not have to think about the issue any more. We do not have to collect, sift or weigh information, or assess arguments for and against courses of action. Instead, when confronted with a choice, we act automatically know what to say and how to act, in the confident knowledge that it will be consistent with our earlier decision. Consistency offers a shortcut through the complexities of life. Even erroneous commitment decisions have a tendency to become self-perpetuating as people add new reasons and new justifications to support the wisdom of the commitments that they have already made. Automatic, pre-programmed and mindless consistency responding allows us to put up barriers to stave off tricky problems. However, others can manipulate our desire for consistency.

At the social level, commitment and consistency is produced through generalized social norms that favour predictability and steadfastness. These are associated with personal and intellectual strength. People who demonstrate these traits, particularly in adversity, are seen as logical, rational, stable, honest and as worthy of occupying positions of leadership and authority. In contrast, non-commitment and inconsistency are considered to be undesirable personality traits. Inconsistent men are perceived as indecisive and weak-willed, while inconsistent women are judged to be flighty or scatterbrained (Allgeier *et al.*, 1979; Asch, 1946). What others think of us is an important part of what we think of ourselves. If our friends tell us that they think we are generous, then we are likely to act generously (Kraut, 1973). Thus, once an active commitment is made, one's self-image is squeezed from both sides by consistency. From the inside, there is a pressure to bring the self-image in line with one's actions, whether verbal or written. From the outside, there is a tendency to alter one's image so as to adjust it to the way others perceive us (Jones and Harris, 1967).

182

To have the power to bind a person, a commitment has to fulfil four criteria. First, it has to be made voluntarily with little or no external pressure. This prevents a later recantation through the excuse that they 'forced me into it'. Free choice is essential for commitment since it is the glue that binds the action to the person, and motivates them to accept the implications of their acts. Second, the commitment should be visible and public, so that they are unable to deny that they made it. Commitments made in public are thus more likely to last. The more public the stand, the more reluctant we are to change it (Deutsch and Gerard, 1955; Fenigstein, Scheier and Buss, 1975: Tedeschi *et al.*, 1971). Company staff appraisals frequently incorporate goal-setting activities where staff publicly (in the presence of the appraiser), commit themselves to achieving certain work performance targets. Third, commitment must be irrevocable, so that it cannot be changed easily. The inability to undo what has been done, narrows our alternatives considerably. Finally, the person should be explicit about the attitudes, values or subsequent behaviour being committed to (Salancik, 1977a).

To use this bias, get your influencee to take a stand on an issue, or agree to do something for you. Start with a small, perhaps trivial, commitment. You can then start to manipulate their self-image. Depending on the circumstances, you might get them to state their commitment in public, perhaps to a group, or to put it in writing and circulate it to a group. A written commitment has the advantage of being irrevocable, since physical evidence exists of what has occurred; it reduces the opportunity for the influencee to forget or to deny it to himself; and it can be used to persuade others by showing that the influencee truly believes in what he had written. Some door-to-door salespeople get their customers to fill in the sales agreement themselves. This helps to overcome the 'cooling-off period' where customers change their minds. Having got their self-image where you want it, your influencee will naturally comply with a whole set of your requests which are consistent with the stand that they have already taken, and which is also consistent with their new self-image (Sherman, 1980). This approach, of starting with a small commitment and building up, is known as the, *foot-in-the-door* technique. Not only does it make your influencee more willing to agree to a subsequent additional and larger request (door opened even wider), it also persuades them to perform a range of favours for you, which are only vaguely connected with the original, little one that they did for you at the start (Dillard *et al.*, 1984; Freedman and Fraser, 1966; Schwarzwald *et al.*, 1979; Jacob, 2001; Girandola, 2002). It has been found that a time delay between requests increases acquiescence. This gap, more than a few minutes but not longer than 24 hours, enables a self-perception change to take place (Beaman *et al.*, 1998).

The act of making a commitment decision itself produces dissonance in a person. There will inevitably be negative aspects of the option chosen, and positive aspects of the option rejected. To reduce such dissonance, the influencee will, in her head, spread apart the alternatives on offer. After her decision is

183

made, she will tend to emphasize the positive aspects of her chosen option, and de-emphasize its negative aspects. She will do the reverse for the option rejected. Having committed herself through a decision, she will then become bonded to it. Market research has discovered that people like a product more after buying and paying for it, than before the purchase. Gamblers are more committed to their bets after having made them than before. In all these examples, it is behaviour that is determining the attitude, and not attitude determining behaviour. Commitment is about an individual becoming bound by their acts. The more committed a person is to a choice, the more negatively they will view other options. For this reason, if you give a person advice that is even broadly consistent with a decision that they have already made on some issue, the more likely they are to take it (Brehm, 1956).

The strength of another person's commitment is affected by a number of factors. First, the size of the request. The larger the first request agreed to by your influencee, the more they will be committed to it (Fern et al., 1986). Second, actions rather than intent. If the influencee actually performs the action that you requested them to, as opposed to simply agreeing to perform the action, the more committed to it they will become (Beaman et al., 1983). Third, the effort and reward involved. The more effort an influencee expends and the less external reward they receive, the more committed they will become. This explains the importance of initiation ceremonies in tribes, schools and some occupations. Going through a lot of pain and trouble to get something, makes it seem more valuable than if were achieved with little effort (Aronson and Mills, 1959). External inducements have to be absent because they would break the requirement for volition. For maximum commitment, the participants have to own what they have done. They have to take inner responsibility for their actions. Finally, it has been found that commitments, 'grow their own legs', making reinforcement unnecessary. Once a commitment is made, people view themselves differently, and convince themselves that this is the correct way to be. They start noticing facts that they previously had not noticed. This process generates additional reasons that they then use to justify their new commitment. Thus, even when the original reason for the change is taken away, their newly discovered reasons may, on their own, be sufficient to support their perceptions that they have behaved correctly (Brownstein and Katzev, 1985; Cialdini et al., 1978; Katzev and Johnson, 1984).

There is a powerful way of simultaneously harnessing the power of both the reciprocation bias and the commitment-and-consistency bias. Instead of asking someone to help you to *do* something, ask them instead to help you *think* how to do something. This will make them feel that your problem is partly theirs as well. By asking for their advice, you have challenged them by giving them a problem to solve, and getting them interested in it. By asking them, 'What would you do?', you not only receive their advice, but you also gain their commitment to a satisfactory solution. By proffering advice, they are making a small commitment to your solution. The consequential change in their self-perception will cause them to believe that they like you as a person (otherwise, why would they be helping someone whom they did not like?). The very act of advising commits them to you, and this further cements your alliance and friendship. The operation of this psychological process leads us to an intriguing possibility. We already know that the principle of reciprocation obligates the favour-requester to the favour-giver. However, and in addition, by asking for a favour, the favour-requester also obligates the favour-giver to them! Letting someone do you a favour, commits them to you. You are offering them the opportunity to get involved. Once they have invested in you, your career or your project, they will not want you to fail, and will make extraordinary efforts on your behalf (Pfeffer, 1992; Regan, 1971). Opportunities to use both techniques in combination should be sought (Goldman, 1986).

Social proof bias

George Kelly said that people acted as naive scientists who explained the actions of others by asking three questions. *Consistency* – does the person behave in the same way in other situations at other times? *Consensus* – do others behave in the same way in similar situations? *Distinctiveness of action* – is she the only one to behave in that fashion? The last two questions focus on the behaviour of people around us. The social proof (or validation) bias states that people decide what to believe or how to act in a situation, by looking at what others believe and do. In situations of uncertainty and ambiguity, they observe and follow others, especially those they perceive to be most similar to themselves. Such similarity is defined in terms of status, social background, dress, manner or language (Festinger, 1954; Hornstein *et al.*, 1968; Tesser *et al.*, 1983). Market research suggests that 95% of people are imitators and only 5% are initiators. Imitating others has several benefits. First, it eliminates the need for mental effort to evaluate a situation on our own. Second, it leads us to hold similar views to those around us. We already know that we like those whose views are similar to our own, and we fear being ostracized or rejected by others. Imitating others avoids both these dangers. Hence, it is not surprising that people are persuaded more by the actions of others, than by any proof that you can offer.

The social proof bias can be observed in operation on a daily basis. Buskers put £1 coins in their baskets, and church ushers 'salt' collection baskets so as to guide congregations as to what is the appropriate donation. Advertisers tell us that a product is the 'fastest-growing' or 'largest-selling'. Some paperback books are advertised as a 'bestseller' prior to their publication! These adverts do not stress the benefits of the product, but instead emphasize that many other people are buying it. Television adverts depict characters similar to their audience, avoiding actors who are too handsome or glamorous. You can use the social proof bias in your own influencing by informing your influencees that many other individuals, who are just like them, have complied with your request, or who are doing the same thing. You can also ensure that the referees on your application form resemble, in terms of their background and status, the person making the appointment decision. In this context, people trust and will follow the advice of people like themselves.

Liking bias

Similarity is one of the two requirements of social proof. It affects a person's liking for you, and that liking encourages their compliance to your requests. People prefer to say yes to those whom they like. This is most clearly illustrated by the party plan approach of Tupperware Home Parties Corporation which arranges for its customers to buy from a friend, rather than from an unknown salesperson. The liking bias is so powerful, that the person concerned does not even have to be present for it to be activated. Often, just a mention of a friend's or mutual acquaintance's name will be sufficient. This can occur face to face, on the telephone or in a letter. Any of these requests may begin, 'Bill suggested that I approach you about'. Your liking for Bill, becomes transferred to the requesting stranger. An element of reciprocation may be involved if you happen to owe Bill a favour. The power of liking through personal contact or acquaintance is so strong, that doorstep salespeople will, after either a sale or even a rejection, ask you for names of friends or acquaintances who might be interested in their product. They can then greet their next prospect with the opening line, 'Miss X suggested that I call on you'. This makes it difficult to turn away the salesperson who is somehow representing your friend.

How do you get your influencee to like you? You can take four specific steps (Cialdini and Goldstein, 2002). First, you should maximize your physical attractiveness. It was noted earlier in the book, that attractive people create an automatic response which psychologists call the halo effect. Having noted their good looks, we automatically and unconsciously assign to them favourable traits such as talent, kindness, honesty and intelligence (Adams, 1977). This applies to both men and women (Signall and Ostrove, 1975; Stewart, 1980; Kulka and Kessler, 1978). Attractive people obtain help when they need it (Benson et al., 1976) and are more persuasive in changing others' opinions (Chaiken, 1979). There is a limit to what nature has endowed you with, and it is a case of making the best of what you have. Hence the importance of good dressing and grooming.

Second, be like the person you are influencing – simpatico. As mentioned earlier, we like people who are similar to us in opinions, personality traits or lifestyle. Similarity can create an instant bond between people. We are more likely to help those who dress like us (Emswiller et al., 1971; Suedfeld et al.,

186

1971); or who claim to have similar interests to our own. The stated similarity may be in occupation ('I'm a student too'); habitation ('I come from London as well'); status ('I'm married too'); or preferences ('I don't like cabbage either'). Trivial as these similarities may seem, they do have an effect (Brewer, 1979; Gonzales et al., 1983; Aune and Basil, 1994). For this reason, some commentators recommend that you manufacture links between yourself and your target influencee as quickly as possible.

Third, take active steps to interact with those people whom you wish to influence. Interaction leads to familiarity, and familiarity is an important factor in liking, affecting a wide range of different decisions (Grush, 1980). We prefer things that are familiar to us and hence will repeat choices that we have made in the past (Zajonc, 1968). Repeated contact with a person, particularly under circumstances of mutual and successful co-operation, on common tasks towards a common goal, will heighten mutual liking. It is because we like people we know well, that networking and visibility are so important in influencing personal opportunities and promotion, and will be discussed in later chapters. Fourth, communicate to the influencee that you like them. This produces return-liking and willing compliance from them (Berscheid and Walster, 1978). We all like to be liked, and are more willing to comply with the requests of others, who show that they like us. Making flattering compliments and giving praise are both ways of communicating liking, as is saying 'I like you' (Drachman, deCarufel and Inkso, 1978; Byrne, Rasche and Kelley, 1974). People tend to believe praise, become helpless when they receive it, and like those who provide it (Jones and Wortman, 1973).

Authority bias

Each of us has a deep-seated duty to authority, and will tend to comply when requested by an authority figure (Milgram 1974). In any society, a diverse and widely accepted system of authority allows the development of sophisticated structures for the production of resources, trade, expansion and social control. Since the opposite is anarchy, we are all trained from birth to believe that obedience to authority is right. Notions of submission and loyalty to legitimate rule of others are accorded value in schools, the law, the military and in political systems. The strength of this bias to obey a legitimate authority figure comes from systematic socialization practices designed to instil in people the perception that such obedience constitutes correct behaviour. Different societies vary their terms of this dimension. As we grow up, we learn that it benefits us to obey the dictates of genuine authority figures because such individuals usually possess higher degrees of knowledge, wisdom and power. We tend to do what our doctor advises. In consequence, deference to authority can occur in a mindless fashion as a kind of decision-making shortcut – 'ask an expert what to do, and do what they say'.

187

When we comply with authority in an automatic fashion, we may be reacting to the symbols of that authority, and not to its substance. We each possess stored patterns for responding to authority which are activated by specific external signs. The two most important symbols are titles and clothing. To trigger the authority bias, you can use your titles and association membership (e.g. B.Sc., M.A.; Independent Consultant) to convey your authority which is based on your expertise. Experts who seem to be impartial are more influential (Eagely *et al.*, 1978). People frequently assume substance from appearance, and clothing can act as an authority symbol that triggers a mechanical compliance. The 'cloak of authority' is easily feigned. It is difficult to resist requests that come from figures wearing authority attire such as uniforms or white coats (Bickman, 1974; Bushman, 1984; Mauro, 1984). The well-tailored business suit communicates authority status, and can evoke deference from total strangers (Wilson, 1968). It is the importance of things and people that make them appear bigger. Since we see size and status as linked, you can substitute the former for the latter by selecting suits with a striped pattern that make you appear taller and hence more authoritative.

Scarcity bias

We all know that things and opportunities that are difficult to obtain are more valued. We use information about an item's availability as a shortcut to decide quickly on its quality. Moreover, as things become less available, we lose freedoms. Since we hate this, we react against it, and want these things more than before. For example, stockpiling coffee if it threatens to be in short supply (Brehm, 1966; Brehm and Brehm, 1981). The scarcity bias operates under two opposing conditions. Scarce items are heightened in value when they are newly scarce. That is, we value those things that have been recently restricted more than those that were restricted all along. Additionally, we are more attracted to scarce resources when we compete with others for them. Scarcity pressures have an emotion-arousing quality that prevents people thinking logically about it. We see it everyday around us. The rarity of stamps and coins establishes their value; shops advertise limited offers, closing-down-on-Friday sales and limited edition cars. Auctions are dangerous places since scarcity and competition combine to arouse emotions and lead you to overbidding. In any scarcity situation, we are not consciously aware why we want something more, only that we do. Since we need to make sense of our desire for an item, we begin to assign positive qualities to it in order to justify our want.

This bias is known by different names. The *playing-hard-to-get techniques*, is one such label, and notes that compliance can be increased if it is suggested that a person, object or outcome is scarce, and hard to obtain. That is why, as an interviewee, inadvertently dropping the information that you have been offered a job by another leading company, is likely to enhance rather than reduce your

188

appeal in the eyes of selectors. The findings were described by Baron and Byrne (2000). It recommends creating the impression that you are scarce and thus hard to get. Related to this is the *deadline technique* which states that increasing compliance can be gained by telling influencees that they have only a limited time in which to take advantage of some offer or obtain some item. This is prevalent in all forms of selling. Notice how, after one deadline offer expires, a new one replaces it immediately. To use the scarcity bias, you simply need to convince your influencee that the item (product, service, idea, proposal, deal) is somehow in short supply and will not last beyond a certain date or time. This may be true or false. Your hard-to-get tactic gives you added appeal, while the deadline tactic places a limit on the person's opportunity to obtain what is being offered. By doing so, the item's perceived value to the influencee rises, and they will be keener to obtain it (Schwarz, 1984). Hence, it is useful for an interviewee to tell selectors that they are applying to other organizations, or have been offered a job by another company.

We shall now turn to the research from decision theory, to examine some further biases that can cause errors of thinking. We have already noted that the pressures of life lead us to use shortcuts when making decisions, and that these involve using a single, highly representative, usually reliable, piece of the total information available. Research into decision-making further suggests that these same time and cost constraints, also limit the quantity and quality of information available to people. Individuals use and retain only a small amount of data in their usable memory. A quick tour of the key observations made by decision theorists includes a number of the most well-known biases.

Ease-of-recall bias

We are biased towards those events that we can recall and imagine most easily. We then go on to believe that they are more probable and more typical than they really are (Tversky and Kahneman, 1974). For example, people overestimate the number of plane crashes and murders of children. The two features that make recall easy are recency and vividness. A recent event is recalled more quickly than one which took place long ago; while a vivid event, because it impressed us emotionally, will be recalled easily even though it occurred in the past. For example, with annual staff reviews, any spectacular success or failure by the appraisee will be easily recalled by the appraiser (vividness). In addition, their job performance in the last three months before the appraisal will be more easily recalled than that occurring in the previous nine months (recency effect).

Let us see how you can use this bias. Dealing with vividness, if you are making a proposal to an audience in competition with others, to place it at the forefront of their minds, you should make it easy for them to imagine. A vivid presentation uses scenario descriptions, hi-tech presentation equipment, and fables, which

189

build upon a small amount of generally acknowledged truth. All these make your proposal memorable to your audience, and thus influential. In the appraisal situation, a single spectacular success will have more impact than consistent good, but unspectacular performance. You also make your proposal both more typical and more probable for them (Alba and Marmorstein, 1987; Russo and Shoemaker, 1989; Slovic and Fischhoff, 1977; Tversky and Kahneman, 1973).

Turning now to recency, we know that advertisers use message repetition extensively. This ensures that the influencing is regularly re-located in the audience's mind. If we hear a thing often enough, we can come to believe that it is true. Repeating the same message over and over again, regardless of its truth can thus create reality. Repetition also creates familiarity, and the section on liking showed that we like people and things that we are familiar with. Obviously, familiarity with a suggestion or idea does not guarantee its acceptance, but the two are frequently linked (Aronson, 1992). The longer and more frequently a message is received by listeners in speech or writing, the more deeply it becomes embedded in their minds. This bias argues for the importance of communicating your job achievements to your boss on an ongoing basis, perhaps in the form of 'you might like to know' memos, whether or not she has formally requested work updates from you.

Information bias

When dealing with information, people frequently fall into the *base rate insensitivity* trap. They under-use information that describes most projects or people, and instead allow themselves to be influenced by the distinctive features of the case being presented. An influencer's vivid and compelling anecdote pushes the general truth out of the audience's mind. For example, you propose the launch of fruit-flavoured crisps. Historical evidence shows that the failure rate for this type of product is about 80 per cent. However, by vividly describing the wonderful product, the receptive market, and the brilliant marketing team who will steer it to success, your audience forgets the 80 per cent base failure rate. Instead of rejecting your proposal out of hand as statistics would lead them to, they give you a hearing, and may even approve your proposal. When such vivid information is absent, the audience will tend to use base rate estimates correctly (Kahneman and Tversky, 1973; Tversky and Kahneman, 1984).

The compelling anecdote acts as a distracter, and the most effective distracters have been found to be superficial impressions, vague indiscretions and wishy-washy, little, biographical summaries. Schwenk (1986) reported that too much weight was given to such information about individuals and companies, and too little attention to pallid, colourless, but nevertheless more reliable and relevant statistical data (Brogida and Nisbett, 1977). However, the latter had little emotional impact on the audience, being less easily recalled and often ignored.

The message to influencers is to use vivid, anecdotal information to draw your audience away from any statistical information which might negatively affect their support for your proposal. Managers are influenced by vignettes, and if your anecdotal information paints a consistent picture, they will not seek other, more objective information (Bar-Hillel, 1989; Einhorn and Hogarth, 1981; Nisbett and Borida, 1975; Meehl and Rosen, 1955: Saks and Kidd, 1980).

Chance bias

People hold serious misconceptions about the operation of chance, and yet the making of realistic assessments of probabilities concerning the occurrence of events is an important aspect of a manager's job. Three aspects of this bias are particularly relevant. First, individuals tend to perceive order in random sets of events. They believe that something will be true for short sequences that is in reality only approximately true for very long sequences, and only rigorously true for sequences near to infinity – for example, the movements of shares on the stock exchange. Second, people wrongly expect random and non-random events to 'balance out', and see chance as a self-correcting process. They fallaciously believe that deviations in one direction, will induce deviations in the other in order to restore some sort of presumed balance. For example, that after four product launch failures, managers incorrectly conclude that a fifth failure is unlikely, even though statistically, the performance of the fifth is totally independent of the previous four. In fact, deviations are not corrected as the chance process unfolds, but only become diluted (Kahneman and Tversky, 1972; Langer, 1975; Tversky and Kahneman, 1971; Hamill et al., 1980).

Third, people like to look for causes of events. We are slow to deduce particular instances from a general truth, but are remarkably quick to infer a general truth from a single vivid experience. A common cause is generality held to indicate the presence of its effect, rather than a common effect of its cause. Thus if two events co-exist, we prematurely jump to the conclusion of causality. By attributing events to one cause or another, we order our world, thereby making things more predictable and controllable in our minds. Part of the explanation for the operation of the chance bias is human beings' intense need to find order and meaning in their lives through seeking reasons for happenings, even in the most random events. This bias can be exploited by the way questionable statistics might be presented, and the way in which the causes and effects of past, present and future events can be implanted in people's minds (Weiner, 1985).

Relationship bias

The *presumed association* or *conjunction bias* draws on the previously described ones, and refers to people's inclination to over-estimate the probability of two events

191

co-occurring, based upon the number of similar associations that they recall easily. When they have to judge what is typical, they lose sight of any objective probability. They consider the simultaneous presence of two normally associated facts, to be more probable than either of the facts occurring separately. This is despite the irrationality of believing that it is more likely that two events to be joined, than that each will happen alone (Kahneman and Tversky, 1973; Tversky and Kahneman, 1983; Shafir et al., 1990). Once a person becomes convinced of such a positive correlation, however illusionary it is shown to be, they will always find new confirmations and justifications as to why their correlation is correct (Bar-Hillel, 1973; Chapman, 1967; Hamilton and Rose, 1980; Kahneman and Tversky, 1979). As before, this bias can be explained by noting that the perception of a relationship where none exists, or a perception of a stronger relationship than actually exists, gives individuals a feeling of predictability and control (Ward and Jenkins, 1965). Moreover, when we expect to see a significant correlation, we are also more likely to notice and recall confirming instances of it, rather than disconfirming ones (Chapman and Chapman, 1967; Einhorn and Hogarth, 1978, 1981). The implication for influencing is that if your proposal can benefit from a historical correlation, even a spurious one, your audience are more programmed to accept it than challenge it – 'The last time sales doubled was during a leap year, next year is another leap year and I believe they will do so again'.

Overconfidence bias

This is the tendency for people to be more confident than correct. They fail to collect key factual information because they are too sure of their assumptions and opinions, and do not acknowledge the actual uncertainty that exists. Overconfidence is greatest in a person's areas of ignorance, exactly where it can do the most damage. In contrast, an individual frequently demonstrates underconfidence on topics in which they are knowledgable. It appears that, as a person's knowledge of a topic decreases, they do not correspondingly decrease their level of confidence. This bias occurs because our experience does not produce a more realistic, self re-appraisal as one would expect. People only actively seek information that confirms their current beliefs, and do not seek or will dismiss any that challenges those beliefs.

For example, following a tentative decision to buy a certain make and model of a car, a person will search for data to support their decision, even though a search for challenging or disconfirming evidence would provide them with more useful insights (Fishhoff et al., 1977; Klayman and Ha, 1987; Skov and Sherman, 1986; Dunning et al., 1990; Vallone et al., 1990). However, it is typically not possible to know that something is true, without checking for possible disconfirmations. Additionally, once they start to think why an idea might be true, it begins to seem true (Koehler, 1991). When influencing, it is useful to challenge the knowledge base of your most vociferous critic. There is a good chance that their confidence about why you are wrong is inversely proportional to their knowledge of the topic.

Hindsight bias

After finding out whether or not an event occurred, individuals tend to overestimate the degree to which they could have predicted the correct outcome. This is the 'we-knew-it-all-along' effect. People are not good at recalling or reconstructing the way a certain situation appeared to them before finding out the results of that decision. While our intuition may be accurate, we tend to distort our beliefs about what we knew beforehand, on the basis of what we found out later. The same phenomenon occurs when people look back on the judgements of others. A corollary of the hindsight bias is that people are less generally surprised by a reported outcome than they should be. That is, they see it as 'obvious' even though, before the fact, they may be undecided (Fishhoff and Beyth, 1975; Slovic and Fishhoff, 1977).

Knowledge of this bias may be of the greatest value if a proposal of yours fails, and others attempt to blame you, claiming that they, 'knew it was wrong all along'. First, you can use your knowledge to point out the existence of the bias. Second, you can look out for the attack on you in which your critic reassesses the relevance of a particular piece of data from the past that is somehow representative of the final observed outcome, for example, a set of sales figures that you used in your presentation. He then claims that the failure, which has now occurred, was predictable. What you need to be aware of is that this person is using hindsight to criticize your foresight judgement. We can note that in the short run, hindsight has the benefit of flattering us to believe that our judgement is far better than it actually is. Hindsight reduces our ability to learn from the past, and to evaluate objectively our decisions and those of others. Since we rely on the results and the hindsight corresponding to them, we will inappropriately evaluate the logic used by the decision-maker in terms of *outcomes occurring*, and not, as we should, by the *methods* employed (Fishhoff, 1975a, 1975b).

Status quo bias

Also known as the *endowment effect* or *minimization-of-regret bias*, this is simply a preference for the current state. People prefer the status quo because the perceived disadvantages of leaving it appear greater than the advantages. When something is designated or identified as being the status quo or the default option, people will prefer it. Indeed, they are willing to take bigger gambles to maintain the status quo, than they would be to acquire it in the first place.

193

The perceived advantages of the status quo increase as the number of available alternatives increases. This mental bias prevents us from ending investments and activities which carry a long history of hopes, disillusionments and risks. We experience regret even when we alter an existing situation that has in the past been neutral to us. We believe that actions and decisions require a greater justification than inaction, such as not deciding or just leaving things as they are. The reason for this is that our brains have a built-in cost for action. If our actions do not succeed or cause us a loss, we regret having acted. Curiously, if we do not act and leave things as they are, and this causes a loss, we will still experience regret, but it will be less. The implication is that, in neutral situations where there is no crisis but a possibility of gain, it is easier to persuade people to do nothing.

Sunk cost bias

Researchers have observed that individuals will often demand much more to give up an object that they currently own, than they would be willing to pay to acquire it anew. The dis-utility of giving up the former is greater than the utility of acquiring the latter (Kahneman and Tversky, 1984; Samualson and Zeckhauser, 1988; Thaler, 1992). While the majority of people have a resistance to over-spend a particular budget, they also have an opposed bias, to invest even more, to bring to fruition a past investment which cannot now be reversed. This produces the phenomenon of, 'throwing good money after bad'. We will add more to it than we would have been willing to spend at the beginning, if we believe that this is the only way to make it pay in the end. We permit past investments to influence our current decisions, when such costs should be excluded from consideration. Rational decisions should be based on comparisons between future gains and future costs. History is full of examples of a commitment to a policy or project known to be unworkable. These include films which go wildly over-budget, American involvement in Vietman, and the Anglo-French government decision to persist with Concorde.

The sunk cost bias leads to escalating commitment and entrapment of the decision-makers. It provides you with a powerful aid to influencing which depends upon the way in which you manipulate information (Arkes and Blumer, 1985). If you want them to continue supporting your no-hope project, you should begin by reminding your audience from the outset of all the money or effort that they have already invested in it. The more money and the larger the effort, the better. Next, cause your audience to attribute the failure so far, to causes which are unlikely to persist in the future (Conlon and Wolf, 1980). Finally, explain the advantages of, and seek approval for, continued spending on a grand scale. Evidence suggests that the existing financial situation and your presentation strategy, will cause social anxiety among your listeners, leading them to ignore information about costs, and increasing their commitment to continued spending (Brockner *et al.*, 1979, 1981, 1982).

Finally, there are some other, less frequently discussed biases (*Economist*, 1999). People appear to be disproportionally influenced by the fear of feeling *regret*. They will pass up gaining available benefits, for a small chance of feeling regret at having failed. They are also prone to *cognitive dissonance* or denial. This is holding two beliefs simultaneously, one of which is manifestly at odds with the evidence, usually because a belief has been held and valued for a long time. Rather than looking at individual decisions in the context of the big picture, they tend to *compartmentalize*. That is, they make a choice about things in one particular compartment without taking account of its implications for things in other compartments. Human beings engage in *magical thinking*, attributing to their own actions, something that had nothing to do with them. In this way, they assume that they have control over events when, in reality, of course, they do not. A lucky investor buys a share that rises, and convinces himself that he is skilful rather than merely fortunate. A common theme running through this field of prospect theory, as it is known, is that people are loss averse rather than risk averse. Loss averse means that they would prefer not to lose £100 rather than gain £100. People regularly miscalculate probabilities.

EMOTIONS AND DECISIONS

Underlying all the discussions in this chapter is the idea that our emotions affect the decisions we make, and that our decisions, in turn, affect the emotions that we experience. By being aware of how feelings affect decisions allows you not only to predict what a person's mood might be after they have made a certain decision, but may also let you influence their decisions by manipulating their feelings. Schwarz (2002) considered the links between emotion, cognition and decision-making, providing insights into the irrational reasons behind many decisions. He summarizes some of the most useful research findings. First, let us consider emotion or feeling at the time of decision-making. Some points are common sense, and one of these is that moods influence decisions (Barone *et al.*, 2000). A person in a happy mood will overestimate the likelihood of a positive outcome, and vice versa. Additionally, an outcome is more likely to be perceived as positive if the person is in a happy mood. This however is not the case if the decision-maker is aware that their current feelings are unrelated to the outcome being considered. The interaction with others is also affected by mood. People in a good mood are more likely to imitate the behaviour of others, and will act in a co-operative way, while those who are feeling sad tend to be less co-operative.

Other findings are less obvious. For example, people are more likely to recall information that is consistent with their current feelings. Thus, knowing how a person is currently feeling about a subject can give you pointers as to what information their decision will be based upon. Mood also affects how people process information. People in a happy mood tend to have a top-down processing approach, paying too much attention to pre-existing knowledge, while giving less consideration to the details at hand. People in a sad mood adopt a more systematic approach, and do the reverse. They both consider more factors, and do so, one factor at a time. This is thought to be because we adjust our approach to our current situation. If things are going badly, there is more need to analyse the underlying facts; if things are going well, if is sufficient to rely on the usual routines, and thus the need for new knowledge is less urgent. It has been found that sad individuals are biased towards high risk-high reward options, while those who are anxious are biased to low risk-low reward ones (Raghunathan and Pham, 1999). The person's mood is likely to affect the perspective or approach that they feel will be most effective.

Turning now to how people might be feeling after they have made a decision, we know that they try to minimize the possibility of regret or disappointment. They experience more regret about what they have done, than what they have not done. In consequence, they may choose a decision alternative that has a more severe and more likely outcome, as long as it means that they have to be less involved in the choosing process. This is useful to know when you are presenting or creating different possibilities for your influencee. Also, people tend to focus excessively on a specific emotional event, and often fail to grasp the full range of factors that are influencing their feelings. Thus, if one aspect of a possible event is likely to create a strong feeling of well-being in a person, smaller, undesired effects may not be evaluated properly, since they will be less visible to the influencee. With respect to risky behaviour (e.g. drug taking), those with greater experience of these activities emphasize the positive effects and reduce the negative ones. In contrast, those with limited experience, tend to avoid the negative effects of these activities. Knowing whether a person is risk-lover, risk-averse, or risk-neutral, can help an influencer to decide what to focus on. It appears that extensive experience of mood-eliciting situations does not improve the accuracy of the predictions for similar situations, and consequently, it is just as difficult to predict future feelings.

Finally, what about our memories of our past feelings? Studies have shown that when people think of past episodes involving an emotional dimension, they do not take into account the full experience. They focus only on two parts of it – the moment of peak intensity and the ending. Surprisingly, people appear to neglect the duration of the feelings. As a result, they might prefer a long experience with a mild ending, in comparison to a short one, with the same degree of stress throughout. This finding can, for example, be used to make people less sorry for what they have gone through, by easing the experience at the end.

196

CONCLUSION

Sanford (1983) offered an explanation of how these various biases operated. He argued that, to understand any problem, you had to link the problem statement with the relevant background knowledge. The quality of the link was determined by how familiar you felt the problem to be. Once you mentally slotted in a framework with which to address your problem, it was difficult to construct a different framework. Moreover, it was easier to insert newly acquired knowledge that fitted your existing framework than to deal with knowledge that did not fit in. What are the consequences of this? From the perspective of memory, information that does not fit into your framework will not be recalled. Initially, 'odd' information that does not fit, will command attention for a while but following a failure to fit it in, it will be forgotten. In contrast, information that fits, even though not fully analysed, will be retained. This is exemplified in the experience of explaining something to someone, when you suddenly realize that you do not fully understand it yourself. You have effortlessly and uncritically absorbed easily fitting, unanalysed information. A second consequence is that once an interpretation of something is made, it is difficult to form a new one. When you do try, the old interpretations that exist in your memory, keep creeping back in. Being unable to form alternative models, blocks both your logical reasoning and your creativity. In order to think creatively, you have to first break out of your current modes of thought.

The topic of decision-making bias is one of the most fascinating aspects of the entire literature of influencing theory. Much of this work was pioneered by Kahneman and Tversky (2000), and has been discussed by Gilovich (2002). However, much of it complex to explain, and is best done with the aid of extensive examples which space precludes here. Readers are therefore referred to the work of both Cialdini (2001a) and Bazerman (2001). These authors provide a lively and highly accessible introduction to this important field.

Chapter 10

Influencing behaviour

You can dodge your responsibilities but not the consequences.

Anon.

INTRODUCTION

An early approach to influencing was proposed by John Watson, and developed by B.F. Skinner. It is called *operant conditioning* and it seeks to encourage desirable behaviour while discouraging undesirable behaviour. It has been applied to many different aspects of life including the organizational context (Campbell *et al.*, 1985; Huberman, 1964; Luthans and Martinko, 1987; Nord, 1970; Organizational Dynamics, 1973). Operant conditioning, or behaviour modification as it is more commonly known, is based on three assumptions. First, that what needs to be changed is not the individual, but some aspect of their *behaviour*. Second, that the person ultimately responsible for behaviour change is the person themselves. Third, your responsibility as the influencer is to bring the problem behaviour to their attention, get them to acknowledge that it is indeed causing difficulties, and assist them to modify it so that it becomes acceptable to all concerned. This chapter describes a set of procedures that are based on the principles of behaviour modification. For illustrative purposes, it will focus on the organizational situation of a manager influencing a subordinate.

MODIFYING BEHAVIOUR

Let us begin by considering the first of these assumptions. Earlier chapters have considered both verbal and non-verbal behaviour. Behaviour includes all aspects of a person that can be directly observed by another (timekeeping, production output, absence), while excluding everything that cannot (their personality, attitudes, beliefs, values and motivation). The behaviour modification approach argues that you do not need to change the person, but some aspect of their behaviour. When an employee is frequently late for work, you do not want them to

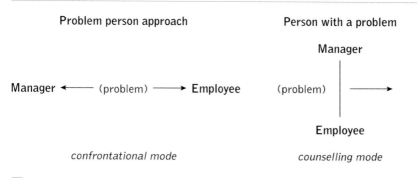

Figure 10.1 *Two contrasting approaches to influencing people*

become a different person, you just want them to start punctually. If you try to change a person's behaviour, you can be said to be taking a 'person with a problem' approach, whereas if you seek to modify their attitude or even personality, you are taking 'problem person' approach. The difference between the two is summarized in Figure 10.1.

INDIVIDUAL RESPONSIBILITY FOR BEHAVIOUR CHANGE

The 'problem person' approach sees the manager as responsible for changing the behaviour of an employee. It recommends punishing staff for misbehaving, or bribing them for complying. However, when you treat people like children, they will respond like children. Such a parental approach creates in employees feelings of dependency, resentment, anger, hostility and apathy. In contrast, the 'person-with-a-problem' perspective holds that ultimately, it is the employee's responsibility to regulate their own behaviour, and if you treat the employee as an adult who has a problem to solve, then they are more likely to respond like an adult. In this second approach, managers do not abrogate their responsibility for maintaining efficiency; however, they ensure that their employees recognize that they may have a behaviour problem to solve, and help them to do so. This is the second assumption of this approach.

What are the advantages of taking a person-with-a-problem approach for the manager and for the employee? For the manager, it makes the interaction less personal, and hence, less stressful. The focus is upon the other person's behaviour, and not upon them as an individual. Second, behaviour is more objective, its occurrence can be counted. Again, this makes the situation less personal. Third, since behaviour is 'produced' by the individual, you can help them to increase, reduce or stop the production of it. Finally, the approach offers flexibility. Old behaviours can be modified or eliminated, and new behaviours learned. There are also benefits in this approach for the

199

employee. First, being criticized is often an embarrassing and stressful experience. If the focus of discussion is upon their behaviour and not them, this can distance both parties, making the process less emotional. Second, since the occurrence of the problem behaviour is counted, this objectivity allows the employee to assess the magnitude of the problem himself or herself. Third, as the employee produces the behaviour, they can change it. This gives them control of the situation, enabling them to generate their own alternatives, and thus maintain their dignity. Finally, the approach allows them to learn new, acceptable behaviours, while sustaining and enhancing a good working relationship with you.

MANAGING THEIR BEHAVIOUR

The third assumption concerns your role as their boss. This is to identify their problem behaviour, bring it to the employee's attention, and assist them in finding a solution. As mentioned, a focus on the problem behaviour changes the relationship from a confrontational to a counselling or advisory one. You are helping the employee to address and solve their own problem. This helps you in a number of ways. It helps to maintain your relationship with the person better than if you had disciplined them. It motivates the individual to improve their performance. It does this by stressing their positive achievements and improvements in the future, rather than getting bogged down in recriminations about the failures of the past. It helps the employee develop their own problem-solving skills which, while being focused on this problem, can be used by them to address similar problems in the future. Finally, it allows you to make your own positive contribution to finding an acceptable solution, provided that the employee takes the main responsibility for behaviour change. To summarize, the focus is on the individual employee's behaviour, which is to be changed by them, with your help. The 'person-with-a-problem' approach uses a seven-step sequence.

Check the area of their problem

Checking the nature of the problem can ensure that you understand its boundaries. It also reminds you that employees' performance problems are frequently similar, that the range of problems is predictable, and that the skills developed in helping one employee can be used with another. The list in Table 10.1 identifies common behavioural problems experienced by company employees, as well as some found in the non-work contexts with spouses, partners, friends and others. Once you have located the behaviour that is causing you a problem, you should note down its main features as you see them. This will help you clarify your thoughts about the matter.

200

Table 10.1 *Identifying the employee's problem*

Work

1   Poor attendance

2   Poor timekeeping

3   Is resistant to change

4   Fails to delegate

5   Appraises others badly

6   Produces unsatisfactory written reports

7   Makes poor public presentations

8   Produces insufficient work

9   Fails to work to deadlines

10   Produces shoddy/slapdash work

Non-work

11   Leaves the flat untidy

12   Fails to do her share of cooking

13   Turns up late for dates

14   Complains about the food in all restaurants

15   Is rude to me

16   Is late in producing her portion of the rent

17   Does not co-operate

18   Disturbs others with his music

19   Is aggressive

20   Never plans ahead

Highlight their specific problem behaviour

Highlight the observable behaviour that concerns you. You identify the actions that illustrate this behaviour (that can be seen or heard, and hence can be counted). Highlighting can be contrasted with *tagging* which means placing a tag or a label on a person's lapel to describe that individual's unobservable, inner state. Tagging makes assumptions and inferences about the employee and their personality, and can elicit a negative, emotional reaction. It can be found in staff appraisal forms which ask whether the appraisee possesses drive, loyalty, vision or initiative. How can you see loyalty? The main problem with tagging is that it fails to specify in sufficient detail the unsatisfactory behaviour and gives no guidance as to how it might be usefully changed. Hence, as the influencer, once you have identified the general area of your concern, restate the problem in terms of one or more highlighted statements. For example, in the case of the problem area of poor attendance, the highlighted behaviour might be: *is frequently absent from work*. After this first attempt, look again at what you have written, and decide if you be can be more specific about the problem behaviour using questions such as: What makes you say that? What specifically has occurred? What evidence do you have? What examples can you give?

Analyse the frequency of the problem behaviour's occurrence

Analysis involves measuring the individual's problem behaviour. It is important because it allows you to confirm that their behaviour is indeed worse than the average; and it also provides you with facts (e.g. actual absence dates and frequencies) that you can use in your discussion. A highlighted behaviour can be analysed either directly or indirectly. In the direct approach, you assess the *behaviour itself* by keeping a note of its occurrence, and noting this down (e.g. number of days the employee is absent in a month). With the indirect approach, you focus on the *results* of the behaviour. This is achieved by studying documents and the reports of others (e.g. has the person included recommendations in her proposal as requested). It has been argued that if their problem behaviour is having an impact upon their current work performance, or the performance of those around them, or is likely to affect the individual's future or career, then it is legitimate to help and encourage them to change it.

Causes of behaviour

What are the causes of an employee's problem behaviour? You begin by focusing on the specific problem behaviour of the employee that was highlighted in step two. Next, you go back, and ask what events or conditions preceded the employee's highlighted behaviour, and which may have *triggered* it off? Finally, you consider the *consequences* for the individual of their highlighted behaviour. That is, what happened to them after they have manifested the undesirable behaviour. Let us consider them in turn. To ascertain the triggers, you need to ask the questions listed in Table 10.2.

The triggers for a person's undesirable behaviour may be found in the properties of the *individual* (causes 1–3), that is, their personal circumstances which can affect their ability to do their job. In the *fit* between the job and the person (causes 4–6), for example, the job's level of difficulty or challenge. There may have been a selection problem, the wrong person being chosen for the job. The trigger could be in the properties of *management style* (causes 7–9) with respect

Table 10.2 *Possible triggers for highlighted behaviour*

1	Is there a difficulty in their personal, family or domestic situation?
2	Is there a health problem?
3	Is the person (unsuitably) modelling their behaviour on another's?
4	Does the person possess the personal ability to achieve the required performance (e.g. have they been trained?)
5	Is the job too difficult?
6	Is the job too simple and lacking in challenge?
7	Are the job goals to be achieved clear to them?
8	Do they receive sufficient external motivation, such as money?
9	Have they received feedback on their past performance?
10	Have they been given sufficient resources with which to do the job (e.g. equipment, information, a budget)?
11	Is there anything others do or say that could prompt the undesirable behaviour?
12	Are their working conditions conducive to satisfactory job performance?
13	Is the organizational structure satisfactory, in terms of rules and supervision?
14	Are there special situations or events that precede the undesirable behaviour?

to goal definition, the reward system and the ability and willingness to communicate about poor and excellent performance. In the properties of the *organization* (causes 10–13) with respect to physical facilities and the organizational structure of rules and procedures; or in the properties of the *situation* (cause 14), in that a certain event or set of circumstances may occur just before the undesirable behaviour occurs. Next, you should consider the *consequences* for the individual of their highlighted behaviour. That is, what happens to them after they have manifested the undesirable behaviour? You are interested primarily in the consequence that follow for them personally. Following the undesirable behaviour, the employee may:

1 be rewarded in some way by his co-workers or someone else;
2 receive feedback on her behaviour;
3 be disciplined by being reprimanded or given a formal verbal or written warning;
4 be given more or less interesting, easier or more difficult, future assignment;

203

5 be given recognition;
6 be promoted;
7 receive financial or non-financial benefits.

A positive, encouraging consequence of the employee's behaviour increases the likelihood of that behaviour being repeated, while a negative, discouraging consequence will decrease that likelihood. If may even be the case that you, as his manager, may be inadvertently reinforcing the undesired behaviour. Behavioural consequences for an individual are not all the same. They differ in terms of their *impact*, with some consequences directly affecting the employee's behaviour, while other consequences primarily affect those around him. They differ in terms of *timing*, with some consequences being immediate (occurring within the same or next day), while others are delayed (occurring a week or more later). Finally, consequences differ in terms of their *probability* of occurrence, with some being certain and others being uncertain. Under normal circumstances, personal, immediate and certain consequences, have a greater affect on a person than those which affect others, are delayed or which are uncertain. Influencing involves identifying the causes of the gap between the employee's actual and required behaviour. To be most effective, you have to prepare for your meeting with the employee to discuss their behaviour problem. Thinking about the likely causes, in terms of likely triggers and consequences, can help you to agree a plan to close the performance gap.

Examine the problem behaviour with the employee

Your interview with the employee is concerned with helping them to take responsibility for their own behaviour, correcting it and moving back to accepted standards of performance. The interview is a positive rather than a negative thing. So how do you start? Plan your interaction before you begin. Specifically, state the objective that you want to achieve ('At the end, he/she will'). Decide an *indicator* to measure if you have achieved it ('He/she will suggest at least two options for dealing with the problem'). Finally, *plan your behaviour*, detailing what you will say and do during the meeting to reach the objective. Having explained the purpose of the interview step, let us now consider the six distinct phases that make up the interview. Each one makes a contribution to a successful outcome.

Introduce your concern

In the first phase of your interview with the employee, introduce your concern about their performance in a neutral manner. Your aims are to get them not only to admit that there is a problem, but also to take responsibility for solving it. The key technique in this step is to ask a general question in a neutral manner about your area of concern, and then to keep quiet and listen to their answer. If they ask, 'What do you mean?', just repeat the question. Your questions might take the following form:

Concern	Question
Absence	Colin, I've asked you in today to find out your feelings about the level of staff absence within the department.
Lateness	Jean, I want to know how you feel about people coming to work late.

At this stage, be careful *not* to ask:

Problem	Question
Absence	Colin, why are you absent from work so often?
Lateness	Jean, why are you so frequently late for work?

The first set of questions is rather more subtle than they appear. Some employees, who might be referred to as Responders, may be aware of their problem already, and be willing to discuss it there and then, Mentally, Responders will add on to your question, the phrase, *'especially yours/you'*. Indeed, they may even answer their own question, starting their sentence with the word, 'I', as shown below.

Problem	Question	Employee answer
Absence	Colin, I want to know what your feelings are about absence in your department. *Especially yours.*	I've been taking rather more time off than usual because of my wife's illness.
Lateness	Jean, I want to know about how you feel about people coming to work late. *Especially you.*	I don't seem to be able to rouse myself in the morning, to get in on time.

If the employee does not take the hint, we can call him a Defender. It means one of two things. Either he knows that he has a problem behaviour but is unwilling to discuss it without further prodding, or he may be genuinely unaware that he has a problem behaviour which is affecting his job performance. This second category of Defenders can be identified by their replies to your general question. These will not contain any reference to their own problem behaviour. For example:

Problem	Question	Employee answer
Absence	Colin, I want to know what your feelings are about the level of absence in your department.	A few people are occasionally absent, but it's no big deal.
Lateness	Jean, I want to know how you feel about people coming in to work late.	The odd person comes in late, but it's usually due to traffic or some problem at home.

Clarify or describe the problem behaviour

If, in answer to your generalized question, the Responder admits that they are aware of their performance deficiency, then your task now becomes that of specifying with them what exactly the problem behaviour is. This process involves comparing their *actual* performance with the *desired* performance. If you have had an earlier discussion about this same problem, you will need to provide details about what has or has not happened since your last meeting. The undesirable behaviour should be described specifically, and supported with numerical evidence from the third step of Analysis. Such objectivity encourages the process of problem-solving.

In the case of the Defender, if she is reluctant to admit that she has a problem behaviour, or is unaware of any performance deficiency, then you have to identify for them exactly what the problem is. As before, this process involves you comparing their *actual* performance with the *desired* performance. The difference between Responders and Defenders is that the latter are likely to become angrier or more defensive than the former. This stems from their unwillingness to discuss their deficiency, or surprise at learning that there is a problem. The procedure here is exactly the same, except that you need to give the Defender time either to express her anger at your comment, or to absorb the criticism. Once they have taken your points on board, you again specify that part of their work behaviour that needs changing.

Express your views about the situation

In this phase of the interview, confirm the seriousness of their inappropriate behaviour, and secure their agreement to examine ways of changing. You should express both your thoughts and your feelings about the employee's problem behaviour. State how it is impacting on them in terms of their work performance and future in the organization, the performance of their co-workers and your own performance as their manager. The aim here is not to give you the chance to 'blow off steam'. Indeed, it is essential that you conduct this phase without becoming excited, threatening or angry. Instead, you are seeking to convey to them just how seriously you are treating the issue. As before, be specific about the effects, remembering that the employee may just be failing to think through the repercussions of their actions or inactions. Many may be genuinely surprised and embarrassed at having these consequences pointed out to them. This phase is not completed until the employee both agrees that he or she has a problem and expresses a willingness to explore the problem with you.

Investigate causes of the problem behaviour

What are the reasons for their undesirable behaviour? You will have some idea because you will have already considered the triggers and consequences in step four which dealt with causes. However, by asking the employee for the reasons, you raise their self-esteem by showing that you want to hear their side of the story. It also indicates to them that you are wanting to help them. As they give their excuse or rationalization, listen carefully without interrupting, and try to understand how the employee is feeling (angry, disappointed, embarrassed). The issue can be emotional for them. Even if you feel that you are hearing the 'same old story', you should not pre-judge the issue, or show disbelief. You can confirm that you understand what they are saying by paraphrasing their comments, without necessarily agreeing with their facts, beliefs or interpretations. As you listen, look out for examples of triggers and consequences which might be contributing to their undesirable behaviour. Having heard the employee out, question him about the effect of the various triggers and consequences that you have thought about earlier. The aim is to check your hunches so as to pin down the cause of their problem behaviour.

Question	Hunch
1 Are you having any difficulties at home?	Women often absent themselves if a child is ill (trigger).
2 Are you finding the job too difficult?	Some people avoid the stress of too difficult a job by absenting themselves from it (trigger).
3 What was the reason you were absent last time?	Are there any special situations or events that precede this behaviour e.g. backlog of work? (trigger).
4 What happens when you get back to work after an absence?	Insufficient feedback from absentee's supervisor (consequence).

207

Generating solutions

Summarize what has been discussed and agreed so far, and encourage the employee to generate possible solutions that would fill his performance gap. Begin by restating that their current performance is unacceptable, and remind them that it is their responsibility to change it. Since the employee owns the problem, he should also ideally, own the solution. For this reason, it is important not to suggest any solutions at the start of this phase. Instead, begin by asking them for their ideas about how they might change their own behaviour in a way that meets the requirements of the job. By inviting suggestions, you will gain their commitment to change. Listen to each suggested idea, and ask questions for clarification if required. Avoid making any value judgements or assessments before all their ideas have been produced. It is rare but possible, for an employee to have no idea as to how he may solve his own problem, even if he is willing to. In such circumstances, you should have prepared for two or three possible and acceptable solutions. You would then present these to them for evaluation.

Evaluating solutions

Here you are evaluating each of the solutions that the employee has produced, or that you have produced for them. Remember, that the chosen solution has to be acceptable to both of you. However unacceptable to you the employee's suggestions may appear, do not dismiss them out of hand. Instead, respond by stating, 'I understand what you're saying, and here's another point of view. Let's look at them both, and see if we can put them together'. Rather than presenting your solution alternatives, look for opportunities to incorporate these as part of the employee's suggestions. Try to narrow down acceptable ways of changing the person's behaviour to two, both of which would be equally acceptable to you. Then ask them to choose the one which they prefer.

Agree on the specific action to be taken

The final face-to-face task is to gain the employee's agreement and commitment to make specific changes. Have them agree to a timescale within which this will be done, and set a follow-up date to review progress. Your aim is to help them to solve their problem by thinking through the specific, concrete actions that they can take in implementing the change (e.g. arranging for a telephone wake-up call). Where appropriate, offer support and information (e.g. 'We could put a card in the canteen asking if anyone would be willing to give you a lift to work'). If the employee gets annoyed or upset, just remain calm and re-state the work performance standards, explaining that he should now begin thinking about how these might be achieved. Finish the interview on a positive note by

208

focusing on the future. Confirm that the action that the employee has chosen will allow him to overcome the problem, and indicate your confidence in his ability to do this.

Changing triggers and consequences

After the meeting, you have another task to do. Based on your preparation and subsequent meeting, you need to consider altering the employee's work environment by adding, removing or modifying the triggers and consequences associated with their problem behaviour. A change in a person's behaviour can be stimulated by the application of one or more of six change techniques. The skill is knowing when to introduce each. The first technique changes the triggers of behaviour, and is called a *prompt*. A prompt is anything that you do to move another person to action. Prompts occur before behaviour and are designed to get it going or to guide its direction. A common prompt is a No Smoking sign. Prompts also include rules, schedules, signs, verbal requests, orders, traffic lights, performance plans and yellow lines on warehouse floors. A trigger can also be changed by *modelling*. This refers to setting an example for someone else. Imitation is a powerful method of learning, and this technique uses the principle of, 'do as I do' (Bandura 1969, 1977a, 1977b).

Turning now to changing consequences, *reinforcement* is the term given to providing a positive outcome for any action a person takes that increases the likelihood of its being repeated. When we systematically design work environments to make reinforcers follow desirable behaviour, we are taking advantage of this tool for change. Some after-the-act reinforcers include applause, social, verbal or written recognition; letter of appreciation; positive feedback; being asked for suggestions; smile, and so on. A related technique is *removing negative consequences*. If a negative consequence follows a desirable behaviour, that desirable behaviour may stop. A third technique is *extinguishing*. You extinguish by preventing reinforcers from following an undesirable behaviour. Another approach is to *reinforce opposite behaviour*. This is decreasing undesirable behaviour by crowding it out with other, opposite or incompatible behaviour. Rather than punishing sloppy appearance, you reward neat dressing. Many managers and organizations find that reinforcing punctuality is more effective than punishing lateness.

Finally, you can introduce a *negative consequence* which is any event which follows an undesirable behaviour and which decreases the likelihood of that behaviour happening again. Undesirable behaviour can be decreased or stopped by introducing negative consequences which did not previously exist. For example, there may have been no cost to coming into work late. By introducing a deduction of pay for repeated lateness, you have introduced a negative consequence for an undesirable behaviour which had not previously existed. However, this technique can cause resentment; tends to produce only temporary suppression of the undesirable behaviour; and does not teach new, desirable behaviour. Some of these new prompts and consequences may be agreed to with the employee at the interview, while you may implement others independently in an effort to sustain and support the agreed behaviour plan.

Monitor performance and follow-up interview

The final thing to be done is to check on the employee's behaviour and performance prior to the agreed review date. If this is the first follow-up interview, and the employee has changed his behaviour, praise them, and encourage continued good performance. In fact, once you note that the new behaviour has been established, go and see the employee at their work location to reinforce the desired behaviour by congratulating him. In follow-up interviews, if the employee has not changed their behaviour, remind them of their failure, but stress particularly the fact that they have broken your agreement. If may be that the employee is unable or unwilling to live up to the agreement, and it is debatable whether they want to keep their job. In such circumstances, it may be necessary to implement the statutory disciplinary procedure of verbal warning, written warning and ultimately, dismissal.

Chapter 11

Assertive criticism

Criticism is a study by which men grow important and formidable at very small expense.

Samuel Johnson

INTRODUCTION

We think of criticism as 'jumping down someone's throat', 'showing them up' or humiliating them. Yet the first meaning of criticism in the dictionary is, 'the art or act of analysing or evaluating'. The word 'criticism' comes from the Greek word *kritikos* which Aristotle used to mean, 'able to discern or judge accordingly'. Despite its definitional neutrality, the word has acquired a negative connotation. The synonyms that are often suggested for criticize are blame, censure, condemn, denounce or reprehend. Researchers have found that flaw-finding is the traditional and dominant way that managers use to encourage change in employee behaviour. When this negative connotation of criticism is considered within the context of interpersonal relations, and is linked with the need of individuals to protect their own egos, it is not surprising that most people experience being criticized as a negative event which involves personal attack and hurtful exchange. In this chapter, criticism is defined as the process whereby you tell people what it is that they are doing which you consider to be wrong or which bothers you, and help them to adjust their behaviour (Giblin, 1956). On the positive side, criticism has the power to motivate and has historically been a powerful force for change.

It is also not surprising that most people dislike criticism and seek to avoid it. That applies as much to the criticism-giver as to the criticism-receiver. People being criticized report feeling hurt or humiliated, and find it difficult to accept that they are not doing their job adequately. The critics fare no better. They find it embarrassing, and do not want to hurt the feelings of the other person. Most worrying of all, they do not know how the other person will respond to their criticism. We know that criticizing is one of the most difficult and least liked interpersonal tasks that managers do at work. Yet for all that, the receipt of criticism is the means through which we improve our performance, and the giving of criticism represents one of the key influencing opportunities in the workplace. Clearly, there must be different types of criticism, which have different effects on both the critic and the criticism-receiver. Paul (1988) said that criticism can be either constructive or destructive. Constructive criticism focuses on problems and helps the person being criticized to improve; concentrates on behaviour and not on personality; strengthens relationships; builds trust; is two-way; reduces stress; avoids conflict; and helps the employee to develop and grow. It was the absence of these eight features which, in Paul's view, characterized destructive forms of criticism.

CRITIC'S BEHAVIOURAL STYLE FOR CONSTRUCTIVE CRITICISM

Glaser (1990) argued that a critic's behaviour differed on two major dimensions. First, with regard to their *respect for self*. Those who had low respect for themselves were frequently not willing to share their thoughts, feelings, past experiences, reactions with others. In a sense, they were saying to themselves, 'I'm not OK' as a person. Others, in contrast, had a high respect for themselves, and communicated their thoughts and feelings to others. Such a willingness was based on a belief that, 'I'm OK' as a person. The remainder fell somewhere along the continuum. A second source of difference was their *respect for others*, defined as a person's willingness to afford others the same rights as they afforded themselves. Some people had little respect for the opinions, feelings and reactions of others. They were saying to those they criticized, 'You're not OK'. At the other end of this scale were those who defended the rights of others, taking a view of the person being criticized as, 'You're OK'. The remainder fell in between. These two dimensions are independent of each other as is shown in Figure 11.1, and you can be high or low on both of them.

Glaser's two dimensions distinguish four dominant critic communication styles, each with its own attitudes and behaviours. Habitually, people tend to use the three which produce destructive forms of criticism – passive, manipulative or aggressive styles. Such use may be the result of habit or of a one-off success which is then repeated and never changed. The different styles affect your ability to influence others. You can change from any of the first three styles to the assertive one which is associated with a constructive form of criticism.

Passive criticizing style

A passive critic's approach is motivated by feelings of sadness, fear and discomfort. Passives are quiet, withdrawn and deferential. They operate from the standpoint

Figure 11.1 A model of interpersonal influence
Source: Glaser, 1990: 3

that they are worth less than others. Passive critics are people who are inhibited, self-denying, lack confidence in themselves and are conflict-avoiding. They do not respect themselves, and assume that others are more important than they are. In consequence, they fail to stand up for themselves. A Passive ignores his or her own needs, in an attempt to satisfy the needs of others. As a result, they experience feelings of low self-esteem, frustration and sometimes withdrawal. They express their thoughts and feelings in such a self-effacing manner that they invite others to ignore them. Their anger is turned inwards, and other people are accorded more rights than the person accords themselves. In transactional analysis (TA) terminology, Passives are saying, 'I'm not OK – You're OK'.

If you have identified yourself as a Passive, then your main problem is a lack of self-confidence. You avoid taking responsibility or committing yourself to ideas or people. Instead, you end up complying. You find others making excessive demands of you which you find difficult to refuse. If you act non-assertively, you may feel more comfortable because you are not risking the pain of people confronting you or disliking you. You may choose to be passive just for a quiet life. You may feel virtuous because you are being unselfish and self-sacrificing. However, a constant denial of your needs will lead to a drop in self-esteem which will cause frustration and internal tension. You are inviting people to take advantage of you if you are passive. A passive criticizing style may be so weak that the

213

person's error fails to be communicated to them. Passives are the bystanders in organizations who allow others to do things to them. One of the first steps towards developing self-confidence is to realize that you are responsible for yourself, and that you influence others through your own behaviour.

Open Aggressive criticizing style

The Open Aggressive critic has a positive self-attitude, but fails to take account of the needs of those whom she is criticizing. In TA terminology, they are saying, 'I'm OK – You're not OK'. Such people are domineering, pushy, self-centred and engage in self-enhancing behaviour. When criticizing others from a position of anger, openly aggressive people will frequently adopt an accusatory tone ('You've really screwed it up this time'). At the extreme, they may even be abusive, threatening and authoritarian. Non-verbally, Open Aggressives glare, finger-point and make angry movements towards the other person. Their approach to criticism is based on their feelings of hostility and irritation. They behave in domineering, sarcastic and opinionated ways. In certain circumstances, their behaviour achieves their short-term goals, for example, with timid or less powerful individuals, or in situations where hours of gentle persuasion may have failed. Additionally, such behaviour gives an Open Aggressive a feeling of power as they see others fearfully doing their bidding. However, the benefits rarely last long since they depend on negative power. They force short-term compliance rather than achieving long-term commitment. Openly aggressive criticizing tends to be counter-productive as the resentment of those who have been intimidated seeks an outlet in some form of retaliation.

Concealed Aggressive criticizing style

The person who uses a concealed aggressive criticizing style has both a negative attitude to himself and low consideration for others. Unlike Open Aggressives who are open about their negative feelings, Concealed Aggressives do not feel secure enough to be open about their own anger or disapproval. In consequence, they manipulate others and are subversive. They convey their thoughts and feelings in subtle and underhand ways. For example, by giving their subordinates boring, repetitive work to do so that they apply for a transfer. They are usually demotivated and depressed individuals. They have a negative voice tone, expression and actions. Their behaviour is destructive, both to themselves and to others with whom they interact and criticize. Concealed Aggressives may speak coldly, bang desk draws or be sarcastic. In TA terminology, they are saying to themselves, 'I'm Not OK – You're Not OK'. Such attitudes may have been generated by changes in their lives over which they had no control, or over which they were not consulted about. For example, job relocation decisions, redundancy, lost promotions.

If you have identified yourself as a Concealed Aggressive, then your main problem when criticizing others constructively is that you are unaware that you lack confidence in doing so. You find it difficult to trust either yourself or others. You expect others to be devious towards you, and you experience yourself as being devious towards them. You have negative thoughts about yourself and others. As a Concealed Aggressive, you may be able to get people to do what you want without having to risk refusal by asking them directly. However, the danger is that by not asking them directly, people may misunderstand what you want. In the long term, this strategy will not work because people dislike being manipulated and, when they find out what you are up to, you will lose their co-operation and respect.

Assertive criticizing style

Being assertive means standing up for your own rights in a way that does not infringe the rights of others. It involves expressing your needs, wants, opinions, feelings and beliefs in a direct, honest and appropriate way; being open and flexible; and genuinely concerned with the rights of others, yet at the same time, willing to establish your own rights. Assertives make things happen and create opportunities for themselves; feel able to be open with others; communicate with people at all levels; respect their own actions; know their own limitations and accept them. Assertive behaviour is thus fundamental to you as an influencer because it allows you to express disagreement without creating unnecessary conflict. It allows you to make requests and state your views in a confident manner. It lets you co-operate with others in solving problems in a way that leaves everybody reasonably satisfied with the outcome. As an Assertive, you develop more confidence in setting goals and making decisions, and can cope with criticism, whether valid or not, without becoming defensive, critical or feeling guilty. It means that you can deal with difficult people and situations more effectively. Assertives respect both themselves and others. They stand up for their rights and this allows them to communicate their own thoughts and feelings to others, without violating their rights. Assertives are saying to themselves, 'I'm OK and You're OK'.

Being assertive does not mean getting what you want every time. Assertives always risk being refused because they state clearly what they want. When you state your opinion, you risk being disagreed with, and so you risk confrontation with others. You cannot influence by acting assertively, without saying no, causing disappointment or having confrontations. However, this risk can be reduced if you remember that assertiveness is about respecting the other person as well as yourself. If you behave assertively, your relationship with the other person will survive your disagreements with them. Assertive communication is a long-term influencing approach that permits others to understand clearly what you want

215

and where you stand on an issue. By making your position clear, you build trust with others, and they go along with you because you are consistent. Because you respect your own needs, those around you will not feel manipulated or brow-beaten. You thereby increase your own self-respect, and win the respect of others. Overall, you are likely to get more of what you want in both the short and the long term. The assertive criticizing style is the only one that solves problems, allows you to stand up for your rights, and secures the commitment and co-operation of others. The other three styles, in various ways, produce temporary solutions, create new problems, divest others of their rights and secure only compliance. For this reason, assertiveness theory is a useful perspective from which to approach criticism (Townend, 1991).

PRINCIPLES OF ASSERTIVENESS

Assertiveness is based on the principles of equality, respect and responsibility. The principle of *equality* sees you and me as being of equal value, irrespective of the differences in the positions that we might occupy in the organization. It holds that I have a right to say what I think and feel, and have a duty to listen to what you say. Thus, when you criticize me, I must listen to your criticism of me, but it is my responsibility to decide what to do with that criticism. When a person com-municates assertively, he or she feels calm and comfortable, and their behaviour is self-assured and confident. The second principle of assertiveness is *self-respect*. To build self-respect, remind yourself of your rights, irrespective of what organi-zational position you hold. This gives you the confidence to stand up for yourself, but remember that others have these rights too. You have the right to:

1   be treated with respect as an intelligent, capable and equal human being;
2   have and express opinions, views and ideas which may be different from other people's;
3   have these opinions, views and ideas listened to and respected;
4   set your own priorities;
5   be the judge of your own behaviour, and be independent of the judgement of others;
6   have needs and wants and ask others to respond to them;
7   say no to a request without feeling guilty;
8   make mistakes;
9   change your mind;
10   take responsibility for the consequences of your behaviour;
11   ask for more information;
12   decline responsibility for other people's problems;
13   deal with others without being dependent on them for approval;
14   choose not to assert yourself.

216

Finally, the principle of *responsibility* holds that you are responsible for your own feelings and actions, and that the other person is responsible for theirs. This principle is manifested in the use of 'I-language'. Since you are seeking to change others' behaviour, your criticism will be perceived as personal, and they may react defensively or aggressively. Much criticism is offensive because it oversteps a person's permitted psychological space, as when they are made to feel guilty, blamed, put down or rejected. They react by losing respect for you, and reject your criticism of them since to accept it would result in a reduction of their self-esteem. The main cause of this effect is often the use of the word 'you' at the start of your sentence, as in, 'You made a mess of that'. The alternative is to say 'I', which keeps your message within your rights. Saying, 'I feel frustrated with your performance whenever'. You can speak for yourself in this way, but have no right to speak for the other person. You can speak openly, honestly and directly to them, if you speak your own mind, rather than preface the message with a manipulative 'you'. Not only does this show that you are taking responsibility for your own thoughts and emotions, but it is also less accusatory than 'You-language'.

Compare the following two sentences. 'You make it difficult for us to meet production targets when you're late for work', with 'I find it difficult to meet production targets when you're late for work'. The second sentence states the problems, without putting the other person down. When putting forward a proposal at a meeting, say, 'I'd like to suggest' rather than, 'Don't you think that'. Avoid using 'one' or 'you' ('One might try' or 'You could go for a'), and recognizing that 'we' is a non-assertive word, which is best used consciously and selectively, when influencing a group, by making it appear that it is their idea, rather than yours that they are adopting. Another reason for using 'I' is your wish for the other person to change their behaviour. Whether they are happy with their actions or not, they have chosen them. This causes you a problem because you want to do something about it. By prefacing your message with 'I', you are emphasizing the effect that their behaviour is having on you and those around you.

CONDITIONS FOR GIVING CONSTRUCTIVE CRITICISM

Before assertively criticizing someone, you should ask yourself a number of questions. First, are you the appropriate person to do the criticizing? For example, when a colleague from another department provides you with inadequate data, should you criticize her yourself, or is it better to raise the issue with her boss who might be the more appropriate person to do the criticizing? Second, is your criticism of the person justified? To decide this, you need to clarify your standards and values. These provide you with criteria against which to check the person's work performance or job behaviour. Clearly, the person must already be aware of these beforehand. Criticism against unspecified criteria is both unfair and can create resentment. Third, is the person capable of improving? If the answer is no, then it is inappropriate to criticize. If a secretary cannot use a word-processing package correctly because she has not been taught, then criticizing her is inappropriate. In such a situation, her self-esteem will be reduced, her typing will not improve, and you will become annoyed at the lack of progress. The solution to this problem is not to criticize but to provide extra training.

The fourth question is when and where to criticize? While there are no golden rules, the following guidelines can help to reduce a person's defensiveness. Constructive criticism should not be given so soon after the unsatisfactory behaviour that you are still in an emotional state, and may respond sarcastically or in an accusatory manner. Nor should it be so long delayed that the link between the error and the criticism is severed. Criticism should be given in time for the person to do something about it, and early wrong steps rectified. In terms of where to criticize, the natural tendency is at their work location, which frequently means in front of or within earshot of others. Some critics also believe that the person will be less inclined to argue back when others are present. However, people prefer to discuss their shortcomings in private. Scheduling a meeting in your office, holding all telephone calls and having a non-confrontational seating arrangement, can all establish the right atmosphere. Although perhaps a little more formal, the benefits outweigh the costs.

GIVING AND RECEIVING CRITICISM

The objective of constructive criticism is to maintain and enhance the self-esteem of the person being criticized; clarify the problem to be solved; and generate a solution that is acceptable to both of you. To achieve this, your criticism needs to be prepared, and will therefore be planned rather than spontaneous. As the critic, you need to think through your objective beforehand. Ask yourself what aspect of the person's behaviour do you want to change; and what are your real motives for doing this (to make yourself feel better, to punish the individual, or to improve their job performance?). You decide what message you want to communicate; and how this might be done so as to reduce its recipient's defensiveness. Weisinger (1989) recommends actually writing out in advance what you are going to say, and rehearsing it aloud when alone, to check out how it comes across. Such planning and practice helps you decide how best to criticize constructively.

In contrast, when you receive criticism from others, you have no control over the timing or approach of the critic. If that person is unskilled, and if her criticism is potentially destructive, then you will need to engage in a 'damage limitation' exercise. You will seek to maintain your self-esteem in the face of the attack, gain an objective and clear understanding of the problem, ascertain if their criticism is valid, and if so, agree a mutually acceptable solution to solve the problem. Paul (1988) offered a '3C' approach to constructive criticizing which consisted of three steps which she labelled, Communicate, Clarify and Commit. Since the process between you and the critic is interactive, these three steps do not form a rigid sequence, but represent a cycle through which the parties may go through a number of times. Hence, after being criticized but before responding, take a few deep breaths, count to five and give yourself time to think. Aggressive or passive responses are instinctive, unthinking reactions, while an assertive response is, by its nature, fractionally delayed. You need time to put your brain into gear before your mouth gets moving.

COMMUNICATE

In the communication step, said Paul, you defend yourself from poorly given, destructive criticism. You do this by using the assertive technique of fogging or negative assertion. There are five different ways to protect yourself by using the fogging technique.

Fogging/negative assertion

You respond to the critic's aggressive or manipulative behaviour by calmly acknowledging the possibility that there may be some truth in what they say, while still allowing yourself to remain your own judge of what to do with their comments. In essence you are signalling that you hear what they are saying, without either agreeing or disagreeing with their comments. Fogging allows you to receive personal criticism without becoming defensive or anxious. It can take one of several forms that Paul suggests:

Agree with any truth in their statement.

CRITIC:	'You were the last person to submit an assignment.'
YOU:	'That's right, I did hand it in very close to the deadline.'
not	'What's the sweat, I wasn't late!'
or	'I am so extremely sorry not to have handed it in earlier.'

Agree with the possibility, however slight, that the critic is right.

CRITIC:	'You gave me the wrong information.'
YOU:	'Yes, the data I supplied you with, could very well have been incomplete.'
not	'What do you mean "wrong" – you were lucky to get anything!'
or	'It was foolish of me not to have checked the information.'

219

Agree with the logic of the critic's statement.

CRITIC: 'Your absences are very inconsiderate to others.'
YOU: 'I can see why you think that I am inconsiderate.'

not   'Look, I was ill in bed you dope!'
or   'I really will try to be more thoughtful in future.'

Allow for the possibility of improvement.

CRITIC: 'You were absent again.'
YOU: 'Yes, I'm sure that my attendance could be better.'

not   'Your attendance isn't exactly brilliant, either, you know.'
or   'I promise not to be absent again.'

Empathy

CRITIC: 'You're really being very selfish.'
YOU: 'I can see how you might feel that I'm being selfish.'

not   'Of course I'm not selfish – you're far too sensitive.'
or   'You're right. I'm sorry.'

The protective technique of fogging not only helps you to avoid feeling bad about yourself after a 'put down', it also puts your critic into a more constructive frame of mind by calming them down. Remember, they are criticizing you because they feel that you have caused a problem. Before you can sort the issue out rationally, the critic has to come off their emotional 'high' and begin discussing the problem unemotionally. Communicating assertively, that is, acknowledging that you have heard their complaint, can begin this process of problem-solving.

CLARIFY

Paul labels her second step, *clarifying*, which in transactional analysis theory, goes by the label of Negative Enquiry. Clarifying can further assist in bringing your critic out of their emotional state. Clarifying means asking the critic to be specific about his complaint. In practice, this means that instead of labelling you as 'incompetent', 'uncommitted' or 'unfair', he has to pinpoint examples of your behaviour which led him to make that assessment of you. The concepts of *highlighting* and *tagging* were introduced in the previous chapter on influencing

220

behaviour, and are relevant here. Asking your critic to identify your problem behaviour forces him to talk in specifics instead of generalities. This in turn moves him from the emotional plane to the rational. It is useful to paraphrase his comments to check your understanding. Paul suggests several clarification techniques using negative enquiry.

Negative enquiry

Negative enquiry probes the negative aspects of criticism in order to get more information. You prompt the critic for examples, which enable you to get at the real information, or to exhaust them. Many critics will offer generalized, unspecific, personal criticism not wholly based on factual evidence. You question them calmly about these. For example:

CRITIC: 'I don't think you're being fair to others.'

YOU: 'Could you tell me exactly in what way you think that I'm not being fair to others?'

CRITIC: 'You really have been "stand-offish" lately.'

YOU: 'Oh, can you tell me in what way I've been acting like that?'

In questioning your critic, focus on yourself and not on your critic, 'What is it about me or my work that is wrong?'. Actively encourage criticism. You will gain more useful information from your critic if you verbally and non-verbally convey the message to them that you would like them to tell you more. Listen closely to the words they use, and help the critic to focus on exactly what is wrong.

YOU: 'You say I'm dressed badly? What is it about the way I'm dressed that's not right?'

CRITIC: 'Well, your suit for one thing. Just look at it. It hasn't been pressed for a month.'

YOU: 'Then it's my suit not being pressed that makes you say that I look badly dressed?'

CRITIC: 'Yes – well, that's one thing.'

Analyse their criticism by continuing to ask specifying questions like who, what, when, where, how, how many, how much, which one? 'On which occasion did my suit appear crumpled?' Avoid 'why?' which can be aggressive. Exhaust the critic by asking, 'Is there anything else about my suit that is wrong?' or 'Is there anything other than my suit that makes you say that I look badly dressed?'. Other enquiries that you can make of the critic are:

221

'What causes you to feel that . . .?'

'What causes your concern about . . .?'

'What is it about this report that is wrong . . .?'

'What makes you say . . .?'

The process of asking for clarification does not mean that you admit that your critic is necessarily correct. Clarification helps you to understand the critic's viewpoint. You may discover that you disagree with him, or that they have misunderstood something. Alternatively, you may find that they are absolutely correct, and that you have indeed been negligent in some way. However, you cannot make such a judgement until you have first understood their point. The clarification step ends with both parties exchanging views and coming to a restatement of the problem which both can agree with. Unless this is achieved, then the next step is impossible, since no one will search for a solution for a problem they do not believe exists.

COMMIT

Paul's commitment step involves finding a mutually acceptable solution to the problem and getting the agreement of your critic to its implementation. This is what transactional analysts call a 'workable compromise'. It assumes that the critic has a valid point about your behaviour. The critic may offer a solution which would solve the problem, and will seek your support for it. Alternatively, they may ask you to suggest some possible solutions, in the way described in the previous chapter. All possible solutions can be evaluated and the best one chosen. The final stage involves gaining the verbal commitment of the other person, which needs to be done directly and explicitly. Your critic will state what you have agreed and what is to happen now. They will conclude with the unambiguous question, 'Will you do that?'. Once you feel that you can take criticism from others without experiencing stress yourself, you will be in a position to criticize others constructively. As we have seen, criticism is just another way of influencing people around you to change their behaviour.

TECHNIQUES OF ASSERTION

So far, two techniques of assertion have been described, *fogging* and *negative enquiry*. There are a number of others you can use when assertively criticizing others, or when you want to avoid being manipulated by others when they criticize you. These all involve slight changes in what you say. Use some of the suggested words and phrases described here, appropriately adjusted to suit yourself. By speaking assertively, you will begin to hear yourself using these assertive words, and you will thus start to think and feel confident, and later to act assertively. Each technique incorporates the assertive principles of equality, self-respect and responsibility discussed earlier (Lindenfield, 1986; Fensterheim and Baer, 1975; Stubbs, 1986).

Minimal effective assertion

This simply involves telling people, in the least threatening manner, what you want them to do or not do. You state your needs and check with the other person that you are not violating theirs. For example, you might say, 'We have a tight deadline on this report. I want you to work overtime on it tonight. How does that fit in with your plans?'. Here you are stating your requirements, but are also inviting the other person to say whether or not they have a problem. When they tell you their problem, you will be in a position to negotiate a compromise. You have shown you respect both your own needs and theirs.

Saying no

You can say no to a request without either feeling guilty yourself or causing the other person offence. However, before doing so, listen carefully to their request. Make a judgement as to whether you want to do the task, taking into account your other interests, priorities and commitments. Having checked, say clearly and unambiguously and with a firm tone of voice, 'No, I don't want to or will not do that'. Make sure that the word 'no' is in your sentence. Be gracious and not brusque. Do not make excuses, there is no requirement on you to give the requester a reason if you do not want to. If it makes you feel better, suggest an alternative person for the task. End the discussion, either by changing the subject or by physically leaving. Sort out any guilt you may feel later. You can only do so much.

Many people feel unhappy with refusing a request in an assertive manner, and feel that by rejecting a request, then they are at the same time rejecting the person. If you are one of these, use empathy to soften your refusal. Do this by throwing in an, 'I'm sorry' to make yourself feel better, but do not apologize profusely 'I'm sorry, I cannot cover for you tonight, I really would have liked to help you out'). This indicates to your questioner that their request has been heard, and that you are sorry that you cannot comply. Empathy however does not require you to supply a reason for a negative response. You can choose to offer them a compromise if you want to, but do not take over the ownership of their problem. Faced with your refusal to their request, the supplicant will either do the task themselves, or will find someone else who will be pleased to do it. Life goes on.

Understanding assertion

Glass (1991) suggested the following assertive phrases to incorporate into your critical statements to others. These can soften your criticism and tells them that you care about and will support them. Using these phrases avoids hurting the person's feelings, and prevents a defensive response on their part:

- You may find it useful to . . .
- You may want to think about . . .
- May I suggest something to you?
- I'm on your side, so do not take what I'm about to say negatively.
- I want you to know that I have your best interest at heart when I say . . .
- Please don't feel offended, but it is important that we should discuss . . .
- You may not be aware of it . . .
- It's difficult for me to tell you this.
- I know you don't mean anything by it.
- I know it's hard for you to . . ., however, . . .
- I see what you mean, however, you may not have all the facts . . .

Discrepancy assertion

This is where you identify contradictory pieces of information or views in a person's statement. For example, when they said they want some more free time to pursue their interests, while stressing the importance of continually being on the job. Since the two are inconsistent with each other, you point out the discrepancy to the person.

Interrupting the process

With this assertive technique, you respond not to the content of another person's communication, but to its process. That is, you talk to them about how they are talking to you. That is, you tell the other person what effect their communication style has on you. For example, you may say, 'When you talk to me in that way, *I feel* that you don't really want my opinion'.

Using silence

Instead of interrupting and arguing with someone who is in a highly emotional state, you can choose to just let the other person vent their anger and wind down, before proceeding with your discussion. Silence is a powerful communication device. Many people feel very awkward about silences in face-to-face communication, and feel the need to fill these with talk. However, after a confrontational message, it is entirely appropriate, to give the other person time to think, and ideally to come up with a proposal that satisfies both parties. Your message is likely to have been complete and self-contained. The effect of your silence is to indicate to them that you have delivered your honest, direct message, about your common problem, and that you are awaiting their answer. This is the best way to make your point. If you talk to fill in the silence, there is a danger that you will dilute your message, and provide them with an escape route.

Paraphrasing

Paraphrasing was suggested earlier in the Clarifying stage. It involves, repeating in your own words, what you have heard the other person say to you or reflecting their feelings; and checking that you have understood them correctly. Not only does this help to deal with criticism, but it is also a vital part of active listening. Paraphrasing allows you to control the direction of the response because you can re-state that part of their message that you feel is the main reason for concern, while ignoring the other 'noise' in their communication. Here are some examples of paragraph openings: 'It seems to you then'; 'What I hear you asking is'; 'Then you feel that'; 'I understand that you'; and, 'If I heard you correctly, you'.

Broken record

If you want people to comply with your requests, but not get into an argument with them, you can state your wishes or demands very simply, and stick to them. Choose a phrase with which you feel comfortable, and then, like a damaged, old-style vinyl record, which jumps in the groove, and repeats the same section over and over again, you keep to your point in the face of the other person's persistence e.g.:

CALLER:	'Are you satisfied with the quality of your existing widows?'
YOU:	'Maybe, but I'm not interested in buying double glazing.'
CALLER:	'Are you interested in saving on heating bills?'
YOU:	'Yes, but I'm not interested in buying double glazing.'
CALLER:	'Do you want to increase the value of your property?'
YOU:	'Yes, but I'm not interested in buying double glazing.'

Do this without becoming emotional, and remain calm, reasonable and composed. This technique can be used when you are in conflict, but you have to resist the temptation to justify or answer the questioner. It is also useful when refusing unreasonable requests, asking questions for clarification, expressing feelings or values when others are not listening. In all these circumstances, you may be trying to make a point but the other person seems to be ignoring your request, or is trying to distract you with other issues. You continue repeating until your message gets across to them.

225

However

This is not really an assertive technique, but rather a vital linking word in an assertive conversation. In the bargaining process, avoid the word, *but*, which is a stopping word. It is used to negate what you have said in your sentence up to the point of its use. For example, 'Your suggestion has merit, but', is understood by your listener to mean that her suggestion lacks merit. Instead of 'but', use the word, 'however', which is a linking word. For example, 'Your suggestion has merit, however, I would like us to consider mine alongside it'.

What are the advantages to you, and indirectly to your organization, of developing your assertiveness? From a career standpoint, it may help to ensure that your true merit and potential is adequately recognized and rewarded. From a personal standpoint, being assertive makes you feel better about yourself. There may well be less chance of becoming too domineering or of feeling powerless in situations. The recognition that you are responsible for your own behaviour, feelings and thoughts, will lead to less blaming of others, and less excusing of your own mistakes or inadequacies. You will save both time and emotional energy through worrying less about offending others. There are many books on assertiveness and they can be found in the popular psychology sections of all the major bookshops. Anyone wishing to develop their assertiveness skills can benefit from reading them.

Chapter 12

Influencing strategies

Few are open to conviction, but the majority of men are open to persuasion.

Johann Wolfgang von Goethe

INTRODUCTION

An influencing strategy is a plan to achieve a goal, and a great deal of research has been conducted into them (Ansari, 1990; Ansari and Kapoor, 1987; Case *et al.*, 1988; Falbo, 1977; Franklin, 1975; Marwell and Schmitt, 1967; McDonald and Keys, 1993; Schilt and Locke, 1982; Vecchio and Sussman, 1991; Wayne and Ferris, 1990; Wright and Taylor, 1994; Ringer and Boss, 2000; Higgins *et al.*, 2003). The problem for influencers is too much rather than too little advice. They need to know what strategies are available and when they are best used. This chapter uses the findings of a study conducted by Kipnis *et al.* (1984) into how managers influenced their own managers, co-workers and subordinates. They identified seven influencing strategies: reason, friendliness, coalition, bargaining, assertiveness, higher authority and sanctions. Each will be dealt with in depth, and will then provide the basis for further consideration of influencing approaches.

Reason

Reason describes a strategy of influencing which relies on the presentation of data and information as the basis for a logical argument that supports a request. You are saying to the influencee, 'I shall explain the reasoning behind my idea'. It involves planning and preparation on the part of the influencer, who arranges her facts and arguments in a way that convinces the influencee. The basis of the influencer's power is their own knowledge and ability to communicate the information. Reason is the most widely used strategy in organizations, and is the first choice when influencing bosses and subordinates. If the information and logic presented is challenged or is suspected, then the reason strategy is inevitably weakened.

Friendliness

Friendliness is a strategy that depends on the influencee thinking well of the influencer. This can be accomplished by, 'acting friendly', showing sensitivity and understanding ('I'll come and see you when you are less busy'), creating goodwill (perhaps by a joke) and using flattery. For example, consciously deciding to compliment someone on a recent achievement before making your own request. As a strategy, friendliness involves a strong emotional component since it plays upon the influencee's feelings. Your use of this influencing strategy will be based on your own personality, interpersonal skills and sensitivity to the feelings and attitudes of others. Friendliness is most frequently used with co-workers, but is also used with subordinates and superiors. It is nearly as widely used as reason. Influencers are most likely to use friendliness when they seek personal favours, help with their work, or when their organizational power base is weak. Overuse of this strategy can lead other people to suspecting your motives and your work competence.

Coalition

Coalition is mobilizing other people in the organization to support you, and thereby strengthening your request. You operate on the premise that there is power in numbers. If many people make the same request or argue for the same action, the influencee is more likely to grant the request. Your power when using this strategy is based on your alliances with others in the organization. These supporters may be used to show similarity of view, or be brought in as go-betweens. In the latter case, you might ask a colleague to persuade someone on your behalf, because they know them better than you. Coalition is a complex strategy that requires substantial skill and effort. Nevertheless, it is widely used, mainly when influencing co-workers and bosses. Coalition is used to attain both personal and organizational goals, but is usually applied as a back-up strategy. Its use is not without its dangers, and overuse can create the impression that you are conspiring against the influencee.

Bargaining

Bargaining is influencing through negotiation and the exchange of benefits based upon the social norms of obligation and reciprocity. It comes down to, 'If you do this for me, I'll do that for you'. The influencer reminds their target of past favours that they have received from them, or promises future ones. Implied in this strategy are the notions of finding common ground, equity and compromise. In short, the influencer relies on a trade that involves making concessions in exchange for getting what they want. What the influencer has to trade is derived from two sources – their own time, effort and skill, and the organization's resources over which the influencer has control. Bargaining is common, but is used more with co-workers than subordinates or bosses. It is primarily applied when the influencer seeks personal benefits. Its weakness is that it creates obligations in the future that the influencer must fulfil.

Assertiveness-insistence

Kipnis *et al.* use the term assertiveness to refer to an influencing strategy which involved influencing people through your insistent, forceful manner. In this sense, their use of this term is different from its common usage as described in the previous chapter. To emphasize this difference, while still retaining the original label, this influencing strategy will be re-labelled assertiveness-insistence, to emphasize that the behavioural style involved is closer to the aggressive end of the continuum. An assertive-insistence influencing strategy involves overtly making strident verbal statements such as, 'I should like you to do this'; repeating your request in an unfaltering tone; and regularly reminding the influencee of your request. More covertly, it can involve setting deadlines, deciding who attends certain meetings, deciding which items will be included on an agenda, how the issues will be framed, and which alternatives will be considered. Assertiveness-insistence gives the impression that the influencer is 'in charge' and expects compliance with their wishes. At times, visible emotion and displays of temper will also be present. It is used more with subordinates than with co-workers and superiors.

Higher authority

Higher authority is an influencing strategy that uses the chain of command and outside sources of power to influence the target person. Kipnis *et al.* limited themselves to the situation of the influencer appealing for the support of senior people who had power over the influencee. For example, saying to a co-worker, 'If you do not accept this proposal, I'll have to take it to our boss'. However, there are additional applications of this strategy. Higher authority can be used when framing your requests. For example, claiming that you are expressing senior management's preferences as in, 'I know the divisional head would go along with this proposal'. Another application is not appealing to a person with higher authority to gain agreement, but to a higher order of ethical or moral values. For example, saying to the influencee that, 'I'm asking you because it is the right thing to do'. You might invoke company tradition or its value system if your organization has a strong corporate culture. It is most often used as a backup strategy when the influencer does not expect the influencee to agree to her request, and tends to be used slightly more often on co-workers. Overuse of this

229

strategy can undermine your relationship with both your influencee (who may feel that you are threatening them), and the person with the higher authority (who expects you to sort out your own problems and not bother them). Perhaps the *threat* of higher authority is as far as you would realistically wish to go.

Sanctions

Sanctions can be either positive or negative, and involve either desirable benefits or undesirable consequences. 'If you finish this project, you will get a promotion, if not, you will spend another year in this job.' The use of sanctions is a classic approach to influencing people and may seem to be an obvious influencing strategy. However, its use clearly depends on the influencer's ability to provide rewards and administer punishments. Even so, this is the least favoured of all the influencing strategies studied. Kipnis believed that it was primarily managers who used sanctions on their subordinates as a last resort. However, as we shall see, sanctions can also be used by staff on both their bosses and co-workers. They have to be used carefully since a failure to follow through can lead to a loss of credibility. Used in moderation, they can be effective, but repeated or used excessively, they will lead to resentment.

CHOOSING INFLUENCING STRATEGIES

The popularity of the seven strategies was found to vary depending on the direction of influence – upwards towards managers, down towards subordinates, or laterally towards co-workers. The popularity of the strategies are shown in Table 12.1. Commentators have grouped these seven influencing strategies in different ways. They have labelled reason, friendliness and bargaining as primary strategies, ones that an influencer would use initially. The remaining four – assertiveness, higher authority, coalition and sanctions – have been termed 'backup' strategies, which tend to be used when the initial strategy has been rebuffed.

Another way of grouping the strategies is first to ask whether their appeal to the influencee is primarily emotional or rational; and whether the focus is on the influencer acting alone (self) or in association with others. These two questions produce a classification framework that is shown in Figure 12.1. Two fundamental questions remain. How should the influencing strategy be applied, and when should it be used? We shall now address these two questions.

Reason

Reasoning involves presenting facts and data to develop a logical argument which supports your suggestion. The Thinker personality type described in Chapter 8 would respond well to a reasoning approach, and would be interested in the

Table 12.1 *Preferred order of use of influencing strategies*

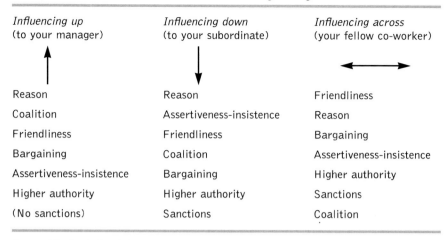

Influencing up (to your manager)	Influencing down (to your subordinate)	Influencing across (your fellow co-worker)
↑	↓	←→
Reason	Reason	Friendliness
Coalition	Assertiveness-insistence	Reason
Friendliness	Friendliness	Bargaining
Bargaining	Coalition	Assertiveness-insistence
Assertiveness-insistence	Bargaining	Higher authority
Higher authority	Higher authority	Sanctions
(No sanctions)	Sanctions	Coalition

Source: Kipnis *et al.*, 1980

		FOCUS	
		Self	*Others*
APPEAL	Emotional	Friendliness	Higher authority
	Rational	Assertiveness Sanction Reason	Bargaining Coalition

Figure 12.1 *Classification of influencing strategies*

details and documentation which they needed in order to come to a decision. When using this influencing strategy with a Thinker, develop your ideas adequately, and organize your information logically. Explain to them how your idea works and how you reached your conclusions. The use of reason requires preparation time, thought and good communication skills. The impact of information, evidence and arguments on the decision-making process has been extensively studied by many writers (Borgida and Nisbett, 1977; Reinhard, 1988; Reyes *et al.*, 1980). Logical argument plays an important part in this strategy. Figure 12.2 shows Toulmin's (1958) depiction of the argumental process.

231

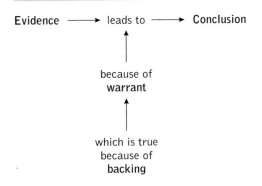

Evidence ⟶ leads to ⟶ Conclusion

↑

because of
warrant

↑

which is true
because of
backing

Figure 12.2 *Toulmin's argumental process*

We infer from *evidence* (data, facts) to a *conclusion* by means of the connector of a *warrant* or general proposition. The warrant gives support because of *backing*. In the examples below, the warrant which provides the backing, is introduced with the word *because*. This is intentional as Langer *et al.* (1978) found that this word acts like a trigger, eliciting automatic compliance from influencees:

Evidence	University X produces excellent graduates.
Warrant	Because Robyn graduated from University X.
Conclusion	Robyn may be expected to perform well in this job.

Evidence	Government survey statistics show that the cost of living is rising sharply.
Warrant	Because, through long experience, we know that this leads to increased wage demands.
Conclusion	We may expect the unions to seek a large pay rise.

Evidence	For the reasons given workers will demand increased wages.
Warrant	Because management, caught in the cost–price squeeze, will resist such demands,
Conclusion	A period of industrial strife is likely to ensue.

Influencers appear to like using reason to persuade, perhaps feeling comfortable with making the, 'facts speak for themselves'. Moreover, influencees prefer to be given reasons when asked to do things. An explanation creates intrinsic motivation allowing an influencee to agree to something that they accept as being a good idea. Influencing through reasoning enhances an influencee's self-esteem when they feel they are being treated as thinking human beings who have a need to understand what they are doing. That is why it is used as a first choice influencing strategy. All the other strategies involve a higher degree of actual or potential interpersonal contact which influencers may prefer to avoid. Reason was most often used when the objectives sought were primarily to the benefit of the company rather than the influencer, and when the influencer's organizational power and expectations of success were high. Additionally, influencers who used rational argument considered themselves to be more intelligent, competent and thoughtful (Rind and Kipnis, 1999).

Sillince (2002) built upon the work of Toulmin and examined the effectiveness of different forms of argumentation. His model identifies three ways in which an arguer can become more persuasive. First, the arguer must select the most appropriate combination of argument dimensions (familiarity, evidence, simplicity) for their particular organizational context. Second, each context has its own rhetorical requirements, requiring appropriate rhetorical forms. Third, the arguer must integrate the four elements of context (arguer, context, topic and setting) in a way that shows empathy for their audience; balances promises and warnings; while remaining tactically flexible to allow a switching of positions. Sillince's model is impossible to summarize briefly, but merits detailed study by those planning to use reasoning as their major influencing strategy.

Friendliness

As the basis for influence, friendliness cannot be simply turned on in the way you might choose to use reason or threaten to appeal to higher authority. It involves creating and maintaining a positive relationship with the influencee beforehand, and then drawing upon that connection to achieve your objective. Although friendliness is often explained by reference to some magical personal attraction between two people, there are steps that you can take to become friendly with someone. The first of these is just to be near them because we make friends on the basis of opportunity. Such physical proximity also increases the frequency of contact, and we are attracted to those with whom we have frequent contact (Festinger et al., 1950; Saergert et al., 1973). Second, you can use some of the ingratiation strategies discussed in Chapter 5, especially flattery and opinion-conforming, which are particularly designed to make your personal qualities appeal to your influencee, and thus gain their friendship (Blackburn, 1981; Mechanic, 1962; Jones, 1964).

A third option suggested by Davies (1999) was to make your influencee feel important, thereby enhancing their self-esteem. You might do this by asking them for their help or advice in a way that shows that you respect their expertise ('I'm well aware that you know a lot about'). Research shows that subordinates who seek and follow the advice of their boss are seen in a more friendly way than those who either do not ask for assistance or who do so but not follow the advice given (Dossett and Greenberg, 1981; Wortman and Linsenmeier, 1977). You

233

do not need to grovel or be apologetic, but do let them know that they are in a position to help you. If you cannot think of any help or advice that you want, you could ask them a question to which you already know the answer, and feign gratitude and interest. Being asked for advice, and thanked for past help given, is also flattering.

Drummond (1991) recommended asking influencees questions about themselves to make them feel important. The first time they will be surprised, the second time they will expect it, and the third time they will look forward to it. Many people see the world as a lonely place in which no one really cares about anyone else. Such people will be naturally attracted to those who show a personal interest in them, and will want more of that pleasant attention. Consequently, when you show an interest in someone, they will be flattered, and will respond positively towards you. This works even with the most powerful and senior people in an organization. However, since you want to avoid over-familiarity, it is best to start asking them questions of a general nature, and finishing up with those which relate to their personal interests. This friendship creation technique establishes valuable bonds, and a fund of goodwill.

Coalition

The power of coalitions as vehicles for influence is demonstrated in the history of trade unions, professional associations and consumer boycotts. Coalitions can be used for both personal and organizational purposes to influence co-workers and managers. In forming a coalition, look for those with similar interests and power. Ask who enjoys the company of top management, gets their name mentioned in talk and publications, and is generally sought after? Such individuals are typically upwardly mobile, are expanding their responsibilities, have up-to-date information, and frequently secure new projects and responsibilities. They are the most valuable people to have in your coalition.

When organizing a coalition, avoid being perceived as either subversive or a pressure group. Take care to observe all the rules, protocols and traditions of the company, and ensure that you both go through the proper channels and remain within the chain of command. Always keep your communication positive with others by stating what you will do rather than what you won't do. While senior management gets nervous when people talk about problems or the past in general, they respond positively to opportunities and the future in the broad sense. So offer your coalition proposals such as, 'a more productive solution that we can use in the future'.

Third, talk about what is observable. As a coalition, describe conditions as you see them, and the results that follow from them. Avoid any discussion of coalition members' motivations or attitudes. Fourth, never overstate problems. This will ensure that others see you as a professional alliance addressing a critical need, and not as a bunch of zealots. Fifth, stick to problems and operate in areas in which coalition members are perceived as experts, have credibility and in which they will be able to exercise the most influence. Operate openly as a coalition, avoiding secret communications. Provide each other with ongoing contact and support since this is the basis for keeping a coalition together.

Reserve your use of the coalition strategy for really important issues. Your request of your allies should be in reasonable proportion to the debt that they owe you. For those who owe you a great deal, you can legitimately ask them to ally themselves with you, despite their reservations. You should never commit your allies without their approval, by for example, quoting or using their names in communications. Tell them what role you want them to play – sign a document, be cited, or to give you actual assistance at a meeting or a presentation. Avoid both lost causes and disastrous victories which sacrifice your power and credibility in a no-win situation. For maximum influencing impact, your allies should be seen by your target influencee as objective, and as thinking on their own. Hence, infrequent use of this influencing strategy maximizes its impact. Consider your moves, not just personally, but in terms of your allies' situations. Merely having others present and 'on your side', may be sufficient to influence an outcome in your favour. Be aware that a coalition approach automatically puts influencees on the defensive and increases their chances of losing face in public.

Bargaining

Chapter 7 considered motivation, and introduced Cohen and Bradford's (1991) eight-step approach to bargaining. This framework is useful for those implementing a bargaining strategy. Much of the literature on bargaining and negotiation emphasizes the distinction between *interests* and *positions*. Typically people adopt positions on issues, and address the conflict of positions. They see their goal as being to agree to a position, and are surprised when they reach an impasse. It is more useful to begin by identifying others' interests, which are the desires and needs that people have. Your position is what you have decided upon, while your interest is what caused you to so decide. For every interest, there usually exist several equally acceptable possible positions. Moreover, behind opposing positions may lie many more common interests than conflicting ones. We frequently and wrongly assume that because another person's position is opposed to ours, their interests must also be opposed. Closer examination may actually reveal shared and compatible interests.

So positions are concrete and specific, while interests may remain unexpressed, intangible and inconsistent. How do you identify the other person's interests? First, you might put yourself in their shoes and examine each position they take and ask why they might take it. You can ask them what their basic concern is in putting forward their proposal, or what they hope to achieve. Second, you can ask why the other party objects to your proposal, the question of 'why not?'. Third, you should recognize that they will be trying to balance several interests, perhaps reflecting different, incompatible constituencies. You may be able to inquire informally how their interests relate to the positions being taken. Bargaining is a useful influencing strategy when seeking personal benefits, provided what is exchanged is of equal value.

Research has assessed women's willingness to engage in bargaining behaviour in order to influence others. Babcock and her colleague concluded from their study that women may do worse then men when they win a job because they take a different approach to negotiation (Babcock and Laschever, 2003). With respect to pay offers, they simply accept the initial pay offer that they have been offered. Only 7 per cent of women negotiated their pay up, compared to 57 per cent of men. This reluctance to bargain appeared to extend further. The conclusion drawn was that women feel uncomfortable with negotiating because they consider that it is inappropriate; that they are not entitled to ask for more; or they think that it may damage their relationship with the other person. They then end up feeling unhappy and resentful when their male colleagues receive better treatment (*Economist*, 2003b).

Assertiveness-insistence

Assertiveness-insistence is a backup influencing strategy. It involves behaviours such as checking up on the influencee and repeatedly reminding them of your needs; confronting them or pointing out that the rules require it; simply ordering them or demanding that they do what you want; setting a deadline for them; telling them it must be done or that they suggest a better way of doing it. Assertiveness-insistence was most used when the objective was to the benefit of the organization, when the influencer's expectations of success were low and when their organizational power was high. This strategy is associated with an autocratic style of leadership. It is most effective when the influencer possesses all the information required, and when the time available to implement the decision is short. Used effectively, it can overcome an influencee's resistance, but if used ineffectively, it can create ill will and resentment. It therefore tends to be used as a backup strategy when the influencer encounters resistance to their initial strategy. Its excessive use can engender or escalate resistance.

Higher authority

Your earliest exposure to higher authority as an influencing strategy may have been in the playground of your first school when a classmate threatened to, 'Get my dad on to you'. Later, teachers may have threatened to report your behaviour to the head teacher. Drummond (1991) discussed how people find it convenient to hide behind rules claiming that, even though they are bad, they have to be followed ('I'm sorry, I'd like to help, but these are the rules that prevent me'). Invoking higher authority, whether of rules or senior people, may indeed serve your purpose. However, if it is used on you, you can act to change their perception of the rule in question, by arguing that it is counter-productive to efficiency, or will result in unfairness, and thus should not be upheld. If your argument, based on sense and justice is rejected, then an appeal to higher authority by you would be appropriate. Another way of using higher authority when seeking to persuade others to withdraw their proposal is to state that, 'The boss won't approve' or 'Head office won't buy it.' Higher authority is one of the backup strategies which tend to be used as a last resort.

Sanctions

While the use of a negative sanction can cause resentment, it nevertheless represents a means of influencing. The threat must matter to the person, and should be pitched at the right level. It must be something the person wishes to avoid, with consequences sufficiently severe to motivate their behaviour. It must also carry within it the notion that desirable behaviour will be rewarded. People are more motivated to seek to attain a desired reward than to avoid an unpleasant punishment. Promises of reward vary in terms of the degree that they depend on the influencee's performance. A *non-contingent* reward requires no further action on their part. You give them a benefit now in the hope of eliciting the desired behaviour in the future. They gain the benefit which increases their satisfaction, reduces their resentment and promotes a more positive attitude towards you. In contrast, a *contingent* promise depends on future satisfactory performance, and is useful when the influencee cannot see a clear link between the behaviour you desire, and the reward that you will give them. Here you are using the promise of a reward to spell out in greater detail, the existing relationship between the desired behaviour, and your granting of a reward. You must decide what would motivate the person to respond, and whether it is in your power to grant it. Beware of overuse. If you always promise them something when they seem to be reluctant, you will end up rewarding their reluctance, and thus actually increasing their resistance.

Can you reward and punish your boss? Kipnis *et al.* believed not, and excluded sanctions as an upward influencing strategy. In contrast, Quick (1988) and Rowntree (1989) argued that you can. One strategy is to identify aspects of your boss's job that they dislike doing, for example, talking to salespeople or clients. If your boss complains about such a task, offer to do it for her. You might take on their more routine and boring tasks as well. Another strategy is to cover for your boss, that is, to take over temporarily some of her responsibilities if she is exceptionally busy. For example, you can suggest she delegates some of her work to you. A third strategy is supplying skills which your boss lacks, which can result in her coming to rely on you for expertise, ideas and suggestions on topics about which she is not well informed. What all these tasks have in common is that none of them appear in your own job description. Provided that your boss accedes to your requests, you can reward her by continuing to do these tasks; if she refuses, you can punish her by ceasing to do them without incurring any formal penalty.

INFLUENCING UPWARDS AND DOWNWARDS

Influencing upwards

Influencing upwards is probably the most important and the most difficult task for a new recruit. Downs and Conrad's (1982) research, reported in Chapter 5, may be interpreted as equating an effective subordinate with an influential one. Case *et al.* (1988) investigated long-term, upward influencing activity. They found that successful influencers used supporting documentation and data (the reason approach), as well as repetition and persistence (a form of assertiveness). The majority avoided coalition, despite the fact that the support of others frequently resulted in success. When allies were used, staff personnel were found to be the most useful when persuading superiors. These influential subordinates were more likely to be rewarded financially, enhanced their advancement potential, and found themselves in an improved position to exert still further influence on their superiors. They also reported feeling more confident about their relationship with their bosses (Schilt and Locke, 1982).

How do the conditions under which a subordinate-influencer attempts to influence their boss, determine which influencing strategies they use? Farmer *et al.* (1997) examined this question. The authors distinguished three influencing strategies – hard, soft and rational. A hard strategy incorporated the strategies of assertiveness-insistence, upward appeal and coalition. In this strategy, influencers believe that they control meaningful reinforcements for the influencee, either through direct control of rewards for compliance or by manipulative threats for non-conformity. More broadly, the stress is upon forms of pressure, invocation of legitimate authority and manipulation of individuals. While subordinates lack power, they do have the ability to threaten. In contrast, soft strategies are less aggressive and more psychologically controlling. They include the influencing strategies of friendliness, consultation, inspirational appeals and exchange (reminding influencees of past favours done for them). Soft strategies tend to use personal power and power-sharing. These were designed to achieve superiors' compliance by either making the influencer more appealing or by offering some attractive future payback in return for compliance. Rational strategies, stress logic, reason and rationality. They use persuasive arguments, logical explanations and supporting information. They offer the superior a course of action (complying with the influencing request) that would maximize the expected value of some outcome important to them. The rational strategy was found to be the one used most often (Farmer and Maslyn, 1999).

What factors affected the choice of upward influencing strategy? Four variables have been found to be important. First, the degree of the influencing subordinate's Machiavellianism (that is, their inclination and ability to manipulate others). The second variable is their locus of control which refers to the extent to which the influencer believes that they have control over their environment). The results reveal that a hard influencing strategy was used by juniors on their seniors, when the former had a high level of both Machiavellianism and education. A soft strategy was associated with higher levels of education, self-monitoring and having an external locus of control. The last of these meant that you believed that external factors, rather than yourself, controlled situations. Highly educated individuals working at a different location from their superior used a rational influencing strategy. This was a situation where interpersonal interaction was limited. Overall, the results suggest that high Machs and well-educated people are more self-confident in pushing for things that they want from their bosses.

A third variable affecting the choice of strategies are the personality traits of the upward influencing subordinate. Cable and Judge (2003) found that, with respect to the Big Five personality trait clusters, those employees scoring high on extroversion were more likely to use inspirational appeal and ingratiation when influencing their boss; those scoring high on agreeableness were less likely to use legitimation or pressure; and those high on conscientiousness were more likely to use rational appeal. Finally, juniors took into account the leadership style of their managers when influencing them. Their boss might be a transformational leader, that is, someone who treats relationships with followers in terms of motivation and commitment, influencing and inspiring them to give more than mechanical compliance, and to improve organizational performance (Buchanan and Huczynski, 2004). If so, subordinates were more likely to use consultation and inspirational appeal. However, if their boss's leadership style was laissez-faire, subordinates were more likely to use exchange, coalition, legitimation and pressure strategies. The main point for the consideration by the subordinate influencer is whether you are allowing your personality to determine which influencing strategies to use on your manager.

Influencing downwards

Managers' attempts to influence downwards will obviously affect employees' feelings and behaviour. Hinkin and Schriesheim (1988) studied the relationships between managers' power, influencing strategies and organizational consequences.

239

They asked middle managers to assess the power and influence strategies used by their bosses, and their own job satisfaction and commitment to their company. The different types of power identified by French and Raven (1959) – legitimate, expert, personal, coercive and reward – were matched with the influencing strategies of Kipnis *et al.* (1984), and correlated with levels of job satisfaction, satisfaction with their boss's technical and human relations skill, and their own commitment (as opposed to compliance) to organization goals. The study found that employees preferred being given a rational explanation for complying with the directives of their manager, and responded positively. As an influencing strategy, reason had a strong positive correlation with both legitimate and personal power, and a less strong one with reward and expert power. Employees often complied with their managers' requests because they were required to. When they considered a strategy to be illegitimate and inconsistent with their expectations of their boss's behaviour, their performance deteriorated over time, in the absence of continued supervision. In contrast, when they believed an influencing strategy to be appropriate, they accepted the directive and continued consistently to perform satisfactorily without the need for tight supervision.

The managers questioned considered friendliness, bargaining and coalition to be acceptable, but these generated neither job satisfaction nor a feeling of organizational commitment in them. A manager's use of assertiveness-insistence had a strong positive correlation with the use of coercive power and negative sanctions. Hinkin and Schriesheim concluded that employees disliked being threatened or strong-armed. However, they reacted less negatively to influencing strategies which they perceived as being sanctioned by the organization, than to those which they felt stemmed from their boss's own personality. Nevertheless, both assertiveness-insistence and negative sanctions were judged to be outside the domain of expected or desired boss behaviour. The influencing strategy found to have the strongest correlation with both employee satisfaction and organizational commitment was reason. The process is summarized in Figure 12.3. Other studies show that as influencing bosses move higher up the organizational hierarchy, they are more likely to use hard influencing strategies like assertiveness-insistence (Somech and Drach-Zahavy, 2002).

Research has identified three main responses to influencing attempts: commitment, compliance and resistance (Yukl and Tracy, 1992; Yukl *et al.*, 1993; Yukl *et al.*, 1996). Why do subordinates resist their managers' attempts to influence them? Using the distinction between hard, soft and rational influencing strategies discussed earlier, Tepper *et al.* (1998) found that subordinates considered soft and rational ones to represent fair treatment. These strategies were seen as demonstrating respect for subordinates' abilities and technical knowledge, and signalled a desire to improve manager–subordinate relations. In contrast, hard strategies were seen as unjust and were resisted. They were considered to doubt subordinates' competencies and abilities. Subordinates' resistance was reduced

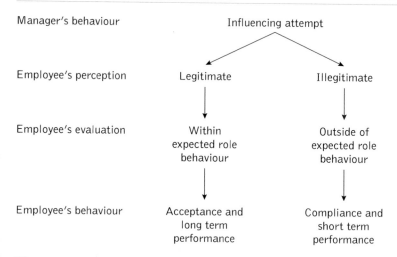

Figure 12.3 *Managers' influencing strategy and employee response*

Source: Hinkin and Schriesheim, 1988: 50. © 1988 AM MGMT ASSN (J). Reproduced with permission of AM MGMT ASSN (J) in the format of Other Book via Copyright Clearance Center.

when hard strategies were used alongside soft ones. Rational strategies generated less resistance than hard strategies. The content of the request also made a difference to the resistance encountered. If there was little or no ambiguity in the request it was less likely to be resisted than an unclear or ambiguous request. Additionally, requests considered as interesting or important by the influencee, generated more commitment to them. This suggests the importance of making a request sound more enjoyable or important than it actually is. The main message from this research is to maximize the chances of success.

TYPES OF INFLUENCEES AND INFLUENCERS

Chapter 8 suggested that influencees differed in terms of their type of personality. Those of a particular type, are more likely to respond to one influencing strategy rather than another. Hence, intuitively, matching personality type to influencing strategy, in the manner suggested in Table 12.2, may increase the chances of success. In addition, influencers have been found to combine influencing strategies to form broader influencing styles (Kipnis *et al.*, 1984; Farmer and Maslyn, 1999). *Bystanders* either never used any of the seven influencing strategies, or only did so occasionally. They exercised little influence in their company. *Captives* were individuals who often used only one or two influencing strategies, but not the others. They restricted their choices, using the same ones irrespective of the situation. *Shotguns*, were people who used a widest range of strategies in their persuasion attempts. However, they paid insufficient attention

Table 12.2 *Match between personality type and most effective influencing strategy*

| Your influencing strategy | Personality type of influencee | | | |
	Director	Socializer	Relater	Thinker
Assertiveness	+	–	–	–
Bargaining	+	0	0	0
Coalition	–	0	+	0
Friendliness	0	+	+	0
Higher authority	–	–	–	–
Reason	0	0	0	+
Sanctions	–	–	–	–

Notes: (+) = most favoured; (–) = not favoured; (0) = indifferent

to their choice and thus did not always successfully match the strategy with the requirements of the situation. Finally, *Tacticians* used three or four influencing strategies on a regular basis, and were able to vary these when required. Case *et al.* (1988) gave the example of a Tactician influencing upwards. This person first convinced his subordinates of the merits of his plan and encouraged them to mention their support to his boss (coalition); he then presented a logical rational presentation to his superior (reason); and followed this up with persistent reminders which were used until the influencing attempt was successful (assertiveness-insistence).

A more empirically based 'matching' approach is suggested by Williams and Miller (2002). Their research was conducted on 1,684 executives from the automotive, retail and hi-tech industries. Subjects described their decision-making tendencies which the researchers subjected to cluster analysis. They found five predominant types based on a combination of personality type and decision-making style. These authors recommend that influencers should determine who the chief decision-maker is among any group of executives, and then to tailor their arguments to match that person's style. Their style descriptions, and even labels, bear a remarkable similarity to the personality types described earlier in the book, thus providing confidence in the validity of the classification system being proposed. The types were as follows.

- *Charismatics* are easily intrigued and enthralled by new ideas, but experience has taught them to make final decisions based on balanced information, not just emotions. They are typically enthusiastic, captivating, talkative and dominant. When persuading Charismatics, one should use buzzwords such as results, proven, actions, show, watch, easy, clear, focus. Fight the urge to join in their excitement, and focus instead on results. Make simple, straightforward arguments, use visual aids to stress the features and benefits of your proposal.

- *Thinkers* are the most difficult executives to persuade. They are impressed with arguments that are supported by data. They tend to have a strong aversion to risk and can be slow to make a decision. They are cerebral, intelligent, logical and academic. The buzzwords to use with them are quality, academic, think, numbers, intelligent, plan, expert, proof. When persuading a Thinker, have lots of data ready. Thinkers want as much information as possible, including all pertinent market research, customer surveys, case studies, cost–benefit analyses, and so on. They want to understand all perspectives of a given situation.

- *Sceptics* tend to be highly suspicious of every data point presented, especially any information that challenges their worldview. They often have an aggressive, almost combative style and are usually described as 'take charge' people. They are demanding, disruptive, disagreeable and rebellious. Buzzwords to use are feel, grasp, power, action, suspect, trust, demand and disrupt. When persuading a Sceptic, you need as much credibility as you can garner. If you have not established enough clout with a Sceptic, you need to find a way to have it transferred to you prior to or during the meeting. For example, by gaining an endorsement from someone the Sceptic trusts.

- *Followers* make decisions based on how they have made similar choices in the past or on how other trusted executives have made them. They tend to be risk-averse. Followers are responsible, cautious, brand-driven and bargain-conscious. Key buzzwords to use are innovate, expedite, expertise, similar to and previous. Followers tend to focus on proven methods; references and testimonials are big persuading factors. They need to feel certain that they are making the right decision, specifically, that others have succeeded in similar circumstances.

- *Controllers* abhor uncertainty and ambiguity, and they will focus on the pure facts and analysis of an argument. They are logical, unemotional, sensible, detail oriented, accurate and analytical. Buzzwords to use include details, facts, reason, logic, power, handle, physical, grab, and 'just do it'. Your argument needs to be structured and credible. The Controller wants details, but only if presented by an expert. Don't be too aggressive in pushing your proposal. Often, your best bet is simply to give her the information that she needs and hope that she will convince herself.

How does gender affect use of influencing strategies? Since managerial advancement is based significantly on a manager's successful use of influencing strategies, it is a crucial element in career progression. Stereotypically, men are expected to use direct influencing strategies, such as assertion, jokes and threats, while women are expected to use indirect strategies including charm, appearance, ingratiation and compliments. Aguinis and Adams (1998) investigated the real differences between men's and women's use of influencing strategies. The experiment showed that managers of both genders, who used a direct style were perceived as having more reward, coercive, legitimate and expert power, than those using indirect styles. Such direct managers were perceived as being more effective, more self-confident, emotionally stable, industrious, leaders and logical, as compared to indirect managers. Requests made by direct managers met with less resistance, more compliance and commitment than those made by indirect managers. Thus choice of style was more important than gender. Perceptions and evaluations of female and male managers are more strongly determined by their organizational position and use of influence strategies than by biological sex. It appears that a woman's reluctance or lack of opportunity to use direct influencing strategies may be the major impediment to her advancement. When she has the possibility and inclination to do so, she is perceived as an effective leader and can progress up the organization.

OBSTACLES TO EFFECTIVE INFLUENCING

Studies into ineffective influencing identified four common obstacles (Kipnis *et al.*, 1984). First, ineffective influencers were found to match their strategy unthinkingly, to the direction of their influencing. For example, perhaps always using friendliness with their bosses, bargaining with their co-workers and assertiveness with their subordinates. Such stereotyped, automatic responding limited their flexibility to customize their strategy to fit different people and circumstances. All the seven strategies have the potential of being used effectively in the appropriate circumstances, and this includes the application of sanctions on managers and co-workers which has already been discussed.

Second, ineffective influencers underestimated the amount of resources they had access to which were valued by other organizational members. The effect of this was twofold. First, they hesitated to influence others at all, and became in Kipnis's terms, bystanders in the company. Second, when they did decide to influence, unawareness of resources restricted their choice of strategies. Chapter 7 on motivation introduced Cohen and Bradford's (1991) concept of organizational currencies. All influencers in an organization, irrespective of their position, have access to various currencies. The aim is to discover which you possess, and to use these when applying your influencing strategy.

Third, some influencers simply give up when faced with a refusal, while others rigidly persist with their strategy despite its not working. Both are examples of inflexibility. In contrast, successful influencers are flexible, and recognize that

244

they can switch strategies to overcome resistance. To change effectively between primary strategies, for example, from reason to bargaining, requires preparation beforehand. Equally important is knowing when and to which backup strategy to escalate to. For example, after using friendliness to persuade their boss, when faced with a refusal, the influencer should consider the backup strategy of coalition, rather than escalating immediately to higher authority or sanctions.

Fourth, people influence others to achieve either organizational or personal goals. Ineffective influencers automatically matched their strategy to one or the other. For example, they believed that when seeking promotion (personal goal), they should use friendliness and bargaining, but not assertiveness or sanctions. Similarly, when persuading others of the value of an absence reduction programme (organizational goal), they should only use reason and coalition, but not friendliness. As before, the automatic selection limits their flexibility to customize their strategy to fit the context. All the seven strategies have the potential of being used to achieve both personal and organizational goals, and in the first instance, all seven should be realistically evaluated.

Additionally, the degree to which an organization is in a state of change can have an impact on which influencing strategies are the most appropriate. Those used in relatively stable organizational conditions may be inappropriate in rapidly changing ones. During a period of rapid change, power relations between individuals can become modified; responsibilities obscured and dependencies and hierarchies altered. In such uncertain organizational settings, different influencing strategies need to be used. In their study of an organization undergoing change, Gravenhorst and Boonstra (1998) found that the three most used strategies, and ones which were most effective in gaining commitment, were rational persuasion; inspirational appeals and consultation.

CONCLUSION

This chapter has presented a range of different influencing strategies identified by Kipnis *et al.* (1984). To be an effective influencer, you need to be able to select the most appropriate influencing strategy for any given situation. In order to do this, you should ask yourself five questions. First, consider the objective of your influence. Are you seeking to achieve organizational or personal goals? Second, whom are you influencing? Specifically, what is your influencee's position in the organization, personality type and primary needs. Third, what resources do you have access to that are valued by the influencee. Fourth, what are your own bases of power that can help to implement most effectively the chosen strategy? Finally, which are the most important organizational factors that provide the environment for your influencing attempt. These can shape influencees' interests and responses. For example, a production manager may reject a marketing executive's attempts to change his production schedule to accommodate a rush job, because the production manager's bonus depends on his keeping costs down, and this is facilitated by long, unchanging production runs. The failure to persuade here is due to the nature of the company's reward system. Success and failure may be linked to other organizational factors such as company structure, technology, culture or mission.

Chapter 13

Influencing a group

All history is a record of the power of minorities, and of minorities of one.

Ralph Waldo Emerson

INTRODUCTION

A group consists of between four and fifteen people, and influencing it is similar to influencing an individual, but with three important differences. First, you will have competition, other people will want to talk, and they will have opinions of their own. Second, you will receive both the support and the opposition of others. Third, the group dynamic will be an added factor. A group can develop a mood and momentum of its own, and this can act to your advantage. Influencing a group at a meeting provides you with valuable opportunities. You have the chance to increase your visibility in the organization, to sell yourself and your ideas, and to extend and develop your network, both inside and outside the organization. Since others consider meetings to be a waste of their time, your attempts to come over as forceful and effective, will be relatively unfettered. An impressive performance will get you noticed, and help you to get on. Every meeting attended by you and a senior manager is both a prospective job interview and a current job evaluation. Meetings are also a good place to prepare for public speaking. Many of the skills learned are transferable. Meetings, however, involve a greater element of two-way exchange than a public presentation, so anticipating and answering questions will be important, as will using your listening skills. You will prepare your opening and closing remarks carefully, rehearsing them before-hand, and taking advantage of your smaller audience's needs and interests by personalizing your presentation (Glaser and Smalley, 1992).

CHALLENGING THE MAJORITY VIEW

Logically, influencing a group in a meeting should be avoided if at all possible. Given the number of one-to-one strategies available, it is much easier to talk to each person individually and strike a deal privately, than to seek to persuade all of them at the same time. Indeed, the most astute managers keep influencing as far away from meetings as possible (Hodgson and Hodgson, 1992; Ng and Van Dyne, 2001). When committees do meet, they often only formally rubber-stamp agreements that have been made outside them. Meetings are rarely places where proposals are put together for the first time. However, if you are forced to persuade in the meeting situation, here are some suggestions about what to do. Persuading a majority of members opposed to your view is a difficult task. Given the power, authority, prestige and material resources possessed by powerful groups in organizations, it is a wonder that not all change is either top-down or majority-led. However, history shows us that powerless minorities, can and do influence powerful majorities. Conflict resolution is at the heart of the minority-influencing-the-majority process.

From the perspective of an individual disagreeing with a majority, the arguments of the latter tend to be accepted passively with little mental activity, and are assumed to be correct. An individual dissenter will ask, 'Why do I not see or think like them?'. In contrast, a majority in conflict with a minority stimulates the former to think why and how it might be wrong, thereby challenging its own views. By making your dissent visible, you focus attention on yourself as a minority who has an alternative, coherent point of view. The majority then wonders, 'How can that person see what he sees, think what he thinks?'. If you, as the minority member persist, the majority will try to see what you see, and to understand what you understand. Such thinking by the majority unconsciously leads it to see things differently – the first step in the process of conversion (Moscovici, 1980). Conflict with a majority which assumes itself to be holding the correct position, induces superficial, unthinking agreement, whereas conflict with a minority stimulates thinking about, and understanding of, their point of view. Studies show that those who believed that they were part of a minority, perceived that they would face greater social pressure, and thus generated more initial thoughts about the issue being discussed than those who thought that they were part of a majority.

In the former situation, the focus of attention is on the conflict of responses, while in the latter case, it is on a conflict of perceptions ('Tell us what you're thinking, and we'll tell you where you're mixed up'). You provide the majority with information that either challenges their image of themselves or which is unexpected. This disrupts the established group view, eliminates past certainty, leaving them feeling uncomfortable, anxious and guilty. Your alternative view, stirs things up, brings arguments to the surface, and these together generate and reinforce the climate of change, encouraging others in the group to begin thinking differently for the first time (Buchanan and Boddy, 1992).

An influencer should challenge existing arrangements and views in the group, encourage conflict and dissent, and facilitate argument and debate. The process of influencing thus becomes coping with and negotiating conflicts between the individuals present. Your intervention will have moved the group to a position of disequilibrium in which members seek new information about themselves and the situation, and may begin to redefine their beliefs. Feeling uncertain and anxious, and disliking conflict and disagreement, the group members will seek to make compromises, converge on different views, or conform to the deviant position. As the deviant, you should demonstrate your certainty, confidence and commitment to your point of view, and signal that you will not move or compromise. This signals to the others that the only way for them to restore group stability and coherence is for them to shift to your position.

Your influence over the majority will be greatest when they are unsure of themselves; when the situation is unclear or ambiguous; when uncertainty reigns; when you offer compelling, quality evidence; and when individual group members' convictions on an issue are low (Tesser *et al.*, 1983). In these circumstances, people will affiliate with others for social comparison purposes. Influence in a group is not unilateral but reciprocal. Every member, irrespective of rank, both influences and is influenced by others (Maass and Clark, 1986; Moscovici and Lage, 1976; Moscovici and Faucheux, 1972; Moscovici and Lage, 1978; Moscovici and Mugby, 1983: Mugby, 1982). While you may be lucky enough to inherit such conditions when you enter the meeting room, it is much more likely that you will have to create them yourself in the minds of your opponents (Gerard and Rabbie, 1961; Gerard, 1963). Based on his experience, Conger (1998) identified four essential steps for a persuader: establishing credibility; framing goals that establish common ground with influencees; reinforcing your position by using vivid language and compelling evidence; and connecting emotionally with the audience. We shall explore these themes throughout this chapter.

SETTING INFLUENCING OBJECTIVES

If a meeting is unavoidable, then you first need to set your objectives. Make your goals and needs explicit – 'if you don't ask, you don't get'. Ask yourself how you might pursue your objective if you succeed? This enables your communication to be goal-orientated, and stops others leading you off track. One way of focusing your thoughts is to write a draft of the minutes of the forthcoming meeting beforehand. This will force you to think about your objective, and will help you to guide the discussion in the desired direction. In setting your objective, keep it simple and specific. Complicated ideas and large propositions are hard for an audience to grasp, especially when they differ significantly from you in their own views. To help your listeners understand and accept your arguments, break them down into small understandable bits. Where possible, show that some of the component parts of your ultimate goal have already been accepted or agreed by them (Fisher, 1964; Ikle, 1964). A proposal put assertively by you,

249

may succeed for no other reason than that the group lacks alternatives, or that the other options on offer appear ambiguous or less well-defined than your own.

GAINING AND BRIEFING SUPPORTERS

We noted earlier that the existence of a minority destroys group unanimity by casting doubt on the predominant view. It also frees those in the majority who may have self-censored their own doubts, to express them and perhaps switch to the minority position. However, you will need to secure at least two supporters pretty rapidly, because a minority of one is perceived as very confident but incorrect, their dissent being attributed to some personal defect. However, a minority of three confident and competent individuals is significantly more influential than one (Moscovici and Lage, 1976; Nemeth *et al.*, 1977). This is provided that it is not categorized as an idiosyncratic outgroup. As a minority, you must be seen positively as 'one-of-us', and as sharing the basic group values and objectives, while disagreeing about the means to achieve these. No one in the majority will want to join you unless you are an in-group minority (Mugny and Papastamou, 1982). The greater the similarity between you and the majority group members that you are seeking to influence, the faster their behaviour change will occur (Sutton, 1982a). Whatever the difference in your position, your proposals should be perceived as contributing to the common good.

Briefing your supporters is therefore an important task. If you are launching a proposal at a meeting, test it beforehand by approaching some of the key decision-makers on an individual basis, and seek their support for it. Consider postponing its launch until you have revised it into a form that will gain widespread support. At the meeting, ensure that your supporters are present since there is strength in numbers. Get them to ask you the questions that you can answer well, and prime them to bring in relevant information and viewpoints that aid your case. An alternative strategy is to arrange for two colleagues to voice initially the opposing majority view, and then to defect publicly over to your side. Minority group members who have defected from the majority are especially persuasive for the others (Levine, 1989). Such orchestration of support will be vital in the face of resistance and counter-suggestions. Whichever strategy is adopted, you will need to brief your backers in advance of the meeting so as to avoid any inconsistencies in their language or approach. However, do not lose the element of surprise (Buchanan and Boddy, 1992; Davies, 1991a; Quick, 1990). This is an application of Kipnis's coalition-influencing strategy discussed in the previous chapter.

SPLITTING UP THE MAJORITY

You can separate individual group members from the majority norm that prevents them from supporting you by asking them to justify their positions. As they do so, point out any inconsistencies, problems or weaknesses. Get them regularly to re-assess their position during the discussion, and do not allow them to hold their position by default. Critically examine any generalizations and distinguish between opinions, speculations and facts. When presented with facts (e.g. statistics) test them or challenge their validity. Do your homework beforehand. Since facts are stronger then opinions, use them to counter the beliefs, hunches and the prejudices of others. However, facts do not 'speak for themselves', so explain the point that you are making to your audience.

Increasing defections can create a snowball effect among the remaining members of the majority who become persuaded by the new emerging consensus (Nemeth, 1986). Pfeffer (1992) noted that once consensus begins to develop in one direction, it is difficult to stop it. The minority picks up the members of the majority who are most willing to compromise (Moscovici and Mugny, 1983). For maximum effect, the growing minority must be perceived as forming a consensual sub-group, rather than a collection of individual deviants (Kiesler and Pallak, 1975). As the size of a minority increases, so does its perceived competence and its influence over the members of the reducing majority. According to Pfeffer, what occurs is not decision-making but decision-happening or decision-unfolding. Given the social nature of the process, it is important to brief your allies to provide proof of the social consensus around your viewpoint to the still wavering or opposed members of the group. Repeat your message, and point out how many others agree with you.

Once your position strengthens and you move into a slight majority, the use of confrontation may become appropriate. Ask members of the new minority, 'Where do you stand on this?' and continue to examine critically their generalizations. Use the group to pressure the remaining minority. Being different from others induces instability and uncertainty in self-evaluation, while similarity provides stability and confidence. In contrast, feedback about one's objective correctness or competence reduces the influence of others (Festinger, 1954; Wilder, 1977). In this way, the power of social proof is brought to bear upon the last few non-conforming members. People become committed to their decision because the process of agreeing makes each person believe that their position is correct.

ANTICIPATING COUNTER-ARGUMENTS

The group members will be prejudiced for or against your proposal, or else neutral towards it. You should expect your idea to be opposed, know where the opposition is likely to come from, what it is based on, and how to deal with it. Your audience's 'hidden agendas' will determine their response to your proposal. Such agendas arise because people are anxious that the proposal may result in some unpleasant consequence for them. They may fear that their access to information, responsibility, influence, autonomy or power base in the organization will be adversely affected. They will therefore attempt to undermine the meeting using subterfuge and deception, concerned that if their true aims were revealed, major opposition would result that would make the pursuance of their aims more difficult.

As the influencer, the onus is on you to discover in advance what their concerns might be so as to meet them, and thereby secure support for your proposal. Design your proposal to minimize objections and offer opportunities for trade-offs. When fear is the cause of a hidden agenda, its removal will eliminate it. However, subterfuge, that is, secrecy aimed at gaining more for one person in the meeting than others, is difficult to bring out into the open. Individuals will go to great lengths to avoid being detected. However, a precaution that you can take as a junior staff member, is to align yourself with a senior manager and thus secure their support. Alternatively, you could warn your objector off, by letting them know that senior management will challenge their dissent to your proposal. A third option is to appeal to higher-level values or standards, such as customer care or integrity, which all the meeting's participants share. Anticipate counter-arguments and dispose of them in your discussion. If someone raises an objection after you have spoken, show by your response that you are already aware of it. In doing so, you will diminish its importance. In contrast, if you fail to antici-pate and acknowledge their point, then the objector's words will carry more force with other group members.

MANAGING MEANING AND DEFINING REALITY

The meeting-in-progress is a micro-world, temporarily separated from reality. Reality is not objective, but depends on the way that people interpret facts and information. Meanings are in people not in objects, and they reflect the perspec-tives or frames of reference within which individuals operate. Group members will all have different definitions of the same situation, based on their different perceptions of it. These are not fixed, and you can re-define reality for them to your advantage. Thomas Aszasz, the famous psychotherapist once said 'define or be defined'. You will want to control the definition of things and events. This includes definitions of 'success', 'failure', 'relevance', 'priority' and everything else.

Pettigrew (1985) recommended managing the perceptions that others have of the meaning of your proposals. For example, by introducing your proposal with a metaphor such as a war, a soccer match or an evolution, you set the frame for the ensuing discussion. What is crucial is not what is real, but what is accepted as real. In this sense, much influencing is symbolic activity (Prus, 1989; Sederberg, 1984). The corollary of this is that you should remain detached to avoid being seduced into others' definitions of the situation. Most people, however, are reactive, blinkered and drift along, accepting at face value what they are told, and never realizing that reality is political. If someone says there is a crisis, then they believe it.

252

Different definitions of the situation depend on which facts are selected, emphasized and presented. Hence, in this sense, there are no such things as hard facts. Evidence that is said to be compelling or incontrovertible can be challenged. By raising doubts in people's minds, you get them to re-define their reality. A group member may initially accept information from another as being trustworthy evidence, only to reject it later, when its status is re-defined. Conformity to a view is often motivated by a desire to form an accurate view of reality, and to act correctly. Here, conformity is increased by uncertainty about the correctness of one's own judgement, and the ambiguity of the situation. That same conformity is reduced by the perceived uncertainty of others (Deutsch and Gerard, 1955). An ambiguous, difficult or complex issue, for example, 'Should we enter a new product market', cannot be resolved entirely through a test of physical reality (what will happen). This leads to a feeling of uncertainty, and a need for information to reduce that uncertainty. The uncertainty, in turn, creates a dependence on others for valid information, who thus become influential. We conform to the responses of those whom we perceive to provide accurate evidence about reality. The main weapon of definition is language (see Chapter 3). It makes a difference if your proposal seeks to 'introduce cuts in capital expenditure' as opposed to 'increasing investment at a slower rate'. Euphemisms can assist you. Rather than recommencing increasing taxes, which can stimulate opposition, you might seek ways to 'enhance revenue'. If you are unsuccessful, you can always explain it away as a 'success deficiency'.

CONTROLLING THE DECISION CONTEXT

You can achieve your influencing objectives by influencing the group members indirectly by controlling the frame within which they view and decide the issues at a meeting. Here are five ways in which this can be done.

Purpose

Pfeffer (1992) argued that defining a meeting's *purpose* was a critical, if neglected, influencing device. Meetings usually set an objective, agree a course of action, solve a problem or make a decision. You might change the issue to be discussed by the group from, 'Should we do this?' to 'How we are going to do this? – let's solve the associated problems of implementation'. By setting the terms of a discussion before or at the start of a meeting, you can affect how the issues are perceived and discussed. You can impose your meaning on the issues by couching your questions about an agenda topic in terms of potential risks or gains; as costs or benefits; or as important and innovative or unimportant and traditional. The statement of the meeting's purpose will affect the type of information that you collect, distribute, emphasize or understate in the reporting of your material.

253

For example, if you are seeking approval for a major capital project, but feel that it will be rejected at this time, you may judge it prudent not to define the group purpose as, 'deciding whether or not the project should go ahead', but merely, 'to secure agreement to proceed with a feasibility study'. The latter aim may attract majority agreement, whereas the former may not. At any time you can choose to ask for action, agreement, a vote or a deferral from the group.

Agenda

Since few people regard agendas as an influencing tool, you can use them to affect the group's decision process and outcome unobtrusively. An agenda determines what is discussed at a meeting. To prevent a problematic issue being considered you exclude it from the agenda. If it does appear, you get it removed from the agenda at the very start of the meeting. Finally and most desperately, you filibuster or re-schedule it be discussed at a later meeting (preferably next century). All these tactics stop a decision-issue from ever surfacing within the group context. On the other hand, if you want change, you must get your issue onto the public decision agenda, and have it discussed by the group members. The raising of issues in public has the symbolic significance of challenging those in power, and permits the development of coalitions and political bargaining between individuals who are interested in it. Control of the meeting agenda is therefore crucial. Look at its length, and the items on it. Does your proposal stand out as significant, or will it be competing with a range of other pressing items? Should you put your proposal in at this time or wait? Can your proposal be subsumed under any of the other, otherwise competing, agenda items? Can you challenge any of the items on the agenda, and have them removed in order to let yours in? (Bachrach and Baratz, 1963).

Order of voting

The order in which a group makes decisions can affect the outcome of your proposal in ways that few influencers appreciate (Plott and Levine, 1978). A fixed agenda limits the information available to group members about the preference patterns of others. It is only when they vote or speak that these become apparent, and this in turn is determined by the agenda sequence. When given a fixed amount of time for a discussion, the agenda order determines the limits that will be allocated to various items, including which will receive the least attention. Hence, it may be wise to leave your controversial proposals to the end when they might get through 'on the nod'. Since agendas also represent a sequence of decisions that are taken publicly and with choice, they entail commitments that can change group members' attitudes and perceptions. What is decided about agenda item number four will affect item number five (Salancik, 1977b).

In this way, you can use the agenda to build escalating commitment from group members to your preferred course of action, which in other circumstances would be impossible (Schwenk, 1986).

Elsbach and Elofson (2000) showed that the way in which people explain decision-making, that is, presenting its rationale, affects the way that they are perceived by the group in terms of their trustworthiness and competency. The way that a decision was labelled and the language used affects trustworthiness. An explanation that is difficult to understand may be construed as a cover-up, or as an attempt to make its refutation difficult. Easy-to-understand language improves perceptions of trustworthiness. Decision-makers who used difficult language were perceived as detached and cold. Those using colloquial language were perceived as sensitive to human issues and dynamics. Groups seek to make swift but acceptable decisions. The basis for their evaluation of a decision may come down to the simplicity of the language used, and its relevance to them. If the decision is of little personal relevance to the group's members, they will look at the legitimacy of the decision-making process, and the credibility of the decision-maker, rather than to the decision's actual content. The researchers recommend that managers ensure that the language they employ, and their labelling of decisions, is well crafted so as to maximize their competency-based trustworthiness.

Decision criteria

Decision criteria refer to the basis upon which your proposal will be evaluated. You should aim to secure an early agreement from the group to apply your preferred decision criteria. For example, if a project is typically evaluated on maximum pay-off, act to change that criteria to lowest cost or maximum quality. Using this criterion, you then assemble those statistics that are most favourable to your case. Bedoyere (1990) said that people select the criteria of judgement which most reliably indicate their success to others, and which provide them with the most comforting results. Our ability to apply different standards of judgement is considerable. Indeed, the philosopher and mathematician, Blaise Pascal (1658) said that, 'The art of persuading consists as much in pleasing as in convincing'.

Decision frames

Decision framing is limiting the issues and decisions for group members to consider. Psychologists use the term, *segregation*, to refer to people's tendency to draw narrow boundaries around a problem, and allow it to become the immediate and exclusive centre of their attention. If your presentation of the problem sounds reasonable, the group members will accept it in the form that you have formulated it, and will avoid considering the many other possible conceptualizations of it. Moreover, you can also constrain their decision solutions by limiting the choice alternatives that you offer them. Once your options are presented, it takes effort for others to extend that list. The majority of decision-makers lack the time and mental capacity to cope with more than a few options anyway; they encourage their subordinates to bring them, 'solutions not problems'; and they typically seek a satisfactory rather than the best alternative (Simon, 1960). It is people's mental laziness that makes decision framing an effective influencing device (Tykocinski *et al.*, 1994; Smith and Petty, 1996).

Presenting the decision choices

We actually know a great deal about how to frame decisions so that they will have the maximum influence on group members. Bazerman (2001) and Russo and Shoemaker (1989) summarized the extensive body of research on this topic. First, people dislike losses and will seek to avoid them. They are *risk averse* to positively framed choices, and risk-seeking to negatively framed choices. When offered a choice between, on the one hand, a guaranteed £300, and on the other, a 33 per cent chance of £600, people will opt for the former (Kahneman and Tversky, 1979: Tversky and Kahneman, 1981). They treat risks concerning perceived gains differently from risks concerning perceived losses. It is more painful to lose £30 than to gain £30. Moreover, people value the reduction of uncertainty more, when the outcome was initially certain, than when it was merely probable. They will prefer a proposal that appears to offer 100 per cent certainty of a £30,000 gain, to one that offers an 85 per cent probability of a £45,000 gain. This is called a preference for *pseudo-certainty*. People will make decisions not only to protect themselves against risk, but also to eliminate the worry caused by any amount of risk (Tversky and Kahneman, 1981). So in framing your suggestion, show your audience how your proposal avoids a loss. How much they will lose by not adopting it, rather than only how much will be saved or gained.

People evaluate outcomes relative to a *reference point* which they use to assess the appeal of a proposal. Is £20,000 a lot? It is if their reference point is £5,000, but not if it is £100,000. Since group members will be using different reference points, act to establish a point that is to your advantage. Another finding concerning measurement relates to the use of *yardsticks*. For example, with respect to cost savings, percentages may be better than absolute figures. Is £1,000 saved on a £2,000 deal, better than £1,000 saved on a £5,000 deal? The sum saved remains the same in both cases, but it is perceived differently when expressed as a percentage or as an absolute figure. So choose the most influential way of expressing what you have done. If you have completed a project budgeted at £100,000 for £90,000, express your achievement as a £10,000 saving for the company. If you went over budget to £110,000, say that you remained within 10 per cent of the budget.

If it is in your interest to dramatize an insignificant problem, express it as ratio rather than as a percentage. You can shock your group by telling them last year 1-in-20 employees experienced some sort of industrial accident in the company, and that your budget should therefore be doubled to deal with this major problem. The fact that 95 per cent of employees did not suffer any injuries needs to be rapidly glossed over. The 'one-in-so-many' is a popular device used by all forms of media to make their viewers and readers indignant about what are essentially non-problems.

People value a series of small gains more than a single gain of the same amount summed up. They also experience one large loss, less badly, than an identical loss, suffered in multiple, smaller parts. This is because they value initial gains from a reference point more highly than they value subsequent gains. They feel worse about initial losses than about subsequent losses. In the light of this finding, when negotiating with your group about your proposal, you should not give in on a number of issues all at once. Instead, let them feel each victory independently. When explaining the benefits of your proposal, do not display all its positive features at once, but present and have them evaluate each, one at a time (Thaler, 1985).

Finally, you should consider the effect that the timing of choices has on decisions. We would rather have a desirable commodity today, than a month from now. Would you prefer a delay of a month before receiving a negative outcome, rather than getting it immediately. The perceived difference between getting a good outcome now, versus a month from now, was found to be larger than the difference between getting a good outcome twelve months from now versus thirteen months from now. People become more impatient when they can 'smell' a good outcome. This creates an, 'I want it now' mentality, which they will not acknowledge, but which will unconsciously bias their decision-making. This occurs when they focus on a single element of a positive outcome. In contrast, when presented with a range of positive outcomes, they will space these out more in time, wanting some now, and some later. Thus, how you frame choices in terms of immediate and distant outcomes, will affect your group members' responses (Schelling, 1984; Thaler and Shefrin, 1981; Loewenstein, 1987).

WRITING BEFORE AND AFTER THE MEETING

A written document circulated by you to the group members before the meeting, can focus their attention and frame the decision-issues. Whatever your meeting's objective, a written proposal carries more weight than a spoken one, even if the others have not read it. The written format gives the appearance of rationality, thereby reducing the impact of any verbal counter-arguments which, by contrast, come to be seen as spontaneous and less well thought out. Documents can galvanize others into action by requiring them to respond or forcing them to commit themselves in writing. Frame your written proposals in a format that approximates the rational model used by the majority of companies. This sequence consists of identifying the problem, generating alternative solutions, choosing a solution, implementing it and reviewing it. By implying that change implementation will follow these logical steps, group members come to feel that, 'things are being done properly', and this ritual also helps you to establish your personal legitimacy and credibility (Buchanan and Boddy, 1992).

To gain the approval of others, your text should fit current company values and ideals, and use arguments and justifications that are acceptable within that culture, and attractive to senior management. Avoid words like *discover, study, devise, monitor, explore, investigate, define, review* and *revise*. They imply procrastination and convey the idea that the analysis, which should have been carried out before your proposal was made public, has yet to be completed. The implied need for further study suggests that you do not fully understand the problem, and that there is going to be a delay. Instead, use words like *reduce, cut, grow, remove, eliminate, meet target, improve, maintain, challenge* and *do*. These words convey understanding, action and progress. It is common for proposals phrased in one format to be rejected, but then, when re-phrased with other arguments, to be accepted.

The benefits of circulating your written ideas ahead of time have just been discussed. However, making a live presentation of your ideas at the meeting itself also has benefits. It allows you to define reality for the other meeting participants much more vividly. By presenting, you gain attention, minimize interruptions, facilitate understanding and allow yourself to concentrate on favourable data. One of the reasons why proposals may be rejected by a committee is that its members do not understand them. A presentation increases understanding, and carries more weight than the presentation of documentary evidence alone (Schwenk, 1986). A combination of both is probably the ideal solution, provided that time is available.

Finally, writing the minutes of the meeting is another way of manufacturing reality. The person who writes these possesses the power that comes from the opportunity to manipulate the description of the atmosphere of the discussion, the arguments expressed and the decisions recorded. Even when there is a style of minute-writing, there remains scope for manipulation because decisions are often vague, thus giving the minute-writer freedom to decide how they are to be worded. Minutes are legally admissible documents and the sooner after the meeting they are written the better, so indicate the date of their writing.

USING TIME

Timing is an influencing variable in a group setting in that issues and events have a quality of ripeness. There is a time to act and a time to delay. The scarcest resource in an organization is attention, and attending to something has an oppor-tunity cost. Choosing the right time to advance your ideas is crucial. A good idea presented at the wrong time will be ignored. One reason why persistence often pays off is because the act of regularly re-presenting your idea for group approval increases your chances of hitting the right moment in time. Being early and moving first, can also give you an edge. When it is difficult for others to undo what you have achieved, your actions will serve as the basis for further negoti-ations. You can then set the terms of the debate and the framework for subsequent actions. Being first provides the advantage of surprise. Nice people finish last, having given the opposition time to mobilize.

Another way to use time to influence is to make people wait for you to arrive. It is said that punctuality is the virtue of the bored. By being late you call atten-tion to yourself, and force others to consider your implicit power over them. The Duke of Wellington's advice to latecomers was, 'Never apologize, never explain'. Others may pay more attention to you, to encourage you to arrive on time in the future, which again reinforces their dependence on you. Waiting is an act of behavioural commitment. You have to justify waiting to yourself. One way of self-justifying this waste of time is to enhance cognitively the value of the thing or person being waited for (Schwartz, 1974). The opposite of delay is the deadline. The faster you are able to persuade another, the more the advan-tage lies with you and vice versa. Deadlines favour you if you have the momentum, and convey a sense of urgency and importance. When the discussion moves in your favour, set a deadline by saying, 'We need to decide this now', even if this is not really necessary. Moreover, proposals made near the deadline for a decision, are often more likely to pass than those that surface earlier.

INTRODUCE WITH FEAR

How do you gain the approval of neutral or hostile individuals to your proposal? The research data suggests some specific techniques. First, arouse their desires and concerns before making your proposal. Introduce it as being vital to orga-nizational survival, competitiveness or profitability. Make it even more immediate by relating it to pressing company needs. Above all, link it to members' personal concerns so as to engender an emotional response from them. Explain what it can do for their job security or career development. By creating a felt need that a change is required, you unfreeze them, and trigger their speedier agreement. In this context, a mild level of fear has been consistently associated with increases in listener acceptance. However, attitude change only results in agreement and changed behaviour when you not only expect your group members to change, but also specify the direction of the change and method of its implementation. Unless both are provided, your group will become more rigid, defensive and hostile to your proposal (Leventhal, 1970; Sutton, 1982b).

259

You can highlight threats from outside the company to justify your proposals. Exploit or even invent a crisis. To maintain your credibility however, your invented crisis needs to materialize, so play safe and put it in the future ('We need to act now to avoid a crisis in two years' time'). In those two years, everyone in the room, including yourself, will have moved on. Such arguments are more powerful than those based exclusively on personal aspirations or empire building. However, the former should not be excluded, since pure altruism can raise suspicion, and reduce your trustworthiness. Others understand that personal motives can be a source of drive, energy and ambition, and are perceived as legitimate, provided that they are expressed in the right way. Hence, you can let them know that you have nothing to gain personally from your proposal, if that is the case; or state but underplay any advantages to you; or you can be bold, and explain the advantages to you, but adding the equal or greater advantages to the organization. Such an explanation will give added credibility to all your subsequent points (Buchanan and Boddy, 1992).

WORDS AND PHRASES

Choice of words and phrases during a group meeting is crucial. The use of verbal influencing was examined earlier in the book. There is an influencing principle which we have already encountered which states that once an influencee has agreed with you, they are more amenable to your persuasion. This is generally know as the, yes-technique. It is based on the idea that establishing empathy with your listeners is the basis for influencing them, and that by agreeing with you at the start, the influencee wants to continue being on your side. You are in effect putting words into his mouth, and thus his mind. He believes what is in his mouth. The stated *yes*, is the verbal equivalent of a salesperson getting a foot in the door. By accepting your statements, he is taking responsibility for them. The easiest way to get a yes response from your audience is to ask a question or make a statement to which the answer has to be yes. Such opening lines include: *have you found*; *would it be fair to say*; *do you sometimes find*; *in your experience*; and *have you ever wondered why?*

There are other applications of the yes-technique. You can structure a yes-set by ending your own statements with an 'OK' or 'Yes' – '*You're wanting to increase the rate of return, Yes?*'. The final word softens, and literally asks for a sign of agreement – a nod, a yes or an, 'ahuh'. With a statement like, *do me a favour and look at these reports, OK?*', the OK becomes an anchor, softening the command to a point that makes it sound like a request, instead of the order that it really is. You can use these repeatedly throughout your discussion, not just at the beginning and end. A third way to create a yes-set is to say something, and then follow it with a, *do you see?*, *is that alright?* or *do you follow?* Psychologists call this checking understanding, but when associated with a manifestly simple idea, procedure or explanation, this technique acts as a yes-elicitor. A fourth way is to turn an obvious statement generalization or some trite saying, into a question. For example, from 'Customers expect good service' to 'Don't all customers expect good service?'. This request for producing verbal and mental agreement builds bridges between you and your influencees. The final technique is to repeat back or paraphrase what the influencee has just said, while at the same time nodding your head in agreement – 'You like the time schedule.' The aim of your nod in the statement is to communicate friendliness and acceptance, and this acts to generate a yes-response. After you have established a positive climate, you make the point or proposition with which you want your listeners to agree. It may be that you are unable to secure agreement from the group to your full proposal. Nevertheless, you may get their agreement to part of it or to the fact that you are raising an important issue for consideration (Freedman and Fraser, 1966; Seligman et al., 1976; Lewicki and Litterer, 1985).

Reid and Ng (2000) examined how an influencer could project a favourable image of themselves in a group situation through conversation. The more a person participates in a group discussion, the greater is their perceived influence. To make yourself appear more powerful, talk more! The group unconsciously establishes a norm of speech content. When the content of your utterance is consistent with the group norm, your influence increases; if it is inconsistent with it, your influence decreases. Imagine a manager is holding a meeting with her subordinates to discuss poor results. The workers are annoyed at management's restrictions which make it hard for them to achieve their targets. The manager can exert the greatest influence by first agreeing that the restrictions do indeed hinder them (an utterance that conforms to the group norm). She thus increases her influence among the group members. Then she can still tell them what they do not want to hear (i.e. that they will have to work still harder), yet she will continue to be liked by them as their manager. Reid and Ng's findings suggest that, to be influential in a group, make sure that your opinions are known, either by turn-taking or interrupting in a group discussion. This demonstrates your power. Second, once you have gained your turn, say things that are not too controversial, but at the same time, that do not state the obvious.

Studies over the years have revealed numerous other verbal devices for influencing. Henri Tajfel suggested creating granfallons ('proud and meaningless associations of human beings'). Groups can be given a feeling of identity on the flimsiest of pretexts. A product or service can be given a 'personality' so that its buyer is given a sense of belonging to a special group. Additionally, create factoids which are facts that did not exist before you created them, and which are difficult to undo. Use 'slice of life' imagery by vividly describing a situation to enable group members to imagine the benefits of the consequences of your proposal. Choose your message words carefully. For example, 'There is no alternative' or 'best ever'. Words can both deceive and create misconceptions. Use decoys to

261

compare an idea with an inferior one. This produces a context effect that makes the influencer's idea look better than it really is. Speechwriters distinguish between blah words, colour words and power words. Blah words are forgettable. Colour words are vivid but do not generate an emotional reaction that can be assessed. Power words grab attention without actually saying anything. Power words include 'interesting', 'unusual', 'decisive', 'hot', 'exciting', 'new', 'critical', 'urgent' and 'compelling'. To maintain a group's attention, feed them a steady diet of power words.

PROPOSAL CONTENT

The content of your proposal and the way in which you present it to the group, can affect its acceptability. Kanter (1983) recommended that it should be *trial-able*, capable of being piloted before a full commitment was made with all the associated effort and expense; *reversible*, could be changed back to today's status quo if necessary; *divisible*, had a number of independent aspects; *concrete*, had tangible outcomes; *familiar*, recognizable and within the members' comfort zone; *congruent*, consistent with existing company policy, practice and values; and *sexy*, excited the listeners. Incorporating some of these features in your proposal can help to secure agreement.

If you have to put forward anti-arguments to your proposal, wait until enough pro-arguments have been given to achieve a predominantly favourable perception for the consideration of the later, anti-ones. The first impression becomes the lasting impression under certain circumstances. These include, when what you tell them now, will be incompatible with what you will tell them later; when you get group members to take a publicly committing action after you have presented the points you want them to accept, but before you provide them with contradictory arguments; when the issue is unfamiliar to your group; and when your listeners have only a superficial interest in the issue you are presenting. Under these four conditions, group members will begin to identify with you as a person whose beliefs seem viable to them. The key here is to increase or prolong the stress in the audience, thereby altering their thinking processes, impairing their judgement, and increasing their openness to suggestibility. In this state, their conversion to your viewpoint, when it comes, may be unexpected and dramatic.

Finally, there are five ways of making your group's attitude more positive to your proposal. First, you can lead your group members to add a new positive belief about your proposal that becomes prominent in their minds – 'You may not have realized it, but it will save us thousand of pounds'. Second, you can increase the attractiveness of a belief they already hold – 'My preferred candidate for the post is Ms Y who, as you know, is a member of the Institute of X. However, you may not realize how valuable her membership of that institute can be for us'. Third, you increase the strength of an existing positive belief that they already hold – 'You know that one advantage of my proposal is that it will take only ten months to implement. But what you may not realize is that every month saved, represents a financial gain of £10,000'. Fourth, you can decrease the unfavourability of an existing negative belief – 'OK, my proposal only saves £2,000, but then again, the opportunity of saving this amount should not be rejected'. Finally, you could try shuffling your audience's current beliefs around, so that a different set of beliefs becomes prominent – 'Have you forgotten, that last quarter we agreed to outsource our human resources function' (O'Keefe, 1990).

USING NOTES AND GRAPHS

Write notes on what others are saying, especially in the first hour of the meeting during which members position themselves. This shows them that a record is being kept, and it can help you think more clearly before responding. You can jot down a quick note if you want to comment on anything that anyone else has said. Indeed, notes can be used as props during a meeting to break your own flow of thought, if you find yourself developing an unhelpful position. Were you to just stop dead, the group might see you as weak, vulnerable or confused. However, by stopping to consult your notes, you give yourself thinking time. You read them in silence, look up at the audience, refer to something in your notes, and put yourself back on track. You are buying time, fending off an inter-ruption ('I'm just looking for a reference') and maintaining control. Notes can also serve as a diversion and as a way of shifting to another topic. Used effectively, they will make you look well prepared and informed.

Using notes to quote or cite someone is powerful. The citation maybe a previous speaker's words or an authority's research uncovered by you prior to the meeting. Using notes makes it clear to others that you are being careful, thorough and meticulous. Evidence of data collection not only demonstrates knowledge, but also counters opponents' use of phrases such as 'I think', 'I feel' or 'It seems to me that'. Such statements lack the weight of your researched facts. If you have prepared, and your preparation is available to you through your notes, you will have more facts at your fingertips than your opponent, and you will win the argument. Whatever form your notes take, typewritten pages, lists, charts, diagrams, handwritten, they should contain plenty of underlining and highlighting that others can see, but cannot read. Ensure also that you can retrieve and access the required information during the meeting.

Graphs exist to help identify trends and relationships between variables. They are frequently used in group presentations as decision aids. However, they have also been used to persuade viewers. It appears there is no optimal way to design graphs, since appropriateness is based on a combination of graph content, presenter objectives and audience needs. However, some guidelines and rules do exist. For example, that they should be clearly labelled, that design variation should mirror numerical change in data, and so on. The principle underlying how graphs should be correctly presented is that they should be drawn in a manner that leads viewers to reach conclusions consistent with those that they would reach when analysing the underlying numeric data on which the graphs are based. However, established graph presentation guidelines are often violated to create more persuasive presentations to groups by influencing viewers' impressions of the data. Arunachalam *et al.* (2002) studied four types of improperly designed graphs. It is important to stress that in these experiments, the researchers presented subjects with a combination of accurate numeric data and impression-inducing graphs, in order to assess the effect on decision-makers' choices.

Exaggerating magnitude

The first of these improper graphs involved *exaggerating the magnitude* of a trend. This can be done by improperly scaling the vertical axis, either by starting at a number other than zero, or by having a discontinuity in the scale. Both of these devices make the sizes of the intervals on the vertical unequal. For example, the graph at the top of Figure 13.1 is correctly drawn and starts at zero. It shows that sales have increased by about 75 per cent over a five-year period. The height of the bar representing year 5 sales is approximately 1.75 times the height of that representing year 1 sales. In contrast, the graph at the bottom of Figure 13.1 exaggerates sales growth by 100 per cent. Year 5 column is about 3.5 times the height of those representing year 1 sales, although the numeric increase is only 75 per cent. This distortion is achieved by either not starting at the origin (zero) or else not indicating a discontinuity on the scale. This can easily make a small rise or fall look more significant than it is. This is the most commonly found improper graph design, and is often found in annual reports and business media.

Masking

A second device is *masking*. This is done by distracting the reader from evaluating changes in the data being graphed. For example, one can present two variables, that differ in magnitude, on the same graph. The observer will tend to focus on the changes in the greater magnitude variable. Put another way, changes in the smaller magnitude variable will be hidden by those in the larger one. For example, one can hide the fact that sales are rising but earnings are declining, by displaying both on the same graph as shown in first of the three graphs in Figure 13.2. Here, the black column represents sales while the white column shows earnings. See how the first combined graph, differs from the next two, separated ones.

Accurately drawn graph

100 % proportionality distortion

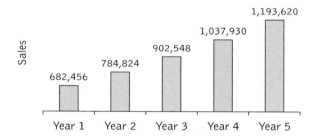

Figure 13.1 *Example of 100% proportionality distortion*

Source: From Arunachalam *et al.*, 2002: vol. 16, no. 2, 187. Reprinted with kind permission of American Accounting Association

Year reversal

A third device is *year reversal*. This involves reversing the sequence of years on the x-axis. It can make a negative trend look positive. The reason is that we are used to reading left to right. The top histogram in Figure 13.3 shows a declining sales trend over succeeding years, with the most recent year shown in the fifth column. The bottom histogram in that figure shows the same sales data. However, it presents the most recent sales data in the first column.

Negative values

The final contrivance is to *omit negative values*. By not letting the graph drop to the negative side of the x-axis, the negative values become less visible, and trends may appear both smoother and less variable. In Figure 13.4, contrast the presentation of the very poor middle year in the top histogram, with the not-so-good, but seemingly not disastrous one, in the bottom histogram.

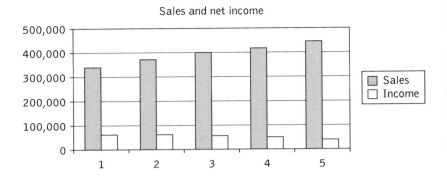

Correct approach; Separate graphs for sales and income masking

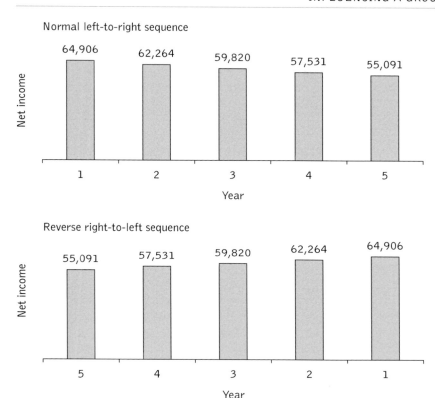

Normal left-to-right sequence

Figure 13.3 Example of year reversal

Source: From Arunachalam *et al.*, 2002: 189. Reprinted with kind permission of American Accounting Association

In these experiments, when these improperly designed graphs were presented, the accurate numeric data was always also included and displayed on the graphs themselves. Viewers could therefore check, if they wanted to, the numeric data with the graph display. However, researchers found that subjects were more likely to choose an alternative when graphs were designed to indicate a more favourable impression of the data, than when the graphs were accurately drawn. Several reason are suggested. One of these may be that people seek to minimize their cognitive effort, and find it easier to compare slopes of graphs than numerical data. Another reason may be that people have difficulty detecting subtle errors, especially when the data remain internally consistent. Hence, many decision-makers are not aware that graphs may be inaccurately drawn, and the effect therefore goes unnoticed and uncorrected.

The implications of this research for you, as an influencer at group presentations, are significant. You can use graph design not only to influence impressions,

Negative numbers explicitly graphed

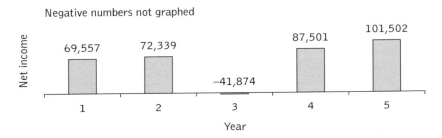

Negative numbers not graphed

Figure 13.4 *Example of omission of negative numbers*

Source: From Arunachalam *et al.*, 2002: 189–90. Reprinted with kind permission of American Accounting Association

but also to direct your audience's attention to specific aspects of the data set, thereby guiding their decision-making in the direction of your choice. Additionally, the fact that people are happy to ignore correct numerical data and make judgements on improperly designed visuals, has wider ranging implications for influencing people within organizations. Moreover, it should allow you to assess critically the graphs which appear in the presentations of others, and not least those that appear in companies' annual reports.

DILUTION EFFECT

The dilution effect refers to the observation that providing neutral or irrelevant information weakens a judgement or impression that you make (Zukier, 1982). You need to guard against it in both your verbal and written presentations. Do not dilute a good argument, either by providing additional, weaker points yourself, or by providing these in response to an invitation from a group member ('Are there any other reasons why we should accept your proposal?'). Your opponent will listen to you recounting your progressively weaker arguments, will spot the weakest, pounce on it, and dismiss your case, strong arguments and all. One or two strong points are more powerful than many weak ones. A weak argument does not strengthen an already strong one, but actually detracts from it. The dilution effect can be used to change your image to your audience. If your group members do not like you for whatever reason, you can reduce their negative image of you, by including information about yourself that is irrelevant to the proposal being discussed. For example, your background, your marital status or the number of your children. The dilution effect makes you appear more similar to the group members, more average, and thus more like everyone else in the room. As an average person, you will be seen to be less likely to be of super-intelligence or terribly negative.

SPEAKING TO THE GROUP

Make your remarks short, simple and clear, thus showing that you are worth listening to. Fluent and self-confident speakers are most influential. Talk to the whole group, and not just to the individual who appears to be agreeing with you, otherwise you will alienate the others. When speaking, make regular eye contact with all members, to make them feel that you are speaking to them personally. You can be a clear communicator by labelling your behaviour. Signal verbally that you are about to ask a question, make a proposal or offer a solution. This gains the attention of the whole group. Whenever given a choice, make a positive rather than a negative comment, about what should be done rather than what must be avoided. Such speech gains you credibility as someone who seeks solutions and inclines listeners to your proposal. Present your case by speaking calmly, which is more effective in getting people to change their minds than forceful threats or shouting. People react negatively to language which they perceive as being too intense, and those who are under external pressure to make a decision, are especially receptive to low intensity language, and will reject proposals couched in highly emotional tones (Bowers, 1964). So control any strong feelings that might lead you to oversell your idea by presenting it too fervently.

It is inevitable that someone will oppose your proposal, or will wish to promote theirs. So remain calm while they state their case fully (Giblin, 1956). If they are loud, remind yourself that they may have poor communication skills, and that their aggression may be the only way that they have of expressing themselves. Interruption is the single most irritating interpersonal habit. The person with something on his chest has his 'mental set' all geared up for talking, and will not listen to you. Bite your tongue if you have to, but let the other person finish. Once they have finished, summarize what you have heard them say since this signals that you have listened, and have understood them. Vocalizing another's ideas helps you to remember them better. When people find that they are being listened to, their initial fear of having to fight for attention to make their point fades. They then often become less defensive, present their points in a more reasonable way, and generally become more willing to listen to you. When you speak and listen actively, the norm of reciprocity, encourages the other group members to do the same. Remember also that the worst time to state your position on a topic is immediately after the other person has stated their contrary position. Avoid antagonizing opponents by contradicting them immediately and directly. Delay a little, and instead, offer your proposal as a solution to their problem.

If, in their presentation, the objector verbally attacks you, resist the temptation to 'win' the argument. Instead, just thank them for their feedback, and move on with the positive aspects of your case. Any personal retorts only deflect you from your primary objective of persuading the group. When you do respond, think and respect the questioner's needs, and endeavour to see things from their point of view, however much you may disagree with them. Avoid the common, knee-jerk response of *yes-but* which contains the subtle message of opposition and disagreement. Its effect is destructive, even if expressed as, 'Yes, that may be right, but'. It triggers a defensive response from your opponent just when you want to establish rapport (Rafe, 1990; Glass, 1991). If you cannot agree with the speaker's statement say, 'I can understand how you might believe that, and'. If you cannot agree say, 'I can respect your feelings, and'. At anytime, you can maintain rapport by saying, 'I appreciate your desire to [ ], and'. The replacement word, *and*, removes the opposition implied by *but*, and communicates your desire to be agreeable. The word, *however*, is also a good substitute for but ('*Yes*, you have a good point, *however*, have you considered'). These verbal tactics prepare your opposer to be more receptive to your suggestion, and to consider the issue in another way. At the same time, they allow you to speak on the topic without having to attack the rightness of the opposer's views. Another way of responding to an objector is to mention first any points on which the two of you agree, and only then those over which you disagree. You can communicate your disagreement by pre-fixing your opposing view with, 'Let me play devil's advocate for a minute'. Alternatively, you might compliment your opposer which may disarm them ('I think Fiona has put her case exceptionally well').

Pause before you answer. A short pause shows that you are thinking about a point just made, whereas too quick a response indicates that you have no time for their problems or concerns. Only a slight pause is acceptable, since a longer one may leave you appearing indecisive or trying to evade a definite answer. You can get help from other group members if you need it. For example, if you get boxed in by challenges, say, 'I'm obviously not making myself clear', or, 'I haven't done justice to this, can someone else clarify the point for the others?'. This places the blame on yourself for a less than adequate presentation, and avoids blaming your listeners for their failure to understand or to agree with you. Most importantly, it does not devalue your message and maintains its consistency. Avoid rushing to justifying or defending your view against their criticism too much or you will look defensive. Just acknowledge it with a nod. Your pause or silence can lead to another group member providing you with ammunition which can be fired when ready. Alternatively, that person may respond on your behalf. If neither happens, when you do respond, you will not be speaking defensively. Silence among group members does not necessarily signify neutrality.

Use 'we-language' to create a feeling of group consensus. The word, 'we', engenders a feeling of togetherness and co-operation that can never be stated outright. It carries an impact out of all proportion to its size. So say, 'Something that we could consider is', in preference to, 'I think we should'. Davies (1988) suggested some other influential phrases. Preface your proposal with, *'rightly or wrongly'*. This acts to anticipate and pre-empt resistance and criticism, and disarms most of the counter-arguments before they can be expressed. Without stating it obviously, you are showing that you have considered arguments for and against your decision, have weighed them up carefully, and you have now come to a considered decision. Your listeners will be reluctant to jump in with an over-hasty criticism of what is essentially a considered decision by you. Another useful phrase, this time to gain attention, is, *'It's as you were saying earlier'*. People always prick up their ears to hear repeated what they have already said. Try using, *'Here are two ways of looking at this'* which is a gentle way of introducing a controversial idea to forestall its immediate rejection. Finally, experiment with, *'What Jill says is quite correct'*. Use this phrase if you want to be one up on Jill. It nicely implies that you are the real expert, and that Jill is merely playing at it, and has on this occasion struck it lucky. However, Jill cannot object to your comment, since, on the face of it, you are simply agreeing with her and are backing her up.

Single communication and single persuasion attempts are rarely successful. You need to repeat your message and your arguments throughout the meeting, and in different meetings. Persevere with the simple repetition of your message ('Is it beyond reasonable doubt?'). Such repetition may appear to be redundant, but will keep the issue alive, and will reinforce the points that you want your listeners to have in front of them. If your presentation is lengthy, then throughout it, you will need to remain confident, consistent and calm, even under pressure. The consistency of your message will be considered to be a sign of your certainty and commitment to your viewpoint. Hence, avoid any behaviours that contradict your message. Other aspects of public speaking are discussed in the next chapter.

DEALING WITH INDIVIDUALS' RESISTANCE

Group influencers are recommended to assess other people's reactions to your ideas, and tailoring your response to their type of resistance. Group members are not just 'for' or 'against' your proposals. Fox (1999) suggests seven categories of resistance, which are summarized in Table 13.1. He explains that in a meeting, one might experience different types of resistance from the different participants.

He suggests identifying those who have the power to help or hinder you; and who control key resources. It is these who should be the primary focus of your influencing attempts. Another technique is to address different people in the group with different parts of your message. Car adverts often stress both vehicle speed and reliability.

Table 13.1 *Categories of resistance*

Resistance	Response to that resistance
Actively hostile	The aim is to stop them working against you, and move them to a neutral stance. Interact with them at a personal level, so that they can get to know you. Build a positive relationship with them by first focusing on areas of your agreement, before considering your disagreements.
Hostile	The aim is to convince them that you are being careful, fair and logical. Show that you understand their viewpoint. Support your statements with reliable, factual evidence. Clarify areas of your agreement and disagreement. Ask for small concessions from them, while trying to work towards a mutually acceptable solution.
Neutral	Associate your point with a neutral person's feelings, values and concerns. Stress the connection between their interests or position and your proposal. In this way secure their support. Keep your points simple and descriptions vivid, repeating both in different ways. Stress both mutual gains and mutual losses.
Undecided	Tip the scales in your favour by focusing on your side of the issue. Avoid an overly balanced presentation. Cite expert opinion and examples. Break your proposal into smaller action suggestions that the person can accept. Reinforce and follow up your points so that person does not regress into indecision.
Uniformed	Inform them by stressing your expertise, experience and background. Discuss only your point of view, and ignore the other. Do not 'over-inform' but allow them to ask clarifying questions. Make your presentation lively and interesting.
Supportive	Make their support of your position active and enthusiastic. Tell them what you want them to do, and get them to do it quickly. Use vivid testimonials and examples to reinforce their commitment. Show them the benefits of your approach. Prepare them for encounters with hostile people, showing how they should defend themselves.
Actively support	Keep them active, encouraging them to share their views with your non-supporters. Try to unite them against a common enemy. Reinforce their enthusiasm with your own.

Source: Based on Fox 1999 (www.foxperformance.com/consulting1.html)

TURNING OPPOSITION AROUND

During a long discussion, it is important to check where other members stand on the issue; whether they understand what is being proposed; and whether you all have a common understanding of the stage that the discussion has reached. Such checking helps to clarify points, overcomes misunderstandings and creates mutual trust. Most importantly, it identifies who is for and against your proposal. After the summary, find a common point of reference – one of which you can both agree on (e.g. 'doing nothing is not an option'). Then present your viewpoint, and ask the other person to summarize what they understood you to have said (Glass, 1991). Listen in a way to be able to understand and explore another's position. What strengths and weaknesses do others see in your proposal? How serious are these weaknesses? Evaluate any objections made.

People usually respond to another's proposal by saying what they dislike about it, while ignoring what they do like. So do the opposite, reward your opposer when they say something with which you agree. Research tells us that people are most likely to repeat behaviour which is rewarded (Skinner, 1953; Homans, 1961). To do this, first acknowledge the point that they have made ('That's an interesting point, I hadn't thought of that'). This separates out the key statement they make from others they may have made earlier. It simultaneously distinguishes those parts of it which you like and agree with, from those which you do not. You can then express your appreciation to them for saying things that are favourable to your argument. Compliment and encourage them to go further. If the other person makes a concession, and gives you something that you want, reward them by making a concession in return.

Every opposing majority group will consist of both strong opinion leaders and the uncommitted or disinterested followers. Some of the latter may neither have a view on your proposal nor will be affected by it. Some will 'go with the flow' of the meeting, perhaps just wanting to be on the winning side, irrespective of which that is. Others will conform to the positive expectations of another person due to their desire for social approval and acceptance. We know that people compare themselves to others who are most like them in terms of background and opinion, in order to determine what is the correct, appropriate or desirable behaviour.

PUBLIC COMMITMENT AND CONFORMITY

Should you avoid or encourage group members at the start of a discussion to state publicly where they stand on an issue or how they respond to your proposal? The argument for this tactic is that it gives you an early indication as to whether you are alone, in a small minority or a member of the majority. It also forces them to justify the positions that they take, which is particularly useful if they are against you. As they justify their stand, you can make a mental or written note of any inconsistencies, problems or weaknesses, and raise these later in the discussion. The argument against this tactic is that a verbal, public commitment to a position locks an individual into it, preventing them from easily changing their mind. Internally, they bond themselves to their early position, and externally fear losing face or appearing inconsistent to others if they subsequently change their minds. There is therefore no definitive answer in the research as to which is the best tactic to use.

If you do seek an early public statement and find that they are hostile to your proposal, you will have to 'uncommit' group members from their public statement. Unbinding a person from their previous commitment can be done by suggesting that they were not really responsible for their original decision in some way (Pfeffer, 1992). This might be because they faced external pressure (no free choice); the original information on which they made that decision has been superseded or found to be inaccurate; or that the situation has now changed. All these explanations offer them a 'way out', and the freedom to re-choose. Pfeffer was adamant that you should avoid directly attacking the decision that they made earlier, since this will merely elicit a string of justifications. You need to allow them to change their mind without having to admit that they were mistaken. All this emphasizes the desirability of persuading people on a one-to-one basis, outside the meeting room, or voting secretly within it (Tetlock and Manstead, 1985).

What should you do if you want to change your position, yet still maintain your own credibility in group members' eyes? You should use a two-step strategy. First, portray yourself as the kind of person who is open-minded and courageous enough to change their position ('I know, I said we should disband our personnel department, but I have listened to the arguments that you have made for keeping it, and now believe that you are right'). Next, explain that conditions have changed since you took your original position ('Three months ago, when I said we should disband it, there was not as much government legislation on workplace relations').

QUESTIONING TO PERSUADE

Questions are a powerful yet neglected influencing tool, since they can raise doubts in influencees' minds, and help them to accept your propositions. Applying the Socratic teaching method, you can use questions to communicate your proposal. Unskilled influencers believe that influencing is synonymous with talking at their influencee. In the final analysis, it is the influencee who influences him or herself, with the influencer creating an 'information environment' in which such self-influencing can occur. You get them to realize the strength of your case by asking them questions which reveal the legitimacy of your case, and encourage them to perceive your proposal differently. Moreover, in generating their own

answers, the influencee gains a feeling of solution-ownership. In the group situation, questions can avoid your having to disagree directly with someone. Rather
than saying, 'What you've said doesn't support your argument', you just ask,
'How does what you've said support your argument?'. Drummond recommended
turning your suggestions and proposals into questions so as to foster a sense of
collectiveness – 'I suggest we . . . what do other people think?'. What if you
are unable to respond to a question? Do what politicians do. They ignore the
question; acknowledge the question without answering it; question the question;
repeat the question; verbally attack the questioner for asking it; decline to answer;
give an incomplete answer; answer another question; or claim to have already
answered the question (Day, 1989).

GROUP OWNERSHIP AND COMPROMISE

Another fundamental principle of influencing is that people will agree and commit
to proposals in which they have participated and with which feel involved.
So you may have to choose between getting your idea accepted, and taking credit
for it. No one likes to feel that they are being sold or told something. We prefer
to feel that we are buying of our own accord and acting on our own ideas. So
how can you transfer that feeling of the ownership of your idea to group members?
Four approaches have been identified. The *their-original-thought-strategy* helps them
to have the right idea in the first place. Begin by asking members to define what
their priority is in the situation. Next, list what has already been done towards
achieving that stated goal. Then, highlight the gap or difference between the two,
based on the information you have obtained. Finally, offer your idea as a way of
filling that gap. However, if you say, 'You should do X', you are not facilitating
ownership. So instead, say, 'Do you think that we ought to do X?'. If they agree,
this form of speech will leave them owning your idea.

The *hitching strategy* links your idea to a thought or a value that a group member
has expressed earlier in the discussion ('Jane, you stressed the importance of
quality, I feel that my proposed training programme is an extension of what you
are saying'). Hitching your idea to the person's original comment makes it easy
for them to accept it as no more than a logical extension of what they themselves have already been thinking about. Rejecting it would produce in them a
feeling of inconsistency. The *amendment strategy* requires you to structure your
idea into a form which makes it easy for others to suggest changes to it during
the meeting. Once they offer these, you quickly incorporate them into your idea,
thus making it half theirs. Alternatively, before the meeting, ask people for help
in preparing your idea. People are flattered to be asked, and once they have
contributed, even in a minor way, they assume a sense of ownership for it.

Finally, with the *explanation strategy*, you select an opponent to explain your
idea to the other group members under the pretence of clarifying your thoughts

to everyone else. Whatever their misgivings about your idea, to maintain their own reputation and credibility, they will have to ensure that they present your idea clearly and objectively (if not enthusiastically) to the others. Having explained it in this way, there is a chance that, to avoid cognitive dissonance (saying one thing, believing another), the opposer may re-align their internal views on the matter with their external verbal presentation, and come to see your idea more positively. Each of the four strategies involve giving away your idea to some degree. However, you may be able to retain the official ownership of your proposal, and thus the kudos that goes with it, by literally having the last word on the item ('So we've agreed that, shall we move on?'); by summarizing it for the meeting minutes being taken by someone else, 'Following my proposal, the meeting agreed'); or by writing the minutes of the meeting yourself.

COMPROMISING AND LOSING

When the majority of the group have difficulty in accepting your proposal, you should compromise or adjust it without losing poise or credibility. Skilled influencers always concede something to find some point of agreement. If the specificity of your proposal is a barrier to its acceptance, then make it wider and more generally applicable, by clouding it with abstractions. Do this carefully as too vague and abstract goals do not attract committed support. If the complexity of your proposal is a barrier to its comprehension and acceptability, then re-state it in simpler terms. If simplicity and narrowness of focus is the obstacle, relate it to other issues and dimensions. Present it as challenging and interesting, while at the same time safe and uncontentious. Consider giving in on a minor point, the other person may reciprocate by conceding something on a major one.

Whatever the outcome, victory or defeat, do not gloat, cry or be angry (until later). You will not win every time. When you lose, do not take it personally. Separate your proposal from yourself. Do not become angry with those who decided against you, or carry on arguing with them after they have rejected it. Do not confront them individually as they may start bearing a grudge against you when you make your next proposal. You can certainly express your disappointment with the decision assertively, but then confirm your position as a team player, by supporting the majority decision, and working to implement it successfully, even though you may not personally favour it.

You should lose in such a way that you can maintain your relationship with the other group members, and avoid burning any bridges behind you. Just say to them, 'Well, I lost that one', and let them take their win this time. Your job is to build contacts for the next engagement, so do not destroy the precious and time-consuming work that you have put in the past by the way that you handle failure. It is said that we learn more from our failures than from our successes. Find out why you lost. One reason for maintaining good relations with your opposers is that you can ask why they rejected your proposal. On important issues, you should make contingency plans ahead, should you fail. Finally, do not react to defeat by playing it safe, and avoiding risking failure in the future. Top managers attribute their success to making the right decision in only 50 per cent of cases.

Chapter 14

Influential public speaking

He who wants to persuade should put his trust not in the right argument but in the right word. The power of sound has always been greater than the power of sense.

Joseph Conrad

INTRODUCTION

Organizations consider public speaking to be a vital managerial skill. Interestingly, our assessment of the credibility of the content of a speaker's ideas is largely based on their performance, even though there is no logical relationship between what is said and how it is said. We noted earlier, that Mehrabian (1972) had estimated that 55 per cent of the impact that individuals made on others came from non-verbal signals, and Chapter 2 considered this topic. However, according to Mehrabian, a further 38 per cent of the impact came from how people spoke. Stewart (1976) reported that, 'management is a verbal world whose people are usually instructed, assisted and persuaded by personal contact rather than on paper'. Talking and listening occupy between a half and three-quarters of a manager's time. It is therefore not surprising that managers prefer to be told things, rather than having to read them for themselves. This chapter concentrates on influencing a large group of people, and thus complements the preceding one on small group influencing. It will not discuss the mechanics of how to give presentations, but will focus upon the psychology of influencing a large group of people. It will offer advice on how best to present yourself, structure and sequence your material, and 'read' your audience, so as to give your message the maximum persuasive impact.

Persuasive public speakers have realistic objectives. They know what they can reasonably talk their audience into, within the parameters of the time available and the audience numbers present. Talking them into a small, specific change is more realistic than a large one. Large changes normally require small group or one-to-one discussions. For example, in a health promotion lecture, encourage them to eat one extra item of fruit each day. To communicate your message effectively, it must be received by your audience; attended to; understood; believed; remembered and acted upon (Therkelsen and Fiebich, 2001). How might this be done?

PRESENTER CHARACTERISTICS

Persuasion is partly achieved through the force of a speaker's personal character. The presenter speaks in a way that makes an audience feel that he or she is credible. Aristotle referred to this as *ethos* – or the perceived character of the speaker. He felt that a speaker's behaviour revealed whether he was of high character, intelligence and goodwill, and this acted to create a persuasive influence. Operationally, ethos can be defined as credibility. We believe people whom we judge to be credible. Aristotle said, 'we believe good men fully and more readily than others . . . his character may almost be called the most effective means of persuasion he possesses'. Your credibility depends heavily on the way that you present yourself to others, specifically on your composure, sociability and extroversion (Carbone, 1975; Greenberg and Miller, 1966; McCroskey *et al.*, 1980). The psychological construct of credibility breaks down into a number of interrelated concepts. These are perceived expertise, charisma, consistency, self-confidence and trustworthiness. The word perceived is important. You need to say and do certain things to manage the impression that you give to your audience.

Expertness

If others perceive you as an expert, whether you are one or not, you will be able to exercise influence over them, so the key issue is creating the perception of expertise in the minds of others. The reputation that precedes a speaker affects the audience' perception of the truth and value of the content of their speech (Naftulin *et al.*, 1973;). Often, we 'know to see' rather than 'see to know'. So, communicate your expertise to the audience at, or before, the start of your presentation begins. For example, if seeking to convince a group about investing in safety improvements, quote the relevant legislation; if you possess a law degree, ensure they know; or attend a one-day seminar on health and safety legislation and write an article on the subject for the company newsletter (King, 2002). At the start of your speech, summarize your expertise on the topic, or brief the chairperson to introduce you by telling the audience about what qualifies you to speak on the subject as an expert. During your presentation, cite a variety of highly credible and highly trusted research sources to enhance your own perceived expertise (Cantor *et al.*, 1976; Warren, 1969; Hovland and Weiss, 1951).

279

Charisma

Charisma is the nearly magical ability of some individuals to influence others through the sheer force of their personality. Charismatic leaders are able to attract and inspire others towards improved performance and engender respect from them. Research has revealed three predominant clusters of qualities. Charismatic leaders were judged to be dynamic (enthusiastic, inspiring, outgoing, sociable and jestful); insightful (considered as bright, intellectual, wise and competent); and confident (secure, unflappable and not meek). These charisma-inspiring behaviours are capable of being incorporated into your behavioural skills repertoire (Atwater et al., 1991; Bass and Avolio, 1990; Kozubska, 1997; Conger et al., 2000). So, how might you make yourself more charismatic and attractive to your audience? Likable communicators are most persuasive (Chaiken and Eagly, 1983; Eagly and Chaiken, 1975; Mills and Aronson, 1965). If an audience warms to you, it will listen to you, and more irrationally, will believe you (Bedoyere, 1990). This is regardless of your overall expertise or trustworthiness. People who are liked and admired by others, that is, who possess personal power and can influence through the use of the friendliness strategy, exert greater influence than those who are not liked. People associate the attractiveness of a communicator with their message. We are influenced by those people we like. We will comply even if we know that they are trying to influence us, and stand to gain personally from doing so.

To be liked, you need to be pleasant, pretend to like the others, show interest in their concerns, praise them and, at least initially, support their views. A friendly, open person is easier to talk to, to like and therefore to believe in, than someone who is distant, abrasive or haughty. Another tactic is to become known to them before your presentation starts. All things being equal, the more familiar an item or person is, the more attractive they are judged to be (Zajonc, 1968). Third, open with humour, although not necessarily a joke or a contrived story. It is easy to like someone who has made you laugh. Laughter binds a group together. Make informal comments about circumstances that are common to you and your audience. This helps them to identify you as someone to whom they can relate. However, avoid any self-deprecating remarks. These signal a lack of self-confidence to your audience, and can endanger your expert status. The greater the similarity between yourself and your audience, the greater will be their acceptance of your ideas (Sutton, 1982). Moderately extroverted speakers come over as more credible, than highly extroverted or introvert types.

In a large public speaking situation, perceived confidence and sincerity is enhanced by using phrases such as, 'I believe' or 'I am sure'. Wearing glasses should be avoided. Few of the great charismatic orators in history wore glasses while speaking, and research showed that not wearing them increases audience agreement (Maslow et al., 1971). Why should this be so? Atkinson (1984) explained that

280

humans are the only primate species in which the coloured irises are framed by visible areas of whiteness (called sclera). He claimed that the evolutionary significance of this had to do with the communicative importance of our eyes. The whites of our eyes make it relatively easy for audience members to track even slight speaker eye movements over long distances. Eye contact with voice control are therefore crucial. Gazing at an audience, that is, looking at them in a steady and intense way, at or near the point of completing your statement; delivering more loudly than surrounding speech passages; delivering with greater pitch or stress variation; markedly speeding up or slowing down; and using a variety of other non-verbal gestures, all adds to the appeal of your message for the audience.

Speaking from memory without notes, communicates spontaneity, with the speaker being perceived as being more genuine, authentic and trustworthy (Atkinson, 1984). Freed from notes, you can add emphasis with carefully co-ordinated head, hand and arm movements. These are particularly important when presenting to a large audience. You will be able to sustain longer continuous eye contact with your audience, and monitor and respond to them. Keeping them constantly under surveillance is also a means of keeping their attention. Your body language will signal to your audience the effort that you have put into the delivery of your speech. Be enthusiastic and totally involved with your audience. Use emphatic, colourful language and gestures. Your dynamic, friendly and extro-verted behaviour, will produce a positive audience encounter. Forward-looking people, concerned with the future are more credible than negative, backward-looking ones.

Consistency and self-confidence

Amongst the determinants of minority influence identified by Moscovici (1985) was consistency. A minority that unswervingly sticks to its position is influential (Moscovici, Lage and Naffrechoux, 1969). To quote Oscar Wilde, 'We dislike arguments of any kind; they are always vulgar and often convincing'. Hence, you must persevere with the simple repetition of your message, avoiding behaviours that might contradict the message, and presenting a logical system or demon-stration. Street corner orators, politicians on hustings 'walkabout' and religious preachers, are all aware of the importance of this. Consistency in both influ-encer message and behaviour are vital because it is considered a sign of their certainty and commitment. The influencer's message must be perceived as coherent, different, plausible, natural and corresponding to reality (Muscovici, 1985; Nemeth and Wachtler, 1973; Nemeth and Wachtler, 1974; Staats, 1968). Message repetition adds to the persuasive impact of the message. However, it is not the simple physical repetition of the message, but the psychological meaning attributed to consistency, that is important.

281

Consistency conveys self-confidence (Nemeth and Walchter, 1974). By being firm and forceful, you prompt the audience to reconsider their position. People perceived as qualified experts who are also confident and committed to a view, are most likely to influence the attitudes of others, especially low-esteem people. In contrast, being perceived as nervous by your audience reduces your credibility. It is only nervous people who have something to hide. A person who is hesitant, confused or uncertain when giving information is not as convincing as someone who appears to know what she is talking about (Reardon, 1991). So remain confident, consistent and calm, even under pressure. Your ability to communicate natural enthusiasm, sincerity and spontaneity, all take the sharp edge off persuasive communication, and make people less resistant.

Trustworthiness

Trustworthiness refers to whether you are perceived as reporting accurately what you know. It denotes the anticipation that you will act in a manner consistent with an audience's interests, and specifically, that they will be able to maintain control of their fate through you (Prus, 1989). Since trust involves their, 'betting on the future', all assessments of trust are based on assumptions or anticipations. While their trust in you will not guarantee your success, its presence or absence can affect your influencees' willingness to make the commitments that you want them to. Once you gain their trust, it will not only be taken for granted by them in their later dealings with you, but will also shape their preferences to come and deal with you personally (Barber, 1983: Luhmann, 1980).

Behaviourally, trust development involves three strategies. First, is *portraying integrity*. Since your audience depends on you to define effective applications of your proposal, you can foster trust by presenting your ideas in ways which are consistent with their interests. Another way to portray integrity is to convey honesty. Take the opportunity to speak against your own self-interest, since this will raise your trust-rating. If the audience feel that you have nothing to gain, and maybe something to lose, by convincing them, they will trust you more (Ostermeier, 1967; Swenson *et al.*, 1984; Walster *et al.*, 1966a; Walster *et al.*, 1966b). Where possible, give precise numbers not rounded ones and use the printed word. Another means of projecting integrity is to explicitly personalize your relationship with your listeners by taking their perspective into account when presenting your proposal. Be attentive to your audience, and provide them with explicit indications of your appreciation ('This item is for you', 'you are important to me'). While this may be interpreted as an appeal to vanity, this represents a viable means of generating trust. Also, spending extra time with your audience is important, as the popularity of encores at the ends of concerts attests.

A second trust-enhancement strategy is supplying your listeners with *evidence of your proposal's quality*. Since quality can only be known after your proposal has been implemented (and rarely even then), you are seeking to 'objectify' its quality or correctness in advance of your listeners committing themselves to it. You therefore need to demonstrate your idea by having them witness, handle or sample it. This fosters familiarity, and things that are familiar are liked. The 'you-try-it' demonstrations promote obligations amongst participants. Having sampled, they will feel that they are acting inconsistently if they do not follow through. Providing abstract evidence to gain audience confidence, for example, through references to testing, quality control and conditions of use, can be effective. Since trust is based on, 'what others would concur with', you can indicate any external consensus on the wisdom of supporting your proposal. Testimonials from those who have adopted a similar proposal evoke high levels of credibility. Only with such information will your audience be able and willing to define your proposal as a good choice.

Third, during your speech, communicate your high moral character to your audience. Do this by stressing your fairness; stating that you have studied both sides of the issue; verbalizing your concern for enduring values (large truths, general principles); and by stating the clear set of beliefs that you strongly hold. Such oratory will appeal to your audience's emotions (which are influentially more powerful), than to their intellect. Make visible your similarity with the audience's values, attitudes and goals. Research on personality shows that we are most influenced by our closest associates, friends and relatives. Audiences respond positively to speakers who broadly share common categories and strategies in thinking about the world. So, perceived similarity will lead the audience to hold you in high esteem (Schachter, 1951). Finally, make your audience believe that you are acting spontaneously.

PRESENTER BEHAVIOUR

Your speech, however short, will last a very long time for your audience, compared to normal conversation. However, it is not just an issue of time. In public speaking, the normal turn-taking of conversations is suspended. Your main problem is boring your audience before you have had the chance to change their minds. Because your presentation offers your listeners no opportunity to speak, this weakens their basic incentive to pay attention. Therefore, the pressure is on you to attract, sustain and upgrade the attentiveness of your audience members who might otherwise be inclined to go to sleep. The most important means of doing this is through *variety*. The brain's perceptual system is organized is such a way that repetitive stimuli are quickly ignored. In altering their public speaking style, many novices discover that those behaviours that they find most appealing in presenters when they are listening, are the most embarrassing (but not diffi-cult) ones to incorporate into their own presentation style. An audience's attention has to be continually fought for throughout an entire speech. This is achieved by attending to *paralanguage* which includes voice, speech pace and pause, pitch, volume and clarity.

Voice

Galen, the Greek philosopher, said that what goes on in your head and heart is reflected in your voice (Glass, 1991). He asserted that it was the voice, and not the eyes that mirror the soul. The voice remains important, and a nasally weak, inaudible voice, or a gruff, gravelly one, is perceived by an audience as reflecting negative feelings. Let us now consider specific aspects of the physical speech production system, to see how this can be made most effective. A controlled, confident voice is a valuable asset. It may be a natural gift, or can be developed through voice coaching. When others like the way you sound, they will listen far more readily to what you have to say. Your breath provides the basic power to your voice. It is invaluable for feeling and sounding in control. When you control your breath efficiently, you gain control over voice volume and pitch, and this in turn, reduces your stress and adds to your confidence. To do this, inhale and then slowly exhale. Our bodies often do this automatically when we sigh or yawn. To breathe efficiently you need to get the maximum use from the bottom part of your pear-shaped lungs. When you breathe in, there should be little audible sound, and you should be able to feel your stomach muscles releasing outwards as the dome-shaped diaphragm beneath the lungs drops downwards. Your ribs should swing outwards. As you breathe out, you will feel your stomach muscles flattening as the diaphragm rises upwards (Roloff et al., 1998).

Breathe from your stomach, breathe in, tummy out; breathe out, tummy in. Think about your breathing by placing your hand on your stomach. To practise, every time you breathe in, extend the out breath. Count one on the first out breath, two on the second, three on the third, and build up to seven. When you are able to speak at a meeting, prepare yourself by taking a few slow, controlled breaths out, rather than gulping large amounts of unnecessary air in. When you get anxious, you take shallower breaths and you do not release air as frequently as you do normally. This is called hyperventilation. As a result, you get a build-up of carbon dioxide, which gives you shortness of breath and a faster heartbeat. To release tension before a presentation, you need to oxygenate yourself. Take air in through your nose, hold it for three seconds, then, gently and slowly, exhale through your mouth for six seconds. You will feel your abdominal muscles contracting as you let all the air out through your mouth. Do this ten times. On the fourth time you will feel a little light-headed. Don't worry, the feeling will go away. You should end up feeling better and less anxious.

Speech pace and pause

Like physical movement, a quick, jerky pace of speaking suggests to your audience that you do not enjoy speaking, that you are nervous, and that you are not confident in what you are saying. Pace refers to rate of delivery – the number of words that come out of your mouth a minute (usually about 120), and the use of the pause. It is better to err towards a rapid rate of delivery than a slow one. You will sound quick thinking rather than ponderously pompous. If you want to motivate and inspire people with a sense of mission, speed up and communicate a sense of enthusiasm behind your message.

If you need to convey authority and reassurance, be less hurried. Speech pace variety is achieved by speeding up for some sections of your speech, and slowing down for others. Stereotypically, we judge someone who is a slow speaker to be slow in their thoughts and decisions, as well as a bore. In contrast, the person who talks too quickly is judged to be 'slick'. The truth may be more complicated, and based more on the, 'people like people like themselves' principle. If the audience are predominantly slow talkers, than a fast talker will be viewed with suspicion and vice versa. The faster a woman speaks, the higher her pitch will be. Speaking too fast may appear to make her babble, and she will be perceived as nervous or over-anxious. As the barrister develops his talk to the jury, he needs to speak more slowly, giving the listeners a chance to process cognitively his arguments (Smith and Shaffer, 1991). The use of the speech pause communicates power and is the equivalent of physical stillness. It is also equates with underlining in writing. Inserting a pause helps you to keep audience members listening, encourages them to absorb the important point that you are saying; it gives you time to recover and prepare physically and mentally for what you will say next; and it permits you to consider the reactions of your audience before moving on. Become personally comfortable with the pause, and do not feel that you need to fill it with non-words such as *um* or *er*. Vary your pauses to keep people listening to you. This will also assist your composure.

Pitch

The pitch and tone of your voice is determined by resonance which is the use of the available air space in the body. A high-pitched voice resonates in the head, while a low-pitched one resonates in the chest. Most of us resonate in the mouth. Your voice pitch reflects how relaxed you are. When nervous, you will raise the pitch of your voice, for example, when trying to gain a concession from someone in authority. Your pitch may rise uncontrollably because of inadequate breath control or throat tension. A whispery or a mumbling voice lacks power, invites interruptions and implies a lack of confidence. A squeaky voice signals helplessness, while a monotone sends people to sleep and suggests that you are not interested in your topic. Each person has a range from high to low. Men's vocal chords are longer and thicker, so their natural pitch is lower. Pitch is often determined by habit, imitation or jaw tension. Evaluate your own voice and select an appropriate pitch. Find a pitch that is low but comfortable. A strong, positive voice gives the impression of a strong, positive individual, even if you are shaking in your shoes.

285

Raise your awareness of your own voice, and get others to give you their impressions of it. Listen to the evenness of the sounds that a person's voice creates. A wavering tone can be caused by the muscles of the chest and throat not contracting smoothly, and therefore not producing a regulated air flow. This often indicates nervousness or some other strong emotion. Avoid a low, inaudible voice or statements which tail off. Avoid ending statements on an up-note which makes them sound like questions. A whispered monotone seldom convinces anyone that you mean business, while shouting arouses defensiveness. A level, well-modulated versatile style, with inflection and varying speed is convincing. Check that you are breathing efficiently and that your neck and throat are relaxed. Nod your head gently, and see if you can talk at the same time without tensing your neck. Practise your breath control by letting your breath drop low into the lungs and then sighing and yawning as you breathe out. Both activities are excellent for relaxing the throat.

When we speak, we use pitch patterns. An upward inflection conveys a very different message from a downward one. Try saying, 'I'd need you to do that for me' using a rise at the end (sounds tentative and open to negotiation). Repeat it using a fall at the end (sounds resolved and definite). If you have difficulty hearing pitch, use a finger like a baton to conduct yourself, lifting it as you rise in pitch, and lowering it as you fall. Use pitch to reinforce your message. Play around with pitch to make your recommendation first sound like a suggestion, and then like a question. Use changes of pitch to create variety in your speech. To sound more authoritative, breathe from the diaphragm with full-depth breaths starting from the stomach. Record your voice, play it back and then repeat at a lower pitch. Record a tape of a famous actor, and imitate their voice. Train yourself to use speech patterns that are conversational and crisp, and which gain you credibility.

Voice coaches teach men and women to sound firmer, relaxed, more assertive and more confident. Voice pitch affects listeners' perceptions of communicator authoritativeness, competence, dynamism and character (Bradac and Mulac, 1984; Dubois and Crouch, 1975; Glaser and Smalley, 1992; Hosman, 1989; McCroskey and Mehrley, 1969). Few managers would feel it to be quite right to hire a voice coach, yet management is primarily about influencing others verbally. It is therefore curious that the other professions whose main job is to influence with the voice-actors, politicians and barristers, have no qualms about hiring speech therapists. For both professional women and men, voice coaching may represent a useful personal investment in their development (Miller et al., 1976).

Volume and clarity

Listeners associate confidence and presence with clear, audible speech. To maintain your audience's attention, your voice volume should be sufficient to deliver your words to them where they are sitting. They should not have to come to collect them. Once again, good breath control is important. We hear our own voices, not just through our ears, but also through the bones in our heads. None of us therefore hear ourselves as others hear us. This makes it difficult to estimate just how much volume we are using. To speak loudly and clearly, your speech organs – jaw, larynx, tongue and lips – need to be relaxed and mobile. To relax, release the jaw by yawning, stretching the lips forwards and backwards, chewing vigorously. Poor voice projection can be the result of a reluctance to use much energy in the muscles of your lips. Remember that listeners also read your lips. Practise reading and talking while exaggerating your articulation, then check in the mirror to lessen the exaggeration until it looks acceptable.

Clarity of speech refers to the way that we make our consonants sound. We express vowels (a, e, i, o, u) through the mouth; and consonants (all non-vowels) through the nose. If we pass too much air through our nose, then our vowels get lost. To test this, pinch your nose between your thumb and forefinger and say *man*, the *a*-sound should be distinct. If it is not, then you are passing too much air through your nose. Speech is what happens in your mouth cavity and lips. The contact of the mouth, interrupts the flow of air. To make the sounds *be*, *me* and *pe*, we use the lips; for *de*, *te* and *ne*, we use the tip of the tongue and the hard palate at the back of the upper teeth; and for *ge*, we use the soft palate and back of the tongue.

How well you produce these sounds, determines how clearly you come over to your audience. To articulate properly, your upper lip muscles need to be flexible. During interviews for example, your facial muscles tend to freeze up, and the strain can cause twitching. For this reason, an interviewer's trust in a job applicant increases over the course of their meeting, as the latter's facial muscles relax and he or she becomes more expressive. Actors receive voice coaching to increase clarity, but the rest of us can usefully practise our childhood tongue twisters such as Betty Botter, the Neath Police and Red Lorry – Yellow Lorry. Finally, you can take note of Glass (1991) who cited Gallop's survey of the most annoying speaking habits. Some of these refer to one-to-one and small group discussion, while others are relevant to the public speaking situation (Table 14.1).

Clear speech is important because an audience unconsciously associates it with clarity of thinking. If you miss out some letters, it is the equivalent to wearing scruffy clothes. The audience may confuse your speech with your personality, assuming that like your speaking style, you are slapdash and pay little attention to detail. Non-fluencies in speech include vocalized pauses ('uh uh') and superfluous repetition of words or sounds ('you know'); corrections of slips of the tongue; and articulation difficulties. As the number of these increase, the speaker is rated lower on competence, but not necessarily on trustworthiness (Miller and Hewgill, 1964; Sereno and Hawkins, 1967). The variety principle here involves interspersing periods of loud speech with low and medium volumes. All three have to be clearly audible to your audience.

287

Table 14.1 Annoying talking habits

Habit	% annoyed
1 Interrupting while others are talking	88
2 Swearing	84
3 Mumbling or talking too softly	80
4 Talking too loudly	73
5 Monotonous boring voice	73
6 Using filler words ('um', 'you know')	69
7 A nasal whine	67
8 Talking too fast	66
9 Using poor grammar or mispronouncing words	63
10 A high-pitched voice	61
11 A foreign or regional accent	24

Source: Glass, 1991: 166–7

Audience distance

Morgan (2001) advocates what he terms a 'kinesthetic' approach to public speaking. His view is that presentations are less about facts and information that you put over to listeners, and more about the *connection* that you make with them. He discusses visceral, personal and emotional connections which, he claims, make the audience trust you and act on your statements. Morgan suggests identifying individuals in the audience who can act as proxies for the whole audience; varying the distance between yourself and the audience; moving into the personal space (1.5–4 feet) of proxies to recount an anecdote or make a plea ('I need your help to turn this round'); opening with a personal parable embodying the overall presentation theme, told in the proxies' personal space; and then draw back into public space (4–12 feet) to outline the topic. The speaker should then re-enter personal space to layout their proposed solution, and encourage the audience to own it. Challenge the audience to implement the solution by asking them to take immediate physical action, e.g. by introducing themselves to their neighbours. Ensuring that physical movements are synchronized with the verbal message is crucial. Gestures of openness and receptivity (e.g. spreading arms), help to create connection. The speaker must read the cues provided by the audience along four dimensions: open–closed, engaged–disengaged, allied–opposed and committed–uncommitted, and adjust the presentation as required.

288

MESSAGE CHARACTERISTICS

Content

New is better. Merely repeating the previous arguments or presenting old information is unlikely to be influential. Your audience has already evaluated and rejected it. Thus you need to *offer new information* in the form of statistics, studies, opinion polls, that support argument. Salespersons are taught to *sell benefits not features*. 'A flexitime system allows staff attendance in the office to be monitored' is a feature. 'Flexitime will allow you to meet both your work and home commitments' is a benefit. Since an audience is more influenced by a benefit, you need to explain to them how exactly they will personally gain by supporting your idea or proposal. Providing action alternatives is also crucial. It is not enough just to argue against something, you need to *specify alternative actions* that are credible, for them to follow.

Since people resist change, they are unlikely to want to replace their own views with yours. Hence, you need to show them that *your position is consistent with theirs*. You have to devise a way to let them see that accepting your position does not mean changing their own. Your audience is looking for a link between wants and beliefs, and your offerings. If, as the presenter, you can demonstrate a consistency between your ideas, values and goals and theirs, your audience will not resist. A vivid, *simple demonstration* or a *simple statement* can often cut through complex arguments. Prepare ahead and think how you can show them (perhaps physically) your points. Allow your audience to *save face*, when changing their mind to support your position. By giving them an excuse to change their mind, a way out, you provide them with a bridge to cross over to your side, rather than having to make a leap of faith (Nisbett *et al.*, 1981).

Emotional appeal

The importance of stirring your audience's needs and emotions at the start of your presentation has been mentioned previously. After these have been aroused, present information which satisfies these. This sequence produces greater acceptance than an order which presents the information ahead of needs-arousal (Cohen, 1957; Cohen *et al.*, 1955; Brembeck and Howell, 1952). It is the focus on emotions and not intellect that distinguishes the persuasive from the non-persuasive speaker. To get your audience to accept your suggestions, you should generate emotions of greed, fear or guilt in them. Demonstrating how your suggestion will benefit from them, while providing them with specific instructions on how they should implement your proposal will increase their support for you (Sutton, 1982; Leventhal 1970). Speaker messages with a moderate fear-appeal, which were accompanied by vivid descriptions of undesirable possible outcomes, coupled with optimistic suggestions of how to avoid these, were found to be more

289

effective than those with medium to strong fear appeal (Hovland *et al.*, 1953). To generate fear, it is less effective to threaten harm to your influencee directly. It is much better to choose a significant third party. While health campaigns tell drinkers and smokers directly that they could die as a result of their actions, it is more effective to tell them that their actions could leave their children parentless or could damage their new born offspring. The second argument is much more influential because it utilizes guilt. The use of guilt is a popular way of influencing among several religions. TV programmes and posters campaigns soliciting money for good causes all seek to make you feel guilty and thus to contribute.

MESSAGE STRUCTURING

How your message is structured can also have a major effect on your success in influencing your audience, as every barrister talking to a jury in a courtroom knows. Limiting the amount of information presented is important. In public speaking, *less is more*. Research shows that people recall most information when you limit it to a maximum of seven pieces, plus or minus two. Five or three is even better. Having previously listed the different ideas that you want to communicate, cluster them under a few main headings. This is called *chunking*, and it prevents not only the dilution effect but also your audience from experiencing information overload. You can expect your message to be narrowed by your listeners, and the parts that stand out the most will receive most of their attention. The larger an audience, the more difficult it is to hold its attention, and the more limited the verbal forms that you can use to convey your ideas. Here are some sets of verbal devices to overcome these difficulties.

Decisions on how to structure your message depend on six main variables. These are how knowledgeable your audience is about the topic; how favourably they perceive you as a person; whether they are initially opposed to your view; whether you are the only speaker on the platform; whether a decision is required from the audience; and when that decision will be made. Your audience's prior level of information will affect whether you present your proposal on its own, or present the counter-arguments to it as well. If they are well informed about the issue, they will be less impressed by simplistic, one-sided arguments. They will want to hear constructive arguments supporting your view, as well as important opposing points which are then attacked and dismissed. The well-informed already know some of the counter-arguments and, if you do not mention them, they will assume that you are unaware of them; unfair about them, or are unable to refute them (Hovland and Mandel, 1952; McGuire, 1964). When making your two-sided presentation, either present your pro-arguments and then refute the con-arguments (called the 'support-then refute' strategy), or interweave the pro- and con-arguments. Both these presentation strategies have been found to be preferable to the 'refute-then-support' approach, where you refute the opposition's arguments, before introducing your own supporting ones (Bettinghaus, 1966; Zimbardo *et al.*, 1977).

In contrast, one-sided proposals are most impactful when your audience is uninformed about the topic under consideration. It will thus not know what counter-arguments are missing, and may be confused by these if you do provide them. A one-sided, pro-argument is also most effective when the audience is already favourably predisposed to you and your message; when that message will be the only one to be presented on that occasion; and when you want immediate, though temporary, opinion change (Crawford, 1976). McCroskey *et al.* (1972) argued that one-sided arguments can immunize receivers against subsequent counter-arguments, since your original persuasive message will have taken the counter-arguments into account ('Some people will tell you that what I say is not so. Let me say'). If your audience is heterogeneous in terms of knowledge, and you have to provide the con-argument in a single presentation, the items which you present first will dominate the impression your audience receives. If you want to promote your proposal but are compelled to present the case against as well as for it, begin with the pro-arguments, and only then move on to those con-arguments. It is likely that your audience will receive the incompatible information without realizing that there are any contradictions or inconsistencies. Make your presentation in one, continuous flow, and do not break or signal when the con-views are being expressed.

Where you position your message affects your influence as a public speaker. As the only speaker, you should place any communication that is highly desirable to the audience first, and follow it with less desirable communication. Desirable also includes agreement. Start by showing where you agree with them, since this establishes a positive relationship with audience members, and decreases their resistance to your message. This produces more opinion change than the reverse order. This is because the audience members become favourably disposed to you, since you have associated desirable points with them (McGuire, 1957). Second, as human beings, we are programmed to judge a situation very quickly. This so-called *halo effect*, means that our initial judgement influences the way that we interpret subsequent experience and information (Asch, 1946; Luchins, 1957). Additionally, people want to maintain existing patterns, and do not want to be confused with new facts. We notice and recall evidence that supports our existing view, and ignore conflicting data. Indeed, we frequently avoid making investigations that might lead us to find contradictions (Burgoon and Burgoon, 1975; Jones, *et al.* 1968).

Do not place your main point in the middle of your presentation. When a topic is familiar, interesting or controversial for an audience, make your point early, and expose the listeners to the primacy effect (first items presented tend to be remembered and create a pattern for subsequent information). For uninteresting, unfamiliar and uncontentious topics, make your main point at the end, using the recency effect (last item presented tends to be remembered (Rosnow and

291

Robinson, 1967). When your persuasive message proposes a solution to a problem, state the problem first, then the solution, because this is usually more interesting and more understandable for the listeners. When you agree with your listeners on some points but not others, discuss the points of agreement first before considering your areas of disagreement. This order raises your listeners' evaluation of you, and makes them more receptive to your claims in the disputed areas (Fisher, 1993). If you begin with the points of disagreement, this antagonizes your audience. This is why when talking to a hostile audience, politicians begin their speeches, with a point of agreement, however general, e.g. 'We can all agree that there needs to be change' or 'I think we all agree that we need to discuss the matter'.

What about the gap between the audience's original view and that advocated by you? If an audience strongly disagrees with your viewpoint, and you have high credibility with them, you should present your position in its most extreme form and not tone it down so that it does not seem to be too different from their own. The reason for this is that all human beings have a strong desire to be right, and to perform reasonable actions. When you come along and disagree with them, it makes them feel uncomfortable because it suggests that their actions or opinions are wrong, or are based on misinformation. The greater the disagreement, the greater the discomfort. To reduce the discomfort, the audience members will often change their opinions to match what they hear. The greater the disagreement therefore, the greater the change (Aronson *et al.*, 1963; Zimbardo, 1960). In contrast, if your credibility with the audience is slim or non-existent, you will produce maximum opinion change by producing only a moderate discrepancy between your views and theirs.

What if you are presenting your proposal in public, in competition with another speaker? Should you go first and make a first impression in the audience's mind (primacy effect), or last and have your points most easily remembered by them? (recency effect) The answer depends on whether and when the audience decides between the two proposals (Figure 14.1). Assume you and your opponent are to present your proposals one after another. If there is a gap between the first speaker and the second, for example, a break for coffee, and the second speaker's presentation is then quickly followed by an audience decision, then the recency effect operates and it is wisest to go second (Miller and Campbell, 1959; Lund, 1925). This is because the interference of the first speech on the second speech will be minimal, and audience retention will be working in your favour, through the recency effect.

In contrast, if your audience's decision is several days away, you should speak first, because the primacy effect will operate. The primacy of your speech will interfere with the audience's ability to learn your opponent's arguments. With the decision days away, the differential effects due to memory are negligible. If, in addition, after hearing your position, you can get your audience to make a response which publicly indicates their support for your position (e.g. a show of

Recency effect: go second

First argument ⟶ (coffee) ⟶ Second argument ⟶ Verdict
            (break)

Primacy effect: go first

First argument ⟶ Second argument ⟶ (days') ⟶ Verdict
                              (break)

Figure 14.1 *Turn-taking and the recency and primacy effects*

hands in support), you will reduce the effectiveness of the subsequent opposing presentation even more. This is because any public expression of a view, whether verbal or written, tends to freeze subjects in that view, and makes them resistant to the other side of the argument. People often make up their minds before hearing the counter-case anyway. Having done so, the audience will rehearse their position in anticipation of having to defend it. They will then not pay attention to the subsequent contradictory information in the second presentation (Hovland *et al.*, 1957; Hovland, Campbell and Brock, 1957; Lund, 1925; Zimbardo and Ebbesen, 1970).

You always have the choice of using either a deductive or an inductive argument to sequence your presentation. With a deductive approach, you tell them what you want them to do, e.g. vote to support your proposal. For the remainder of your presentation, you supply reasons and arguments for this course of action. With the inductive approach, you give reasons and make arguments that lead to the inevitable conclusion. In this version, you reveal your aim at the end, after you have supported it with many reasons. Of the two, the deductive approach is more generally effective. It is easier for your audience to follow; allows you to tell them what they need to know and why, and allows them to take in your arguments supporting your objective. With the inductive approach, the audience does not know what point you are wanting to make until the end. There is therefore a danger that they might misunderstand the argument and evidence that you have presented. However, the inductive approach can be recommended if the audience is hostile to your aim or message. In such case, using it will allow your arguments and evidence to be heard, and this may reduce your audience's resistance to your position. Tell your audience what you want them to do clearly and precisely. Do not assume that they already know. In his summary of Aristotle's advice on how to structure an argument to present it to an audience, Thompson (1999) distinguished different types of rhetoric. One of these, *deliberative rhetoric*, was used to persuade listeners about some future action. His depiction of Aristotle's five-point plan is shown in Table 14.2. Thompson (1999) offered an

293

alternative to Aristototle's argument arrangement, which took the form of a four-part story, and which was favoured by the management consultants, McKinsey and Co. This structure is particularly effective in presentations whose main purpose is to identify and then to solve a problem. This format is shown in Table 14.3.

Table 14.2 Aristotle's five-point plan

1 Used in the introduction to create goodwill and to put the audience in a receptive frame of mind.	*Bait*: a story or statement which arouses audience interest
2 The factual background description which is clear, brief and persuasive.	*Problem or question*: posed that has to be solved or answered.
3 Proof, usually beginning with a proposition. The proof of the case involves showing the benefits that will result, and appeals to the listeners' interests. Refutes likely objections and the case of adversaries.	*Problem or question*: you resolve the issues that have been raised
4 The speaker reserves their strongest appeal, to self-interest or a higher plan, for the climax. Specifically, your own material should be amplified; your adversary's case diminished; summary or recapitulation; end with inspiring emotion	*Payoff or benefit*: you state specific advantages to each member of the audience of adopting the course of action recommended in the solution or answer.
5 Call to action: you state the concrete actions which should follow from your presentation.	

Source: Based on Thompson (1999) *Persuading Aristotle*, London: Kogan Page, 23–5

Table 14.3 Four-part story

Situation: Tell the audience briefly what they already know which sums up the issue that is the focus of the presentation (e.g. staff problem; market share, financial difficulty).	This is designed to be a brief synopsis or overview of conditions which will already be known to the audience. It is important to avoid creating disagreement at this stage.
Complication: Identify a problem which threatens the viability of the status quo.	This may take the form of rising or falling customer numbers; new competitors; technological developments, etc.
Question: The complication identified raises a question.	What can be done? What options are available? What should be done next?
Answer: A solution or hypothesis is presented.	It is described in detail to the issues raised by the question.

Source: Based on Thompson (1999) *Persuading Aristotle*, London: Kogan Page, 25–7

Both argument structures can be effective, although the five-pointer is favoured by salespeople when asking an audience to buy their product or service. The bait at the beginning grabs audience interest creating a high level of their involvement, while the call to action at the end is a request to buy. The simple, logical structure makes it easy to put together rapidly an effective presentation. In contrast, the four-parter, claims Thompson, works best as a spoken or written report for a client. It assumes that the audience is already interested, and persuaders are advised to get to the answer stage within one minute, or risk losing their listeners' attention.

LINGUISTIC TECHNIQUES

Claptraps

The first set of devices were identified by Atkinson (1984) who called them claptraps. A claptrap was a way of catching audience applause (trapping the claps) in a public meeting. By using a claptrap, the speaker instructed an audience, in a step-by-step manner, towards a precise moment in the very near future in their presentation, when they were to all do the same thing, at the same time – that is, clap! Amongst the most well-known claptraps are, 'Ready, steady' and 'Hip, hip'. The former leads to a race start, while the latter evokes a coordinated audience cry of 'Hooray!'. The most common and most effective claptrap was the *two-part contrast*. This comes in the form of contrasts such as 'day and night', 'us and them' and 'young and old'. The making of a contrast between items is an adaptable and widely used technique for packaging and delivering applaudable messages. Some well-known examples are John F. Kennedy's, 'Our task is not to fix the blame for the past, but to fix the course for the future', and George Orwell's, 'All animals are equal, but some are more equal that others'.

The second most effective claptrap was the *list of three*. Its appeal lies in its air of unity and completeness. Amongst the well-known lists in history are Ceaser's, 'I came, I saw, I conquered', and the saying, 'Try, try and try again'. Finally, there was the *puzzle-solution format* which sets the audience a problem, and then provides them with a solution. For example, you can start your presentation by saying that you are going to talk about the single biggest cause of absence from work, and a little later reveal that it is back pain. These three claptrap formats can be effectively used in combination as well as singly. Their successful application depends upon the presenter's careful choice of and stress on words, timing, and the use of pauses. Atkinson's findings support the general proposition that how presenters spoke was as, if not more, important than what they actually said.

295

Statements, examples, facts and inferences

Another message communication device is the statement–example–inference technique. You make a statement or assertion, and then give an example, preferably a fact. This brings your statement to life and involves the imagination of the listeners. It allows them to understand exactly what you mean, and begins the process of their incorporating it into long-term memory. Then finish with the inference. Using facts rather than opinions to support your arguments, strengthens your message and is more persuasive to an audience. Evidence is the proof offered by influencers to support their claims. Eye-witness accounts are compelling (Brigham and Bothwell, 1983), and factual evidence can counter an opposer's opinion (Baumeister and Darley, 1982). Audiences recognize some information as 'first hand', for example, a demonstration, and assign it higher evidentory status than hearsay evidence. When confronted with conflicting evidence from different sources, listeners will experience dissonance, and will give greater credence to evidence based on their own or others' sense experiences (Rosenthal, 1972).

However, facts do not 'speak for themselves'. Audiences frequently draw different conclusions, and make different interpretations from those you intended as a speaker. Hence the importance of stating your conclusions to the audience unambiguously. O'Keefe (1990) found that where the speaker included an explicit conclusion or recommendation, the persuasive effect was greater. So, do not allow your listeners to make up their own minds about what you say or show them, but draw the conclusions for them (Cope and Richardson, 1972; Hovland and Mandell, 1952; Leventhal *et al.* 1967; Tubbs, 1968; Weiss and Steenbock, 1965). Audiences are willing to change their attitudes or behaviour, provided that they are presented with facts that they have not previously considered. Even if information is not really new, it can be made to appear new (McGuire, 1968; Haskins, 1966; Hovland and Mandell, 1952; Fine, 1957; Weiss and Steenbock, 1965; Sears and Freedman, 1967).

Stories, analogies and metaphors

This is a third set of presentation devices which engender emotions, but are frequently neglected. Hundreds of people can be effectively communicated with using stories, analogies and metaphors. While logic shrinks in the mind of the listener and is quickly forgotten, emotion expands and seizes the imagination. A good *story* will remain in the influencee's mind, long after everything else is forgotten. So ensure that you include a personal (ideally tear-jerking) story in your presentation (Conger, 1998). Metaphors, stories, analogies and anecdotes have been used for hundreds of years. Jesus spoke in parables, while Abraham Lincoln and Ronald Reagan made their most powerful points through metaphors and anecdotes (Thompson, 1999; Bowers and Osborn, 1966). Since you need to develop quick rapport with your audience, metaphors and stories can create a comfortable atmosphere and rarely cause resistance. Practically no one objects to a well-chosen story. Often, you can have a character in a story make a point which you cannot yourself.

Another approach is to use *analogy* to attract attention. An analogy is an inference from a parallel case which uses resemblances from other features. How did Philip Crosby, quality guru and author of *Quality is Free* persuade managers of the importance of quality, given the mundane nature of the topic? He said that quality resembled sex. Everybody was for it; felt they all understood it; thought that execution was only a matter of following natural inclinations; and that all problems associated with it were caused by other people. When you say that something resembles something else, you are using an analogy. Finally, there are *metaphors* which proceed through implicit or explicit assertions that A is B. We use metaphors when seeking to understand one element of our experience in terms of another. For example, the company is an organism, a brain, a prison, a machine. It is a way of thinking, and a way of seeing that pervades how they understand your point.

How do these devices work? Analogies grip the audience's attention because they are like a film in the cinema. They click into the minds of listeners through the relevance of the relationship between the characters. People naturally think in terms of 'mind-pictures', and that is what makes them so powerful. These three tactics directly match the way that the human mind works, customizing whatever it encounters. When you hear the word 'dog', you mentally recall a picture of a dog that you know, rather than dogs in general. You automatically customize a story or metaphor that you are told by relating it to your life and experience. It takes no effort, your mind does it for you. When you hear a story of success, you relate it to yourself, and identify with it. The only way that you can understand the experience of any other human being is by relating that re-counted experience to a real or hoped-for experience of your own. For this reason, a story simplifies things for the audience. Metaphors work so well because they help listeners to visualize and re-live that experience.

By telling appropriate stories and using suitable metaphors, you can get your listeners resonating to the emotional appeal of your chosen topic. When you tell a story of a happy customer, your listener will recall the time when she was pleased with a product. That memory carries with it a positive feeling for her. Because it is emotional, it expands into her consciousness. Stories operate by systematically recreating good feelings in the audience. They lead an audience from an initial feeling of security to conviviality, to high esteem, to happiness, to pride in ownership and on to whatever you have in mind for them. A good sales story can trigger the emotions of pride of ownership, safety, love, adventure or anything else that is positive. People will not necessarily accede to your

297

request or accept your proposal solely on the basis of logic. Stories arouse emotions upon which people act, even if they subsequently seek out logical justifications for their emotionally based decision.

Do some stories work better than others? In constructing a story of your own, ensure that it is relevant to your objective and to your audience, and that it makes the point. This ensures that listeners will identify with it, and recognize its relevance to the issue being discussed. Tailor the language and word pictures to appeal to the listeners. Keep the stories simple, even if the listeners are well educated. People like good, short stories and know them by a number of different names: nursery rhymes, legends, myths, fables, fairy tales and parables. They enjoy being told stories and will reward you for doing so.

Rhetorical devices

There are several useful rhetorical devices that you can incorporate into your speech that will have an impact on your audience. The first of these is using antithesis. *Antithesis* is putting two opposites near each other in a sentence ('We find ourselves rich in goods, but poor in spirit'). Kushner (1999) explained how to create an antithesis. First pick two opposite, words, phrases or concepts. Write a sentence with one of the opposites, in each half of the sentence. To balance it, put an equal number of words in each half. Place these opposites in approximately identical positions in their half of the sentence. The closer the opposites appear to each other, the more dramatic the antithesis will sound. Keep it short and simple, rather than long and cluttered ('Dying is easy, comedy is hard'); and try to end it on a positive note ('Stop talking, start acting'). More ambitious speakers can try the double antithesis, which puts two opposites in each part of the sentences ('We are good at making war, but bad at making peace'). Alternatively, they might attempt the version of an antithesis where the opposite in each half of the sentence is the word order itself ('Let us never negotiate out of fear, but let us never fear to negotiate').

Hyperbole is another word for exaggeration. It is used in common parlance ('I've been waiting forever'), and is effective in emphasizing a point during a presentation. *Allusion* is a reference to a person, object or event from literature, mythology or Bible ('Sorting out the problems was one of the labours of Hercules'). *Alliteration* is the use of a phrase whose words all begin with the same sound. ('Whinging whingers wanting woe'). *Similes* are like metaphors except that they are directly stated comparisons of one thing to another ('As strong as an ox'). They often contain the words 'like' or 'as', to make the comparison. *Rhetorical questions* is one asked by the speaker for effect, to which an answer from the audience is not required. Rhetorical questions focus the listeners on a topic, and are used as introductions, transitions or conclusions.

A *catchphrase* is an effective way of drawing your audience's attention to a key point. Advertisements on television, radio and posters are full of them – 'Because it's your stuff'; 'No pain, no gain'. These phrases 'catch' in your memory. Every time that you think about one of them, you automatically think about the product. The author accidentally devised a catchphrase when lecturing on personality. To distinguish personality type from personality trait, he wrote, 'You have a trait, but you fit a type'. That catchphrase appears in some of his students examinations answers. Before speaking to an audience, choose an important point that you want to stress, build a catchphrase around it, and repeat it endlessly.

Humour and surprise

These constitute a fifth set of presentation devices that also focus on audience emotions. All are startling to the listener and act as tension releasers and mind-set breakers. They change influencees' emotions and perspectives. Greatbatch and Clarke (2002) suggest that *humour* performs four primary functions: it creates and maintains social cohesion and group solidarity; attacks others in socially acceptable ways to enhance your self-esteem at the expense of others; it gains you the approval of others; and it manages your embarrassment, fear or stress, in a threatening situation. Humour works by developing good feelings, positive attitudes and a lighter atmosphere. It creates positive emotions that draw listeners closer to you. It helps you to build rapport and trust, and opens up a more favourable mutual attitude. Humour helps us forget the drabness of our lives, and brings sunshine into it. It gives us fresh perspectives. It may make the audience more carefree, less tense and more congenial. Humour itself involves surprise and mild confusion. A newer and slightly more startling experience can shift your listeners away from a fearful and tense mental attitude, when we all laugh and share our humanity with each other. Most organizational members practise keeping the lid on their emotions throughout the day. They are accustomed to handling tension, pressure and difficult situations. However, laughter will break these wide open. They are not used to handling laughter, and few of them have any defence against it. Greatbatch and Clarke (2002) identified a number of laughter-inducing approaches used by management gurus in their public presentations. These included criticizing or praising managers from another organization in order to question or compliment common practices found there; emphasizing the remarkable or absurd characteristics identified in these institutions; mentioning the actions of individuals in non-management surroundings: and inducing laughter about one's own shortcomings.

Surprises like mystery quests and special attractions, capture members' attention, which you need, before you can secure their agreement. Because surprise and confusion create a need for new input, they are ideally suited for those who would not normally listen to you. If you are making a proposal, say something confusing, 'This proposal of mine is a bad investment'. Your listeners are taken aback, since it is not what they had expected to hear. You get their immediate attention since they were expecting the opposite. Your listeners wonder why you, a sane person, would make such a statement. It reassures them that this is not going to be a high-pressure encounter; they become more relaxed, and more receptive to what you have to say. You go on to elaborate that your proposal is bad – from a short-term perspective – but excellent from a medium to long-term standpoint. By the end of your presentation, your audience feel that they are making a good choice in following your recommendations.

Surprise and confusion work by signalling to the listener that they need still more information to re-establish their equilibrium. It shows them that they are not in control as they had thought. Exceptionally rigid people, who have had a long history of ignoring information presented in a straightforward manner, may respond to these tactics. Once they are in a state of uncertainty ('unfrozen'), they may become more receptive. These techniques are a form of mild shock treatment which needs to be carefully used in terms of the listeners' values and beliefs. People appreciate humour and are willing to pay for it. Comedians are amongst the highest paid entertainers in show business.

AUDIENCE FEATURES

You must decide why people should listen to you. If you cannot, then there is no reason to give a presentation. You have to give your audience an incentive to pay attention. To do this, relate your proposal to their needs, or create a perception of needs in them and then promise to fill it. Rafe (1990) discussed audience personality and motivation which was based on the idea of four personality types encountered in Chapter 8. Using the classifications of Thinker, Director, Relater and Socializer, it is possible to adjust the content and process of your communication to influence each type. Some audiences can be so homogeneous, that a single message can be applied to all. A speech to an audience of businesspeople can reasonably assume that they are all Director-types, and your presentation material can be tailored accordingly. Similarly, an audience of academics might be treated as Thinkers. If you have not been briefed beforehand, it is safest to assume that your audience is composed of Socializers. These are people who are open and indirect, slow, easy, relaxed, amiable, receptive to new information, and welcome any interest that you show in their needs and interests. Adapt your presentation to meet the needs of this type of group until, through verbal or non-verbal feedback, you learn that they are predominantly of a different type.

When you face an audience, its members will be supportive, and will attend in order to gain information which will be of benefit to them. While listening to you giving your speech, such an audience functions on the third level of

Maslow's needs hierarchy – belonging. Just being part of an audience, being with others, makes this possible. The situation stresses membership, sharing and participation. So, build your talk on their sense of belonging if you want to influence them to accept your message. This allows you to establish an emotional bond from the start. Then, select an esteem level need such as achievement, recognition or competence, which is appropriate and appeals to your listeners. Show them how, by accepting your proposal, they can meet their need in this area. As Maslow said, motivated individuals (and your audience is motivated to at least be attending your presentation), will automatically seek gratification at the next level, once their present need has been filled. So you might start at level three, 'We are all here to participate in the seminar, and share the ideas on offer', and move to level four, 'the information that you will acquire will increase your sense of personal achievement'.

Only personal contact prior to the presentation can accurately assess the feelings of individual members of a large audience to your proposals, but even this will not guarantee that you will catch the mood of the audience with more than average precision. To do that requires innate sensitivity. One framework that can help you to analyse your audience was suggested by Hodgetts and Gibson (1991) and is shown in Figure 14.2. Their audience analysis grid aims to discover

Audience friendliness

	1 Friendly	2 Neutral	3 Disinterested	4 Hostile
4 Resistant to learning	(A) Show them personal profit from presentation	(B) Need a dramatic start to grab interest	(C) Stress benefit of this presentation given the fact they're there anyway	(D) Find and emphasize important benefit for them
3 Neutral to learning	(E) Get them involved in the presentation	(F) Use ice-breakers or humour to get their attention	(G) Get their interest fast	(H) Concentrate on benefits of learning
2 Little knowledge: eager to learn	(I) Pedagogy important for best results	(J) Quickly give them the facts they want	(K) Give them the facts: don't waste time trying to be friends	(L) Emphasis on education
1 Knowledgeable	(M) Straightforward presentation	(N) Warm them up by referring to their expertise	(O) Find a point to grab their interest	(P) Identify source of hostility and try to defuse it

Audience knowledge and willingness to learn (left axis)

Figure 14.2 Audience analysis grid
Source: Hodgetts and Gibson, 1991: 405

where, 'the audience is coming from', so that the presenter can respond most effectively and influentially. The grid uses two variables. The first is *audience knowledge and willingness to learn*, and the second is *audience friendliness*. The former estimates the amount of prior knowledge that the audience possesses about your topic, and how prepared they are to learn from you. The latter dimension assesses whether the audience is friendly, neutral, disinterested or hostile to you. Obviously, these can only be subjective judgements that you, as the speaker, can make beforehand. From the beginning of your presentation, both verbal and non-verbal audience feedback can lead you to alter your initial assessment. Once you have categorized the audience, Hodgetts and Gibson recommend a choice of sixteen different presentation strategies. Interestingly, the same grid can be used to decide whether to present a one-sided or a two-sided argument of your case, as described earlier in this chapter. For example, with an uninformed but friendly audience (cell I), you would be most influential by using a one-sided argument.

Chapter 15

Influencing through networking

To percolate you need to circulate.

INTRODUCTION

Earlier in the book, it was stressed that many new graduate recruits into organizations naively believed that to succeed and to be promoted, it was sufficient for them to work hard, and that their hard work would be recognized and rewarded. If hard work is necessary but not sufficient in itself, what else is required? More specifically, how do companies choose amongst competing candidates for the declining number of managerial posts? The explanation that organizations give for public consumption can be labelled the rational view, and states that they see their employees as their most valuable resource, and seek to make the best use of their skills. Posts are therefore filled by those individuals who are considered to be best fitted to carrying them out. For this reason, careful selection is conducted, which benefits both the individual and the company. This view stresses that selection is based on merit. The company ignores irrelevant or non-functional criteria such as applicants' family connections, membership of clubs or pandering to the social prejudices of selectors. Instead, it is an applicant's track record that counts. This rational view stresses objectivity, and the application of clearly defined, quasi-scientifically determined, selection procedures and techniques.

Several writers have challenged this view (Thomas, 2003). Pfeffer (1981a) wrote that, 'A belief in the merit-based and non-political aspect of careers in organizations is there to maintain the legitimacy of the organization's internal labour market and to help assuage the feelings of those who earn less than others in the organization . . . This value is articulated repeatedly, and comes to be believed by those involved in the process'. The contrasting political view of organizations emphasizes that selection for a post is determined less by merit, than by the personal preferences of power holders, and by the organizational politics to be discussed in the next chapter. Barlow (1989) argued that assessment for

303

promotion was performed by a, 'network of colleague relations' linking oper-
ating managers to each other and to their superiors, rather than through any
formal appraisal system. This author concluded that influencing these higher-level
gatekeepers who controlled access to promotion, was a more effective means of
getting promoted than getting a good appraisal. Another study, this time of
plateaued and non-plateaued managers by Gould and Penley (1984), showed that
salary progression was most linked to networking. The research evidence therefore clearly suggests that networks play a major, if not decisive part, in promotion
decisions. This is despite what the company says publicly, and what it would
want you to believe. The research message from the research studies is clear, if
you want to get ahead, get into networking because, along with communications
skill, networking is one of the keys to career success.

CONNECTEDNESS

An important aspect of any company's political landscape are peer networks, that
is, clusters of colleagues at the same organizational level. These are circles of
acquaintances who can provide you with reputation and information. These supply
you with connection power which is defined as, not so much what you know,
as who you know. Your capacity to influence is partly based on your extensive
network of contacts. A poll carried out by the Dentsu Institute for Human Studies
in Tokyo (Fortune, 1991) asked American and Japanese individuals what they
felt was needed to get ahead in life. Although the responses varied between the
nationalities and the age groups within them, having 'good connections' accounted
for between 23 per cent and 35 per cent of all the responses. Job performance
is not a sufficient condition for career advancement in most organizations, and
may not even be necessary (Granovetter, 1974; Kanter, 1977). Social similarity,
social background and social contacts was in many cases more important, and
often sufficient in themselves. The politics of careers evaluates jobs and positions
in terms of the contacts that they may provide, and strategic career moves are
made to develop social similarity and identification with senior management
personnel who are in a position to allocate rewards and promotions.

Your connection power will rise as people identify you as someone worth
being associated with. You may use your network to connect different people
with each other, or put in a good word for someone. 'Having the ear of the
chairman' reflects this particular power base (Kaplan, 1984). It implies that you
have good access to senior management, and can lay other people's interests
before the chairman at some time in the future. Knowing that some senior
managers support your proposal can strengthen it when you put it to the group.
By challenging you, your opponents are also challenging them. The sponsorship
of your proposals by senior and respected figures is therefore critical. However,
you need to avoid 'tainted' members, that is, associating with senior staff who

are only temporarily influential, or whose influence has waned within the organization. Kotter (1985a) stressed the importance of developing personal relationships with relevant parties, and then using these to communicate, educate, negotiate, or to reduce or overcome most kinds of resistance to co-operation. Before meeting someone, you should find out a little about them and their work. Also, join societies, professional associations, and clubs where the powerful go. Get yourself elected on to committees. It increases your visibility, even though it may be time consuming.

WHAT IS NETWORKING?

Kakabadse (1983) defined networks as, 'interest groups which are formed for non-organizational reasons', and considered them to be of vital importance in promotion. He distinguished four types. Networking behaviours refer to individuals' attempts to develop and maintain relationships with others that have the potential to assist them in their work or career. There are different types of networks. First, *practitioner networks* which consist of people who are linked through a common training or professional concern. These may be formal associations (e.g. accountants) or loose groupings of employees who share a common professional identity (the computer staff). Second, *privileged power networks* draw together those who possess substantial positional power. These operate as exclusive clubs in which the mighty celebrate and enhance their elite status, and access is by invitation only. Third, *ideological networks* consist of people who share a concern to advance certain broad policies and objectives. Admission to them is afforded on the basis of commitment to shared ideals and programmes. Finally, *people-oriented networks* form around shared feelings of personal warmth and familiarity which persist as long as members find their continuing association personally worthwhile. These are the friendships groups to which members are admitted on the basis of their personal identification with existing participants. While this type of network might coincide with an existing departmental grouping, it is just as likely to cross it. Michelli and Straw (1999) offer a somewhat different categorization distinguishing *personal networks* that consist of friends and family; *organizational networks* originating from teams and project groups; *professional networks* that include associates, colleagues and clients with common work interests and tasks; and *strategic networks* that cover inter-organizational situations.

To be influential within an organization, you need to be connected to other people, and have access to information. Social networks are the means by which such connections are established. Networking is the practice of actively using your network connections of contacts to keep yourself informed about what is happening inside your organization. Additionally, networks usually also extend to individuals outside your current organization. Networking is about developing and maintaining contacts; creating opportunities to meet new people; using people

305

and being used by them. Networking is important because it gives you access to people, and through them, to information. Having information and knowing people, in turn gives you information power and connection power, which are the basis for exerting all types of influence within the organization. Why should networks be so important?

NETWORKING FOR INFORMATION

All these networks operate to further the interests of their members, providing them with access to information unavailable through the official system. Information is the lifeblood of all organizations. It can alert you to forthcoming developments in the company; the emergence of new power figures and the decline of old ones; and helps you to establish a relationship with your peers. It gives you the key with which to understand the power dynamics of the organization, pointing out where the power was, is now, and where it is going to. Not having information means that you are surprised by events. This makes you powerless and helpless, not in control of situations, and lacking a choice of response options. For these reasons, setting up a system to provide information on an ongoing basis is a priority for those who want to exert influence within a company. Research also showed that general managers do not rely as much on the formal processes of planning, organizing and controlling as had been thought. Instead they pursue broad-ranging and informally specified agendas of problems. They address these through an extensive network of organizational contacts, rather than through the formal organizational structure (Kotter, 1979).

NETWORKING FOR PROMOTION

One particular interest that a network can promote is that of career progress in a company. A network can be used to influence superiors who are in a position to influence, or to make promotion decisions. Research has consistently confirmed the importance of social networks and of networking, in getting promoted. Thomas (2003) made the point succinctly, 'in management what you know and what you have achieved will seldom be sufficient for getting ahead. Knowing and being known in the networks of influence, both for what you have achieved and for who you are may be essential'. In the 1950s, Coates and Pellegrin (1957) studied the informal factors that affected success in promotion. They found that a majority of these referred to an individual's membership of, and participation in, various social networks.

In the 1980s, one study compared 'successful' managers, defined by the speed of their promotion through the company level ascended, divided by time in the organization; with 'effective managers', defined by the managers' unit performance and subordinates' satisfaction and commitment. The latter were those

Table 15.1 *The activities of successful and effective managers: % of time devoted to four clusters of activity*

	Successful	Effective	Successful and effective	All managers
Traditional management	13	19	34	32
Routine communication	28	44	31	29
Human resource management	11	26	15	20
Networking	48	11	20	19

Source: Luthans *et al.*, 1988

managers who both 'delivered the goods' and 'maintained high employee morale (Luthans *et al.*, 1988). The two groups differed in terms of the time they devoted to four clusters of tasks. These were traditional management (planning, decision-making); routine communication (exchanging information and paperwork); human resource management (staffing and training) and networking (interacting with outsiders, socializing and politicking). Table 15.1 shows that successful managers differed from effective ones mainly in terms of the time that they devoted to networking activities.

Another aspect of networking for promotion is helping your network members and allies obtain positions of power. Minztberg (1983, 1985) reported a number of political games played in organizations. One of these was named 'The Young Turks' game which was played by young managers, close to, but not yet at the centre of power. Their goal was to become holders of formal authority by means of initiating major institutional or strategic changes. Another game, which could involve peers, was called, 'Strategic Candidate'. Here, managers at the same level promoted one of their own group into a key position, so as to increase their power. Networks are as important for the downwardly mobile as for those ascending the corporate ladder. Tom Peters, the management guru, stated that during times of organizational upheaval and job losses, it was important to look after your network, since when you were made redundant, you would look to it to look after you.

SOCIAL DEFINITIONS OF PERFORMANCE

Networks exert the greatest influence on promotion decisions when an organization's formal criteria for promotion are either indistinct or difficult to measure objectively. Much of what managers do is innately intangible and, in addition, much of it is done in teams. For these reasons, it is difficult to attribute success or failure to any one team member. Therefore, professional and management performance in organizations, comes to be socially defined. Companies lack objective, quantifiable measures of attributes such as leadership potential. In consequence, their staff selectors and promotion committees look outside, to help them define and to evaluate the everyday behaviour of staff that they regularly witness inside their own organizations. How often do staff gain internal promotion after announcing that they have been offered a more senior post with higher salary in another company?

Since success in companies is socially defined, your long-term career progress depends as much on being seen as promotable and valuable to the company, as contributing to its bottom-line profits. In these circumstances of performance ambiguity, the impression management technique of self-promotion can have a great impact. Projecting an image of yourself to your bosses as someone who is both promotable and valuable can be more important than any actual, tangible achievement. In different ways, your networks can provide you with the means through which such image projection can be achieved. As large organizations are by definition impersonal, networking becomes one of the few ways of gaining visibility for yourself with others.

Since senior staff will look outside the company to assess your potential, one strategy is to join professional organizations, community groups and social clubs. In this way, you will meet, and become known by, an ever-wider circle of people. As your network expands, it will come to the attention of your company that you are 'well known'. Rather conveniently, they will forget that you are well known for activities which are not related to your work. Perhaps a case of 'being famous for being famous?'. You can be more than a member of these organizations by taking a leadership role within in them. By serving on the committee of an external organization, you create the impression that you possess attributes required for promotion. In the process, and as a bonus, you establish social relationships with fellow members which can be useful for business and subsequently, for job-hunting purposes.

DISCOVERING THE COMPANY CULTURE

Successful networking depends on knowing how your own organization works. Even as a new recruit, you need to allocate time to learning about the formal organization as depicted in the organizational chart and the job descriptions. It means seeing how your job and the work of your section fits in with others. In a new job, arrange to meet new colleagues to find out about their jobs, and their view of the organization and its members. Do not stop there however. Find time to investigate the informal system as well. While it may be less visible, it is important, connecting as it does, the different people in your new organization. Understanding how this informal network operates, and becoming a part of it, will not only enhance your information power, but will also provide you with an effective base from which to influence. For example, if you do not realize that it is the senior manager's secretary who schedules meetings, then you can waste a lot of time influencing the wrong person.

The key questions are: 'Who is in charge here?' and 'Whom do I need to influence either directly or indirectly?'. The person who has the power to grant your wish may not necessarily be the job-title holder (Bryce, 1991). Young or recently appointed staff who have a negative view about power and the need to influence, may well feel that joining and fitting into a network is an irrelevant and time-wasting activity. However, not being in a network has its own dangers and costs. It prevents you from seeing the political environment accurately and effectively 'working the system'. The more politically astute people around you will come to gain recognition, and rise in influence and seniority, perhaps at your expense.

ENTERING AN EXISTING NETWORK

When joining an organization, you enter an existing and well-established informal network. These networks are essential to join because they exchange information about key company issues; put you in contact with people you need to know, educate you in the accepted ways of behaving in the company and explain to you how things get done. Joining an existing network is like joining a select club to which you have to be recommended. You will need to find the gatekeeper who recruits new members. Make contact with them, either formally or informally, at a company social event or through working with or for them on projects. Maybe get to them by asking for their advice or seeking their help on some work that you are involved in. As in any elite club, you will ask them to sponsor you. Building a network is important for all managers, but it is probably harder, yet most important, for women. Their numbers are slowly rising in the managerial ranks but they still represent a minority in most companies. Although contacts with other women managers are an essential first step, they need to be extended to men, if real influence is to be exercised.

Joining any informal group will mean adhering to certain rules or norms. Some individuals, perhaps those who are newly employed as graduate trainees, may resent the idea of having to conform. Yet membership of any group demands conformity to certain rules of behaviour and dress. This is irrespective of whether the group concerned is the playground gang at the primary school or the board of a major international company. Quite simply, you cannot be both a group member and not conform. The two actions are incompatible. Indeed, we know that members who support the values and practices of the group network, are also those who can exert the greatest influence over its members. Conversely, your reluctance or inability to conform, perhaps because of a major difference in values, attitudes or practices between yourself and others, will mean a failure to exert influence. In such circumstances, you may have to reconsider whether you feel able to continue as a member of that network or that organization. Informal networks are just as dynamic as organizations. Individuals change and economic and political factors advantage some groups while disadvantaging others. For this reason, you need to be constantly monitoring changes and testing reality. Is your network still centrally located with respect to 'where the action is' or has it become marginalized (and you with it) as the situation has moved on? Once you are in this informal group, exert influence through it. Adhere to its rules and avoid challenging its central values and habits.

THE GRAPEVINE

Joining a network also means joining the communication system that links the different parts of a company's informal network together. This is the 'grapevine' and is a natural part of all organizations. A grapevine and a rumour mill are not synonymous. Rumour may indeed be a part of the grapevine – the injudicious and untrue part that is communicated without factual evidence to support it. Rumours should be stopped as soon as possible as they tend to distort future happenings, which come to conform to the rumour. It has been estimated that between 75 per cent and 95 per cent of grapevine information is correct, even though the information may be incomplete in itself. Being personal and flexible, a grapevine can penetrate any company security screen, and is faster than any formal communication system. Unlike a chain communication structure, in which A tells B and B tells C, the grapevine uses a cluster chain in which A tells three or four people, only one of whom will pass the message on, and that person will usually tell more than one other person. As the information bulletin ages, and the number of those knowing it increases, it gradually dies out because those who receive it do not repeat it. The reason why not everybody passes on a piece of information is because a grapevine is more a product of a situation than of a person. People are active on a grapevine when events cause them to be so. In periods of excitement or insecurity, the grapevine will be most active. At these times you need to pay extra attention to it. The greatest spread of information occurs immediately after it is known. People are most apt to feed the grapevine when their friends or work colleagues are involved. Since the grapevine operates largely by word of mouth and observation, it is most active in office situations that regularly bring people into contact with each other. If you find yourself being bypassed by the grapevine, it may mean that your own personal channels of communication need improving.

OPERATING IN A NETWORK

Once you have joined an existing network, you will make it the foundation for a private network of your own. This is because your career goals, personal circumstances and background will be unique to you, and thus you will need particular individuals to support these. Your formal position in the organization will either be a help or hindrance in extending your network. If your job allows you to be with others (proximity), it will require you to interact with them. Employees most easily develop informal relationships with people who work close to them. It is important to occupy a critical or high-uncertainty position in a department's formal structure, in preference to having a standardized, routine job with little discretionary decision-making and low visibility. Influence can be gained by coping with critical organizational uncertainties. Power builds on power. Not holding a critical formal position may make it difficult for you to become central to an informal network (Kanter 1977). Your formal position notwithstanding, there are concrete steps you can take. Having joined, begin networking by observing, listening, questioning and assessing. Organizations are full of clues to indicate what is going on. A person with a white face and bags under his eyes is under pressure. A senior manager doing her own photocopying suggests something secret that her secretary cannot be trusted with. Sudden increases in numbers of meetings; people huddled in groups; closed office doors of people not wishing to be disturbed; people wearing suits rather than sports jackets, are all indicators of something going on. Just walking through the office with your eyes and ears open is getting close to the information.

EXTENDING YOUR NETWORK

In recent years, the vogue for networking has given it an unwarranted mystique. To start networking, you need a pen, a telephone address book and some printed business cards with your name, job title, organizational affiliation and contact address, phone number and email address. Some people also buy a box or wallet that store other people's cards. Have it in one place ready to use. Make it flexible and expandable. To broaden your network, first go to places and attend events where you will meet other organizational members. Second, once there, establish friendly relations with the people you meet. Make the first contact. When you see someone who you would like to have in your network, take the risk and introduce yourself. Chapter 3 on verbal influencing gives you some advice on that. Finally, use these relationships to learn about the company. You should make the effort to attend company events such as product launches, social and sports events, training and inter-departmental projects, even if you have little intrinsic interest in them. They give you the opportunity to meet new people who work in different parts of the company, and you will thereby gain a broader and clearer perspective on the organization as a whole. You can start building your network by keeping names and locations of people whom you meet at these events, and arrange to meet for lunch or after work. You will soon learn that there is a system in every organization that bypasses large sections of the formal channels of authority.

Extend your network outside your company for both short- and long-term purposes. Making contacts with people inside the firm can help you meet your immediate difficulties and short-term objectives. Contacting those outside is also important, especially to gain inside information about job opportunities in other industry sectors and organizations. One estimate is that only 30 per cent of professional and managerial jobs are publicly advertised. The remainder are filled by the cheaper, swifter and perhaps more reliable medium of personal recommendation of a network member. For this reason, meetings of professional associations and chambers of commerce, can extend your personal network. Participating in a part-time Master of Business Administration (MBA) programme at your local university can put you in touch with managers at similar levels to you from other organizations.

Both internal and external contacts need to be maintained and nursed even when you do not require anything immediately from them. Contacts will resent your contacting them only when you want a favour. The maintenance of long-term contacts need not be onerous. It may involve three or four lunches a year where each member updates the other on current activities and future objectives. These can highlight needs, and give the people involved the opportunity to exchange relevant publications (e.g. journal articles) or put each other in touch with others who can help them in some way. The annual Christmas card reinforces these continuing long-term links.

MENTORS AND SPONSORS

Amongst the members of your network, ensure that you have both a mentor and a sponsor. A mentor serves as your guide to the organization, providing you with help, support and information. Your mentor will not be your immediate boss, but is normally a senior or long-serving manager, in the same or another department. These people are willing to help younger employees. Some companies have instituted formal mentoring programmes for their new recruits. If you work in one that has not, you will have to identify and persuade a manager to act as your mentor (Missirian, 1982). In addition to providing information, Kram (1983) saw mentors offering, 'psycho-social functions' which are those aspects of the relationship that can help to build your confidence by enhancing your sense of competence, clarifying your identity and increasing your effectiveness in the job. This is achieved by role modelling, acceptance-and-confirmation, counselling and friendship. A study by Markiewicz et al. (2000) suggested that in organizational and work contexts, women were disadvantaged in informal friendship networks in contrast to formal channels. Women had more restricted and less powerful informal associations. Hence they relied more on formal application processes for promotion, whereas men used their informal contacts to take faster advantage of promotional opportunities. However, those women who had received

312

mentoring in early and middle career, achieved higher incomes and more promotions than those who had not.

The sponsor's role is different from that of a mentor. A mentor does not necessarily provide you with the opportunities that a sponsor can. To progress upwards within an organization, you need a senior, powerful person who will give you the opportunity to prove yourself; will put your name forward for the good, high-visibility jobs; and will defend you when you make a mistake. Their primary role is making introductions for young people, to get them more effectively through the system. Your sponsor's inside knowledge can help you to make the right career decisions. They can provide you with advice on company politics, and give you access to the powerful coalitions in the organization (Missirian, 1982). One senior manager can play the role of both your mentor and sponsor.

To progress upwards, you will need powerful friends to back you. Without them, one mistake could result in your downfall. However, ally-building is not just a defensive strategy. You do not need to be a genius to succeed to the top of an organization. If you are good at getting sponsors, then competence will be enough. Sponsors will help you on an ongoing basis, if they believe in you. That is why once they adopt you, you will not need to ask for their help directly on every occasion. Before a senior manager agrees to act as your sponsor, they will want to get to know you so as to assess your potential, and to ensure that their support will not backfire on them. For this reason, interacting with them, through networking, is fundamental.

Finding a sponsor is creating another form of alliance with a person who can promote your interests. *Sponsored-mobility* refers to the fact that a small group of senior managers determine who gets the most desirable jobs in the company. It stands in contrast to *contest mobility*, where there is open competition for the best jobs. Sponsors can do three things that will generate power for you. First, they can look after and fight for your interests. Stand up for you at meetings if controversy is raised, and promote you if promising opportunities become available. Second, if you are a junior manager, they allow you to bypass the hierarchy, and short-circuit cumbersome procedures. You can contact them informally, but the interchange can produce formal results. Finally, who your sponsor is, sends an important signal about you to others. You bask in your sponsor's reflected power. It shows that you have the backing of an influential person.

GETTING STARTED

Calano and Salzman (1988) have suggested a number of useful principles to guide your networking activities. Networking should become a priority item in your weekly work schedule. It is useful to decide upon a target number of new relationships that you want to establish during the next twelve months, perhaps five. Another measure of your network's effectiveness is to be able to answer most of your questions with no more than five, and ideally three telephone calls. Your chosen contacts and speed of response time ought to be integrated with and support, your career goals. You should raise your visibility by writing articles in the company newsletter, or by grasping the opportunity to speak to groups and clubs. Once people know that you exist, they will contact you, thus making the task of network expansion easier and quicker.

Build your informal network carefully. Go for quality of contact, rather than quantity, all the way up and down the organization. Select your fellow networkers on the basis of what information they possess and what real influence and control they exert, rather than on the formal company position that they happen to occupy. Drummond (1991) stressed the importance of having secretaries in your network. They tend to operate in a network anyway, trading information with other secretaries. They know who is on the way up (and down). Never press for information, just be polite, friendly and stop for a chat, build the relationship and keep listening. Once rapport is established, you can safely stimulate the flow of conversation by asking if the boss is in? (his whereabouts will be revealed, always useful). What sort of mood is he in (if under pressure, find out who is after him and why). How are things? (allows exasperation to be vented, and usually produces the latest news). Since your own secretary, if you have one, will be in the network, give the appearance of mutual trust and confidence, while saying less than you know.

However busy you may be, get out from behind your desk and out of your office, and visit others around the building. Call in on them for an occasional chat, ask them how they are getting on and what's new? In your own cubicle, be approachable. If you have an office, leave your door open and through your style, manner and voice, communicate your willingness to be visited or interrupted. If you drop in on others, they will understand that you do not mind being visited by them. Managers attach more credence to information supplied by those they see frequently than infrequently (Drummond, 1991a).

Ensure that you cultivate the right sources. Since gathering information is an involved process done on a continuing basis, no one person is likely to possess all the information that you will require. Some people have access to unique information by virtue of their position or professional expertise. There will be others whose opinions and sound judgement means that they can be trusted. Still others seem to get hold of rumours ahead of everyone else. Still others are compulsive talkers and will quickly insert into the rumour mill any information that you care to provide them with. The reliability and value of all your contacts will soon become apparent to you. To be asked for information, and to be able to provide it, can be empowering for the individual being asked. By requesting information from them, you are fulfilling their need to demonstrate their possession of information power. In this way, both of you gain. The more sources of information that you have, the more knowledgeable you will become.

314

Of course, it will be up to you to collate, interpret and act on the information that you have gathered.

Take the trouble to reciprocate regularly. Be discriminating about how you use your network contacts so as to ensure that your actions help you and do not offend them. When someone does help you, reinforce their action by taking the trouble to thank them either verbally or in writing. Doing this will strengthen your bond with them. These same people will also be interested in what you know. They will not feed you information forever without getting something back in return. So you must be prepared to release some of your information to them, and not expect immediate short-term benefits. If your own network contacts are plentiful and reliable, you will have access to information that will be of equal interest to them as well. Make a conscious effort to obtain information that is likely to be of more interest to them than you, just to have something to swop. In addition, make a point of passing on what you can on a regular basis, and not always to the same people. The more you sow, the more you will eventually reap. Cialdini's theory of reciprocation suggests that network members will be motivated to pass useful information your way, if you have done the same for them in the past.

Be a promoter of others. Speak regularly to members of your network and, if you find someone with a need, offer to share a contact them. You will be doing both parties a favour, by fulfilling the needs of one, while providing an opportunity to the other. Your own value and esteem will rise in the eyes of both. Be alert to information flagging significant future developments. Not all the information that you will receive will necessarily be usable immediately. Some types of information allow you to act now, in order to gain a benefit later. A contact may tell you that a new division is being established in six months time, which will be recruiting staff internally. With this knowledge you can use the time to update yourself about the area, and be in a strong position to apply for the more senior posts in it, once the decision is formally announced and recruitment has commenced. You can go further and be prepared to take advantage of opportunities that may arise. For example, before you attend a company social function, you could think what you want to get out of it network-wise. You would therefore ensure that you brought sufficient business cards with you to exchange, should you meet someone appropriate.

Another ongoing network management task is to keep your list of contacts updated. They should reflect your current and future concerns, issues, interests and opportunities, and not past ones. You may want to de-couple yourself from past contacts, which is easily done by not taking the initiative to pass them information, or by not reciprocating when they pass you theirs. Updating takes extra effort, especially if your career goals are to move to a different department or organization. If you are in Personnel or Human Resources and you want to move into Marketing, and the two departments are on different sites, establishing contacts will take more effort. You may attend company functions that bring together employees from all parts of the organization. You will need to identify those from the marketing department in the group. Company training courses, social and sports clubs, also attract a cross-section of the whole company. Establishing external contacts can be done by attending public training courses run by training consultancies or business schools, and national conferences in the relevant industry sector (Welch, 1980).

Like a journalist, protect your sources. You have an obligation to protect the person who has passed information on to you which is not generally available to others. They should not suffer or be inconvenienced by what they have told you. If you are asked about the source of any information, feign an inability to remember. A network is a democracy. Unlike the members of a traditional hierarchical, formal organization, your network partners inside of the company are your equals and should be treated as such. Even if you are the departmental manager, the lady in the print room who puts your work ahead of others is an equal. Treat all information with care. Amongst the information that you will gain will be gossip. The safest rule is not to pass it on, irrespective of how many others may want it. It can be used by others for mischief with malice. If you name comes to be associated with it because others do not protect their sources as diligently as you do, you will pay a high price for it. Some people will offer you gossip in the hope of receiving some back. Resist the temptation.

Once you have a network, do not be shy or embarrassed to use it. Contact the people if you need help, and follow up their offers of assistance if they make them. Maintaining a network is an ongoing activity that you do at a low level, rather than intermittent task that you occasionally blitz. Successful organizational relationships are built on mutual advantage. Boe and Youngs (1989) felt that networkers should be open-minded, seeing networking an on-going process which affects all aspects of their lives. Finally, sell the idea of networking to others. Your network will be stronger if other people in it have active networks of their own. Encourage your associates to network both inside and outside your company. Share your enthusiasm and help everyone to profit from it.

CONCLUSION

Discussing contemporary organizational life, Robert Jackel commented that people must not only look up in an organization, but continue to look around at their peers in order to establish alliances, and develop what he calles an interpretative community that will support you when the value of your work becomes an issue. This concerns what other people say about you, and your reputation in an organization becomes central. This in turn implies that you are constantly having to prove yourself, not just to your boss but also to your peers. This in turn generates a deep and pervading sense of anxiety which is a core feature of middle management work. Although many observers have felt that the last few years have been a period of extraordinary tumultuous change, Jackel argues that the regular pattern in the corporate world is one of continuous upheaval. Change and turnover of personnel at the top, puts pressure on those in the middle and lower ranks to keep an eye on what the shifts in the organizational structure are or might be so that they will be nimble enough to form new alliances should the necessity arise. Indeed, in large companies, a great deal of people's time is consumed with organizational politics.

Different individuals approach networking differently. Some people may be reluctant, and may need to be encouraged and taught to do this (Oaff, 2000). Travers *et al.* (1997) examined the attitudes towards networking of women from the USA, UK and Spain. They labelled each group. American 'instrumentalists' placed most focus on active learning and the use of their network as an arena for self-projection. British 'developers' used networks for developing self-confidence and as a place to learn, rather as one through which to do business. Spanish 'socialites' placed the greatest importance on the social aspects of networking, and were less interested in career contacts than the other two groups. Another study sought to discover the personality traits of people who networked successfully. It found that they possessed high self-esteem; were extroverted; and held favourable attitudes to workplace politics (Dougherty and Forret, 2001).

Chapter 16

Influencing through power and politics

Power is the pivot on which everything hinges. He who has the power is always right; the weaker is always wrong.

Niccolo Machiavelli

INTRODUCTION

'In the real world of organizations, the "good guys" don't always win' (Robbins, 1989). Demonstrating openness, trust, objectivity, support and similar humane qualities in relationships with others, does not necessarily lead to improved managerial effectiveness or career success. There will be times when, to get things done, or to protect your interests against the manoeuvring of others, you will have to get tough. That is, you will have to engage in 'politicking'. We can distinguish between *power*, which is the property of the organization system at rest, with *politics*, which is the study of power in action. Organizational politicking involves engaging in activities to acquire, develop, retain and use power, in order to obtain your preferred outcomes in a situation where there is uncertainty or disagreement about choices. Anyone seeking to implement change within an organization (a change agent) fits this description, and Buchanan and Badham's (1999) book offers the most useful, detailed guidance and advice in this field. Politicking concerns the actions that you take to influence the distribution of advantages and disadvantages within your organization (Allen *et al.*, 1979; Farrell and Petersen, 1982). The study of politics is the study of who gets what, when and how.

A survey report from the Roffey Park Management Institute confirmed that politics was a central feature of organizational life. A total of 24 per cent of respondents said that it was the norm in their organizations, 70 per cent said that political behaviour had increased; 45 per cent admitted engaging in it, giving significant reasons for doing so; and 45 per cent considered it to be essential in order to get things done within the organization. Only 3 per cent reported that they engaged in politicking because they enjoyed it, which was the same figure as those wishing to attain power and influence people (Holbeche and McCartney, 2002). It has been noted that a common trait amongst those who do not progress up the organization, despite their potential, is a belief that their ability and performance will shine through. They feel that they can keep their head down, get on with their jobs, and are not required to do anything more. However, it seems, if you want to get on, you need to engage in politicking, and opting out is not an option.

Dr Cheung-Judge (Lewis, 2001) observed that many gifted business practitioners remained stuck in their jobs by failing to use socialized power effectively. In contrast, those that had reached the top, had networked, built teams and had personally sought to make a personal impact on the organization. Once people get to the workplace, their desire to practise politics has often faded. Moreover, some of them did not believe that they possessed power, while others do not want to play the power game. Mann (1995) noted three reasons for women's reluctance to engage in organizational politics. These were their lack of confidence; a lack of competence; and a distaste for politics. The careers website, MMXI, revealed that most people do not believe that politics would do them any good. Only 39 out of 1,000 people canvassed cited office politics as an important factor in promotion to the top, with 420 believing luck to play an important role. This shows how ill informed the majority of your work colleagues are likely to be.

WHAT IS POWER?

Power is an abstract concept that is difficult to define. However, most writers agree that it is the capability of one person to overcome others in achieving their desired goal or result. As such, power is the basis of influence. At work, we each have some capacity to influence both other people and the daily events in the organization. However, the more power you have, the more you are able to influence these. As a newly recruited graduate, you may see company politics as a distasteful activity which should be avoided, and which is conducted by those lacking integrity. However, not involving yourself in the politics of the organization has its costs. It means evading your responsibilities, condemning yourself to being less effective than you could be, and placing yourself at the mercy of those who have gained power and who know how to use it. These same people can prevent you from reaching your goals.

In contrast, possessing power gives you the freedom, choice and ability to carry out your responsibilities, control your destiny and influence your environment. Although a total focus on the task to the exclusion of politics is possible in a favourable economic climate, in a period of retrenchment and change, your lack of political awareness and sensitivity may put at risk your past achievements. You can become over-focused on doing your job, forgetting that the completion

319

of most of your tasks requires the co-operation of others. Among the causes of management failure are political incompetence, political naivete, and the inability or unwillingness to perform effectively the required political tasks in the organization (Kotter, 1985a, 1985b). If you want to contribute positively to your company, you need to understand how to acquire power, and exercise the influence that it offers you. Gaining power allows you to survive in an organization, behave in a way that suits you, and permits you to promote the goals which you think are important. Politics and power are value neutral. They can be used by unscrupulous individuals to pursue their own goals at the expense of others, or they can be used to work with others, to achieve common team goals, and to accomplish organizational objectives. If you do not have a natural inclination to be political, you may have to develop one.

ORGANIZATIONS: RATIONAL OR POLITICAL?

In the previous chapter, the distinction between the *rational* and the *political* models of organization was introduced. From school and university, we learned that life is a matter of individual effort, ability and achievement. In the classroom, interdependence is minimized. The contest is between you and the course material to be learned. Co-operation between pupils is frowned upon, and may even be considered cheating. We also learned that there are right and wrong answers. Life is presented as a series of challenges called problems-to-be-solved. Once you are shown the correct approach or answer, it is self-evident. The emphasis is on discovering the right answer. Our educational experience is one of independent action, centralized control, orderly decision-making and rationality. People who pass exams are rewarded, while those who fail do not progress. Information and rules guide actions. Our entire pre-work experience therefore predisposes us to accepting a rational model of organizations whose main features are summarized on the left hand side of Table 16.1.

However, on entering a work organization, you suddenly discover that to accomplish anything, you need your colleagues to share the same goals. Your private knowledge and skill, so useful in the classroom, are insufficient within the organization. Success comes from working with and through others, and depends on how well different individuals co-ordinate their efforts. Organizations are like football teams rather than collections of golfers. Companies are therefore interested not only in your individual achievement, but also in your ability to work in a team. Hence their stress on this during the selection process. It is power that transforms individual interests into co-ordinated activities that accomplish organizational ends (Zaleznik and Kets de Vries, 1975). Moreover, in the organization, things are seldom clear-cut or obvious. We lack an instructor, problems are multi-dimensional and yield multiple methods of evaluation. The consequences of our decisions are often only known long after the fact, and

Table 16.1 *Rational versus political models of organization*

Organizational characteristic	Rational model	Political model
Goals, preference	Consistent across participants	Inconsistent, pluralistic within the organization
Power and control	Centralized	Decentralized, shifting coalitions and interest groups
Decision process	Orderly, logical, rational	Disorderly, characterized by push and pull of interests
Rules and norms	Norm of optimization	Free play of market forces; conflict is legitimate and expected
Information	Extensive, systematic, accurate	Ambiguous, information used and withheld strategically
Beliefs about cause–effect relationships	Known, at least to a probability estimate	Disagreements about causes and effects
Decisions	Based on outcome-maximizing choice	Result of bargaining and interplay among interests
Ideology	Efficiency and effectiveness	Struggle, conflict, winners and losers

Source: Based on Pfeffer, 1981: 31

then only with ambiguity. Slowly and perhaps painfully, you come to realize that organizations are more political than rational, as depicted on the right-hand side of Table 16.1 (Martin and Simg, 1954; Michener and Suchner, 1971; Schein, 1977).

WHY ARE ORGANIZATIONS POLITICAL?

Organizational life is about differences. It is rare for a company to have a single, unambiguous, clearly defined objective. Figure 16.1 summarizes Pfeffer's (1981) explanation of how, in complex organizations, tasks are divided up into departments. *Differentiation* refers to the specialization of both departments and employees' jobs in an organization by task. This division of labour enables an organization to achieve certain economies. However, it also has a number of divisive consequences. First, it creates differences in goals and understandings about what the company does, or should do, because each department is assigned its unique goal as part of the differentiation process. Marketing's task may be to maximize sales, while Production's may be to minimize costs. Such objectives are frequently in conflict. Second, different departments receive different sets of information. Marketing receives data on sales, while Production receives data on

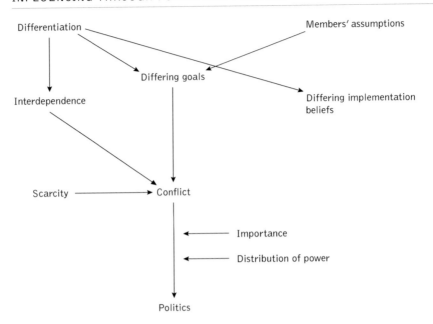

Figure 16.1 *Conditions producing the use of power and politics in organizational decision-making*

Source: Based on Pfeffer, 1981a: 69

costs. This causes parochialism, with each employee seeing the world through their own department's perspective.

Third, differentiation creates *interdependence* between people and departments, where the actions of one affect the other. It thus ties groups and individuals together, making each concerned with what the other does and gets. Fourth, differentiation also causes the creation of differences in *beliefs* about how something should be done. Fifth, company members bring different *assumptions* with them as to how things should be done. These are based on their socialization, background, training and on analysing business problems. All these differences create the potential for disagreement and conflict. A sixth requirement for power and politics to come into play is *scarcity*. Resources that are defined as scarce are perceived as being valuable (Brehm, 1966; Leavitt, 1954; Worchel *et al.*, 1975). Labelling a resource as scarce produces a vigorous action to obtain it, and more dissatisfaction with its apparent unavailability.

Will these conditions inevitably result in politics and the use of power? They will if two further conditions are met. First, if the resource or issue is *important*. It depends on how critically it is perceived. The use of power requires time and effort, so therefore it needs to be important. Second, a wide *distribution of power* needs to exist in the organization. Political activity, bargaining and coalition formation only occur when power is dispersed, and not when it is centralized at the top, or with one person. Which organizational resources are judged to be most scarce and important, and hence most open to politicization?

Ganz and Murray (1980) identified the following: promotions and transfers, hiring, pay, budget allocation, facilities and equipment allocation, delegation of authority, interdepartmental co-ordination, personnel policies, disciplinary penalties, work appraisals, grievances and complaints. What these all have in common is that the organizational decision-making procedures and performance measures associated with each of them is highly uncertain and complex; the competition among individuals and groups for them is strong; managerial discretion is high; and decisions have widespread consequences including success or failure at work, and upward superior and lateral, inter-unit relationships (Beeman and Sharkey, 1987). The last of these is an aspect of organizational integration, and is the most difficult to subject to routinization and techno-economic rationality.

POLITICS AS MANAGING MEANING

Ferris *et al.* (1991) argued that politics concerned the deliberate attempt to 'create, maintain, modify or abandon shared meanings'. Meanings are not inherent properties of situations but represent our responses to them. Shared meanings provide guidelines for our future interpretations and behaviours. We have already examined meaning-management in the small group context in Chapter 13. The same process occurs at the organizational level where politics are used to manage the meaning to produce desired outcomes. In companies, the ambiguous nature of the work environment provides a fertile background for the struggle to impose shared meanings. As one moves up the organization, both objectives and criteria become increasingly nebulous and unclear. Such ambiguity contributes to a desire for uniformity of beliefs, and leads to individuals seeking to establish consensus in their opinions, within a context of ambiguous stimuli (Nemeth and Staw, 1989). People are therefore highly susceptible to the influence of others in creating the impression of shared meaning.

Politics includes the use of strategies to maintain your power against others who want to take it away from you. It includes both long-term manipulation of relationships in order to improve your position, and *also* short-term actions to give you a tactical advantage (Tyson and Jackson, 1992). Politics is about overcoming the problem of resolving situations where different organization members bring different values to their work, and consequently do not share meanings with one another (Kakabadse, 1983). Bolman and Deal (1991) summarized this political view of organization, seeing goals and decisions as emerging from bargaining, negotiation and jockeying for position by individuals and coalitions. These coalitions were composed of varied individuals and interest groups which

323

possessed enduring differences of values, preferences, beliefs, information and perceptions of reality. The political model of organization is thus very different from the rational model.

COMPANY CULTURE

Pfeffer (1981a) noted that to influence successfully, you needed to make an accurate judgement about your organization's political culture, landscape and power distribution. Each company has its own unique culture which is its system of shared meanings. Culture consists of a set of unwritten norms that employees accept and understand. Company cultures differ widely. Some encourage their employees to take risks, while others do not. In some organizations the feedback to employees about the consequences of their actions is rapid, in others it is delayed. Deal and Kennedy (1982) distinguished *tough guy*, *bet-your-company*, *work-hard*, *play-hard* and *process* cultures. To succeed, your political strategy must be compatible with the company culture. The best way to find out about your company's culture is to investigate the performance appraisal system, and discover the criteria used for determining salary increases, promotions and other rewards. The answers that you obtain should tell you what kind of behaviour pays off in your organization. The crucial thing here is to focus on what the company does, and not what it says it does. Actions not words should guide your understanding of the organization's culture.

The political culture within a company will impinge upon how people interact, and how they will influence those around them. People have different personalities and these affect how they will react to political behaviour in organizations. Witt *et al.* (2002) studied how that culture affected persons with different personality traits. They chose three of the traits from the Big Five (Costa and McRae, 1992) – conscientiousness, agreeableness and extroversion. Conscientiousness was typified in industrious, dedicated employees who were often perfectionists, dedicated to their jobs, hard working and following rules. Those scoring high on this dimension were unlikely to be affected by a high level of organizational politics, while those who scored low would be. The latter understand that being rewarded for work done is a political act, and this will result in their having low job dedication. Agreeableness involves being courteous, flexible, trusting, good-natured, co-operative, altruistic, tender and modest. Highly charged political environments will have less affect on those high on this dimension than those scoring low. The reason may be that the former are predisposed to being highly helpful and co-operative. Extroverts are very sociable, talkative and assertive. Extroverts are not affected by very political situations since they are adept at creating their own social networks, place themselves in the information loop, and are not affected by uncertainty in the workplace. Introverts, in contrast, will lack these traits and are likely to be unaware about management decisions.

POLITICAL LANDSCAPE

The division of labour means that some departments are more central and contribute more directly to the primary goals of the organization than others. A company's political landscape therefore consists of departments and people who possess differing amounts of power. What are the true indicators of power in your organization, and how powerful are the different departments on this criteria? To assess an individual's power within departments, you can see if they have the ability to intercede successfully on behalf of someone in trouble; secure a desirable placement for a talented subordinate; or gain approval for expenditure beyond the budget. A second consequence of division of labour is the creation of interdependence. In order for one department to achieve its objectives, it requires the co-operative effort of another. While this may cause conflict, it also creates opportunities for coalition as individuals work with, and through others, to get things done.

To facilitate its implementation, a decision will often be delayed in order to get as many interests as possible behind it. Internal alliances are founded on common interests among participants who need one another. Once an issue is highlighted on which there are common positions, potential coalitions can form. Hence, you need to identify individuals, units and departments with whom you share a common view, and take time to talk to these with whom you disagree so as to persuade them over to your viewpoint. Remember, most important decisions are made outside meetings. Discuss each issue, and reach agreement on a one-to-one basis. Build your coalitions on good interpersonal relationships with liking, trust and respect. A long-term relationship based on reliability and a motivation to work with others, is a better foundation than a short-term exploitation of a current situation. Coalitions survive over time because each party recognizes a commonality of interests. We shall now consider the different types of power in an organization, and see how each can be developed.

REWARD POWER

This is the power to give rewards to those who comply with your requests. To do this, you must control the resources from which those rewards flow. So, as quickly as possible, position yourself where you have or can approve budgets. Nothing is as effective in coping with recalcitrant staff as the power to cut off funding for their projects. On the other hand, nothing promotes gratitude and co-operation, like the financial support of others' favourite projects. However, rewards need not be just financial. Chapter 7 reported the work of Cohen and Bradford (1989) who identified a range of rewards which they termed *organizational currencies*, and which could be used to motivate and persuade those around you. People have different needs, and thus would view different currencies as

325

rewards. It is useful to control and dispense required organizational resources, accumulating slack ones, allocating these in exchange for reciprocal favours, obedience or compliance. However, care must be taken if this power is used frequently as influencees may come to expect special rewards from you every time you want them to do something new or unusual. For this reason, it is best to reinforce desirable behaviour only after it has already occurred, to show that you appreciate them as competent and committed people.

COERCIVE POWER

Coercive power is the ability to punish. Often, the threat of coercion is sufficient. A manager may threaten to prevent a pay rise; fire a subordinate; give an unsatisfactory performance evaluation; deny promotion; or withdraw overtime. Coercion encompasses both physical and mental pressure, and succeeds by eliminating the influencee's options (Drummond, 1991). When using it, emphasize to the influencee that there is no alternative, and eliminate the possibility that your requirement is in any way negotiable. You inform the person about the rules and penalties, and warn them before punishing them. Check the situation before acting, and match the punishment to the infraction. Once coercion is used, it must be applied quickly, consistently, uniformly and relentlessly. Punish in private, and always act to maintain your credibility. Because coercion does not build commitment, and only engenders compliance, it should be avoided unless absolutely necessary, since it is likely to cause resentment and undermine your referent power. So if you use it, do so sparingly. Lewicki and Litterer (1985) suggested that coercive power may be used as part of position power when a job requires it. You have to punish the person, 'because the rules demand it'. You should recognize, create and cultivate dependence among those around you, and convert these dependencies into obligations (Kotter, 1979).

POSITION POWER

In a sense, all power is position power, because your company position gains you access to organizational resources. The focus here however, is upon *authority* – the power invested in all organizational positions. A position holder, like an accountant, can legitimately exercise the power within the boundaries of that position. Position power is your ability to make a subordinate feel responsible to you. Position power can be conceptualized as a form of entitlement, and is most clearly seen in military organizations where rank is visibly displayed. For this reason, it is essential to obtain a clear statement in writing of your duties, responsibilities, reporting relationships and scope of authority. This document can act as a defence against attempts to change your job responsibilities, reduce your authority, or change those who report to you, without your agreement. Carli's (1999) review of research on gender and power suggests that women do not command the respect that men do, nor do they seem to use position power as much as men. Hence, in group interactions, women are not considered as deserving of status as men, and group members tend to give them less opportunity to participate and resist their influencing attempts.

Choose your entry, department and job carefully. Research suggests that graduate recruits who enter a company as part of a formal trainee programme do best, since their admission to the scheme is taken as a sign of their career progress potential. Departments possess varying amounts of power and your choice of location will affect both your rate of salary growth and the length of time that you spend in each job. If you begin your career in a high-power department, you will move rapidly through the company, and if you inadvertently choose or are assigned to a low-power department, you could become stuck in it. Finally, in any situation, you accumulate power fastest in a job that allows you discretion (non-routinized action) permitting flexible, adaptive and creative contributions, gives you recognition (being visible to and noticed by others), and relevance (being centrally located to address pressing organizational problems). Act to change your department and job as soon as it becomes clear that it does not possess the desirable features.

Power in an organizational position can often be expanded by gaining control of a unit rich in resources, information or formal authority. At the minimum, prevent your opponents from doing the same. Once you control the unit, modify its structure to expand your territory and sphere of influence. Power is built by controlling as much territory and activity as possible. Once you grab control, you are rarely challenged, and eventually it becomes converted to legitimate authority. Kanter identified factors that contributed to position power and these are listed in Table 16.2.

Most subordinates accept their boss's right to make requests and tell them what to do. However, they do not like being given orders in a way that implies that they are not as good as their boss. Authority is exercised by making polite requests, not arrogant demands. Make your legitimate requests in clear, simple language so that the subordinate understands what is required, especially if they appear confused. If appropriate, explain the reason for the request, so that they understand why it is necessary. They can thus feel that they are following the logic of the situation, rather than acquiescing to your position power. Nevertheless, the subordinate should understand that it is within the scope of your formal authority to make such a request. Finally, you should follow up and verify that they have complied with your request. Reluctant subordinates may wait to see if you are serious enough to insist on compliance. If you do not insist, they may assume that it is safe to forget about it.

327

Table 16.2 *Factors contributing to power in an organizational position*

Factor	Generates power when factor is
1 Rules inherent in job	Few
2 Predecessors in job	None/few
3 Established routines	Few
4 Task variety	High
5 Rewards for reliability/predictability	Few
6 Rewards for unusual performance/innovation	Many
7 Flexibility in use of people	High
8 Approval needed for non-routine decisions	None/rarely
9 Physical location	Central
10 Visibility of job activity to others	High
11 Relationship of task to current company problems	Central
12 Focus of tasks	Outside of work unit
13 Contact with others through the job	High
14 Allows participation in projects, meetings and conferences	High
15 Participation in problem-solving teams	High
16 Advancement prospects of subordinates	High

EXPERT POWER

Expert power is based on the fact or impression that you have most relevant experience and expertise, and that you know the best course of action in a given situation. It was one of the two main types of power used by effective managers. Your expert power increases when you suggest a course of action that turns out to be highly successful; and decreases when your decisions lead to failure. As the problems under discussion change, so too does the opportunity to be the expert. At a meeting, different managers will emerge as most influential on different topics. Expertise can be consciously acquired through systematically seeking specific experiences or gaining qualifications. Carli's study of gender and expert power shows that men are rated as more competent than women even when there is no objective gender difference in performance. To be considered competent, women have to exhibit more evidence of skill than men, and provide explicit evidence of their superiority (Carli, 1999).

To accumulate expert power, foster an image of experience and competence, avoid careless statements and rash decisions. Drummond (1991) advised preserving your power and mystique and never making anything look easy. You should show others your credentials and demonstrate expert knowledge by citing facts and figures, referring to important but not commonly known features, and discussing points from several perspectives. Circulate articles or newspaper clippings which you have written, or to which you will refer. While this may seem gauche – the point is made. Being referred to or quoted in an article or an interview suggests expertise (Lewicki and Litterer, 1985).

To further demonstrate your expertise, introduce a significant piece of information at an appropriate time, or ask a question that can only be asked by a person who knows a lot about the topic being discussed. Weave into your discussion references to significant work that you have performed, names of those with whom you have worked, so as to indicate the quality of the work that you have done. Produce publications that can be cited. An article or a book on a topic suggests expert knowledge. The aim is to establish yourself as the best person to determine which options are possible and which are not. Drummond suggested using phrases like, 'a complete analysis is required', 'a major appraisal is necessary', 'this has major implications for' and 'this underpins our whole strategy'. Accreditation involves the ability to speak with authority communicating that you know what you are taking about. If you sound confident, others will have confidence in you, even if you are talking nonsense. It is effective because it creates certainty in the listeners' minds. The opposite is also true.

The rise in the importance of the expert is partly the consequence of the way that companies have modified the roles of employees who are now encouraged to develop expertise in a relatively specialized field. As a result, problems have to be tackled by teams of such experts, each bringing to bear their own specialist capabilities. Managers responsible for such problem-solving groups have to become competent at handling these often loose collections of experts, each of whom has their own professional axe to grind. It is also partly the result of the fact that external recommendation and sanction are often more powerful than internal arguments. A consultant-as-expert serves to legitimate the decisions reached, and provides an aura of rationality to the decision process. When power is widely dispersed in an organization, individuals holding different positions may be unable to muster enough support for their view to prevail, and an impasse results. The person who can get agreement to hire a consultant and participate in her selection, can break the deadlock to their advantage by introducing a new element. So outside experts will be used more frequently if power is widely dispersed in a company. If power is concentrated, there will be less need to bring in an outside expert to buttress a position, since internal power will be enough to carry the day. These strategies employ power unobtrusively and legitimate decisions which have to be made, but about which there is a disagreement concerning both the definition of the situation and favoured action. The use of an outside expert results in the less visible use of power in decision-making.

Buchanan and Boddy (1992) recommend buying in an outside consultant who may even be briefed in advance on the anticipated contents and conclusions of their report. Thus, the manager saying, 'The consultant says we ought to do this' is more influential than, 'I say we should do this'. Your listeners will often be responsive to such a power play. In making everyday judgements, people use judgement heuristics which were discussed in Chapter 9 to speed up and simplify thinking (Chaiken, 1987). Such heuristic says, 'If an expert says so, it must be true'. In this context, listeners actually ignore the expert's arguments, and allow themselves to be convinced just by the consultant's status as expert. Somewhere deep in their subconscious the word expert triggers associations of such individuals who excel in their domain; work with large meaningful patterns; solve problems quicker and with few errors; have superior memories; can conceptualize issues more deeply; and spend more time qualitatively analysing problems (Glaser and Chi, 1988). Once you introduce your chosen expert consultant, your audience will accede to your recommendation. Consultants are presumed to be

Table 16.3 *Techniques for undermining the credibility of other experts*

Strategic rejection	Just reject their report (if you have the power and self-assurance).
Invisible man	Avoid the individual so as to prevent any discussion at all.
'Bottom drawer it'	Send a memo praising their technicality, then put it away and forget it.
Mobilize political support	Call in favours from your colleagues.
Nitty gritty tactic	Question the minor details, highlight any minor mistakes so as to discredit the whole report.
Deflection	Deflect discussion away from substantive areas by focusing on less important matters in the report.
But in the future	Argue that while the data may be historically accurate, it does not consider future changes.
Further investigation required	Send them away to collect more data, either by changing the terms of reference, or by following up any interesting issues raised in the original report.
Scapegoat	Identify a suitable scapegoat who can be raised as a threat to any proposed change
Emotional tactic	Appeals to their emotions – such as personal consequences of the action.

Source: Pettigrew (1974: 24–30). Republished courtesy of Emerald www.emeraldinsight.com.

objective, expert and expensive. The first two characteristics ensure legitimacy, the third fosters commitment to their recommendations. If your opponent employs an expert, it puts you on the defensive. To undermine this expert's credibility, you might try some of the tactics listed in Table 16.3.

INFORMATION POWER

Francis Bacon said that 'knowledge is power'. Information is the life-blood of all organizations, and that it is the main currency of exchange between its members. Information is power if there are those who need it, and who are willing to trade something for it. Information power resembles expert power except that, in this case you are not presenting yourself as an authority on a particular topic, but as the one who has information not possessed by others. There are two dimensions of information power, gaining and using it. Both affect how influential you are. To gain information, you need to position yourself in networks through which relevant information flows. Without these, you are isolated. You may have to become involved in regular meetings with individuals inside and outside the organization, and subscribe to relevant journals. Such actions ensure that the information which you can provide is up-to-date, relevant and will be sought by others. This includes not only technical information about aspects of the work process, but also information about the firm's social system. Your access to the latter depends on your level of interaction with others. Ensure that you become well placed in your company's communication net, and develop useful social connections with key organizational players. Powerful people have powerful friends.

Three aspects are crucial to becoming centrally located so as to gain the greatest power, and these are summarized in Figure 16.2. First, *between-ness* is important. Place yourself between others in a communication path. For example, the secretary is between you and your boss. The salesperson is between you and your customer. Second, *connectedness* refers to the number of other people with whom you have contact, both within and outside the organization. Provided they contribute to your power, the more the better. Finally, *closeness* or proximity. This is the distance between you and all the other people in your network. Ensure that you can reach other people with as few intermediate steps as possible. The closer you are, the more independent you are since others cannot control your access to the focal person. Where your office, cubicle or desk is located will affect the number of interactions that you have with others, the content of those interactions, who gets to know you, what you get to know, and your relationship with these others (Brass, 1984, 1985; Freeman, 1979). Hence, check how near your desk is to head office, and how near your office is to senior management's. Avoid out of the way locations in god-forsaken postings, unless you are sure that they are necessary stepping stones to the more senior positions. Out of sight, out of mind!

331

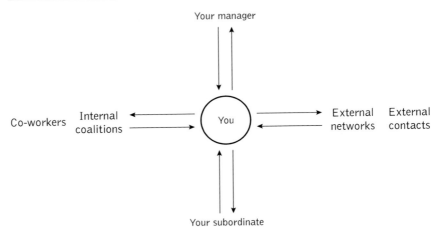

Figure 16.2 *Between-ness, connectedness and closeness in a communication network*

Being central in a communication network is most easily achieved through the careful choice of your job. A low-visibility job is unlikely to lead to relationship building. In contrast, jobs which straddle departments and units, tend to get noticed, allow you to develop contacts across the organization, and thus help you to become more influential through your central position in the communication structure. Staff or assistant-to positions, while they may not carry formal authority, do give you power by providing you with access to key people in the organization. Thus a staff job offers you connection power, while a line job provides you with resources to exert reward or coercive power. Ambitious employees evaluate job opportunities in terms of whether they provide contacts with other company personnel. Your information power depends on your knowing and interacting with others.

Information is power because most people erroneously believe that there are right answers to problems which can be uncovered, illuminated by information and analysis. Rationality is the Achilles heel of organizations. All organizations strive to appear rational, and to be seen to be using the proper procedures (including information and analysis) to justify their decisions. Companies often construct the appearance of legitimate and sensible decision processes to support their intended courses of action, even when these are based on emotion or intuition. Because of this, information power can be used potently and surreptitiously. By following the prescribed and legitimate procedures, your decisions will be perceived to be better and more readily acceptable. The appearance of bureaucratic rationality is essential in making companies appear legitimate (Kramer, 1975; Kramer and Neale, 1998). Hence, you should seek out information, not necessarily to make a decision, but to make it appear that a decision has been made in the correct fashion, that is, on the basis of information and not on uninformed preference or hunch. Decisions made on the latter basis do not produce the same level of comfort or legitimacy, as the former.

You can promote favourable data, and suppress unfavourable data. If in doubt, keep it to yourself. If you have to release information unfavourable to you, then do it before someone else does (limit the damage by taking charge and let others hear it from you directly); preface bad news with good (stating achievements blunts criticism); and do it gradually (release it bit by bit and they might not even notice that you have made a mistake). Finally, knowledge is only power if it can be recalled and deployed when needed. Governments are experts at this, which has come to be labelled 'spin'. The problem is that we forget most of what we learn (Drummond, 1991). So you need to keep a record of potentially significant information, be able to access it and cross-reference it as required. For example, at the start of a project, or when meeting someone for the first time. People who meet you for the first time often reveal a lot about themselves in casual conversation. They only clam up once they discover what you are after. Have a notebook, diary or a dictating machine to hand, as well as a good filing system. Networkers always update their file of contacts.

PERSONAL POWER

Referent or personal power refers to the loyalty of one person to another, based on their desire to please them. Such power is derived from your personal qualities and the relationship that you have with the influencee. It thus differs from the previous types of power which are all, in their different ways, related to organizational position. Your personal power comes both from your ability to convey feelings of personal acceptance and approval to others. It is increased when you are considerate to others, show concern for their needs and feelings, treat them fairly and defend their interests when dealing with superiors and outsiders. It is diminished when you express hostility, distrust, rejection or indifference to those around you, or when you fail to defend the interests of your subordinates or those around you. Carli's (1999) research on gender differences shows that women's greater likeableness gives them greater referent power than men, with people reporting more positive feelings towards women than men.

Personal power is based on the influencee's attraction to you, which itself is a function of your friendliness, gregariousness, congeniality, honesty, candour and integrity. The power derives from your possessing the qualities that are valued and desired by them. Your poise, wealth or confidence, may lead them to identify with you. The influencee wants to be like you. Film, pop and sports stars are adored by their fans, and thus exert personal power. Their capacity to influence young consumers is reflected in the willingness of companies who sell clothes, shoes and soft drinks, to pay them huge sums to advertise their products.

333

Personal power also derives from establishing and maintaining a relationship with the influencee. Since there is a strong link between perceived similarity, liking and attraction, you should work to establish your personal power by building a relationship. Begin by finding out what you have in common with the other person, since common experiences create the basis for deeper knowledge. Then, increase your self-disclosure by telling the other person a little about your feelings and thoughts, as this increases the trust between you. If possible, highlight your mutual interdependence and common fates, in order to encourage a comprehensive exchange of views (Lewicki and Litterer, 1985).

Charisma refers to the nearly magical ability of some individuals to influence others. Research and folklore have suggested that charismatic leaders can inspire others to increase their performance, and engender the respect of others. What are the personal qualities of charismatic leaders? Research has found that charismatic leaders are perceived as dynamic, enthusiastic, inspiring, outgoing, sociable and jestful; as insightful, bright, intellectual, wise and competent; and as confident, secure, unflappable and not meek (Atwater *et al.* 1991; Conger and Kanungo, 1987; Conger *et al.*, 2000). From an impression management perspective, charisma-inspiring behaviours are capable of being taught and learned (Bass and Avolio, 1990). Pfeffer (1981b) felt that we tended to over-attribute power to personal characteristics, believing them to be the sources of power, rather than its consequences. Nevertheless, they may be important to develop, or at least to project to others. The key traits are:

- *Energy*, endurance and physical stamina often triumph over cleverness. If you have energy and strength, you can outlast the opposition, and overcome those who surpass you in intelligence or skill. Your energy, persistence and endurance will inspire those around you, signalling the importance of the task, and what is possible (Gardiner, 1990).
- *Directing* energy in a focused way to avoid wasted effort. The focus may be a single industry or a few organizations, thereby gaining experience of a narrower set of concerns and problems. It allows you to focus in on the details, and learn the names of the key individuals in that sector.
- *Sensitivity* is the ability to read and understand others. To induce a group to pursue your objectives, you must understand their interests, attitudes and how to reach them. Seeing the world from their perspective is the starting point. Find out what the others want and need, and accommodate this in your proposal (Fisher and Ury, 1981; Ury, 1991).
- *Flexibility* involves keeping your goals stable, but your tactics flexible. Use information about others to change your own behaviour, matching it to their needs. Flexibility helps you to acquire allies, as you shift approaches to accommodate different interests. Flexibility comes from focusing on ultimate objectives, while remaining emotionally detached from the

situation. Rigidity hinders the development of support and inhibits tactic changing (Christie and Geis, 1970).

- *Toughness* is the willingness to engage, when necessary, in conflict and confrontation. Sometimes it is important to fight, to be difficult, to make rivals pay for getting their way, rather than what you want. Overcoming the resistance of others implies disagreement. A personal attribute of influential people is a willingness to engage in such conflict with others. Conflict is a sort of anticipatory deterrence in which you let others know that if they do not do what you want, the consequences for them will be unpleasant. Unwillingness to fight by those who dislike conflict results in their being defeated by someone who is less fastidious. People who want to be liked by everyone will avoid conflict. Hence, the most effective exercisers of power are often those who are independent enough not to need the approval or the intimacy of others.
- *Humbleness* is the ability to submerge your own ego temperament, to be a team player, and enlist the help and support of others. Sometimes it is important to build alliances and networks of friendships by getting along with others. The main problem is that your ego can get in the way. So the ability to submerge it and thus get something accomplished is important. This is related to flexibility since it involves trading present restraint at the moment for greater power and resources in the future. Build others up, to gain support from others.

Demonstrating these six traits can increase your personal power. Each relates either to gaining support and allies (sensitivity, flexibility and ego-submersion); or to surviving in a competitive arena (energy-stamina, focus, conflict engagement) (Salancik and Pfeffer, 1977). Use your own sense of humour, enthusiasm, confidence and commitment to infect and stimulate others towards your own way of thinking. Whatever you may feel inside, use your impression management skills to project these positive traits to others. One way of using personal power is to make an appeal that evokes feelings of loyalty from those around. Indicate to them that your request is very important to you, and that you are counting on them for their support and cooperation. Another way, is through role modelling. You behave in the way you want others to behave. If people admire you, they will imitate you, wanting to please you and become more like you. You can thus influence them without the need for making any explicit requests. Buchanan and Badham provide a typology of power tactics (Table 16.4). Basing it on Gray and Starke's (1984) classification system, they add an additional category of more covert and ruthless ('dirty tricks') tactics. Their examples come from interviews and discussions from managers attending executive development programmes in Australia, Britain, Sweden and Finland. They are confident that these represent the taken-for-granted 'recipe knowledge' of many experienced managers around the world.

Table 16.4 Power tactics

Power tactic	Definition and examples
Image building	Actions which enhance reputation and further career; appropriate dress, support for the 'right' causes; adherence to group norms; air of self-confidence. • 'You have got to be seen to be successful at all costs.' • 'Seek to be associated with success; seek the spotlight.'
Selective information	Withhold unfavourable information from superiors; keep useful information from your competition; offer only favourable interpretations; overwhelm others with complex technical data. • 'Exclude others as appropriate from your plans and activities.' • 'Withhold information and dispense misinformation to maintain control.'
Scapegoating	Make sure someone is blamed; avoid personal blame; take credit for success. • 'Blame a predecessor.' • 'Pick your timing to discredit people.'
Formal alliances	Agree actions with key people; create a coalition strong enough to enforce its will. • 'Gain access to key players and information.' • 'Seek the support and affiliation of those in power.'
Networking	Make lots of friends in influential positions. • 'Be mobile . . . out and about, talking networking.' • 'Invite the "right" people to social events.'
Compromise	Give in on unimportant issues to create allies for subsequent, more important issues. • 'Be ready to change your opinions quickly.' • 'Decide how much you are prepared to lose.'
Rule manipulation	Refuse requests on the grounds of 'against company policy' but grant identical requests from allies on the grounds of 'special circumstances'. • 'Ask yourself . . . what can I get away with?' • 'Stay clean . . . never get caught playing the game.'
Other tactics	These examples do not fit under Gray and Strake's headings, and are more covert and ruthless, being concerned with political infighting. • 'When all else fails, do not be afraid to use coercion.' • 'Undermine the expertise of others.' • 'Play one person or group off against another.' • 'Keep a "dirt file".' • 'Do it to them before they do it to you.' • 'Undermine opponents through "whispers in the corridors".' • 'Use "subversives" to plant ideas with other managers.' • 'Use other people to "fire the bullets".' • 'Trash the deal in the details; nit-picking can be an effective blocking tactic.'

Source: From David Buchanan and Richard Badham, *Power, Politics and Organizational Change*, 1999, Sage, London, pp. 27–9. Reprinted with Permission

GENDER AND POWER

Carli (1999) considered three types of power – referent (personal), legitimate and expert power – in relation to gender. She contends that women enjoy higher levels of referent power than men, but that the latter are perceived to possess more legitimate and expert power. She says that women's displays of competence, directness and authority reduce their influence, while men's displays either enhance or have no effect on their influence. In her study, men using a direct and assertive strategy when applying for a job were more likely to be recommended than women using the same strategy. Her research indicates that as long as women behave in the expected manner, i.e. pleasantly and agreeably, people (particularly male colleagues), will be less resistant to their ideas. Men however, are not penalized for using highly assertive, characteristically male, influencing strategies. Furthermore, a female influencer interacting with a male, can overcome his resistance to her influencing, by combining a warm, co-operative style, coupled with competence. Competence, apparently, does not carry sufficient weight on its own, because a woman is seen as lacking the power associated with men.

Carli notes that while people generally like women more, there is a greater belief in male competence, and a perception that they have a greater right to exercise authority and leadership. Men can exploit a wider variety of influencing strategies because they typically possess greater amounts of legitimate power than women. Women are held to a higher standard of performance, having to be better than men, to be considered equally competent. Even when a woman's higher competence is acknowledged, she may still receive a negative reaction. Competent self-promoting women risk being disliked and rejected, especially by men. Irrespective of gender, people use more direct or assertive forms of influence when they feel powerful. Therefore gender influences in influencing strategies are mediated by gender differences in power.

USING POWER

Many writers have, in different ways seen power as the basis of influencing (Phillips, 1997). The six power bases described here underpin the influencing strategies described in Chapter 12. The relationships between the two are shown in Figure 16.3. The greater the range of power bases available to you, the greater will be the choice of strategies that you can use, and the more effectively you will be able to use them. It is only expert and personal power that is likely to produce commitment in the influencee. Position and reward power are likely to elicit drudging compliance, while coercive power is likely to generate resistance. There are therefore three principles which should guide your power management. First, exercise power unobtrusively; legitimate your decisions and

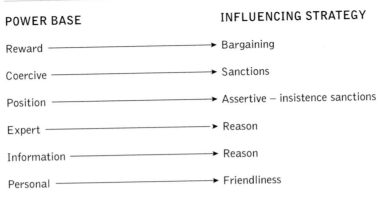

Figure 16.3 *Relationship between power bases and influencing strategies*

actions; and build additional support and power behind a favoured position. Although power is exercised through the politically motivated actions of individuals, the base for that power comes from the larger organizational processes described here.

INCREASING YOUR POWER

How do you increase the strength and number of your organizational power bases? Daft (1992) argued that departments and individuals could increase their power by focusing on the five areas of: dependency, financial resources, centrality, departmental power, non-substitutability and coping with uncertainty. *Dependency* means having something that someone else wants, for example, computer expertise. The greater the number of people who want it, the more powerful you are. Since dependencies are a source of power, create them by ensuring that others have to deal through you if they want something. Similarly, reduce your dependency on others by finding an independent route to what you want, or by acquiring the necessary skill or information yourself.

Control of resources reminds us of the golden rule that, 'The person who has the gold, makes the rules'. Resources can be almost anything that is perceived as valuable. To be useful in the influencing purposes, you can possess them outright, have access to them, be allowed to use them or have rule-making ability to regulate their possession, allocation and use by others (Pfeffer and Salancik, 1978). However, resources are only valuable if you can make others dependent on them. This in turn depends on how much they need what you control, and how many alternative sources there are (Emerson, 1962). So ensure that there are no alternative ways of obtaining access to the valued resources that you

338

control. Resources not already spoken for, so-called incremental ones, are the most precious. Such resources can become addictive. For example, the one-off bonus can become an annual necessity. Indeed, the person or unit offering the incremental resources can gain tremendous power over that part of the organization to which they have been allocated, by making others dependent on them, for example, a PC software support unit. So increase your power by finding unexploited resources. Once people become hooked on them, and have incorporated them into their working pattern and expectations, you can threaten to withdraw them if they do not comply with your request. The key here is recognizing what people need in a given situation, and then creating a resource that will give you control over them.

Centrality refers to the extent to which the work of your department affects the final output and survival of the organization. Division of labour leads to different sub-units having varying amounts of centrality. Sales and Production, are more central than Training, at least in the short term. Centrality is associated with power because it reflects contribution to the organization. Every organization has elements that are important for its success. The centrality of a department changes with the internal and external organizational situation. New strategic contingencies arise which are not yet being satisfied, for example, legal requirements of health legislation. This gives you the chance to move into these new, centrally important areas, and this will increase your power.

Non-substitutability means that a department's function cannot be performed by other, readily available resources. You can assess the non-substitutability of your job by asking yourself some questions. Can you and your skills be easily replaced? If you do not do your job, who else will? If you withhold your service, can the person get it elsewhere? How much does the other person need your support or custom? What are the consequences for the other person if they do not get it? Be careful not to overestimate your power. The job centres are full of people who thought they were indispensable. Your analysis may identify where you have little power currently, and highlight areas where you need to acquire more.

Uncertainty coping refers to departments that cope well with uncertainty and can increase their power. It is not the presence of uncertainty itself, but the ability to reduce the uncertainty on behalf of other departments, that gives it power. For example, the Marketing Department has power to the extent that it can accurately forecast demand for new products. You therefore need to enter areas of high uncertainty in the organization. Identify the key uncertainties and remove them. Stoppages on the assembly line, needed quality on a new product, and inability to predict new demand are all examples of company uncertainties. You will probably eliminate uncertainty only by trial-and-error. That delay is not a problem, it will provide you with experience and expertise that others cannot duplicate.

CONCLUSION

Power is lost as environments and problems change, and new approaches, skills and relationships are needed. Most people are trapped in existing networks of contacts, choices, actions and friendships. We fail to recognize the need for change, never mind how to accomplish it. So, to retain your power, be sensitive to subtle changes in the environment. Understand how a particular set of activities or approaches is effective because it fits the concerns of a particular era. Be flexible enough to accommodate the new reality, even if it means replacing well-known habits. To manage with power, recognize that in every organization there are varying interests. Find out what they are and how they cluster. Identify the different viewpoints of individuals and units on issues of concern, and why they hold them. Recognize that you need to have more power than the opposition, and understand the strategies and tactics through which power is developed and used in organizations.

If someone offers you a position of more prestige or power than you think that you have a right to expect, ask yourself what their motives might be, and what the risks of the situation might be. You may be being brought in without a power base of relationships, or organization-specific knowledge to 'serve an agenda'. Be suspicious of what their agenda might be. The formal position that you hold is sufficient to maintain your power over a long period into the future. Power has many sources and position is only one of them. To hold your position into the future, complement position power with other types of power.

A curious feature of power is that the more you have, the more you get. Once you attain a powerful position, it is easier to accomplish more. Success breeds success. Because you have the resources, you will be highly motivated, and you will motivate those around you. More of your efforts will be successful, and you will be in a position to flexibly interpret and shape policy to meet the needs of particular areas, developing situations or sudden changes. Being seen as powerful by others gains you their respect and co-operation. To shun power and politics, said Bryce (1991), is to put yourself at the mercy of powerful and influential people. It will bar you from many desirable and senior jobs. The reality of business life is that it is about difference — different values, different goals and different interests. There is no clear goal or mission in a company. Your proposal may be correct, but you may lose out because you are not powerful or influential enough. Decisions in organizations are not based only, or even mainly, on logic and rationality. They are determined by power and politics. So you need to be a politician in the sense of understanding and being sensitive to the causes of conflict and the strategies to cope with it. Having power gives you the freedom to influence your environment, and control over your destiny. Gaining power is also about survival, fighting to be yourself and having independence in a competitive world. It is not a substitute for being competent at your job, but is an important complement to it.

Bibliography

Abelson, R.P. (1976), 'Script Processing in Attitude Formation and Decision Making' in Carroll, J.S. and Payne, J.W. (eds), *Cognition and Social Behaviour*, Hillsdale, NJ: Erlbaum, pp. 33–46

Adams, G.R. (1977), 'Physical Attractiveness Research: Towards a Developmental Social Psychology of Beauty', *Human Development*, vol. 20, pp. 217–39

Aguinis, H. and Adams, S.K.R. (1998), 'Social Role Versus Structural Models of Gender and Influence Use in Organizations', *Group and Organization Management*, vol. 23, no. 4, pp. 414–16

Aguinis, H. and Henle, C.A. (2001), 'Effects of Nonverbal Behaviour on Perceptions of a Female Employee's Power bases', *Journal of Social Psychology*, vol. 141, no. 4, pp. 537–49

Al-Jajjoka, S. (2001), *How to Pass Professional Level Psychometric Tests*, London: Kogan Page

Alba, J.W. and Marmorstein, H. (1987), 'The Effects of Frequency Knowledge on Consumer Decision Making', *Journal of Consumer Research*, vol. 14, no. 1, pp. 14–25

Allen, J.S. (1983) *How to Turn an Interview into a Job*, New York, NY: Simon and Schuster

Allen, R.W., Madison, D.L., Porter, L.W., Renwick, P.A. and Mayes, B.T. (1979), 'Organizational Politics: Tactics and Characteristics of Actors', *California Management Review*, vol. 22, no. 1, pp. 77–83

Alessandra, A., O'Connor, M.J. and Van Dyke, J. (1994), *People Smarts*, San Diego, CA: Pfeiffer and Co.

Allgeier, A.R., Byrne, D., Brooks, B. and Revnes, D. (1979), 'The Waffle Phenomenon: Negative Evaluations of Those Who Shift Attitudinal', *Journal of Applied Social Psychology*, vol. 9, pp. 170–82

Amalfitano, J.G. and Kalt, N.C. (1977), 'Effects of Eye Contact on the Evaluation of Job Applicants,' *Journal of Employment Counselling*, vol. 14, pp. 46–48

Anderson, A. (2001), 'The Changing Face of the British Graduate Selection Process', Department of Business and Management, University of Glasgow. Unpublished MA dissertation.

Anderson, N. (1988), 'Re-theorising the Selection Interview', paper read at the BPS Annual Occupational Psychology Conference.

Anderson, N. (1992), 'Eight Decades of Employment Interview Research: A Retrospective Meta-review and Prospective Commentary', *European Work and Organizational Psychologist*, vol. 2, no. 1, pp. 1–32

Anderson, N. and Shackleton, V. (1994), 'Informed Choices', *Personnel Today*, 8 November, pp. 33–4

Ansari, M.A. (1990), *Managing People at Work: Leadership Styles and Influencing Strategies*, London: Sage

Ansari, M.A. and Kapoor, A. (1987), 'Organizational Context and Upward Influence Tactics', *Organizational Behaviour and Human Decision Processes*, vol. 40, pp. 39–49

Applebaum, S.H. and Hughes, B. (1998), 'Ingratiation as a Political Tactic: Effects within the Organization', *Management Decision*, vol. 36, no. 2, pp. 85–102

Arkes, H.R. and Blumer, C. (1985), 'The Psychology of Sunk Cost', *Organizational Behaviour and Human Decision Processes*, vol. 35, no. 1, pp. 124–30

Aronson, E. (1992), *The Social Animal*, New York, NY: Freeman and Company, 6th edn

Aronson, E. and Darwyn, L. (1965), 'Gain and Loss of Esteem as Determinants of Interpersonal Attractiveness', *Journal of Experimental Social Psychology*, vol. 1, pp. 156–71

Aronson, E. and Linder, D. (1965), 'Gain and Loss of Esteem as Determinants of Interpersonal Attraction', *Journal of Experimental Social Psychology*, vol. 1, pp. 156–71

Aronson, E. and Mills, J. (1959), 'The Effects of Severity of Initiation on Liking for a Group', *Journal of Abnormal and Social Psychology*, vol. 59, pp. 177–81

Aronson, E. and Osherow, N. (1980), 'Cooperation, Pro-social Behaviour and Academic Performance: Experiments in the Desegregated Classroom' in Bickman, L. (ed.), *Applied Social Psychology Annual: Volume 1*, Beverley Hills, CA: Sage, pp. 163–96

Aronson, E., Helmreich, R. and LeFan, J. (1970), 'To Err is Humanizing – Sometimes: Effects of Self-esteem, Competence and a Pratfall on Interpersonal Attraction', *Journal of Personality and Social Psychology*, vol. 16, pp. 259–64

Aronson, E., Turner, J. and Carlsmith, J.M. (1963), 'Communication Credibility and Communication Discrepancy as Determinants of Opinion Change', *Journal of Abnormal and Social Psychology*, vol. 67, pp. 31–6

Aronson, E., Willerman, B. and Floyd, J. (1966), 'The Effect of Pratfall on Increasing Interpersonal Attractiveness', *Psychonomic Science*, vol. 4, pp. 227–8

Arthur, W., Woehr, D.J. and Graziano, W.G. (2001), 'Personality Testing in Employment Settings', *Personnel Review*, vol. 30, no. 6, pp. 657–6

Arunachalam, V., Pei, B.K.W. and Steinbart, P.J. (2002), 'Impression Management with Graphs: Effects on Choices', *Journal of Information Systems*, vol. 16, no. 2, pp. 183–203

Asch, S.E. (1946), 'Forming Impressions of Personality', *Journal of Abnormal and Social Psychology*, vol. 41, pp. 258–90

Asher, D. (2000), 'A Weighty Matter,' *Psychology Today*, vol. 32, no. 3, p. 14

Atkins, S. (1982), *The Name of Your Game*, Stuart Atkins Inc.

Atkinson, J.M. (1984), *Our Masters' Voices*, London: Routledge

Atwater, L., Penn, R. and Rucker, L. (1991), 'Personal Qualities of Charismatic Leaders', *Leadership Organizational Development Journal*, vol. 12, no. 2, pp. 7–10

Aune, K.A. and Basil, M.D. (1994), 'A Relational Obligations Approach to the Foot-in-the-Mouth Effect', *Journal of Applied Social Psychology*, vol. 24, no. 6, pp. 546–56

Babcock, L. and Laschever, S. (2003), *Women Don't Ask: Negotiation and the Gender Divide*, Princeton, NJ: Princeton University Press

Bachrach, P. and Baratz, M.S. (1963), 'Decision and Non-decisions: An Analytical Framework', *American Political Science Review*, vol. 57, no. 3, pp. 632–42

Bacharch, P. and Lawler, E. (1980), *Power and Politics in Organizations*, San Francisco, CA: Jossey Bass

Bandura, A. (1969), *Principles of Behaviour Modification*, New York, NY: Holt, Rinehart and Winston

Bandura, A. (1977a), *Social Learning Theory*, Englewood Cliffs, NJ: Prentice Hall

Bandura, A. (1977b), 'Self-efficacy: Towards a Unifying Theory of Behavioural Change', *Psychological Review*, vol. 84, pp. 191–215

Bar-Hillel, M. (1973), 'On the Subjective Probability of Compound Events', *Organizational Behaviour and Human Performance*, vol. 9, pp. 396–406

Bar-Hillel, M. (1989), 'The Base-rate Fallacy in Probability Judgements', *Acta Psychologica*, vol. 44, no. 3, pp. 211–33

Barber, B. (1983), *The Logic and Limits of Trust*, New Brunswick, NJ: Rutgers University Press

Bardack, N.R. and McAndrew, F.T. (1985), 'The Influence of Physical Attractiveness and Manner of Dress on Success in a Simulated Personnel Decision', *Journal of Social Psychology*, vol. 125, no. 6, pp. 777–8

Barlett, K. (1994), 'Only Girls Wear Barrettes: Dress and Appearance Standards, Community Norms and Workplace Equity', *Michigan Law Review*, vol. 9, pp. 2541–82

Barlow, G. (1989), 'Deficiencies and the Perpetuation of Power: Latent Functions of Management Appraisal', *Journal of Management Studies*, vol. 26, no. 5, pp. 499–517

Baron, R.A. (1983), 'The Sweet Smell of Success?: The Impact of Pleasant, Artificial Scents on Evaluation of Job Applicants', *Journal of Applied Psychology*, vol. 68, pp. 709–13

Baron, R.A. (1986), 'Self-presentation in Job Interviews: When There Can Be Too Much of a Good Thing', *Journal of Applied Psychology*, vol. 16, no. 4, pp. 16–28

Baron, R.A. (1997), 'The Sweet Smell of . . . Helping: Effects of Pleasant Ambient Fragrance on Prosocial Behaviour in Shopping Malls', *Personality and Social Psychology Bulletin*, vol. 23, no. 5, pp. 498–503

Baron, R.A. and Byrne, D. (2000), *Social Psychology*, Boston, MA: Allyn and Bacon, 9th edn

Barone, M.J., Miniard, P.W. and Romeo, J.B. (2000), 'The Influence of Positive Mood on Brand Extension Evaluations', *Journal of Consumer Research*, vol. 26, no. 4, pp. 372–85

Barrett, J. (2002), *How to Pass Advanced Aptitude Tests*, London: Kogan Page

Barrick, M.R., Patten, G.K. and Haughland, S.N. (2000), 'Accuracy of Interviewer Judgements of Job Applicant Personality Traits', *Personnel Psychology*, vol. 53, no. 4, pp. 925–7

Bartram, D. (1999), 'Testing and the Internet: Current Realities, Issues and Future Possibilities', *Selection and Development Review*, vol. 15, no. 6, pp. 3–12

Baskett, G.D. (1973), 'Interview Decisions as Determined by Competency and Attitude Similarity', *Journal of Applied Psychology*, vol. 57, pp. 343–5

Bass, B. and Avolio, B. (1990), *The Multifactor Leadership Questionnaire*, Palo Alto, CA: Consulting Psychologists Press

Bates, B. and Cleese, J. (2001), *The Human Face*, London: BBC Consumer Publishing (Books)

343

Bates, G.D. (1995), 'How to Get Others to Like You Instantly', *Journal of Management in Engineering*, vol. 11, no. 3, p. 3

Baumeister, R.F. (1982), 'A Self-presentational View of Social Phenomena', *Psychological Bulletin*, vol. 91, pp. 3–26

Baumeister, R.F. and Darley, J.M. (1982), 'Reducing the Biasing Effects of Perpetrator Attractiveness in Jury Simulation', *Personality and Social Psychology Bulletin*, vol. 8, pp. 286–92

Bavelas, J.B. and Chovil, N. (2000), 'Visible Acts of Meaning', *Journal of Language and Social Psychology*, vol. 19, no. 2, pp. 163–95

Baxter, J.C., Brock, B., Hill, P.C. and Rozelle, R.M. (1981), 'Letters of Recommendation: A Question of Value', *Journal of Applied Psychology*, vol. 66, pp. 296–301

Bazerman, M.H. (2001), *Judgement in Managerial Decision-making*, New York, NY: Wiley, 5th edn

Beaman, A.L, Steblay, M.N., Preston, M. and Klentz, B. (1988), 'Compliance as a Function of Elapsed Time Between First and Second Requests', *Journal of Social Psychology*, vol. 128, no. 2, pp. 233–43

Beaman, A.L., Cole, C.M., Preston, M., Klentz, B. and Steblay, N.M. (1983), 'Fifteen Years of Foot-in-the-Door Research: A Meta Analysis', *Personality and Social Psychology Bulletin*, vol. 9, pp. 181–96

Beauvais, L.L., Leonard, N.H. and Scholl, R.W. (1999), 'Work Motivation: The Incorporation of Self-concept Based Processes', *Journal of Human Relations*, vol. 52, pp. 969–98

Bedoyere, de la Q., (1990), *How To Get Your Own Way in Business*, Aldershot: Gower

Beeman, D.R. and Sharkey, T.W. (1987), 'The Use and Abuse of Corporate Politics', *Business Horizons*, March–April

Beer, M., Spector, B., Lawrence, P.R., Mills, D.Q. and Walton, R.E. (1984), *Managing Human Assets*, New York, NY: Free Press

Bell, D.E. (1982), 'Regret in Decision-making Under Uncertainty', *Operations Research*, vol. 30, pp. 361–81

Bell, N. and Tetlock, P. (1989), 'The Intuitive Politician' in Giacalone, R.A. and Rosenfeld, P. (eds), *Impression Management in the Organization*, Hillsdale, NJ: Robert Erlbaum and Associates

Bem, D.J. (1972), 'Self-perception Theory', in Berkowitz, L. (ed.), *Advances in Social Psychology: Volume 6*, New York, NY: Academic Press

Benson, P.L., Karabenic, S.A. and Lerner, R.M. (1976), 'Pretty Pleases: The Effects of Physical Attractiveness on Race, Sex and Receiving Help', *Journal of Experimental Social Psychology*, vol. 12, pp. 409–15

Benton, A.A., Kelly, H.H. and Liebling, B. (1972), 'Effects of Extremity of Offers and Concession Rate on the Outcomes of Bargaining', *Journal of Personality and Social Psychology*, vol. 24, pp. 73–83

Berger, C.R. and Calabrese, R.J. (1975), 'Some Explorations in Initial Interaction and Beyond: Toward a Development Theory of Interpersonal Communication', *Human Communication Research*, vol. 1, pp. 99–112

Berlew, D.E. and Hall, D.T. (1966), 'The Socialization of Managers: Effects of Expectations and Performance', *Administrative Science Quarterly*, vol. 11, no. 2, pp. 207–23

Berscheid, E. and Walster, H.E. (1978), *Interpersonal Attraction*, Reading, MA: Addison Wesley

Bettinghaus, E.P. (1966), *Message Preparation: The Nature of Proof*, Indianapolis, IN: Bobbs-Merrill

Bickman, L. (1974), 'The Social Power of a Uniform', *Journal of Applied Social Psychology*, vol. 4, pp. 47–61

Blackburn, R.S. (1981), 'Lower Participant Power: Toward a Conceptual Integration', *Academy of Management Review*, vol. 6, no. 1, pp. 127–31

Blackman, M. (2002), 'The Employment Interview via the Telephone: Are We Sacrificing Accurate Personality Judgements for Cost Efficiency?' *Journal of Research in Personality*, vol. 36, no. 3, pp. 208–23

Boe, A. and Youngs, B.B. (1989), *Is Your 'Net' Working?*, New York, NY: Wiley

Bolino, M.C. and Turnley, W.H. (2003), 'More Than One Way to Make an Impression: Exploring Profiles of Impression Management', *Journal of Management*, vol. 29, no. 2, pp. 141–60

Bolman, L. and Deal, T. (1991), *Re-framing Organizations*, San Francisco, CA: Jossey Bass

Bolton, R.H. and Bolton, D.G. (1984), *Social Style/Management Style*, New York: AMACOM

Borgida, E. and Nisbett, R. (1977), 'The Differential Impact of Abstract vs. Concrete Information Decisions', *Journal of Applied Social Psychology*, vol. 7, pp. 258–71

Bowers, J.W. (1964), 'Some Correlates of Language Intensity', *Quarterly Journal of Speech*, vol. 50, pp. 415–20

Bowers, J.W. and Osborn, M.M. (1966), 'Attitudinal Effects of Selected Types of Concluding Metaphors in Persuasive Speech', *Speech Monographs*, vol. 33, pp. 147–55

Bozeman, D.P. and Kacmar, M.K. (1997), 'A Cybernetic Model of Impression Management Processes in Organizations', *Organizational Behaviour and Human Decision Processes*, vol. 69, no. 1, pp. 9–30

Bradac, J.J. and Mulac, A. (1984), 'A Molecular View of Powerful and Powerless Speech Styles: Attributional Consequences of Specific Language Features and Communicator Intentions', *Communication Monographs*, vol. 51, pp. 307–19

Brass, D.J. (1984), 'Being in the Right Place: A Structural Analysis of Individual Influence in Organizations', *Administrative Science Quarterly*, vol. 29, no. 4, pp. 518–39

Brass, D.J. (1985), 'Men's and Women's Networks: A Study of Interaction Patterns and Influence in an Organization', *Academy of Management Journal*, vol. 28, no. 2, pp. 327–43

Brehm, J. (1956) 'Post-decision Changes in the Desirability of Alternatives', *Journal of Abnormal and Social Psychology*, vol. 52, pp. 384–9

Brehm, J.W. (1966), *A Theory of Psychological Reactance*, New York, NY: Academic Press

Brehm, S.S. and Brehm, J.W. (1981), *Psychological Reactance*, New York, NY: Academic Press

Brembeck, W.L. and Howell, W.S. (1952), *Persuasion: A Means of Social Control*, New York, NY: Prentice Hall

Bretz, R.D., Rynes, S.L. and Gerhart, B. (1993), 'Recruiter Perceptions of Applicant Fit: Implications for Individual Career Preparation and Job Search Behaviour', *Journal of Vocational Behaviour*, vol. 43, no. 3, pp. 310–27

Brewer, M. (1979), 'In-group Bias in the Minimal Intergroup Situation: A Cognitive-Motivational Analysis', *Psychological Bulletin*, vol. 86, pp. 307–24

345

Briggs, S.R. and Cheek, J.M. (1988), 'On the Nature of Self-monitoring: Problems with Assessments, Problems with Validity', *Journal of Personality and Social Psychology*, vol. 54, pp. 663–78

Brigham, J.C. and Bothwell, R.K. (1983), 'The Ability of Prospective Jurors to Estimate the Accuracy of Eye Witness Identification', *Law and Human Behaviour*, vol. 7, pp. 19–30

Bright, J.E.H. and Hutton, S. (2000), 'The Impact of Competency Statements on Resumes for Short-listing Decisions', *International Journal of Selection and Assessment*, vol. 8, no. 2, pp. 41–53

Bringhurst, N.C. (2001), 'How Assessing Personality Type Can Benefit You and Your Practice', *Journal of Financial Planning*, vol. 14, no. 1, January, pp. 104–13

Brockner, J. Rubin, J. and Lang, E. (1981), 'Face-saving and Entrapment', *Journal of Experimental Social Psychology*, vol. 17, pp. 68–79

Brockner, J., Shaw, M. and Rubin, J. (1979) 'Factors Affecting Withdrawal from an Escalating Conflict; Quitting Before It's Too Late', *Journal of Experimental Social Psychology*, vol. 17, pp. 68–79

Brockner, J., Fine, J., Hamilton, T., Thomas, B. and Turetsky, B. (1982), 'Factors Affecting Entrapment in Escalating Conflicts: The Importance of Timing', *Journal of Research into Personality*, vol. 16, pp. 247–66

Brogida, E. and Nisbett, R.E. (1977), 'The Differential Impact of Abstract vs Concrete Information on Decisions', *Journal of Applied Social Psychology*, vol. 7, pp. 258–71

Brownstein, R. and Katzev, R. (1985), 'The Relative Effectiveness of Three Compliance Techniques in Eliciting Donations to a Cultural Organization', *Journal of Applied Social Psychology*, vol. 15, pp. 564–74

Bruce, B. (1992), *Images of Power*, London: Kogan Page

Bryce, L. (1991), *The Influential Manager*, London: Piatkus

Bryon, M. (2002), *How to Pass Advanced Numeracy Tests*, London: Kogan Page

Buchanan, D. and Badham, R. (1999), *Power, Politics and Organizational Change*, London: Sage

Buchanan, D. and Boddy, D. (1992), *The Expertise of the Change Agent*, New York, NY: Prentice Hall

Buchanan, D. and Huczynski, A. (2004), *Organizational Behaviour: An Introductory Text*, Harlow: Financial Times/Prentice Hall, 5th edn

Bucher, R. (1970), 'Social Process and Power in a Medical School' in Zald, M.N. (ed.), *Power in Organizations*, Nashville, TN: Vanderbilt University Press, pp. 3–48

Burgoon, M.B. and Burgoon, J.K. (1975), 'Message Strategies and Influence Attempts' in Hanneman, G.J. and McEwan, W.J. (eds), *Communication and Behaviour*, Reading, MA: Addison Wesley, pp. 149–65

Bushman, B.J. (1984), 'Perceived Symbols of Authority and Their Influence on Compliance,' *Journal of Applied Social Psychology*, vol. 14, pp. 501–8

Byrne, D. (1969), 'Attitudes and Attraction' in Berkowitz, L. (ed.), *Advances in Experimental Social Psychology: Volume 4*, New York, NY: Academic Press, pp. 35–90

Byrne, D. (1971), *The Attraction Paradigm*, New York, NY: Academic Press

Byrne, D., Rasche, L. and Kelley, K. (1974), 'When "I like you" Indicates Disagreement,' *Journal of Research in Personality*, vol. 8, pp. 207–17

Cable, D.M. and Judge, T.A. (2003), 'Managers' Upward Influence Tactic Strategies: The Role of Manager Personality and Supervisor Leadership Style', *Journal of Organizational Behaviour*, vol. 24, no. 2, pp. 197–214

Calano, J. and Salzman, J. (1988), *CareerTracking*, Aldershot: Wildwood House

Caldwell, D.F. and Burger, J.M. (1998), 'Personality Characteristics of Job Applicants and Success in Screening Interviews', *Personnel Psychology*, vol. 51, no. 1, pp. 119–36

Campbell, D.E. (1979), 'Interior Office Design and Visitor Response', *Journal of Applied Psychology*, vol. 64, pp. 648–53

Campbell, D.N., Fleming, R.L. and Grote, R.C. (1985), 'Discipline Without Punishment – At Last', *Harvard Business Review*, July–August, vol. 85, no. 4, pp. 162–4 and 168, 170, 174 and 176.

Campion, M.A. and Lord, R.G. (1982), 'A Control Systems Conceptualization of the Goalsetting and Changing Process', *Organizational Behaviour and Human Performance*, vol. 30, pp. 265–87

Cantor, J.R., Alfonso, H. and Zillman, D. (1976), 'The Persuasive Effectiveness of the Fear Appeal and a Communicator's First Hand Experience', *Communications Research*, vol. 3, pp. 93–310

Carbone, T. (1975), 'Stylistic Variables are Related to Source Credibility; A Content Analysis Approach', *Speech Monographs*, vol. 42, pp. 99–106

Carli, L.L. (1999), 'Gender, Interpersonal Power and Social Influence', *Journal of Social Issues*, vol. 55, no. 1, pp. 81–9

Carlson, R.E. (1971), 'Effect of the Interview in Altering Valid Impressions', *Journal of Applied Psychology*, vol. 55, pp. 66–72

Case, T., Dosier, L., Murkison, G. and Keys, B. (1988), 'How Managers Influence Superiors: A Study of Upward Influence Tactics', *Leadership and Organizational Development Journal*, vol. 9, no. 4, pp. 25–31

Cash, T. (1985), 'The Impact of Grooming Style on the Evaluations of Women in Management' in M.R. Solomon (ed.), *The Psychology of Fashion*, Lexington, MA: Heath, pp. 343–55

Chacko, T.I., Olsen, J.L. and Shrader, C.B. (1999), 'Skills and Characteristics Assessed by Recruiters During Campus Interviews and Their Relationship to the Interview Outcome', *International Journal of Management*, vol. 16, no. 2, pp. 207–14

Chaiken, S. (1979), 'Communicator Physical Attractiveness and Persuasion', *Journal of Personality and Social Psychology*, vol. 37, pp. 1387–97

Chaiken, S. (1987) 'The Heuristic Model of Persuasion' in Zanna, M.P., Olson, J.M., and Herman, C.P. (eds), *Social Influence: The Ontario Symposium: Vol. 5*, Hilldale, NJ: Erlbaum, pp. 3–39

Chaiken, S. and Eagly, A.H. (1983), 'Communication Modality as a Determinant of Persuasion: The Role of Communicator Salience,' *Journal of Personality and Social Psychology*, vol. 45, pp. 241–56

Chan, J.F. (1998), 'The Power of Persuasion', *Journal of Property Management*, vol. 63, pp. 76–8

Chaplin, W.F. and Phillips, J.B. (2000), 'Handshaking, Gender, Personality and First Impressions', *Journal of Personality and Social Psychology*, vol. 79, no. 1, pp. 110–17

Chapman, D.S. and Rowe, P.M. (2001), 'The Impact of Videoconference Technology, Interview Structure and Interviewer Gender on Interviewer Evaluations in the Employment Interview', *Journal of Occupational and Organizational Psychology*, vol. 74, no. 3, pp. 279–98

Chapman D.S. and Rowe P.M. (2002), 'The Influence of Videoconference Technology and Interview Structure on the Recruiting Function of the Employment Interview:

A Field Experiment', *International Journal of Selection and Assessment*, vol. 10, no. 3, pp. 185–97

Chapman, L.J. (1967), 'Illusionary Correlation in Observational Report', *Journal of Verbal Reasoning and Verbal Behaviour*, vol. 6, pp. 151–5

Chapman, L.J. and Chapman, J.P. (1967), 'Genesis of Popular but Erroneous Diagnostic Observations', *Journal of Abnormal Psychology*, vol. 72, pp. 193–206

Chatman, J.A., Bell, N.E. and Staw, B.M. (1986), 'The Managed Thought: The Role of Self-justification and Impression Management in Organizational Settings' in Sims, H.P. and Gioia, D.A. (eds), *The Thinking Organization*, San Francisco, CA: Jossey Bass, pp. 191–214

Chiu, R.K. and Babcock. R.D. (2002), 'The Relative Importance of Facial Attractiveness and Gender in Hong Kong Selection Decisions', *International Journal of Human Resource Management*, vol. 13, no. 1, pp. 141–55

Christie, R. and Geis, F.L. (1970), *Studies in Machiavellianism*, New York, NY: Academic Press

Church, A.H. and Waclawski, J. (1999), 'Influencing Behaviour and Managerial Effectiveness in Lateral Relations', *Human Resource Development Quarterly*, vol. 10, pp. 3–34

Cialdini, R.B. (2001a), *Influence: Science and Practice*, London: Allyn and Bacon, 4th edn

Cialdini, R.B. (2001b), 'The Science of Persuasion', *Scientific American*, vol. 284, no. 2, pp. 76–81

Cialdini, R.B. and Ascani, K. (1976), 'Test of a Concession Procedure for Inducing Verbal, Behavioural, and Further Compliance with a Request to Give Blood', *Journal of Applied Psychology*, vol. 61, pp. 295–300

Cialdini, R.B. and Goldstein, N.J. (2002), 'The Science and Practice of Persuasion', *Cornell Hotel and Restaurant Administration Quarterly*, vol. 43, no. 2, pp. 40–50

Cialdini, R.B. and Richardson, K.P. (1980), 'Two Indirect Tactics of Image Management: Basking and Blasting', *Journal of Personality and Social Psychology*, vol. 39, pp. 404–15

Cialdini, R.B, Cacioppo, J.T., Bassett, R. and Miller, J.A. (1978), 'Low-ball Procedure for Producing Compliance; Commitment Then Cost', *Journal of Personality and Social Psychology*, vol. 36, pp. 436–76.

Cialdini, R.B., Borden, R.J., Thorne, A., Walker, M.R., Freeman, M.R. and Sloan, L.R. (1976), 'Basking in Reflected Glory: Three Football Field Studies', *Journal of Personality and Social Psychology*, vol. 34, pp. 366–75

Cialdini, R.B., Vincent, J.E., Lewis, S.K., Catalan, J., Wheeler, D. and Darby, B.L. (1975), 'Reciprocal Concessions Procedure for Inducing Compliance: The Door-in-the-Face Technique', *Journal of Personality and Social Psychology*, vol. 31, pp. 206–15

Cianni, M. and Rombmerger, B. (1997), 'Life in the Corporation: A Multi-method Study of the Experiences of Male and Female Asian, Black Hispanic and White Employees', *Gender, Work and Organization*, vol. 4, no. 2, pp. 116–27

Clore, G.L. and Byrne, D. (1974), 'A Reinforcement Effect Model of Attraction' in Huston, T.L. (ed.), *Perspectives on Interpersonal Attraction*, New York, NY: Academic Press, pp. 143–70

Coates, C.H. and Pelligrin, R.J. (1957–8), 'Executives and Supervisors: Informal Factors in Differential Bureaucratic Promotion,' *Administrative Science Quarterly*, vol. 2, no. 2, pp. 200–15

Cockerill, T. (1989), 'The Kind of Competence for Rapid Change', *Personnel Management*, September, pp. 52–56

Cohen, A.R. (1957), 'Need for Cognition and Order of Communication as Determinants of Opinion Change' in Hovland, C.I. *et al.* (eds), *Order of Presentation in Persuasion*, New Haven, CT: Yale University Press, Chapter 6

Cohen, A.R. and Bradford, D.L. (1989), 'Influence Without Authority: The Use of Alliances Reciprocity and Exchange to Accomplish Work', *Organizational Dynamics*, vol. 17, no. 3, pp. 4–17

Cohen, A.R. and Bradford, D.L. (1991), *Influence Without Authority*, New York, NY: Wiley

Cohen, A.R., Stotland, E. and Wolfe, D.M. (1955), 'An Experimental Investigation of Need Cognition', *Journal of Abnormal and Social Psychology*, vol. 51, pp. 291–4

Condon, J.W. and Crano, W.D. (1988), 'Inferred Evaluation and the Relationship Between Attitude Similarity and Interpersonal Attraction', *Journal of Personality and Social Psychology*, vol. 54, pp. 789–97

Conger, J.A. (1998), 'The Necessary Art of Persuasion', *Harvard Business Review*, vol. 76, no. 3, pp. 84–95

Conger, J.A. and Kanungo, R.N. (1987), 'Toward a Behavioural Theory of Charismatic Leadership', *Academy of Management Review*, vol. 12, pp. 637–47

Conger, J.A. and Kanungo, R.N. and Menon, S.T. (2000), 'Charismatic Leadership and Follower Effects', *Journal of Organizational Behaviour*, vol. 21, no. 4, pp. 747–67

Conlon, E. and Wolf, G. (1980) 'The Moderating Effect of Strategy, Visibility and Involvement on Allocation Behaviour: An Extension of Staw's Escalation Paradigm', *Organizational Behaviour and Human Performance*, vol. 26, pp. 172–92

Constable, J. and McCormack, R., (1987), *The Making of British Managers*, London: BIM/CBI

Constantin, S. (1976), 'An Investigation of Information Favourability in the Employment Interview', *Journal of Applied Psychology*, vol. 61, pp. 743–9.

Conway, M. and Ross, M. (1984), 'Getting What You Want By Revising What You Had', *Journal of Personality and Social Psychology*, vol. 47, pp. 738–48

Cooper, J. and Jones, E.E. (1969), 'Opinion Divergence as a Strategy to Avoid Being Miscast', *Journal of Personality and Social Psychology*, vol. 13, pp. 23–30

Cope, F. and Richardson, D. (1972), 'The Effects of Reassuring Recommendations in a Fear Arousing Speech', *Speech Monographs*, vol. 39, pp. 148–50

Costa, P.T., Jr. and McCrae, R.R. (1992), *Revised NEO personality Inventory (NEO-PI-R) and NEO Five Factor (NEO-FF) Inventory Professional Manual*, Odessa, FL: PAR

Crawford, T.J. (1976), 'Theories of Attitude Change' in Seidenbrg, B. and Snadowsky, A. (eds), *Social Psychology*, New York, NY: Free Press

Curtis, R.C. and Miller, K. (1986), 'Believing Another Likes or Dislikes You: Behaviours Making the Beliefs Come True', *Journal of Personality and Social Psychology*, vol. 51, pp. 284–90

Daft, R.L. (1992), *Organization Theory and Design*, St Paul, MN: West Publishing Company, 4th edn

Dalton, F.M. (2000), 'The Eight Classic Types of Workplace Behaviour', *HR Magazine*, vol. 45, no. 9, pp. 165–75

Daubman, K.A. and Sigall, H. (1997), 'Gender Differences in Perceptions of How Others Are Affected by Self-disclosure of Achievement', *Sex Roles*, vol. 37, nos 1 and 2, pp. 73–89

349

Davies, P. (1991a), *Status: What It Is and How to Achieve It*, London: Piatkus

Davies, P. (1991b), *Personal Power*, London: Piatkus

Davies, W. (1988), *Climbing the Corporate Ladder*, London: Thorsons

Day, R. (1989), *The Grand Inquisitor*, London: Pan Books

Deal, T.E. and Kennedy, A.A. (1982), *Corporate Cultures*, Reading, MA: Addison Wesley

Deaux, K. (1972), 'To Err Is Humanizing; But Sex Makes A Difference', *Representative Research in Social Psychology*, vol. 16, pp. 259–64

De Groot, T. and Motowidlo, S.J. (1999), 'Why Visual and Vocal Cues Can Affect Interviewer's Judgement and Predict Job Performance', *Journal of Applied Psychology*, vol. 84, no. 6, pp. 986–93

Deutsch, M. and Gerard, H.B. (1955), 'A Study of Normative and Informational Social Influences Upon Individual Judgement', *Journal of Abnormal and Social Psychology*, vol. 51, pp. 629–36

Deville, J. (1979), *Nice Guys Finish First*, New York, NY: William Mottow and Company

Dillard, J.P., Hunter, J.E. and Burgoon, M. (1984), 'Sequential Request Persuasive Strategies: Meta-analysis of the Foot-in-the-Door and the Door-in-the-Face', *Human Communication Research*, vol. 10, pp. 461–88

Dion K., Berscheid, E. and Walster, H.E. (1972), 'What Is Beautiful Is Good', *Journal of Personality and Social Psychology*, vol. 24, pp. 285–90

Dipboye, R.L. and Wiley, J.W. (1977), 'Reactions of College Recruiters to Interview Sex and Self-presentation Style', *Journal of Vocational Behaviour*, vol. 10, pp. 1–12

Donkin, R. (2003), 'Being Yourself is a Question of Honesty', *Financial Times*, Appointments, 23 January, p. 10

Dossett, D.L. and Greenberg, C.I. (1981), 'Goal Setting and Performance Evaluation: An Attributional Analysis', *Academy of Management Journal*, vol. 24, no. 4, pp. 767–79

Dougherty, T.W. and Forret, M.L. (2001), 'Correlates of Networking Behaviour for Managerial and Professional Employees', *Journal of Group and Organizational Management*, vol. 26, no. 3, pp. 283–311

Downs, C.W. and Conrad, C. (1982), 'Effective Subordinacy', *Journal of Business Communication*, Spring, pp. 27–37

Drachman, D., deCarufel, A. and Insko, C.A. (1978), 'The Extra Credit Effect in Interpersonal Attraction', *Journal of Experimental Social Psychology*, vol. 14, pp. 458–67

Drummond, H. (1991a), *Power: Creating It, Using It*, London: Kogan Page

Drummond, H. (1991b), *Effective Decision Making: A Practical Guide*, London: Kogan Page

Drzdeck, S., Yeager, J. and Sommer, L. (1991), *What They Don't Teach You in Sales 101*, New York, NY: McGraw Hill

Dubois, B.L. and Crouch, I. (1975) 'The Question of Tag Questions in Women's Speech: They Don't Really Use More of Them Do They?', *Language and Society*, vol. 4, pp. 289–94

Dulebohn, J.H. and Ferris, G.R. (1999), 'The Role of Influence Tactics in Perceptions of Performance Evaluations' Fairness', *Academy of Management Journal*, vol. 42, no. 3, pp. 288–303

Dulewicz, V. (1989), 'Assessment Centres as a Route to Competence', *Personnel Management*, November, pp. 56–9

Dunning, D.D., Griffin, D.W., Milojkovic, J.H. and Ross, L. (1990), 'The Overconfidence Effect in Social Prediction', *Journal of Personality and Social Psychology*, vol. 58, no. 4, pp. 582–92

Eagly, A.H. and Chaiken, S. (1975), 'An Attribution Analysis of the Effect of Communicator Characteristics on Opinion Change: The Case of Communicator Attractiveness', *Journal of Personality and Social Psychology*, vol. 32, pp. 136–44

Eagly, A.H. and Chaiken, S. (1992), *The Psychology of Attitudes*, San Diego, CA: Harcourt Brace Jovanovich

Eagly, A.H., Wood, W. and Chaiken, S. (1978), 'Causal Inferences About Communicators and their Effect on Opinion Change', *Journal of Personality and Social Psychology*, vol. 36, pp. 424–35

Eagleson, G., Waldersee, R. and Simmons, R. (2000), 'Leadership Behaviour Similarity as a Basis of Selection into a Management Team', *British Journal of Social Psychology*, vol. 39, no. 2, pp. 301–8

Economist (1995–6), 'Short Guys Finish Last', 23 December–5 January, pp. 21, 22 and 26.

Economist (1999), 'Rethinking Thinking', 18 December, pp. 77–9

Economist (2002), 'Persuasion', 4 May, pp. 95–6

Economist (2003a), 'The Right to be Beautiful', 24 May, p. 9

Economist (2003b), 'Be a Man', 28 June, pp. 90–1

Einhorn, H.J. and Hogarth, R.M. (1978), 'Confidence in Judgement: Persistence in the Illusion of Validity', *Psychological Review*, vol. 85, pp. 395–416

Einhorn, H.J., and Hogarth, R.M. (1981), 'Behavioural Decision Theory: Processes of Judgement and Choice', *Annual Review of Psychology*, vol. 32, pp. 53–8

Ekman, P. and Friesen, W.V. (1974), 'Detecting Deception from the Body or Face', *Journal of Personality and Social Psychology*, vol. 29, pp. 288–98

Elsbach, K.D. and Elofson, G. (2000), 'How the Packaging of Decision Explanations Affects Perceptions of Trustworthiness', *Academy of Management Journal*, vol. 43, no. 1, pp. 80–90

Emerson, R.M. (1962), 'Power Dependent Relations', *American Sociological Review*, vol. 27, no. 1, pp. 31–41

Emswiller, T., Deaux, K. and Willits, J.E. (1971), 'Similarity, Sex and Requests for Small Favours', *Journal of Applied Social Psychology*, vol. 1, pp. 284–91

Evans, F.B., (1963), 'Selling as a Dyadic Relationship: A New Approach', *American Behavioural Scientist*, vol. 6, no. 9, pp. 76–9

Eysenck, H.J. (1960), *The Structure of Human Personality*, London: Methuen, 2nd edn

Falbo, T. (1977), 'Multi-dimensional Scaling of Power Strategies', *Journal of Personality and Social Psychology*, vol. 35, pp. 537–47

Farmer, S.M. and Maslyn, J.M. (1999), 'Why Are Styles of Upward Influence Neglected? Making the Case for a Configurational Approach to Influences', *Journal of Management*, vol. 25, no. 5, pp. 653–83

Farmer, S.M., Maslyn, J.M., Fedor, D.B. and Goodman, J.S. (1997), 'Putting Upward Influencing Strategies in Context', *Journal of Organizational Behaviour*, vol. 18, no. 1, pp. 17–42

Farrell, D. and Petersen, J.C. (1982), 'Patterns of Political Behaviour in Organizations', *Academy of Management Review*, vol. 7, no. 3, pp. 403–12

Feldman, D.C. (1985), 'The New Careerism: Origins, Tenets and Consequences', *Industrial-Organizational Psychologist*, vol. 22, pp. 39–44

351

Feldman, D.C. (1988), *Managing Careers in Organizations*, Glenview, IL: Scott, Foresman

Feldman, D.C. (1990), 'Risky Business: The Socialization of New Managers in the Twenty-First Century,' *Journal of Organizational Change Management*, vol. 3, no. 2, pp. 16–29

Feldman, D.C. and Klich, N.R. (1991), 'Impression Management and Career Strategies' in Giacalone, R.A. and Rosenfeld, P. (eds), *Applied Impression Management*, London: Sage, pp. 67–80

Feldman, M.S. and March, J.G. (1981), 'Information in Organizations as Signal and Symbol', *Administrative Science Quarterly*, vol. 26, no. 2, pp. 171–86

Feldstein, S., Dohm, F.A. and Crown, C.L. (2001), 'Gender and Speech Rate in the Perception of Competence and Social Attractiveness', *Journal of Social Psychology*, vol. 141, no. 6, pp. 785–806

Fenigstein, A., Scheier, M.F. and Buss, A.H. (1975), 'Public and Private Self-consciousness; Assessment and Theory', *Journal of Consulting and Clinical Psychology*, vol. 43, pp. 348–56

Fensterheim, H. and Baer, J. (1975), *Don't Say 'Yes', When You Want To Say 'No'*, London: Futura

Fern, E.F., Monroe, K.B. and Avila, R.A. (1986), 'Effectiveness of Multiple Request Strategies: A Synthesis of Research Results', *Journal of Marketing Research*, vol. 23, no. 2, pp. 144–52.

Ferris, G.R. and Porac, J.F. (1984), 'Goal Setting as Impression Management', *Journal of Psychology*, vol. 117, pp. 33–6

Ferris, G.R., Russ, G.S and Fandt, P.M. (1989), 'Politics in Organizations' in Giacalone, R.A. and Rosenfeld, (eds), *Impression Management in the Organization*, Hillsdale, NJ: Erlbaum, pp. 143–70

Ferris, G.R., King, T.R., Judge, T.A. and Kacmar, K.M. (1991), 'The Management of Shared Meaning in Organization' in Giacalone, R.A. and Rosenfeld, P. (eds), *Applied Impression Management*, London: Sage, pp. 41–64

Festinger, F.E., Schachter, S. and Back, K. (1950), *Social Pressures in Informal Groups: A Study of Human Factors In Housing*, New York, NY: Harper and Row

Festinger, L. (1954), 'A Theory of Social Comparison Processes', *Human Relations*, vol. 7, pp. 117–40, 232–56

Festinger, L. (1957), *A Theory of Cognitive Dissonance*, Stanford, CA: Stanford University Press

Fine, B. (1957), 'Conclusion-drawing, Communicator Credibility, and Anxiety as Factors in Opinion Change', *Journal of Abnormal and Social Psychology*, vol. 54, pp. 369–74

Fisher, D. (1993), *Communication in Organizations*, New York, NY: West, 2nd edn

Fisher, R. (1964), 'Fractioning Conflict' in Fisher, R. (ed.), *International Conflict and Behavioural Science, The Craigville Papers*, New York, NY: Basic Books

Fisher, R. and Ury, W.L. (1981), *Getting To Yes: Negotiating Agreements Without Giving In*, Boston, MA: Houghton Mifflin

Fishhoff, B. (1975a), 'Hindsight + Foresight: The Effect of Outcome Knowledge on Judgement Under Uncertainty', *Journal of Experimental Psychology: Human Perception and Performance*, vol. 1, pp. 288–99

Fishhoff, B. (1975b), 'Hindsight Thinking Backward', *Psychology Today*, vol. 8, pp. 71–6

Fishhoff, B. and Beyth, R. (1975), 'I Knew It Would Happen': Remembered Probabilities of Once-Future Things', *Organizational Behaviour and Human Performance*, vol. 13, pp. 1–16

Fishhoff, B., Slovic, P. and Lichtenstein, S. (1977), 'Knowing With Certainty: The Appropriateness of Extreme Confidence', *Journal of Experimental Psychology: Human Perception and Performance*, vol. 3, pp. 552–64

Fiske, S.T. and Taylor, S.E. (1991), *Social Cognition*, New York, NY: McGraw Hill

Fitzwater, T.L. (2001), *Preparing for the Behaviour-based Interview*, Crisp Learning, Baldock, Herts: Flex Learning Media

Fleishmann, S.T. (1991), 'The Message of Body Language in Interviews', *Employee Relations*, vol. 18, no. 2, pp. 161–6

Fletcher, C. (1979) 'Candidates' Beliefs and Self-presentation Strategies in Selection Interviews', *Personnel Review*, vol. 10, pp. 14–17

Fletcher, C. (1990) 'The Relationship Between Candidate Personality, Self-presentation Strategies and Interviewer Assessments in Selection Interviews: An Empirical Study', *Human Relations*, vol. 43, pp. 739–49

Fletcher, C. (1999), 'The Implication of Research on Gender Differences in Self-assessment and 360 Degree Appraisal', *Human Resource Management Journal*, vol. 9, no. 1, pp. 39–46

Fletcher, W. (2000), 'Let Your Body Do the Talking', *Management Today*, March

Floyd, K. (1999), To Match or Not to Match: Effects of Behavioural Congruence on Interpersonal Connectedness', *Journal of Social Psychology*, vol. 139, no. 3, pp. 309–22

Fombrun, C.J. (1983), 'Corporate Culture, Environment and Strategy', *Human Resource Management*, vol. 22, pp. 139–52

Forbes, R.J. and Jackson, P.R. (1980), 'Non-verbal Behaviour and the Outcome of Selection Interviews', *Journal of Occupational Psychology*, vol. 53, no. 1, pp. 65–72

Forsythe, S. (1987), 'Effect of Clothing on Perception of Masculine and Feminine Traits', *Perceptual and Motor Skills*, vol. 65, pp. 531–4

Forsythe, S.M., Drake, M.F. and Cox, C.E. (1984), 'Dress as an Influence on Perceptions of Management Characteristics in Women', *Home Economics Research Journal*, vol. 13, pp. 112–21

Forsythe, S.M., Drake, M.F. and Cox, C.E. (1985), 'Influence of Applicants' Dress on Interview Selection Decisions', *Journal of Applied Psychology*, vol. 70, no. 2, pp. 374–8

Fortune (1991), 16 December, p. 87

Fortune (2003), 'Field Guide to Power', vol. 148, no. 3, Europe edition, 11 April, pp. 62–3

Fox, J. (1999), *Influencing and Persuading Others*, Fox Performance Training, CT, www.foxperformance.com

Fox, S. and Spector, P.E. (2000), 'Relations of Emotional Intelligence, Practical Intelligence, General Intelligence and Trait Affectivity with Interview Outcomes: It's Not All Just "G"', *Journal of Organizational Behaviour*, vol. 21, no. 2, pp. 203–20

Frank, L.L. and Hackman, J.R. (1975), 'Effect of Interviewer–Interviewee Similarity on Interviewer Objectivity in College Admission Interviews', *Journal of Applied Psychology*, vol. 60, pp. 356–60

Franklin, J.L. (1975), 'Down the Organization: Influencing Processes Across Levels of Hierarchy', *Administrative Science Quarterly*, vol. 20, no. 2, pp. 153–64

Freedman, J.L. and Fraser, S.C. (1966), 'Compliance Without Pressure: The Foot in the Door Technique', *Journal of Personality and Social Psychology*, vol. 4, pp. 195–202

Freeman, L.C. (1979), 'Centrality in Social Networks: Conceptual Clarifications', *Social Networks*, vol. 1, pp. 215–39

French, J.P.R. and Raven, B.H. (1959), 'The Bases of Social Power' in Cartwright, D. (ed.), *Studies in Social Power*, Ann Arbor, MI: University of Michigan Press

Frieze, I.H., Olsen, J.E. and Russell, J. (1991), 'Attractiveness and Income for Men and Women in Management' *Journal of Applied Social Psychology*, vol. 21, pp. 1039–57

Frisch, D. (1993), 'Reasons for Framing Effects', *Organizational Behaviour and Human Decision Processes*, vol. 54, no. 3, pp. 399–429

Gabbott, M. and Hogg, G. (2000), 'An Empirical Investigation of the Impact of Non-verbal Communications on Service Evaluation', *European Journal of Marketing*, vol. 34, no. 3–4, pp. 384–99

Ganz, J. and Murray, V.V. (1980), 'The Experience of Workplace Politics', *Academy of Management Journal*, vol. 23, no. 2, pp. 237–51

Garber, M. (1992), *Vested Interests, Cross Dressing and Cultural Anxiety*, New York, NY: Routledge

Gardiner, J.W. (1990), *On Leadership*, New York, NY: Free Press

Gardner, W.L. and Martinko, M.J. (1988), 'Impression Management in Organizations', *Journal of Management*, vol. 14, no. 2, pp. 321–38

Gary, J.L. and Starke, F.A. (1984), *Organizational Behaviour: Concepts and Applications*, Columbus, OH: Merrill Publishing, 3rd edn

Gerard, H.B. (1963), 'Emotional Uncertainty and Social Comparison', *Journal of Abnormal Social Psychology*, vol. 66, pp. 568–92

Gerard, H.B. and Rabbie, J.M. (1961), 'Fear and Social Comparison', *Journal of Abnormal Social Psychology*, vol. 62, pp. 568–73

Giacalone, R.A. (1985), 'On Slipping When You Thought You Had Your Best Foot Forward: Self-promotion, Self-destruction and Entitlements', *Group and Organizational Studies*, vol. 10, pp. 61–80

Giacalone, R.A. and Pollard, H.G. (1987), 'The Efficacy of Accounts for a Breach of Confidentiality by Management', *Journal of Business Ethics*, vol. 6, pp. 393–7

Giacalone, R.A. and Rosenfeld, P. (1986), 'Self-presentation and Self-promotion in an Organizational Setting', *Journal of Social Psychology*, vol. 126, no. 3, pp. 321–6

Giacalone, R.A. and Rosenfeld, P. (1989), *Impression Management in the Organization*, Hillsdale, NJ: Erlbaum

Giacalone, R.A. and Rosenfeld, P. (eds) (1991), *Applied Impression Management*, London: Sage

Giblin, L. (1956), *How to Have Confidence and Power in Dealing with People*, Englewood Cliffs, NJ: Prentice Hall

Gifford, R., Ng, C.F. and Wilkinson, M. (1985), 'Non-verbal Cues in the Employment Interview: Links between Applicant Qualities and Interviewer Judgements', *Journal of Applied Psychology*, vol. 70, no. 4, pp. 729–36

Gill, D. (1980), 'How British Industry Selects Its Managers', *Personnel Management*, September, pp. 49–52

Gilmore, D.C. and Ferris, G.R. (1989a), 'The Effects of Applicant Impression Management Tactics on Interviewer Judgements', *Journal of Management*, vol. 15, no. 4, pp. 557–64

Gilmore, D.C. and Ferris, G.R. (1989b), 'The Politics of the Employment Interview' in Eder, R.W. and Ferris, G.R. (eds), *The Employment Interview: Theory, Research and Practice*, London: Sage, pp. 195–203

Gilovich, T. (ed.) (2002), *Heuristics and Biases*, New York, NY: Cambridge University Press

Gioia, D.A. and Sims, H.P. (1985), 'Self-serving Bias and Actor–Observer Differences in Organizations', *Journal of Applied Social Psychology*, vol. 15, pp. 547–63

Girandola, F. (2002), 'Sequential Requests and Organ Donation', *Journal of Social Psychology*, vol. 142, no. 2, pp. 171–8

Glaser, C.B. and Smalley, B.S. (1992), *More Power to You: How Women Can Communicate Their Way to Success*, New York, NY: Time/Warner

Glaser, R. (1990), *Are You Aggressive, Assertive or Passive: Interpersonal Influence Inventory: Trainer Guide*, King of Prussia, PA: Organizational Design and Development, Inc.

Glaser, R. and Chi, M.T.H. (1988), 'Overview' in Micheline, T., Chi, M., Glaser, R. and Farr, M.J. (eds), *The Nature of Expertise*, Hillsdale, NJ: Erlbaum, pp. xv–xxviii

Glass, L. (1991), *Confident Conversation*, London: Piatkus

Goethals, G.R. and Reckman, R.F. (1973), 'The Perception of Consistency in Attitudes', *Journal of Experimental and Social Psychology*, vol. 9, pp. 491–501

Goffman, E. (1959), *The Presentation of Self in Everyday Life*, Harmondsworth: Penguin

Goffman, E. (1971), *Relations in Public*, New York, NY: Basic Books

Goldman, M. (1986), 'Compliance Employing a Combined Foot-in-the-Door and Door-in-the-Face Procedure', *Journal of Social Psychology*, vol. 126, no. 1, pp. 111–16

Goleman, D. (2000), 'Durch flexibles Fuhren mehr erreichen', *Harvard Business Manager*, vol. 22, pp. 9–22

Golightly, C., Huffman, D.M. and Byrne, D. (1972), 'Liking and Loaning', *Journal of Applied Psychology*, vol. 56, pp. 521–3

Gonzales, M.H., Davis, J.M., Loney, G.L., Lukens, C.K. and Junghans, C.M. (1983), 'Interactional Approach to Interpersonal Attraction', *Journal of Personality and Social Psychology*, vol. 44, pp. 1192–7

Gould, S. and Penley, L.E. (1984), 'Career Strategies and Salary Progression: A Study of Their Relationships in a Municipal Bureaucracy', *Organizational Behaviour and Human Performance*, vol. 34, pp. 244–65

Gouldner, A.W. (1960), 'The Norm of Reciprocity: A Preliminary Statement', *American Sociological Review*, vol. 25, no. 2, pp. 161–78.

Granberg, D. and King, M. (1980), 'Cross-lagged Panel Analysis of the Relation Between Attraction and Perceived Similarity', *Journal of Personality and Social Psychology*, vol. 16, pp. 573–81

Granovetter, M.S. (1974), *Getting a Job: A Study of Contacts and Careers*, Cambridge, MA: Harvard University Press

Gravenhorst, K.M.B. and Boonstra, J.J. (1998), 'The Use of Influence Tactics in Constructive Change Processes', *European Journal of Work and Organizational Psychology*, vol. 7, no. 2, pp. 179–96

Gray, J. (1982), *The Winning Image*, New York, NY: AMACOM

Gray, J. (2002), *How to Get What You Want in the Workplace*, London: Random House

Gray, J. and Starke, F.A. (1984), *Organizational Behaviour: Concepts and Applications*, Columbus, OH: Merrill Publishing

Greatbatch, D. and Clark, T. (2002), 'Laughing With Gurus', *Business Strategy Review*, vol. 13, no. 3, pp. 10–18

Greenberg, B.S. and Miller, G.R. (1966), 'The Effect of Low Credibility Sources on Message Acceptance', *Speech Monographs*, vol. 33, pp. 135–6

Greenberg, J.S. and Shapiro, S.P. (1971), 'Indebtedness: An Adverse Effect of Asking for and Receiving Help', *Sociometry*, vol. 34, pp. 290–301

Greenburg, J. (1990), 'Looking Fair Versus Being Fair: Managing Impressions of Organizational Justice' in Staw, B.M. and Cummings, L.L. (eds), *Research in Organizational Behaviour*, vol. 12, Greenwich, CT: JAI Press, pp. 111–57

Griffin, J. (1998), *How to Say It at Work*, Upper Saddle River, NJ: Prentice Hall

Grush, J.E. (1980), 'Impact of Candidate Expenditures, Regionality and Prior Outcomes on the 1976 Democratic Presidential Primacies', *Journal of Personality and Social Psychology*, vol. 38. pp. 337–47

Guy, A. and Banim, M. (2000), 'Personal Collections: Women's Clothing Use and Identity', *Journal of Gender Studies*, vol. 9, no. 3, pp. 313–27

Hakel, D. and Schuh, A.J. (1971), 'Job Applicant Attributes Judged Most Important Across Seven Diverse Occupations', *Personnel Psychology*, vol. 24, pp. 45–52

Hamermesh, D.S. and Biddle, J.E. (1994), 'Beauty and the Labour Market', *American Economic Review*, vol. 84, no. 5, pp. 1174–94

Hamid, P.N. (1972), 'Some Effects of Dress Cues on Observational Accuracy, Perceptual Estimate and Impression Formation', *Journal of Social Psychology*, vol. 86, pp. 279–86

Hamill, R., Wilson, T.D. and Nisbett, R.E. (1980), 'Insensitivity to Sample Bias: Generalizing from Atypical Cases', *Journal of Personality and Social Psychology*, vol. 39, pp. 578–89

Hamilton, D.L. and Zanna, M.P. (1972), 'Differential Weighting of Favourable and Unfavourable Attributes in Impression Formation', *Journal of Experimental Research in Personality*, vol. 6, pp. 204–12

Hamilton, V.L. (1978), 'Who Is Responsible: Towards a Psychology of Responsibility Attribution', *Social Psychology*, vol. 41, pp. 316–28

Hamilton, V.L. (1980), 'Intuitive Psychologist or Intuitive Lawyer?, Alternative Models of the Attribution Process', *Journal of Personality and Social Psychology*, vol. 39, pp. 767–72

Hamilton, V.L. and Rose, T.L. (1980), 'Illusory Correlation and the Maintenance of Stereotypical Beliefs', *Journal of Personality and Social Psychology*, vol. 39, pp. 832–45

Hamlin, S. (1993), *How To Talk So That Others Will Listen*, London: Harper

Harper, B. (2000), 'Beauty, Stature and the Labour market: A British Cohort Study', *Oxford Bulletin of Economics and Statistics*, vol. 62, no. 5, pp. 771–800

Haskins, J. (1964), 'Factual Recall as a Measure of Advertising Effectiveness', *Journal of Advertising Research*, vol. 4, no. 1, pp. 2–8

Hater, S. and Bass, B. (1988), 'Superiors' Evaluations and Subordinates' Perceptions of Transformational and Transactional Leadership', *Journal of Applied Psychology*, vol. 73, pp. 695–702

Heider, F. (1944), 'Social Perception and Phenomenal Causality', *Psychological Review*, vol. 51, pp. 358–84

Heider, F. (1946), 'Attitudes and Cognitive Organizations', *Journal of Psychology*, vol. 21, pp. 107–12

Heider, F. (1958), *The Psychology of Interpersonal Relations*, New York, NY: Wiley

Heilman, M.E. and Saruwatri, L.R. (1979), 'When Beauty is Beastly: The Effects of Appearance and Sex on Evaluations of Job Applicants for Managerial and Non-managerial Jobs', *Organizational Behaviour and Human Performance*, vol. 23, pp. 360–72

Heilman, M.E. and Stopeck, M.H. (1985a), 'Being Attractive: Advantage or Disadvantage? Performance Based Evaluations and Recommended Personal Actions as a Function of Appearance, Sex and Job Type', *Organizational Behaviour and Human Performance*, vol. 35, pp. 202–15

Heilman, M.E. and Stopeck, M.H. (1985b), 'Attractiveness and Corporate Success: Different Causal Attributions for Males and Females', *Journal of Applied Psychology,* vol. 70, no. 2, pp. 379–88

Heriot, P. and Wingrove, J. (1984), 'Decision Processes in Graduate Pre-selection', *Journal of Occupational Psychology*, vol. 57, no. 4, pp. 269–75

Higgins, C.A., Judge, T.A. and Ferris, G.R. (2003), 'Influence Tactics and Work Outcomes: A Meta Analysis', *Journal of Organizational Behaviour*, vol. 24, no. 1, pp. 89–106

Higgins, R.L. and Snyder, C.R. (1989), 'The Business of Excuses' in Giacalone, R.A. and Rosenfeld, P. (eds), *Impression Management in the Organization*, Hillsdale, NJ: Erlbaum, pp. 73–85

Hinkin, T.R. and Schriesheim, C.A. (1988), 'Power and Influence: The View From Below', *Personnel*, May, pp. 47–50

Hocking, J., Baucher, J., Kaminski, E. and Miller, G. (1979), 'Detecting Deceptive Communication from Verbal, Visual and Paralinguistic Cues', *Human Communication Research*, vol. 6, pp. 33–46

Hodgetts, R.M. and Gibson, J.W. (1991), 'The Audience Analysis Grid' in Hodgetts, R.M. *Organizational Behaviour: Theory and Practice*, New York, NY: Macmillan, pp. 404–5

Hodgson, P. and Hodgson, J. (1992), *Effective Meetings*, London: Century

Holbeche, L. and McCartney, C. (2002), *Management Agenda 2002*, Fifth Annual Report, Horsham: Roffey Park Management Institute

Homans, G.C. (1961), *Social Behaviour: Its Elementary Forms*, New York, NY: Harcourt Brace and World Company

Hornstein, H.A., Fisch, E. and Holmes, M. (1968), 'Influence of a Model's Feeling About His Behaviour and His Relevance as a Comparison Other on Observers' Helping Behaviour', *Journal of Personality and Social Psychology*, vol. 10, pp. 222–6

Hosman, L.S. (1989), 'The Evaluative Consequences of Hedges, Hesitations and Inten-sifiers: Powerful and Powerless Speech Styles', *Human Communication Research*, vol. 15, pp. 383–406

Hovland, C. and Weiss, W. (1951), 'The Influence of Source Credibility on Communication Effectiveness', *Public Opinion Quarterly*, vol. 15, pp. 635–50

Hovland, C.I. *et al.* (1957), *Order of Presentation in Persuasion*, New Haven, CT: Yale University Press, pp. 129–57

Hovland, C.I. and Mandell, W. (1952), 'An Experimental Comparison of Conclusion-drawing by the Communicator and by the Audience', *Journal of Abnormal and Social Psychology*, vol. 47, pp. 581–8

Hovland, C.I., Campbell, E.H. and Brock, T. (1957), 'The Effects of "Commitment" on Opinion Change Following Communication' in Hovland, C.I. *et al.* (eds), *Order of Presentation in Persuasion*, New Haven, CT: Yale University Press, Chapter 3

357

Hovland, C.I., Janis, I.L. and Kelly, H.H. (1953), *Communication and Persuasion: Psychological Studies of Opinion Change*, New Haven, CT: Yale University Press

Huber, V., Podsakoff, P.M. and Todor, W.A. (1985), 'A Dimensional Analysis of Supervisor and Subordinate Attributions of Success and Failure', *Journal of Occupational Behaviour*, vol. 6, pp. 131–42

Huber, V., Podsakoff, P.M. and Todor, W.A. (1988), 'An Investigation of Biasing Factors in the Attributions of Subordinates and Their Superiors', *Journal of Business Research*, vol. 14, no. 1, pp. 83–97

Huberman, J. (1964), 'Discipline Without Punishment', *Harvard Business Review*, vol. 42, no. 4, pp. 62–8

Hunsaker, D. and Alessandra, A. (1980), *The Art of Managing People*, Englewood Cliffs, NJ: Prentice Hall

Ibarra, H. (1999), 'Provisional Selves: Experimenting with Image and Identity in Professional Adaptation', *Administrative Science Quarterly*, vol. 44, no. 4, pp. 764–91

Iedema, J. and Poppe, M. (1996), 'The Effect of Self-presentation on Social Value Orientation', *Journal of Psychology*, vol. 134, no. 6, pp. 771–82

Ikle, F.C. (1964), *How Nations Negotiate*, New York, NY: Harper and Row

Imada, A.S. and Hakel, M.D. (1977) 'Influence of Non-verbal Communication and Rater Proximity on Impressions and Decisions in Simulated Employment Interviews', *Journal of Applied Psychology*, vol. 62, pp. 295–300

IRS Employment Trends (2000), *Dressed to Impress*, Report Number 695, pp. 4–6

Jackson, L.A. (1983), 'The Influence of Sex, Physical Attractiveness, Sex Role and Occupational-Sex Linkage in Perceptions of Occupational Suitability', *Journal of Applied Social Psychology*, vol. 13, pp. 33–44

Jacob, C., (2001), 'Fundraising on the Web: The Effect of an Electronic Foot-in-the-Door on Donation', *Cyber Psychology and Behaviour*, vol. 14, no. 6, pp. 705–9

Jecker, J. and Landy, D. (1969), 'Liking a Person as a Function of Doing Him a Favour', *Human Relations*, vol. 22, pp. 371–8

Jennings, H.H. (1959), *Leadership and Isolation*, New York, NY: Longman Green, 2nd edn

Jones, E.E. (1964), *Ingratiation*, New York, NY: Appleton-Century-Crofts

Jones, E.E. and Harris, V.E. (1967), 'The Attribution of Attitudes', *Journal of Experimental and Social Psychology*, vol. 3, pp. 1–24

Jones, E.E. and Pittman, T.S. (1982), *Toward a General Theory of Strategic Self-Presentation*, Hillside, NJ: Erlbaum

Jones, E.E. and Wortman, C. (1973), *Ingratiation: An Attributional Approach*, Morristown, NJ: General Learning Corporation

Jones, E.E., Gergan, K.J. and Jones, R.G. (1963), 'Tactics of Ingratiation Among Leaders and Subordinates in a Status Hierarchy', *Psychological Monographs*, vol. 7, no. 3, pp. 1–20

Jones, E.E., Rock, L., Goethals, G.R. Shaver, K.G. and Ward, L.M. (1968), 'Patterns of Performance and Ability Attribution: An Unexpected Primacy Effect', *Journal of Personality and Social Psychology*, vol. 9, pp. 317–40

Jung, C.G. (1924), *Psychological Types*, New York, NY: Harcourt Brace and Company

Kahneman, D. and Tversky, A. (1972), 'Subjective Probability: A Judgement of Representativeness', *Cognitive Psychology*, vol. 3, pp. 430–54

Kahneman, D. and Tversky, A. (1973), 'On the Psychology of Prediction', *Psychological Review*, vol. 80, pp. 237–51

Kahneman, D. and Tversky, A. (1979), 'Prospect Theory: An Analysis of Decision under Risk', *Econometrica*, vol. 47, no. 2, pp. 263–92

Kahneman, D. and Tversky, A. (1984), 'Choices, Values and Frames', *American Psychologist*, vol. 39, no. 4, pp. 341–50

Kahneman, D. and Tversky, A. (2000), *Choices, Values and Frames*, Cambridge: Cambridge University Press

Kaiser, S. (1985), *The Social Psychology of Clothing and Personal Adornment*, New York, NY: Macmillan

Kakabadse, A. (1983), *The Politics of Management*, Aldershot: Gower

Kanter, R.M. (1968) 'Commitment and Social Organization: A Study of Commitment Mechanisms in Utopian Communities', *American Sociological Review*, vol. 33, no. 4, pp. 499–517

Kanter, R.M. (1977), *Men and Women of the Organization*, New York, NY: Basic Books

Kanter, R.M. (1979), 'Power Failure in Management Circuits', *Harvard Business Review*, vol. 57, no. 4, pp. 65–75

Kanter, R.M. (1983), *The Change Masters*, London: Routledge

Kaplan, R. (1984), 'Trade Routes: The Manager's Network of Relationships', *Organizational Dynamics*, vol. 12, no. 4, pp. 37–52

Katzev, R. and Johnson, T. (1984), 'Comparing the Effects of Monetary Incentives and Foot-in-the Door Strategies in Promoting Residential Electricity Conservation', *Journal of Applied Psychology*, vol. 14, pp. 12–27

Keenan, T. (1997), 'Selection for Potential: The Case of Graduate Recruitment' in Anderson, N. and Herriot, P. (eds.), *International Handbook of Selection and Assessment*, Chichester: Wiley

Kellerman, K. (1984), 'The Negativity Effect and Its Implication for Initial Interaction', *Communication Monographs*, vol. 51, pp. 37–55

Kellerman, K. (1989), 'The Negativity Effect in Interaction: It's All in Your Point of View', *Human Communication Research*, vol. 16, pp. 147–83;

Kennedy, C.W. and Camden, C. (1983), 'Interruptions and Non-verbal Gender Differences', *Journal of Non-Verbal Behaviour*, vol. 8, pp. 91–108

Kenrick, D.T. and Gutierres, S.E. (1980), 'Contrast Effects in Judgements of Attractiveness: When Beauty Becomes a Social Problem', *Journal of Personality and Social Psychology*, vol. 38, pp. 131–40

Kiesler, C.A. and Pallak, M.S. (1975), 'Minority Influence: The Effect of Majority Reactions and Defectors, and Minority and Majority Compromises, upon Majority Opinion and Attraction', *European Journal of Social Psychology*, vol. 5, pp. 237–56

Kimble, P.A. and Damhorst, M.L. (1997), 'A Grounded Theory Model of the Ideal Business Image for Women', *Symbolic Interaction*, vol. 20, pp. 45–68

King, K. (2002), 'The Art of Impression Management', *The Social Science Journal*, vol. 39, no. 1, pp. 31–42

Kipnis, D., Schmidt, S.M. and Wilkinson, I. (1980), 'Intra-organizational Influence Tactics: Explorations in Getting One's Way', *Journal of Applied Psychology*, vol. 65, pp. 440–52

Kipnis, D., Schmidt, S.M., Swaffin-Smith, C. and Wilkinson, I. (1984), 'Patterns of Managerial Influence: Shotgun Managers, Tacticians and Bystanders', *Organizational Dynamics*, vol. 12, no. 3, pp. 58–67

Klayman, J. and Ha, Y.W. (1987), 'Confirmation, Disconfirmation and Information in Hypothesis Testing', *Psychological Review*, vol. 94, pp. 211–28

Klein, M. (1988), *BEST Behavioral Profile*, King of Prussia, PA: Organization, Design and Development

Knights, D. and Raffo, C. (1990) 'Milkround Professionalism in Personnel Recruitment: Myth or Reality?', *Personnel Review*, vol. 19, pp. 28–37

Knouse, S.B. (1983), 'The Letter of Recommendation: Specificity and Favourability of Information', *Personnel Psychology*, vol. 36, pp. 331–41

Knouse, S.B. (1989),'Impression Management and the Letter of Recommendation' in Giacalone, R.A. and Rosenfeld, P. (eds), *Impression Management in the Organization*, Hillsdale, NJ: Erlbaum, pp. 283–96

Koehler, J.D. (1991), 'Explanation, Imagination and Confidence in Judgement, *Psychological Bulletin*, vol. 110, pp. 499–519

Koester, J. (1982), 'The Machiavellian Princess: Rhetorical Dramas for Women', *Communication Quarterly*, vol. 3, pp. 165–72

Korda, M. (1976), *Power*, New York, NY: Ballantine Books

Kotter, J.P. (1979), *Power in Management: How To Understand, Acquire and Use It*, New York, NY: AMACOM

Kotter, J.P. (1985a), *Power and Influence*, New York, NY: Free Press

Kotter, J.P. (1985b), 'How To Win Friends and Influence Co-managers', *Canadian Business*, October, pp. 29–30 and 100–7

Kowalski, R.M. (2002), 'Whining, Griping and Complaining: Positivity in the Negativity', *Journal of Clinical Psychology*, vol. 58, no. 9, pp. 1003–22

Kozubska, J. (1997), *The 7 Keys of Charisma – Unlocking the Secrets of Those Who Have It*, London: Kogan Page

Kram, K.E. (1983), 'Phases of the Mentor Relationship', *Academy of Management Journal*, vol. 26, no. 4, pp. 608–25

Kramer, F.A. (1975), 'Policy Analysis As Ideology', *Public Administration Review*, vol. 35, pp. 509–17

Kramer, R.M and Neale, M.A. (eds). (1998), *Power and Influence in Organizations*, London: Sage

Kraut, R.E. (1973), 'Effects of Social Labelling on Giving to Charity', *Journal of Experimental and Social Psychology*, vol. 9, pp. 551–62

Kristof-Brown, A., Barrick, M.R. and Franke, E. (2002), 'Applicant Impression Management: Dispositional Influences and Consequences for Recruiter Perceptions of Fit and Similarity', *Journal of Management*, vol. 28, no. 1, pp. 27–46

Kroeck, K.G. and Magnusen, K.O. (1997), 'Employer and Job Candidate Reactions to Videoconference Job Interviewing', *International Journal of Selection and Assessment*, vol. 5, no. 2, pp. 137–42

Kulka, R.A. and Kessler, J.R. (1978), 'Is Justice Really Blind?: The Effect of Litigant Physical Attractiveness on Judicial Judgement', *Journal of Applied Social Psychology*, vol. 8, no. 4, pp. 336–81

Kushner. M. (1999), *Successful Presentations for Dummies*, Foster City, CA: IDG Books

Lakoff, R. (1975), *Language and Woman's Place*, New York, NY: Harper

Lambert, T. (1996), *The Power of Influence*, London: Nicholas Brealey Publishing

Langer, E., Blank, A. and Chanowitz, B. (1978), 'The Mindlessness Ostensibly Thoughtless Action: The Role of "Placebic" Information in Interpersonal Reaction', *Journal of Personality and Social Psychology*, vol. 36, pp. 636–42

Langer, E.J. (1975), 'The Illusion of Control', *Journal of Personality and Social Psychology*, vol. 32, pp. 311–28

Lasch, C. (1979), *The Culture of Narcissism*, New York, NY: Warner

Leary, M.R. and Kowalski, R.M. (1990), 'Impression Management: A Literature Review and Two Component Model', *Psychological Bulletin*, vol. 107, pp. 34–47

Leary, M.R., Robertson, R.B., Barnes, B.D. and Miller, R.S. (1986), 'Self-presentations of Small Group Leaders: Effects of Role Requirements and Leadership Orientation', *Journal of Personality and Social Psychology*, vol. 51, no. 4, pp. 742–46

Leavitt, H.J. (1954), 'A Note on Some Experimental Findings about the Meaning of Price', *Journal of Business*, vol. 27, no. 3, pp. 205–10

Lefton, R. (1977), *Effective Motivation Through Performance Appraisal*, New York, NY: Wiley

Lennox, R.D. and Wolfe, R.N. (1984), 'Revision of the Self-Monitoring Scale', *Journal of Personality and Social Psychology*, vol. 46, pp. 1349–64

Lerner, M.J. (1977), 'The Justice Motive', *Journal of Personality*, vol. 45, pp. 1–52

Lerner, M. and Simmons, C. (1966), 'Observers' Reactions to the "Innocent Victim": Compassion or Rejection?', *Journal of Personality and Social Psychology*, vol. 4, pp. 203–10

Leventhal, H. (1970), 'Findings and Theory in the Study of Fear Communications' in Berkowicz, L. (ed.), *Advances in Experimental Social Psychology: Volume 5*, New York, NY: Academic Press, pp. 119–86

Leventhal, H., Watts, J.C. and Pagano, F. (1967), 'Effects of Fear and Instructions on How to Cope with Danger', *Journal of Personality and Social Psychology*, vol. 6, pp. 313–21

Levine, J.M. (1989), 'Reaction to Opinion Deviance in Small Groups' in Paulus, P.B. (ed.), *The Psychology of Group Influence*, Hillsdale, NJ: Erlbaum, 2nd edn, pp. 187–231

Lewicki, R.J. and Litterer, J.A. (1985), *Negotiation*, Homewood, IL: Irwin

Lewis, D. (1991), *The Secret Language of Success*, London: Corgi

Lewis, J. (2001), 'Power Struggles', *Personnel Today*, 30 January, pp. 20–1

Liden, R.C. and Mitchell, T.R. (1988), 'Ingratiatory Behaviours in Organizational Settings', *Academy of Management Review*, vol. 13, no. 4, pp. 572–87

Lievens, F., De Fruyt, F. and Van Dam, K. (2001), 'Assessors' Use of Personality Traits in Descriptions of Assessment Centre Candidates: A Five Factor Model Perspective', *Journal of Occupational and Organizational Psychology*, vol. 74, no. 5, pp. 623–36

Lindenfield, G. (1986), *Assert Yourself*, Ilkley: Self-Help Associates

Lippitt, M. (1999), 'How to Influence Leaders', *Training and Development*, vol. 53, no. 3, pp. 18–22

Loewenstein, G. (1987), 'Anticipation and the Valuation of Delayed Consumption', *Economic Journal*, vol. 97, no. 387, pp. 666–84

Lord, R.L. (2002), 'Traditional Motivation Theories and Older Engineers', *Engineering Management Journal*, vol. 14, no. 3, pp. 3–8

Lott, B (1992), 'The Devaluation of Women's Competence' in Bohan, J.S. (ed.), *Seldom Seen, Rarely Heard, Women's Place in Psychology*, Boulder, CO: Westview Press, Chapter 6

Luchins, A.S. (1957a), 'Experimental Attempts to Minimize the Impact of First Impressions' in Hovland, O. (ed.), *The Order of Presentation in Persuasion*, New Haven, CT: Yale University Press

Luchins, A.S. (1957b), 'Primacy–Recency in Impression Formation' in Hovland, C.I. et al. (eds), *Order of Presentation in Persuasion*, New Haven, CT: Yale University Press, Chapter 4.

Luhmann, N. (1980), *Trust and Power*, New York, NY: Wiley

Lukes, S. (1974), *Power: A Radical View*, London: Macmillan

Lund, F.H. (1925), 'The Psychology of Belief', *Journal of Abnormal and Social Psychology*, vol. 20, pp. 183–91

Luthans, F. and Martinko, M. (1987), 'Behavioural Approaches in Organizations' in Cooper, C.L. and Robertson, I.T. (eds.), *International Review of Industrial and Organizational Psychology*, Chichester: Wiley, pp. 35–60

Luthans, F., Hodgetts, R.M. and Rosenkrantz, S.A. (1988), *Real Managers*, London: Macmillan

Maass, A. and Clark, R.D., III (1986), 'Hidden Impact of Minorities: Fifteen Years of Minority Influence Research', *Psychological Bulletin*, vol. 95, pp. 428–50

McCroskey, J.C. and Mehrley, R.S. (1969), 'The Effects of Disorganization and Non-fluency on Attitudinal Change and Source Credibility', *Speech Monographs*, vol. 36, pp. 13–21

McCroskey, J.C., Jensen, T. and Valencia, C. (1980), 'Measurement of the Credibility of Mass Media Sources' in Rolf, M.E. and Miller, G.R. (eds), *Persuasion: New Directions in Theory and Research*, Beverley Hills, CA: Sage

McCroskey, J.C., Young, T.J. and Scott, M.D. (1972), 'The Effects of Message Sidedness and Evidence in Inoculation Against Counter Persuasion in Small Group Communication', *Speech Monographs*, vol. 39, pp. 205–12

McDonald, M.J. and Keys, J.B. (1993), 'Developing the Influential Manager: Experiences with Deans of Business Schools', *Journal of Management Development*, vol. 12, no. 1, pp. 13–19

McFarland, L.A., Ryan, A.M. and Kriska, S.D. (2002), 'Field Study Investigation of Applicant Use of Influence Tactics in a Selection Interview', *Journal of Psychology*, vol. 136, no. 4, pp. 383–98

McGovern, T. and Ideus, H. (1978), 'The Impact of Non-verbal Behaviour on the Employment Interview', *Journal of College Placement*, Spring, pp. 51–3

McGovern, T.V. and Tinsley, H.E. (1978), 'Interviewer Evaluations of Interviewees' Non-verbal Behaviour', *Journal of Vocational Behaviour*, vol. 13, pp. 163–71

McGovern, T.V., Jones, B.W., Warwick, C.L. and Jackson, R.W. (1981), 'A Comparison of Job Interviewee Behaviour on Four Channels of Communication', *Journal of Counselling Psychology*, vol. 28, pp. 369–72

McGuire, W.J. (1957), 'Order of Presentation as a Factor in "Conditioning" Persuasiveness' in Hovland, C.I. *et al.* (eds), *Order of Presentation in Persuasion*, New Haven, CT: Yale University Press, Chapter 7

McGuire, W.J. (1964), 'Inducing Resistance to Persuasion: Some Contemporary Approaches' in Berkowitz, L. (ed.), *Advances in Experimental Social Psychology 1*, New York, NY: Academic Press

McGuire, W.J. (1968), 'Personality and Susceptibility to Social Influence' in Burgather, E.F. and Lambert, W.W., *Handbook of Personality Theory and Research*, Chicago, IL: Rand McNally, pp. 1130–87

Manis, M., Cornell, S.D. and Moore, J.C. (1974), 'Transmission of Attitude Relevant Information Through a Communication Chain', *Journal of Personality and Social Psychology*, vol. 30, pp. 81–94

Mann, S. (1995), 'Power and Politics in Organizations: Why Do Women Lose Out?', *Leadership and Organization Development Journal*, vol. 16, no. 2, pp. 9–16

Markiewicz, D., Devine, I. and Kausilas, D. (2000), 'Friendships of Men and Women at Work: Job Satisfaction and Resource Implications', *Journal of Managerial Psychology*, vol. 15, no. 2, pp. 161–84

Marks, G., Miller, N. and Maruyama, M. (1981), 'Effect of Targets' Physical Attractiveness on Assumptions of Similarity', *Journal of Personality and Social Psychology*, vol. 41, pp. 198–206

Marlow, C.M., Schneider, S.L. and Nelson, C.E. (1996), 'Gender and Attractiveness Biases in Hiring Decisions: Are More Experienced Managers Less Biased?', *Journal of Applied Psychology*, vol. 81, pp. 11–21

Maslow, A.H. (1943), 'A Theory of Human Motivation', *Psychological Review*, vol. 50, no. 4, pp. 370–96

Maslow, C., Yoselson, K. and London, M. (1971), 'Persuasiveness of Confidence Expressed Via Language and Body Language', *British Journal of Social and Clinical Psychology*, vol. 10, pp. 234–40

Martin, G.N., Barrett, C. and Watson, M. (2001), 'The Effect of Odour Pleasantness and Task Complexity on Task Performance', *North American Journal of Psychology*, vol. 3, no. 3, pp. 491–502

Martin, N.H. and Sims, J.H. (1954), 'Thinking Ahead', *Harvard Business Review*, vol. 34, no. 6, pp. 25–36

Marwell, G. and Schmitt, D. (1967), 'Dimensions of Compliance-Gaining Behaviour: An Empirical Analysis', *Sociometry*, vol. 30, pp. 350–64

Mauro, R. (1984), 'The Constable's New Clothes: Effects of Uniforms on Perceptions and Problems of Police Officers', *Journal of Applied Social Psychology*, vol. 14, pp. 42–56.

Mechanic, D. (1962), 'Sources of Power of Lower Participants in Complex Organizations', *Administrative Science Quarterly*, vol. 7, no. 3, pp. 349–64

Meehl, P. and Rosen, A. (1955), 'Antecedent Probability and the Efficiency of Psychometric Signs, Patterns or Cutting Scores', *Psychological Bulletin*, vol. 52, pp. 194–215

Mehrabian, A. (1965), 'Communication Length as an Indicator of Communicator's Attitude', *Psychological Reports*, vol. 17, pp. 519–22

Mehrabian, A. (1968), 'Communication Without Words', *Psychology Today*, vol. 2, pp. 53–5

Mehrabian, A. (1972), *Nonverbal Communication*, Chicago, IL: Aldine-Atherton

Merrill, D. and Read, R. (1981), *Personal Styles and Effective Performance*, Chilton Book Company

Meyer, J.W. and Rowan, B. (1977), 'Institutional Organizations: Formal Structure as Myth and Ceremony', *American Journal of Sociology*, vol. 83, no. 2, pp. 340–63

Michelli, D. and Straw, A. (1999), *Successful Networking*, London: Hodder Arnold

Michener, S.K. and Suchner, R.W. (1971), 'The Tactical Use of Power' in Tedeschi, J.T. (ed.), *The Social Influence Process*, Chicago, IL: AVC

Milgram, S. (1974), *Obedience to Authority*, New York, NY: Harper and Row.

Miller, G.R. and Hewgill, M.A. (1964), 'The Effect of Variations in Nonfluency on Audience Ratings of Source Credibility', *Quarterly Journal of Speech*, vol. 50, pp. 36–44

Miller, M.G. (2002), 'The Effectiveness of the Door-in-the-Face Compliance Strategy on Friends and Strangers', *Journal of Social Psychology*, vol. 142, no. 3, pp. 295–304

Miller, N. and Campbell, D. (1959) 'Recency and Primacy in Persuasion as a Function of Timing of Speeches and Measurements', *Journal of Abnormal and Social Psychology*, vol. 59, pp. 1–9

Miller, N., Campbell, D.T., Twedt, H. and O'Connell, E.J. (1966), 'Similarity, Contrast and Complementarity in Friendship Choice', *Journal of Personality and Social Psychology*, vol. 3, pp. 3–12

Miller, N., Maruyama, G., Beaber, R.J. and Valone, K. (1976), 'Speed of Speech and Persuasion', *Journal of Personality and Social Psychology*, vol. 34, pp. 615–24

Miller, R.L., Seligman, C., Clark, N.T. and Bush, M. (1976), 'Perceptual Contrast Versus Reciprocal Concession as Mediators of Induced Compliance', *Canadian Journal of Behavioural Science*, vol. 8, pp. 401–9

Mills, J. and Aronson, E. (1965), 'Opinion Change as a Function of Communicator's Attractiveness and Desire to Influence', *Journal of Personality and Social Psychology*, vol. 1, pp. 173–7

Mintzberg, H. (1983), *Power In and Around Organizations*, Englewood Cliffs, NJ: Prentice Hall

Mintzberg, H. (1985), 'The Organization as Political Arena', *Journal of Management Studies*, vol. 22, no. 2, pp. 133–54

Missirian, A.K. (1982), *The Corporate Connection: Why Women Need Mentors to Reach the Top*, Englewood Cliffs, NJ: Prentice Hall

Mohamed, A.A., Gardner, W.L. and Paolillo, J.G.P. (1999), 'A Taxonomy of Organizational Impression Management Tactics', *Advances in Competitive Research*, vol. 7, no. 1, pp. 108–30

Moine, D. (1982), 'To Trust, Perchance to Buy', *Psychology Today*, vol. 24, pp 52–5

Moine, D.J. and Herd, J.H. (1984), *Modern Persuasion Strategies*, Englewood Cliffs, NJ: Prentice Hall

Molloy, J. (1978), *The Women's Dress for Success Book*, New York, NY: Warner

Molloy, J.T. (1975) *Dress for Success*, New York, NY: Warner

Morand, D. (2000), 'Language and Power: An Empirical Analysis of Linguistic Strategies Used in Superior–Subordinate Communication', *Journal of Organizational Behaviour*, vol. 21, no. 3, pp. 235–48

Morgan, N. (2001), 'The Kinaesthetic Speaker: Putting Action into Words', *Harvard Business Review*, April, vol. 79, no. 4, pp. 112–21

Morgan, R.L. (1988), *Selling Professionally*, London: Kogan Page

Morse, G. (2003), 'Why We Misread Motives', *Harvard Business Review*, vol. 81, no. 1, p. 18

Moscovici, S. (1980), 'Towards a Theory of Conversion Behaviour', in Berkowitz, L. (ed.), *Advances in Experimental Social Psychology, Volume 13*, New York, NY: Academic Press, pp. 209–39

Moscovici, S. (1985), 'Social Influence and Conformity' in Lindzey, G. and Aronson, E. (eds), *The Handbook of Social Psychology, Volume 2*, New York: Random House, 3rd edn, pp. 347–412

Moscovici, S. and Faucheux, C. (1972), 'Social influence, conformity bias and the study of active minorities' in Berkowitz, L. (ed.), *Advances in Experimental Social Psychology, Volume 6*, London: Academic Press, pp. 149–202

Moscovici, S. and Lage, E. (1976), 'Studies in Social Influence III: Majority and Minority Influences in a Group', *European Journal of Social Psychology*, vol. 6, pp. 149–74

Moscovici, S. and Lage, E. (1978), 'Studies in Social Influence IV: Minority Influence in a Context of Original Judgements', *European Journal of Social Psychology*, vol. 8, pp. 349–65

364

Moscovici, S. and Mugby, G. (1983), 'Minority Influence' in Paulus, P.B. (ed.), *Basic Group Processes*, New York, NY: Springer-Verlag, pp. 41–64

Moscovici, S., Lage, S. and Naffrechoux, M. (1969), 'Influence of a Consistent Minority on the Responses of a Majority in a Colour Perception Task', *Sociometry*, vol. 32, pp. 365–80

Muchinsky, P.M. (1979), 'The Use of Reference Reports in Personnel Selection: A Review and Evaluation', *Journal of Occupational Psychology*, vol. 69, pp. 551–6

Mugby, G. (1982), *The Power of Minorities*, London: Academic Press

Mugny, G. and Papastamou, S. (1982), 'Minority Influence and Psycho-social Identity', *European Journal of Social Psychology*, vol. 10, pp. 43–62

Mulac, A. (1976), 'Assessment and Application of the Revised Speech Dialect Attitudinal Scale', *Speech Monographs*, vol. 43, pp. 182–9

Mulac, A. and Lundell, T.L. (1980), 'Differences in Perceptions Created by Syntactic–Semantic Productions of Male and Female Speakers', *Communication Monographs*, vol. 47, pp. 111–18

Mulac, A. and Lundell, T.L. (1982), 'An Empirical Test of the Gender-linked Language Effect in a Public Speaking Setting', *Language and Speech*, vol. 25, pp. 243–56

Mulac, A. and Lundell, T.L. (1986), 'Linguistic Contributors to the Gender-linked Language Effect', *Journal of Language and Social Psychology*, vol. 5, pp. 81–101

Mulac, A., Incontro, C. and James, M. (1985) 'An Empirical Test of the Gender-linked Language Effect and Sex Role Stereotypes', *Journal of Personality and Social Psychology*, vol. 49, pp. 1098–109

Mulac, A., Wiemann, J.M., Widemann, S.J. and Gibson, T.W. (1988), 'Male–Female Language Differences and Effects in Same-sex and Mixed-sex Dyads: The Gender Linked Language Effect', *Communication Monographs*, vol. 55, pp. 315–35

Myers, D.G. (1993), *Social Psychology*, New York, NY: McGraw Hill, 4th edn

Myers, I.B. (1962), *The Myers–Briggs Type Indicator Manual*, Princeton, NJ: Educational Testing Service

Myers, I.B. (1976), *Introduction to Type*, Gainsville, FL: Centre for Applications of Psychological Type, 2nd edn

Myers, I.B. and McCaulley, M.H. (1985), *Manual: A Guide to the Development and Use of the Myers–Briggs Type Indicator*, Palo Alto, CA: Consulting Psychologist Press

Naftulin, D.H., Ware, J.E. and Donnelly, F.A. (1973), 'The Doctor Fox Lecture: A Paradigm of Educational Seduction', *Journal of Medical Education*, vol. 48, pp. 630–5

Nahemon, L. and Lawton, M.P. (1975), 'Similarity Propinquity in Friendship Formation', *Journal of Personality and Social Psychology*, vol. 32, no. 2, pp. 205–13

Nelson, D. and Wedderburn, A. (1988), 'Staffing: New and Surer Methods', *Scotland on Sunday*, 25 September, p. 13

Nelson, P. (2002), 'Keeping Candidates in Check', *Personnel Today*, 11 June, p. 12.

Nemeth, C.J. (1986), 'Differential Contributions of Majority and Minority Influence', *Psychological Review*, vol. 93, pp. 1–10

Nemeth, C.J. and Staw, B.M. (1989), 'The Trade-offs of Social Control in Groups and Organizations' in Berkowitz, L. (ed.), *Advances in Experimental Social Psychology*, vol. 12, New York: Academic Press, pp. 175–210

Nemeth, C.J. and Wachtler, J. (1973) 'Consistency and Modification of Judgement, *European Journal of Social Psychology*, vol. 9, pp. 65–79

Nemeth, C.J. and Wachtler, J. (1974), 'Creating the Perceptions of Consistency and Confidence: A Necessary Condition for Minority Influence', *Sociometry*, vol. 37, no. 4, pp. 529–40

Nemeth, C.J., Wachtler, J. and Endicott, J. (1977), 'Increasing the Size of the Minority: Some Gains and Some Losses', *European Journal of Social Psychology*, vol. 7, pp. 15–27

Nevo, B. (1976), 'The Effects of General Practice, Specific Practice and Item Familiarization on Change in Aptitude Test Scores', *Measurement and Evaluation in Guidance,* vol. 91, pp. 16–20

Newcomb, T. (1953), 'An Approach to the Study of Communicative Acts', *Psychological Review*, vol. 60, pp. 393–404

Ng, K.Y. and Van Dyne, L. (2001), 'Individualism–Collectivism as a Boundary Condition for Effectiveness of Minority Influence in Decision Making', *Organizational Behaviour and Human Decision Processes,* vol. 84, no. 2, pp. 198–225

Ng, S.K. and Bradac, J.J. (1993), *Power in Language*, London: Sage

Nisbett, R.E. and Borida, E. (1975), 'Attribution and the Psychology of Prediction', *Journal of Personality and Social Psychology*, vol. 32, no. 5, pp. 53–88

Nisbett, R.E., Zukier, H.A. and Lemley, R.E. (1981), 'The Dilution Effect: Non-diagnostic Information Weakens the Implications of Diagnostic Information', *Cognitive Psychology*, vol. 13, pp. 248–77

Nord, W.R. (1970), 'Beyond the Teaching Machine: The Neglected Area of Operant Conditioning in the Theory and Practice of Management', *Organizational Behaviour and Human Performance*, vol. 4, no. 4, pp. 375–401

Oaff, B. (2000), 'Are You Pleased to Meet and Greet', *Professional Manager*, May, pp. 16–18

O'Connor, J. and Seymour, J. (1990), *Introducing Neuro-Linguistic Programming*, London: Mandala/HarperCollins

O'Keefe, D.J. (1990), *Persuasion: Theory and Research*, Beverley Hills, CA: Sage

Organizational Dynamics (1973), 'At Emery Air Freight: Positive Reinforcement Boosts Performance', winter, pp 43–50.

Ornstein, S. (1989), 'Impression Management Through Office Design' in Giacalone, R.A. and Rosenfeld, P. (eds), *Impression Management in the Organization*, Hillsdale, NJ: Erlbaum, pp. 411–26

Ostermeier, T.H. (1967) 'Effects of Type and Frequency of Reference upon Perceived Source Credibility and Attitude Change', *Speech Monographs*, vol. 34, pp. 137–44

Park, M.B. (1979), 'Women Smile Less for Success', *Psychology Today*, March, p. 16

Parkinson, J.R. (1989), *How to Get People to Do Things Your Way*, New York, NY: McGraw Hill/Contemporary Books

Parkinson, M. (2000), *How to Master Psychometric Tests*, London: Kogan Page

Parsons, C.K. and Cable, D. (1999), 'Assessment of Applicant Work Values Through Interviews: The Impact of Focus and Functional Relevance', *Journal of Occupational and Organizational Psychology*, December, vol. 72, no. 4, pp. 561–6

Pascal, B. (1658), *The Art of Persuasion.*

Paul, N. (1988), *Constructive Criticism: Trainer's Guide*, Ely: Fenman Training,

Paunonen, S.V., Jackson, D.N. and Oberman, S.M. (1987), 'Personnel Selection Decisions: Effects of Applicant Personality and the Letter of Reference', *Organizational Behaviour and Human Decision Processes*, vol. 40, pp. 96–114

Peeters, G. (1971), 'The Positive–Negative Asymmetry: On Cognitive Consistency and Positivity Bias', *European Journal of Social Psychology*, vol. 1, pp. 455–74

Perlini, A., Bertolissi, S. and Lind, D. (1999), 'The Effects of Women's Age and Physical Appearance on Evaluations of Attractiveness and Social Desirability', *Journal of Social Psychology*, vol. 139, June, pp. 343–55

Personnel Today (1993), 10 August, p. 2

Personnel Today (2001), 'RBS Outsources Graduate Hiring', 18 April, p. 1

Personnel Today, (2002), 'Face-to-face Interviews Top Employment Poll Procedure Poll', Yardstick, p. 51

Peters, L.H. and Terborg, J.R. (1975), 'The Effect of Temporal Placement and Attitude Similarity on Personnel Selection', *Organizational Behaviour and Human Performance*, vol. 13, pp. 279–93

Pettigrew, A. (1974), 'The Influence Process Between Specialists and Executives', *Personnel Review*, vol. 3, no. 1, pp. 24–30

Pettigrew, A.M. (1985), *The Awakening Giant,* Oxford: Blackwell

Petty, R.E. and Cacioppo, J.T. (1986), *Communication and Persuasion: Central and Peripheral Routes to Attitude Change*, New York, NY: Springer-Verlag

Pfeffer, J. (1981a), *Power in Organizations,* Boston, MA: Pitman

Pfeffer, J. (1981b) 'Management as Symbolic Action: The Creation and Maintenance of Organizational Paradigms in Cummings, L.L. and Staw, B.M. (eds), *Research in Organizational Behaviour*, vol. 3, Greenwich, CT: JAI, pp. 1–52

Pfeffer, J. (1992), *Managing With Power*, Boston, MA: Harvard Business School Press

Pfeffer, J. and Salancik G.R. (1978), *The External Control of Organizations: Resource Dependency Perspective*, New York, NY: Harper and Row

Phillips, N. (1997), 'Bringing the Organization Back In: A Comment on the Conceptualizations of Power in Upward Influencing Research', *Journal of Organizational Behaviour*, vol. 18, no. 1, pp. 43–7

Pilkington, J.M. (1992), *The Hidden Self*, London: Chancellor Press

Plott, C.R. and Levine, M.E. (1978), 'A Model of Agenda Influence on Committee Decisions', *American Economic Review*, vol. 68, no. 1, pp. 146–60

Pratkanis, A.R. (1988), 'The Attitude Heuristic and Selective Fact Identification', *British Journal of Social Psychology*, vol. 27, pp. 257–63

Prus, R.C. (1989), *Making Sales*, Beverley Hills, CA: Sage

Quick, T.J. (1988), *Power, Influence and Effectiveness in Human Resources*, Reading, MA: Addison Wesley

Quick, T.L. (1990), *Mastering the Power of Persuasion*, New York, NY: Executive Enterprises Publications Company, Inc.

Rafe, S.C. (1990), *How to Be Prepared to Think on Your Feet*, New York, NY: Harper

Raffler-Engel, W. (1983), *Non-verbal Behaviour in the Career Interview*, Amsterdam: John Benjamins Publishing

Raghunathan, R. and Pham, M.T. (1999), 'All Negative Moods Are Not Equal: Motivational Influences of Anxiety and Sadness on Decision Making', *Organizational Behaviour and Human Decision Processes*, vol. 79, no. 1, pp. 56–77

Ralston, D.A. (1985), 'Employee Ingratiation: The Role of Management', *Academy of Management Review*, vol. 10, no. 3, pp. 477–87

Ramsey, M. (1994), 'Support for Work Teams', *CA Magazine*, June, pp. 22–34

Ramsay, S., Gallois, C. and Callan, V.J. (1997), 'Social Rules and Attributions in the Personnel Selection Interview', *Journal of Occupational and Organizational Psychology*, vol. 70, no. 2, pp. 189–203

Rand, T.M. and Wexley, K.N. (1976), *Demonstrating the Effect of Similar-to-Me in Simulated Employment Interviews*, (pamphlet) Pittsburgh, PA: PPG Industries Applied Behaviour Research

Rasmussen, K. (1984), 'Non-verbal Behaviour, Verbal Behaviour, Resume Credentials and Selection Interview Outcomes', *Journal of Applied Psychology*, vol. 70, no. 4, pp. 729–36

Reardon, K. (1981), *Persuasion Theory and Context*, Beverley Hills, CA: Sage

Reardon, K.K. (1991), *Persuasion in Practice*, London: Sage, Chapter 6

Regan, D.T. (1971), 'Effects of a Favour and Liking on Compliance', *Journal of Experimental Social Psychology*, vol. 7, pp. 627–39

Reid, A.S. and Ng, S.H. (2000), 'Conversation as a Resource for Influence: Evidence for Prototypical Arguments and Social identification Processes', *European Journal of Social Psychology*, vol. 30, pp. 83–100

Reinhard, J.C. (1988), 'The Empirical Study of the Persuasive Effects of Evidence: The Status After Fifty Years of Research', *Human Communication Research*, vol. 15, pp. 3–59

Remland, M. and Jones, T. (1994), 'The Influence of Vocal Intensity and Touch on Compliance Gaining', *Journal of Social Psychology*, vol. 134, no. 1, pp. 89–97

Reyes, R.M., Thompson, W.C. and Bower, G.H. (1980), 'Judgemental Biases Resulting From Different Availabilities of Arguments', *Journal of Personality and Social Psychology*, vol. 39, pp. 2–12

Riley, D. and Eckenrode, J. (1986), 'Social Ties: Sub-group Differences in Costs and Benefits', *Journal of Personality and Social Psychology*, vol. 7, pp. 599–609

Rind, B. and Kipnis, D. (1999), 'Changes in Self-perception as a Result of Successfully Persuading Others', *Journal of Social Issues*, vol. 55, no. 1, pp. 141–56

Ringer, C.R. and Boss, R.W. (2000), 'Hospital Professionals' Use of Upward Influence Tactics', *Journal of Management Studies*, vol. 12, no. 1, pp. 92–108

Riordan, C.A. (1989) 'Images of Managerial Success' in Giacalone, R.A. and Rosenfeld, P. (eds), *Impression Management in the Organization*, Hillsdale, NJ: Erlbaum, pp. 87–101.

Robbins, S.P. (1989), *Training in Interpersonal Skills*, Englewood Cliffs, NJ: Prentice Hall

Robertson, I.T. and Makin, P.J. (1986), 'Management Selection in Britain: A Survey and Critique', *Journal of Occupational Psychology*, vol. 59, pp. 45–57

Robertson, I.T. and Smith, M. (2001), 'Personnel Selection', *Journal of Occupational and Organizational Psychology*, vol. 74, no. 4, pp. 441–72

Roehling, M.V. (1999), 'Weight-based Discrimination in Employment: Psychological and Legal Aspects', *Personnel Psychology*, vol. 52, no. 4, pp. 969–1016

Roloff, M.E., Paulson, G.D. and Vollbrecht, J. (1998), 'The Interpretation of Coercive Communication: The Effects of Mode of Influence, Powerful Speech and Speaker Authority', *International Journal of Conflict Management*, vol. 9, no. 2, pp. 139–61

Rosenbaum, M.E. (1986), 'The Repulsion Hypothesis: On the Non-development of Relationships', *Journal of Personality and Social Psychology*, vol. 51, pp. 1156–66

Rosenfeld, P., Giacalone, R.A. and Riordan, C.A. (2002), *Impression Management: Building and Enhancing Reputations at Work*, London: Thomson Learning

Rosenthal, P. (1972), 'The Concept of Paramessage in Persuasive Communication', *Quarterly Journal of Speech*, vol. 58, no. 1, pp. 15–30

Rosnow, R.L. and Robertson, E.J. (1967), *Experiments in Persuasion*, New York, NY: Academic Press

Ross, J. and Ferris, K.R. (1981), 'Interpersonal Attraction and Organizational Outcomes: A Field Examination', *Administrative Science Quarterly*, vol. 26, no. 4, pp. 617–32

Ross, P. (1989), *Ask for the Moon and Get It*, London: Thorsons.

Rowntree, D. (1989), *How to Manage Your Boss*, London: Corgi

Rucker, M., Taber, D., Harrison, A. (1981), 'The Effect of Clothing Variation on First Impression of Female Job Applicants: What to Wear When', *Social Behaviour and Personality*, vol. 9, no. 1, pp. 54–64

Rudman, L.A. (1998), 'Self-promotion as a Risk Factor for Women: The Costs and Benefits of Counterstereotypical Impression Management', *Journal of Personality and Social Psychology*, vol. 74, no. 3, pp. 629–45

Russo, J.E. and Shoemaker, P.J.H. (1989), *Decision Traps: Ten Traps to Brilliant Decision Making and How To Avoid Them*, New York, NY: Doubleday

Rynes, S. and Gerhart, B. (1990), 'Interviewer Assessments of Application "Fit": An Exploratory Investigation', *Personnel Psychology*, vol. 43, no. 1, pp. 13–35.

Saergert, S., Swap, W. and Zajonc, R.B. (1973), 'Exposure Context and Interpersonal Attraction', *Journal of Personality and Social Psychology*, vol. 25, no. 2, pp. 234–42

Saks, M.J. and Kidd, R.F. (1980), 'Human Information Processing and Adjudication: Trial by Heuristics', *Law and Society Review*, vol. 15, no. 1, pp. 123–60

Salancik, G.R. (1977a), 'Commitment is Too Easy', *Organizational Dynamics*, vol. 6, no. 1, pp. 62–80

Salancik, G.R. (1977b), 'Commitment and Control in Organizational Behaviour and Belief' in Staw, B.M and Salancik, G. (eds), *New Directions in Organizational Behaviour*, Chicago, IL: St Claire Press, pp. 1–54

Salancik, G.R. and Pfeffer, J. (1977), 'Who Gets Power: And How They Hold on to It', *Organizational Dynamics*, vol. 5, no. 3, pp. 3–21

Salancik, G.R. and Pfeffer, J. (1978), 'Uncertainty, Secrecy and the Choice of Similar Others', *Social Psychology*, vol. 41, pp. 246–55

Samualson, W.F. and Zeckhauser, R. (1988), 'Status Quo Bias in Decision-making', *Journal of Risk and Uncertainty*, vol. 1, pp. 117–25

Sanford, A. (1983), *Cognition and Cognitive Psychology*, London: Weidenfeld and Nicolson

Schachter, S. (1951), 'Deviation, Rejection and Communication', *Journal of Abnormal and Social Psychology*, vol. 46, pp. 190–207

Schaubroek, J. and Lam, S. (2002), 'How Similarity to Peers and Supervisors Influences Organizational Advancement in Different Cultures', *Academy of Management Journal*, vol. 45, no. 6, pp. 1120–38

Schein, V. (1977), 'Individual Power and Political Behaviours: An Inadequately Explored Reality', *Academy of Management Review*, vol. 2, no. 1, pp. 64–72

Schelling, T.C. (1984), *Choice and Consequence*, Cambridge, MA: Harvard University Press

Scherbaum, C.J. and Sheperd, D.H. (1987), 'Dress for Success: Effects of Colour and Layering on Perceptions of Women in Business', *Sex Roles*, vol. 16, nos 7–8, pp. 391–9

Schilt, W.K. and Locke, E.A. (1982), 'A Study of Upward Influence in Organizations', *Administrative Science Quarterly*, vol. 27, no. 2, pp. 304–16

Schlenker, B.R. (1980), *Impression Management: The Self-concept, Social Identity and Interpersonal Relations*, Monterey, CA: Cole/Brooks

Schlenker, B.R. and Britt, T.W. (1999), 'Beneficial Impression Management: Strategically Controlling Information To Help Friends', *Journal of Personality and Social Psychology*, vol. 76, pp. 559–73

Schlenker, B.R. and Weigold, M.F. (1990), 'Self-consciousness and Self-presentation: Being Autonomous, Versus Appearing Autonomous', *Journal of Personality and Social Psychology*, vol. 59, pp. 820–9

Schmitt, N. (1976), 'Social and Situational Determinants of Interview Decisions: Implications for the Employment Interview', *Personnel Psychology*, vol. 29, pp. 79–101

Schwartz, B. (1974) 'Waiting, Exchange and Power: The Distribution of Time in Social Systems', *American Journal of Sociology*, vol. 79, no. 4, p. 841–70

Schwarz, N. (1984), 'When Reactance Effects Persist Despite Restoration of Freedom: Investigations of Time Delay and Vicarious Control', *European Journal of Social Psychology*, vol. 14, pp. 405–19

Schwarz, N. (2000), 'Emotion, Cognition and Decision Making', *Cognition and Emotion*, vol. 14, no. 4, pp. 433–40

Schwarzwald, J., Raz, M. and Zvibel, M. (1979), 'The Efficacy of the Door-in-the-Face Techniques When Established Behavioural Customs Exist', *Journal of Applied Social Psychology*, vol. 9, pp. 576–86

Schwenk, C.R. (1986), 'Information, Cognition Biases and Commitment to a Course of Action', *Academy of Management Review*, vol. 11, no. 2, pp. 298–310

Scott, M.R. and Lyman, S.M. (1968), 'Accounts', *American Sociological Review*, vol. 33, no. 1, pp. 46–62

Sears, D.O. and Freedman, J.L. (1967), 'Effects of Expected Familiarity of Arguments upon Opinion Change and Selective Exposure', *Journal of Personality and Social Psychology*, vol. 2, no. 3, pp. 420–5

Secord, P. and Backman, C. (1964), 'Interpersonal Congruency, Perceived Similarity and Friendship', *Sociometry*, vol. 27, pp. 115–27

Sederberg, P.C. (1984), *The Politics of Meaning: Power and Explanation in the Construction of Social Reality*, Tucson, AZ: University of Arizona Press

Seibert, S.E., Kraimer, M.L. and Crant, J.M. (2001), 'What Do Proactive People Do?: A Longitudinal Model Linking Proactive Personality and Career Success', *Journal of Personnel Psychology*, vol. 54, no. 4, pp. 845–74

Seitz, V. and Cohen, W. (1992), 'Using the Psychology of Influence in the Job Interview', *Business Forum*, vol. 17, no. 3, pp. 14–17

Seligman, C., Bush, M. and Kirsch, K. (1976), 'Relationship between Compliance Missing the Foot in the Door Paradigm and the Size of the First Request', *Journal of Personality and Social Psychology*, vol. 33, pp. 517–20

Sereno, K.K. and Hawkins, G.J. (1967) 'The Effects of Variations in Speaker's Nonfluency upon Audience Ratings of Attitude Towards the Speech Topic and Speaker's Credibility', *Speech Monographs*, vol. 34, pp. 58–64

Shackleton, V. and Newell, S. (1991), 'Management Selection: A Comparative Survey of Methods Used in Top British and French Companies', *Journal of Occupational Psychology*, vol. 94, pp. 23–44

Shafir, E., Smith, E.E. and Osheron, D.N. (1990), 'Typicality and Reasoning Fallacies', *Memory and Cognition*, vol. 18, no. 3, pp. 229–51

Shannon, J. (1987), 'Don't Smile When You Say That', *Executive Female*, vol. 10, pp. 33–43

Sheridan, E. (2000), 'New Tests to Find the Perfect Match: Graduate Recruitment is Improving All the Time', *Guardian*, 21 October, Features, p. 5

Sherman, S.J. (1980), 'On the Self-erasing Nature of Errors of Prediction', *Journal of Personality and Social Psychology*, vol. 39, pp. 211–21

Shiffrin, R.M. and Schneider, W. (1977), 'Controlled and Automatic Human Information Processing, II: Perceptual Learning, Automatic Attending and a General Theory', *Psychological Bulletin*, vol. 84, pp. 127–90

Sigall, H. (1970), 'The Effects of Competence and Consensual Validation on a Communicator's Liking for the Audience', *Journal of Personality and Social Psychology*, vol. 16, pp. 1156–66

Signall, H. and Ostrove, N. (1975), 'Beautiful is Dangerous: Effects of Offender Attractiveness and Nature of the Crime on Juridic Judgement', *Journal of Personality and Social Psychology*, vol. 94, pp. 410–14

Sillince, J.A.A. (2002), 'A Model of the Strength and Appropriateness of Argumentation in Organizational Contexts', *Journal of Management Studies*, vol. 39, no. 5, pp. 585–618

Silvester, J. (1997), 'Spoken Attributions and Candidate Success in Graduate Recruitment Interviews', *Journal of Occupational Psychology*, vol. 70, no. 1, pp. 61–73.

Silvester, J., Anderson-Gough, F.M., Anderson, N.R. and Mohamed, A.R. (2002), 'Locus of Control, Attributions and Impression Management in the Selection Interview', *Journal of Occupational and Organizational Psychology*, vol. 75, no. 1, pp. 59–76

Silvester J., Anderson N., Haddleton E., Cunningham-Snell N. and Gibb A. (2000), 'A Cross-Modal Comparison of Telephone and Face-to-Face Selection Interviews in Graduate Recruitment', *International Journal of Selection and Assessment*, vol. 8, no. 1, pp. 16–21

Simon, H. (1960), *The New Science of Management Decision*, New York, NY: Harper

Sims, H.P., Gioia, D.A, Longenecker, C.O. and Clinton, O. (1987), 'Behind the Mask: The Politics of Employee Appraisal', *Academy of Management Executive*, vol. 1, no. 3, pp. 183–93

Singh, V. and Vinnicombe, S. (2001), 'Impression Management Commitment and Gender: Managing Others' Good Opinions', *European Management Journal*, vol. 9, no. 2, pp. 183–94

Singh, V., Kumra, S. and Vinnicombe, S. (2002), 'Gender and Impression Management: Playing the Promotion Game', *Journal of Business Ethics*, vol. 37, no. 1, pp. 77–89

Skinner, B.F. (1953), *Science and Human Behaviour*, New York, NY: Macmillan

Skov, R.B. and Sherman, S.J. (1986), 'Information-gathering Processes: Diagnosticity, Hypothesis-confirmatory Strategies, and Perceived Hypothesis Confirmation', *Journal of Experimental Social Psychology*, vol. 22, pp. 93–121

Slovic, P. and Fishhoff, B. (1977), 'On The Beginning of Experimental Surprises', *Journal of Experimental Psychology: Human Perception and Performance*, vol. 3, pp. 544–51

Slovic, P. and Lichtenstein, S. (1971), 'Comparison of Bayesian and Regression Approaches in the Study of Information Processing in Judgement', *Organizational Behaviour and Human Performance*, vol. 6, pp. 649–744

Smith, H. (2003), *How to Pass Numerical Reasoning Tests*, London: Kogan Page

Smith, S.M. and Petty, R.E. (1996), 'Message Framing and Persuasion: A Message Processing Analysis', *Personality and Social Psychology Bulletin*, vol. 22, no. 3, pp. 257–68

Smith, S.M. and Shaffer, D.R. (1991), 'Celerity and Cajolery: Rapid Speech May Promote or Inhibit Persuasion Through Its Impact on Message Elaboration', *Personality and Social Psychology Bulletin*, vol. 17, no. 6, pp. 663–9

371

Smith, T.W., Snyder, C.R. and Handelsman, M.M. (1982), 'On the Self-serving Function of an Academic Wooden Leg: Test Anxiety as a Self-handicapping Strategy', *Journal of Personality and Social Psychology*, vol. 42, pp. 314–21

Snyder, C.R. and Higgins, R.L. (1988), 'Excuses: Their Effective Role in the Negotiation of Reality', *Psychological Bulletin*, vol. 104, pp. 23–35

Snyder, C.R., Higgins, R.L. and Stucky, R.J. (1983), *Excuses: Masquerades in Search of Grace*, New York, NY: Wiley Interscience

Snyder, C.R., Lassengard, M. and Ford, C.E. (1986), 'Distancing after Group Success and Failure: Basking in Reflected Glory and Cutting Off Reflected Failure', *Journal of Personality and Social Psychology*, vol. 51, pp. 382–8

Snyder, M. (1974), 'Self-monitoring of Expressive Behaviour', *Journal of Personality and Social Psychology*, vol. 30, pp. 526–37

Snyder, M. (1979), 'Self-monitoring Processes' in Berkowitz, L. (ed.), *Advances in Experimental Social Psychology: Volume 12*, New York, NY: Academic Press

Snyder, M., Tanke, E.D., and Berscheid, E, (1977), 'Social Perception and Interpersonal Behaviour: On the Self-fulfilling Nature of Social Stereotypes', *Journal of Personality and Social Psychology*, vol. 35, no. 9, pp. 656–66

Solnick, S.J. and Schweitzer, M.E. (1999), 'The Influence of Physical Attractiveness and Gender on Ultimatum Game Decisions', *Organizational Behaviour and Human Decision Processes,*' vol. 79, no. 3, pp. 199–215

Somech, A. and Drach-Zahavy, A. (2002), 'Relative Power and Influence Strategy: The Effects of Agent/Target Organizational Power on Superiors' Choice of Influence Strategies', *Journal of Organizational Behaviour*, vol. 23, no. 2, pp. 167–79

Spillane, M. (1993a) *Presenting Yourself: A Personal Image Guide for Men*, London: Piatkus

Spillane, M. (1993b) *Presenting Yourself: A Personal Image Guide for Women*, London: Piatkus

Spillane, M. (2000), *Branding Yourself: How To Look, Sound and Behave on Your Way to Success*, London: Pan

Staats, A. (1968), *Learning, Language and Cognition*, New York, NY: Holt, Rinehart and Winston

Stechert, K. (1986), *The Credibility Gap*, London: Thorsons

Sterrett, J.H. (1978), 'The Job Interview: Body Language and Perception of Potential Effectiveness', *Journal of Applied Psychology*, vol. 63, no. 3, pp. 388–90

Stewart, J.E. (1980), 'Defendants' Attractiveness as a Factor in the Outcome of Trials', *Journal of Applied Social Psychology*, vol. 10, pp. 348–61

Stewart, R. (1976), *Contrasts in Management: A Study of Different Types of Managers' Jobs*, London: Macmillan

Stewart, R.A., Powell, G.E. and Chetwynd, S.J. (1979), *Person Perception and Stereotypes*, Farnborough: Saxon House

Stires, L.K. and Jones, E.E. (1969), 'Modesty Versus Self-Enhancement as Alternative Forms of Ingratiation', *Journal of Experimental Social Psychology*, vol. 5, pp. 172–88

Straus, S.G., Milesb, J.A. and Levesquec, L.L. (2002), 'The Effects of Videoconference, Telephone and Face-to-Face Media on Interviewer and Applicant Judgements in Employment Interviews', *Journal of Management,* vol. 27, no. 3, pp. 363–81

Strutton, D., Pelton, L.E. and Lumpkin, J.R. (1995), 'Sex Differences in Ingratiatory Behaviour: An Investigation of Influence Tactics in the Salesperson–Customer Dyad', *Journal of Business Research*, vol. 34, no. 1, pp. 35–45

Stubbs, D.R. (1986), *Assertiveness at Work*, London: Pan

Suedfeld, P., Bochner, S. and Matas, C. (1971), 'Petitioners' Attire and Petition Signing by Peace Demonstrators: A Field Experiment', *Journal of Applied Social Psychology*, vol. 1, pp. 278–83

Sutton, S. (1982), 'Fear Arousing Communication; A Critical Examination of Theory and Research', in Eiser, J.R. (ed.), *Social Psychology and Behavioural Medicine*, New York, NY: Wiley

Swenson, R.A., Nash, D.L. and Roos, D.C. (1984), 'Source Credibility and Perceived Expertness of Testimony in Simulated Child Custody Cases', *Professional Psychology*, vol. 15, pp. 891–8

Synnott, A. (1996), 'A Sociology of Smell', *Canadian Review of Sociology and Anthropology*, vol. 28, no. 4, pp. 437–59

Tajfel, H. and Billig, M.G., Bundy, R.P. and Flament, C. (1971), 'Social Categorization and Intergroup Behaviour', *European Journal of Social Psychology*, vol. 1, pp. 148–78

Tannen, D. (1990), *You Just Don't Understand: Women and Men in Conversation*, New York, NY: Morrow

Tannen, D. (1995) 'The Power of Talk: Who Gets Heard and Why', *Harvard Business Review*, vol. 73, no. 5, pp. 138–48

Tate, J. (1998), 'The Influence of Gender on the Use and Effectiveness of Managerial Accounts', *Group and Organizational Management*, vol. 23, pp. 267–88

Taylor, S.E. and Thompson, S.C. (1982), 'Stalking the Elusive "Vividness Effect",' *Psychological Review*, vol. 89, pp. 155–81

Tedeschi, J. and Riess, M. (1981), 'Predicaments and Verbal Tactics of Impression Management' in Antaki, C. (ed.), *Ordinary Language Explanations of Social Behaviour*, London: Academic Press

Tedeschi, J.T. (1981), *Impression Management Theory and Social Psychological Research*, New York, NY: Academic Press

Tedeschi, J.T. and Norman, N. (1985), 'Social Power, Self-presentation and the Self' in Schlenker, B. (ed.), *The Self and Social Life*, New York, NY: McGraw Hill

Tedeschi, J.T., Lindskold, S. and Rosenfeld, P. (1985), *Introduction to Social Psychology*, St Paul, MN: West Publishing

Tedeschi, J.T., Schlenker, B.R. and Bonoma, T.V. (1971), 'Cognitive Dissonance: Private Ratiocination or Public Spectacle?', *American Psychologist*, vol. 26, pp. 685–95

Teel, K.S. (1978), 'Self-appraisal Revisited', *Personnel Journal*, July, pp. 364–7

Tepper, B.J. (1995), 'Upward Maintenance Tactics in Supervisory Mentoring and Non-mentoring Relationships', *Academy of Management Journal*, vol. 38, no. 4, pp. 1191–205

Tepper, B.J., Eisenbach, R.J., Kirby, S.L. and Potter, P.W. (1998), 'Tests of Justice-based Model of Subordinates' Resistance to Downward Influencing Attempts', *Group and Organization Management*, vol. 23, no. 2, pp. 144–60

Tetlock, P.E. and Boettger, R. (1989), 'Accountability: A Social Magnifier of the Dilution Effect', *Journal of Personality and Social Psychology*, vol. 57, pp. 388–98

Tetlock, P.E. and Manstead, A.S.R. (1985), 'Impression Management Versus Intrapsychic Explanations in Social Psychology: A Useful Dichotomy?', *Social Psychology Quarterly*, vol. 92, pp. 59–77

Tesser, A., Campbell, J. and Michler, S. (1983), 'The Role of Social Pressure, Attention to the Stimulus and Self-doubt in Conformity', *European Journal of Social Psychology*, vol. 13, pp. 217–33

Thaler, R. (1985), 'Using Mental Accounting in a Theory of Purchasing Behaviour', *Marketing Science*, vol. 4, pp. 12–13

Thaler, R. (1992), *The Winner's Curse: Paradoxes and Anomalies of Economic Life*, New York, NY: Russell Sage Foundation/Free Press

Thaler, R. and Shefrin, H.M. (1981), 'An Economic Theory of Self-control', *Journal of Political Economy*, vol. 89, no. 2, pp. 392–406

Therkelsen, D.J. and Fiebich, C.L. (2001), 'Message to Desired Action: A Communication Effectiveness Model', *Journal of Communication Management*, vol. 5, no. 4, pp. 374–90

Thomas, A.B. (2003), *Controversies in Management*, London: Routledge, 2nd edn

Thomas, P.J. (1987), 'Appraising the Performance of Women: Gender and the Naval Officer', in Gltek, B.A. and Larwood, L. (eds), *Women's Career Development*, London: Sage

Thompson, P. (1999), *Persuading Aristotle*, London: Kogan Page

Tillman, R. and Kirkpatrick, C.A. (1968), *Promotion: Persuasive Communication in Marketing*, Irwin, pp. 148–55

Tjosvold, D. (1978), 'Affirmation of the High Power Person and His Position: Ingratiation in Conflict', *Journal of Personality and Social Psychology*, vol. 8, pp. 230–43

Tolley, H. and Thomas, K. (2000), *How to Pass Verbal Reasoning Tests*, London: Kogan Page

Tolley, H. and Wood, B. (2001), *How to Succeed at an Assessment Centre*, London: Kogan Page

Townend, A. (1991), *Developing Assertiveness*, London, Routledge

Toulmin, S. (1958), *The Uses of Argument*, Cambridge: Cambridge University Press

Travers, C., Pemberton, C. and Stevens, S. (1997), 'Women's Networking Across Boundaries: Recognizing Cultural Agendas', *Women in Management Review (UK)*, vol. 16, no. 2, pp. 9–16

Tretheway, A. (1999), 'Disciplined Bodies: Women's Embodied Identities at Work', *Organizational Studies*, vol. 20, no. 3, pp. 423–50

Tubbs, S.L. (1968), 'Explicit Versus Implicit Conclusions and Audience Commitment', *Speech Monographs*, vol. 35, pp. 14–19

Tucker, D.H. and Rowe, P.M. (1979), 'Relationship Between Expectancy, Causal Attribution and Final Hiring Decisions in the Employment Interview', *Journal of Applied Psychology*, vol. 64, pp. 27–64

Turner, J.C. (1991), *Social Influence*, Buckingham: Open University Press, Chapters 2 and 6

Turnley, W.H. and Bolino, M.C. (2001), 'Achieving Desired Images While Avoiding Undesired Images: Exploring the Role of Self-monitoring in Impression Management', *Journal of Applied Psychology*, vol. 86, no. 2, pp. 351–60

Tversky, A. and Kahneman, D. (1971), 'Belief in the Law of Numbers', *Psychological Bulletin*, vol. 76, pp. 105–10.

Tversky, A. and Kahneman, D. (1973), 'Availability: A Heuristic for Judging Frequency and Probability', *Cognitive Psychology*, vol. 5, pp. 207–32

Tversky, A. and Kahneman, D. (1981), 'The Framing of Decisions and the Psychology of Choice', *Science*, vol. 211, pp. 453–8

Tversky, A. and Kahneman, D. (1983), 'Extensional Versus Intuitive Reasoning: The Conjunction Fallacy in Probability Judgement', *Psychological Review*, vol. 90, no. 4, pp. 293–315

Tversky, A. and Kahneman, D. (1984) 'Judgement Under Uncertainty: Heuristics and Biases', *Science*, vol. 185, pp. 1124–31

Tykocinski, O., Higgins, E.T. and Chaiken, S. (1994), 'Message Framing, Self-discrepancies and Yielding to Persuasive Messages: A Motivational Significance of Psychological Situations', *Personality and Social Psychology Bulletin*, vol. 20, no. 1, pp. 107–15

Tyson, S. and Jackson, T. (1992), *The Essence of Organizational Behaviour*, Hemel Hempstead: Prentice Hall

Ury, W. (1991), *Getting Past No*, London: Business Books

Vallone, R.P., Griffin, D.W., Lin, S. and Ross, L. (1990), 'Overconfident Prediction of Future Actions and Outcomes by Self and Others', *Journal of Personality and Social Psychology*, vol. 58, no. 4, pp. 568–81

van Dam, K. (2003), 'Trait Perception in the Employment Interview: A Five-Factor Model Perspective', *International Journal of Selection and Assessment*, vol. 11, no. 1, pp. 43–55

Vecchio, R.P. and Sussman, M. (1991), 'Choice of Influence Tactics: Individual and Organizational Determinants', *Journal of Organizational Behaviour*, vol. 12, pp. 73–80

Viswesvaren, C., Ones, D.S. and Hough, L.M. (2001), 'Do Impression Management Scales in Personality Inventories Predict Managerial Job Performance Ratings?', *International Journal of Selection and Assessment*, vol. 9, no. 4, pp. 277–89

Vrij, A., Edward, K. and Bull, R. (2001), 'People's Insight into Their Own Behaviour and Speech While Lying', *British Journal of Psychology*, vol. 92, no. 2, pp. 373–90.

Wade-Benzoni, K. (2002), 'A Golden Rule Over Time: Reciprocity in Intergenerational Allocation Decisions', *Academy of Management Journal*, vol. 45, no. 5, pp. 1011–28

Wallace, P. (1999), *The Psychology of the Internet*, Cambridge: Cambridge University Press

Walster, H., Aronson, E., Abrahams, D. and Rottman, L. (1966a), 'Importance of Physical Attractiveness in Dating Behaviour', *Journal of Personality and Social Psychology*, vol. 5, pp. 508–16

Walster, H.E., Aronson, E. and Abrahams, D. (1966b), 'On Increasing the Persuasiveness of Low Prestige Communication', *Journal of Experimental Social Psychology*, vol. 2, pp. 325–42

Walther, G.R. (1993), *Say What You Mean and Get What You Want*, London: Piatkus

Ward, W.C. and Jenkins, H.M. (1965), 'The Display of Information and the Judgement of Contingency', *Canadian Journal of Psychology*, vol. 19, pp. 231–41

Warren, I.D. (1969), 'The Effect of Credibility in Sources of Testimony on Audience Attitudes Toward Speaker and Message', *Speech Monographs*, vol. 36, pp. 456–8

Wayne, S.A., Liden, R.C., Graf, I.K. and Ferris, G.R. (1997), 'The Role of Upward Influence Strategies in Human Resource Decisions', *Personnel Psychology*, vol. 50, no. 1, pp. 979–1006

Wayne, S.J. and Ferris, G.R. (1990), 'Influence Tactics, Affect and Exchange Quality in Supervisor–Subordinate Interactions: A Laboratory Experiment and a Field Study', *Journal of Applied Psychology*, vol. 75, pp. 487–99

Wayne, S.J. and Kacmar, K.M. (1991), 'The Effects of Impression Management on the Performance Appraisal Process', *Organizational Behavior and Human Decision Processes*, vol. 48, no. 1, pp. 70–88

Weiner, B. (1985), 'Spontaneous Causal Thinking', *Psychological Bulletin*, vol. 97, 1, pp. 74–84

375

Weiner, B., Amirkham, J., Folkes, V.S. and Verette, J.A. (1987), 'An Attributional Analysis of Excuse Giving: Studies in a Naive Theory of Emotion', *Journal of Personality and Social Psychology*, vol. 52, pp. 316–24

Weisinger, H. (1989), *Creative Criticism*, London: Sidgwick and Jackson

Weiss, W. and Steenbock, S. (1965), 'The Influence on Communication Effectiveness of Explicitly Urging Action and Policy Consequences', *Journal of Experimental Social Psychology*, vol. 1, pp. 396–406

Welch, M.S. (1980), *Networking*, New York, NY: Harcourt, Brace and Jovanovich

Whiddett, R. and Hollyforde, S. (1999), *The Competencies Handbook*, London: Institute of Personnel and Development

Whiddett, S. and Kandola, B. (2000), 'Fit for the Job?', *People Management*, 25 May, pp. 30–8

Wiens, A.N., Jackson, R.H. and Manaugh, T.S. and Matarazzo, J.D. (1969), 'Communication Length as an Index of Communicator Attitudes: A Replication', *Journal of Applied Psychology*, vol. 53, pp. 64–6

Wilder, D.A. (1977), 'Perceptions of Groups, Size of Opposition and Influence', *Journal of Experimental Social Psychology*, vol. 48, pp. 257–63

Williams, G.A. and Robert B. Miller, R.B. (2002), 'Change the Way You Persuade', *Harvard Business Review*, vol. 80, no. 5, pp. 64–73

Willis, P. (1997), 'Testing Times', *Personnel Today*, 30 October, pp. 26–7

Wilson, A. (2000), 'Tall Men Do Get The Girl', *Psychology Today*, vol. 32, no. 3, p. 16.

Wilson, F.M. (2003), *Organizational Behaviour and Gender*, Aldershot: Ashgate, 2nd edn

Wilson, P.R. (1968), 'Perceptual Distortion of Height as a Function of Ascribed Academic Status', *Journal of Social Psychology*, vol. 74, pp. 72–102

Witt, L.A., Kacmar, K.M., Carlson, D.S. and Zivnuska, S. (2002), 'Interactive Effects of Personality and Organizational Politics on Contextual Performance', *Journal of Organizational Behaviour*, vol. 23, no. 8, pp. 911–26

Wood, R.E. and Mitchell, T.R. (1981), 'Manager Behaviour in a Social Context: The Impact of Impression Management on Attributes and Disciplinary Actions', *Organizational Behaviour and Human Performance*, vol. 28, pp. 356–78

Woodall, M.K. (1987), *Thinking on Your Feet*, Lake Oswego, OR: Professional Business Communications

Worchel, S., Lee, J. and Adewote, A. (1975), 'Effects of Supply and Demand on Ratings of Object Value', *Journal of Personality and Social Psychology*, vol. 32, pp. 906–14

Wortman, C.B. and Linsenmeier, J.A.W. (1977) 'Interpersonal Attraction Techniques of Ingratiation in Organizational Settings', in Staw, B.M. and Salancik, G.R. (eds), *New Directions in Organizational Behaviour*, Chicago, IL: St Clair Press, pp. 133–78

Wright, P.L. and Taylor, D.S. (1994), *Improving Leadership Performance*, Hemel Hempstead: Prentice Hall, 2nd edn

Yapp, M. (2003), 'Assessment Process Need Not Be Torture', *Personnel Today*, 8 July, p. 28

Yate, M.J. (2001), *Great Answers to Tough Interview Questions*, London: Kogan Page, 5th edn

Young, D.M., Beier, E.G.and Beier, S. (1979), 'Beyond Words: Influence of Nonverbal Behaviour of Female Job Applicants in the Employment Interview', *Personnel and Guidance Journal*, vol. 57, no. 7, pp. 346–51

Yukl, G. and Tracey, J.B. (1992), 'Consequences of Influence Tactics Used With Subordinates, Peers and Boss', *Journal of Applied Psychology*, vol. 77, pp. 525–35

Yukl, G., Falbe, C.M. and Young, J.Y. (1993), 'Patterns of Influence Behaviour for Managers', *Group and Organization Management*, vol. 18, pp. 5–28.

Yukl, G., Kim, H. and Falbe, C.M. (1996), 'Antecedents of Influence Outcomes', *Journal of Applied Psychology*, vol. 81, pp. 309–17

Zahn, C.J. (1989), 'The Bases for Differing Evaluations of Male and Female Speech: Evidence Ratings from Transcribed Conversation, *Communication Monographs*, vol. 56, pp. 59–74

Zajonc, R. (1968), 'The Attitudinal Effects of Mere Exposure', *Journal of Personality and Social Psychology Monograph Supplement*, vol. 9, pp. 1–27

Zalesny, M.D. (1990), 'Rater Confidence and Social Influence in Performance Appraisal', *Journal of Applied Psychology*, vol. 75, pp. 274–89

Zaleznik, A. and Kets de Vries, M. (1975), *Power and the Corporate Mind*, Boston, MA: Houghton Mifflin

Zellers, K.P. and Kacmar, K.M. (1999), 'The Influence of Individual Differences on Reactions to Co-workers' Ingratiatory Behaviours', *Journal of Managerial Issues*, vol. 11, no. 2, pp. 234–48

Zimbardo, P. (1960), 'Involvement and Communication Discrepancy as Determinants of Opinion Conformity', *Journal of Abnormal and Social Psychology*, vol. 60, pp. 86–94

Zimbardo, P.G. and Ebbesen, E.B. (1970), *Influencing Attitudes and Changing Behaviour*, Reading, MA: Addison Wesley

Zimbardo, P.G., Ebbesen, E.B. and Malach, C. (1977), *Influencing Attitudes and Changing Behaviour*, Reading, MA: Addison Wesley

Zuckerman, M. (1979), 'Attribution of Success and Failure Revisited', *Journal of Personality*, vol. 47, pp. 245–87

Zuker, E. (1991), *The Seven Secrets of Influence*, New York, NY: McGraw Hill

Zukier, H. (1982), 'The Dilution Effect: The Role of Correlation and the Dispersion of Predictor Variables in the Use of Non-diagnostic Information', *Journal of Personality and Social Psychology*, vol. 43, pp. 1163–74

Index

Note: Page numbers followed by '*t*' refer to tables.

378